Beyond Retention

Cultivating Spaces of Equity, Justice, and Fairness for Women of Color in U.S. Higher Education

A Volume in
Research for Social Justice:
Personal~Passionate~Participatory Inquiry

Series Editors:
Ming Fang He, *Georgia Southern University*
JoAnn Phillion, *Purdue University*

Research for Social Justice: Personal~Passionate~Participatory Inquiry

Ming Fang He and JoAnn Phillion, Series Editors

Beyond Retention

Cultivating Spaces of Equity, Justice, and Fairness for Women of Color in U.S. Higher Education

Edited by

Brenda L. H. Marina and Sabrina N. Ross
Georgia Southern University

Information Age Publishing, Inc.
Charlotte, North Carolina • www.infoagepub.com

Library of Congress Cataloging-in-Publication Data

CIP data for this book can be found on the Library of Congress website:
http://www.loc.gov/index.html

Paperback: 978-1-68123-414-4
Hardcover: 978-1-68123-415-1
E-Book: 978-1-68123-416-8

CONTENTS

v

SECTION V: CULTIVATING HOMEPLACE

SERIES FOREWORD

Research for Social Justice:
Personal~Passionate~Participatory Inquiry

Ming Fang He and JoAnn Phillion

Research for Social Justice: Personal~Passionate~Participatory Inquiry is a book series that features social justice research on life in schools, families, and communities. This work connects the personal with the political, the theoretical with the practical, and research with social and educational change. The studies demonstrate three distinct and interconnected qualities. Each is personal, compelled by values and experiences researchers bring to the work. Each is passionate, grounded in a commitment to social justice and the lives of people and places under consideration. Each is participatory, built on long-term, heart-felt engagement, and shared efforts. Two principle aspects of the inquiries that distinguish them from others are that researchers are not detached observers, nor putatively objective recorders, but active participants in schools, families, and communities. Researchers engaged in this form of inquiry have explicit research agendas that focus on equity, equality, and social justice. Rather than generating traditional educational research outcomes, positive social and cultural change is the focal outcome of inquiry.

Researchers engaged in personal~passionate~participatory inquiry in this series are diverse and their inquiries are far ranging in terms of contexts, people, and geographic locations studied. Their studies reflect new

Creating Spaces of Equity, Justice, and Fairness in Higher Education, pp. ix–xiii
Information Age Publishing

ix

and exciting ways of researching and representing experiences of disenfranchised, underrepresented, and invisible groups, and challenge stereotypical or deficit perspectives on these groups. It is our hope that this
book series will inspire preservice and in-service teachers, educators, educational researchers, administrators, and educational policymakers to
commit to the enactment of educational and social change that fosters
equity, equality and social justice.

The work in this book series draws on diverse research traditions which
promote social justice (Ayers, Quinn, & Stovall, 2009) and the "Democratic Ideal" (Dewey, 1916, pp. 86–88) in education and life. The work of
Du Bois (1903/1994), Cooper (1892/1988), Woodson (1933/1977), Freire
(1970), and Ayers (2006) has also influenced social justice work in terms
of its emphasis on the emancipatory, participatory, and social activist
aspects of research. This work builds upon narrative inquiry (Clandinin &
Connelly, 2000; Schubert & Ayers, 1999), particularly cross-cultural and
multicultural narrative inquiry (He, 2003; He & Phillion, 2008; Phillion,
2002; Phillion & He, 2008; Phillion, He, & Connelly, 2005) in response to
recognition of the complexity of human experience in increasingly diver-
sified societies. These researchers incorporate narrative, story, autobiography, memoir, fiction, oral history, documentary film, painting, and
poetry into inquiries. One special quality of their inquiries that distinguish them from other forms of educational research lies in understanding experience in its own terms rather than categorizing experience
according to predetermined structures and theories (Phillion, 1999).
Their inquiries are "peopled" with characters, rather than filled with categories and labels. In some forms of traditional educational research,
experience is seen, shaped, and written about by the researcher using theoretically derived forms; in effect the experience is determined by the
theory. Experience is the starting point of these inquiries and is in the
forefront at every stage of research. Their inquiries arise from experiences
of researchers and participants, rather than being formulated as abstract
research questions, and they proceed by continual reference to experience
as field texts are collected, analyzed, and interpreted, and as meanings
are crafted.

Researchers engaged in this form of inquiry also draw on critical race
theory (Gutierrez-Jones, 2001; hooks, 1991; Ladson-Billings, 1998, 2003;
Parker, Deyhle, & Villenas, 1999; Stovall, 2005) and use stories to disclose
hidden and silenced narratives of suppressed and underrepresented
groups to counter meta-narratives that portray these groups as deficient
and inferior. They ask themselves questions about what is missing from
the *official story* that will make the problems of the oppressed more under-
standable. By telling counter stories, researchers recognize the importance of commitment to equity and social justice and their obligation to

link inquiry to social and educational change. The explicit aim of democratic and social justice work is to engage with oppressed groups and individuals and empower them to take effective action toward more just and humane conditions.

Three distinct and interconnected qualities, *personal~passionate~participatory*, permeate the process of these social justice inquiries. Researchers not only collect, but often live in the stories of people with whom they engage in inquiry. They position stories collected in historical, sociopolitical, economic, linguistic, and cultural contexts, and contextualize their inquiries within struggles of underrepresented individuals and groups. Stories are presented in lifelike ways; readers vicariously experience complexities, contradictions, and dilemmas of people's lives. There is a sense of "being there" and a sense of urgency for change. The stories told challenge orthodoxy, awaken critical consciousness, and create possibilities for change.

The work featured in this book series, embedded in life in schools, communities and societies on the one hand, and powerful ideas of being human with strong commitment to a just society on the other, are at the heart of social justice work. Researchers begin with conscious reflection on experience to challenge assumptions, "to raise embarrassing questions," and "to confront orthodoxy and dogma" (Ayers, 2006, p. 85). They listen to "issues that marginalized or disadvantaged people speak of with excitement, anger, fear, or hope" (Ayers, 2006, p.88). They learn directly from individuals and communities about problems and obstacles they face and explore possible solutions by drawing upon the experience and knowledge of participants. Researchers demonstrate strong commitment to the plight of their participants and the injustice embedded in the larger society. This commitment permeates every aspect of life, begins with small changes, and expands to larger contexts.

Personal~passionate~participatory inquiry thrives on the researcher's passionate involvement, strong commitment, and unfaltering advocacy for disenfranchised, underrepresented, and invisible individuals and groups. This passion, commitment, and advocacy can not be cultivated in isolation. Rather, it calls for researchers to work with allies in schools and communities, to take to heart the shared concerns of individuals and groups, to build a community to develop strategies for the enactment of educational and social change that fosters equity, equality, social justice, freedom, and human possibility. Such a community can only flourish when the efforts of researchers join with the efforts of all educational stakeholders—preservice and in-service teachers, educators, administrators, educational policymakers, students, parents, and community members. We hope that the inquiries featured in this series will help social justice researchers and workers of this community move beyond boundaries, transgress orthodoxies, and build a participatory movement to promote a more balanced, fair, and equitable human condition. An expanded community, such as this, embodies possibilities and creates hope for more fulfilling, more equitable, more humane lives in an increasingly diversifying world.

REFERENCES

Ayers, W. C. (2006). Trudge toward freedom: Educational research in the public interest. In G. Ladson-Billings & W. F. Tate (Eds.), *Education research in the public interest: Social justice, action and policy* (pp. 81–97). New York, NY: Teachers College Press.

Ayers, W., Quinn, T., & Stovall, D. (2009). *Handbook of social justice in education.* New York, NY: Routledge.

Clandinin, D. J., & Connelly, F. M. (2000). *Narrative inquiry.* San Francisco, CA: Jossey-Bass.

Cooper, A. (1988). *A voice form the South.* New York, NY: Oxford University Press. (Original work published 1892)

Dewey, J. (1916). *Democracy and education: An introduction to the philosophy of education.* New York, NY: Free Press.

Du Bois, W. E. B. (1994). *The souls of Black folks.* New York, NY: Fine Creative Media. (Original work published 1903)

Freire, P. (1970). *A pedagogy of the oppressed.* New York, NY: Seabury.

Gutierrez-Jones, C. (2001). *Critical race narratives: A study of race, rhetoric, and injury.* New York, NY: New York University Press.

He, M. F. (2003). *A river forever flowing: Cross-cultural lives and identities in the multicultural landscape.* Greenwich, CT: Information Age.

He, M. F., & Phillion, J. (Series Eds.). (2008). *Personal~passionate~participatory inquiry into social justice in education.* In *Research for social justice: Personal~passionate~participatory inquiry.* Greenwich, CT: Information Age.

hooks, b. (1991). Narratives of struggle. In P. Mariani (Ed.), *Critical fictions: The politics of imaginative writing* (pp. 53–61). Seattle, WA: Bay.

Ladson-Billings, G. (1998). Just what is critical race theory and what's it doing in a nice field like education? *International Journal of Qualitative Studies in Education, 11*(1), 7–24.

Ladson-Billings, G. (Eds.). (2003). *Critical race theory perspectives on the social studies: The profession, policies, and curriculum.* Greenwich, CT: Information Age.

Parker, L., Deyhle, D., & Villenas, S. (1999). *Critical race theory and qualitative studies in education.* Boulder, CO: Westview.

Phillion, J. (1999). Narrative and formalistic approaches to the study of multiculturalism. *Curriculum Inquiry, 29*(1), 129–141.

Phillion, J., & He, M. F. (2008). Multicultural and cross-cultural narrative inquiry in educational research. *Thresholds in Education, 34*(1 &2), 2–12.

Phillion, J., He, M. F., & Connelly, F. M. (Eds.). (2005). *Narrative and experience in multicultural education.* Thousand Oaks, CA: SAGE.

Schubert, W. H., & Ayers, W. C. (Eds.). (1999). *Teacher lore: Learning from our own experience*. Troy, NY: Educators International Press.

Stovall, D. (2005). A challenge to traditional theory: Critical race theory, African-American community organizers, and education. *Discourse: Studies in the Cultural Politics of Education, 26*(1), 95–108.

Woodson, C. G. (1977). *The mis-education of the Negro*. Trenton, NJ: Africa World Press. (Original work published 1933)

FOREWORD

Sheila T. Gregory
Clark Atlanta University

It is an honor to author the foreword for *Beyond Retention: Cultivating Spaces of Equity, Fairness, and Justice for Women of Color in U.S. Higher Education*. The editors, Drs. Brenda Marina and Sabrina Ross serve as associate professors at Georgia Southern University, a predominantly White institution and have worked in numerous capacities in higher education. Marina has worked in higher education administration as an advisor, as an assistant dean at another predominantly White institution, and currently serves in leadership positions in academic professional associations. Ross, who has worked in higher education since 2001 as an institutional researcher and later as an educator, currently advises doctoral students, teachers graduate and undergraduate courses, and actively serves in various professional organizations. Their personal stories of how they advanced in higher education are not much unlike those you will read in this well-written collection of case studies. Drs. Marina and Ross understand the higher education discourse in general and, more specifically, the discourse associated with the experiences and expressions of women finding their space in the academy. This compilation of narratives provides critical and powerful insights into what it is like to be a woman of color in higher education, particularly in White colleges and universities. In addition to the analyses of the chapters, the coeditors sought out additional women of color administrators who had experienced similar realities in higher education. This value-added component to the book inserts

Beyond Retention: Cultivating Spaces of Equity, Justice, and Fairness for Women of Color in U.S. Higher Education, pp. xv–xvii
Copyright © 2016 by Information Age Publishing

a much needed and targeted dimension that proves to be useful in describing the intersections and interconnectedness of our journeys.

Since my 1999 book, *Black Women in the Academy: The Secrets to Success and Achievement*, African American women continue to be critically sparse in the upper echelons of academia, both in executive administration positions and among the faculty ranks. While some baby steps have been taken, few meaningful advances have been made that are proportionate to the greater numbers of qualified African American women currently obtaining doctorates and seeking academic positions. African American women today still comprise approximately 3% of all full time instructional faculty in the United States, yet only 2.5% of all full-time faculty ranked at assistant, associate, or the full professor level (Digest of Educational Statistics, 2010). *Beyond Retention: Cultivating Spaces of Equity, Fairness, and Justice for Women of Color in U.S. Higher Education* is an important and new extension of my work and the work of many who are dedicated to improving the academic lives and paths for African American and other women educators and scholars of color.

This critical conversation follows my body of research and the work of Collins, Crenshaw and Brayboy, just to a name a few, to better understand the places and spaces where structural barriers still exist and where there are opportunities to thrive. These include the cost and benefits, hybridity, multiple identities, marginalization, advocacy, social capital, organizational citizenship, and crooked rooms described in this book. You will witness situational experiences from graduate school, faculty positioning with hints of White privilege, and glimpses of the glass ceiling effect in place for women of color. There are many valuable lessons learned within every call chapter and response composition. Throughout the text you will also find an undertone of hope that conditions will improve for women of color in academe in the United States. I salute the editors and the contributors for giving the inspiration to keep cracking the glass ceiling in multiple places, until the fight for social justice is no longer required. I applaud the efforts of Drs. Marina and Ross for undertaking the editing of this important book and for bringing to light the thoughtful voices of these academic women and how their lives bring shape to the experiences and responsibilities of all members of the academic community and beyond. I also wish to recognize the unwavering dedication and strength of the contributors who opened their minds, hearts, and spirits to fill the pages of this edited volume. This is no easy or painless feat. Reliving the racialized past of higher education, in an effort to enlighten and improve the lives of others, is a selfless and noble act. Women in general, and African American women in particular, have sacrificed themselves for hundreds of years, to improve the plight of others. I am truly honored to have played this small role in writing the foreword for such a remarkable book.

As you turn the pages of this book and read, through the eyes of these strong, academic women, the struggle and triumphs that they have experienced in their academic journey, you *will* rethink your own reality. Are you just starting out, contemplating if you have what it takes to make it in the academy? Are you one of these women, looking for strategies to survive and thrive? Are you in a position to help make a difference for one, or many qualified academics through meaningful actions, or well-funded policies or programs? What responsibility do you have to make yourself and others more accountable to those who will nurture and train our future nation? Are you part of the problem, or will you commit to be part of the solution?

AUTHOR NOTE

Sheila T. Gregory, PhD, is the author of *Black Women in the Academy: The Secrets to Success and Achievement* and the NAACP Image Award Nominated Book, *Daring to Educate: The Legacy of the Early Spelman College Presidents.* She is the editor of the *Journal of Invitational Theory and Practice* and is a professor in the Department of Educational Leadership and Higher Education at Clark Atlanta University.

REFERENCE

Gregory, S. (1999). *Black Women in the academy: The secrets to success and achievement* (Rev. ed.). Lanham, MD: University Press of America.

Gregory, S. (2001). Black faculty women in the academy history, status and future. *The Journal of Negro Education, 70*(3), 124–138.

U. S. Department of Education. (2010). Digest of educational statistics, 2010. National Center for Educational Statistics (NCES 2011-015). Washington, DC. Retrieved from https://nces.ed.gov/pubs2011/2011015.pdf

ACKNOWLEDGMENTS

From Brenda ...

My purpose and passion for mentoring women in whatever form it may come has played a part in the impetus for this project. First, foremost, and always, I thank God. I am blessed to be a leader, answering the call to serve in academia. Second, I thank my coeditor and colleague Sabrina Ross, for taking the interest and time to embark on this endeavor of composing a manuscript as a service to women.

Third, I am indebted to those who accepted our invitation to share their research, programs, practices, and advice. Each personal experience and narrative has derived greater meaning to my purpose of mentoring women for leadership.

Lastly, and most important, I am thankful and grateful for my husband Frank of 37 years. Without his constant encouragement and patience over the duration of this work, this book may not have come to fruition.

From Sabrina ...

Many people contributed to the development and completion of this project. I am grateful to Ming Fang He for her mentorship, friendship, and unwavering support for this book. I am also grateful to my coeditor Brenda Marina whose determination and steadfast commitment kept our project moving forward in spite of the many competing demands placed on our time.

I would like to extend thanks to the talented and inspirational women who shared their experiences and insights in this text. Their voices under-

Beyond Retention: Cultivating Spaces of Equity, Justice, and Fairness
for Women of Color in U.S. Higher Education, pp. xix–xx
Copyright © 2016 by Information Age Publishing
All rights of reproduction in any form reserved.

score the serious challenges for women of color in academia. Just as importantly, their voices highlight wisdom and strategies useful for resistance and for making the spaces of higher education more just and equitable for all of us working within the often limiting contexts of academia.

Finally, I would like to acknowledge the many women of color and our allies working in higher education who continue to teach for social justice, engage in social justice leadership, and agitate for change in higher education in numerous creatively insubordinate ways. It is my sincere hope that this book contributes to this vitally important work.

INTRODUCTION

Where Do We Begin?

Brenda L. H. Marina and Sabrina N. Ross

The seeds of inspiration for this text were germinated within the precarious terrain of white space—a symbolic and/or geographic site where White culture, values, and ways of acting in the world prevail (Jackson II, 1999; Rebollo-Gil & Moras, 2006). The specific white space that we navigate in our social justice work is a predominantly White institution (PWI) of higher education located in the rural South. Geographic spaces, such as the one within which we work, hold memories and influence lived realities (Hoelscher, 2003; Kincheloe & Pinar, 1991). Our work in rural Southern white space takes place within a context of historical enslavement, frequently contentious race relations, and resistance (Glymph, 2008; Hoelscher, 2003; Pinar, 1991) and this spatial and symbolic context necessarily influences our experiences and our scholarship as Black women and as social justice workers.

Although we work in different fields of education (i.e., higher education administration and curriculum studies), pursued different occupational trajectories to arrive at our current place of employment, and engage in different functions within our university, we discovered that our strikingly similar experiences within the PWI where we work and our use of intersecting lenses of race/ethnicity and gender to interpret those experiences were important sources of commonality. For example, we have both experienced the paradoxical hypervisibility and invisibility (Barnett,

Beyond Retention: Cultivating Spaces of Equity, Justice, and Fairness
for Women of Color in U.S. Higher Education, pp. xxi–xxxviii
Copyright © 2016 by Information Age Publishing

2006; Thomas & Hollenshead, 2001) that comes from working within a predominantly White context. As race/ethnic numerical minorities, we experience hypervisibility because we are sought out whenever "diverse" representation is needed (e.g., accreditation reports, college and university advertising, diversity task forces, etc.), yet we also experience invisibility because we are underrepresented in leadership positions and our unique concerns and needs are rarely acknowledged. As another example, we have both worked ourselves to the point of exhaustion in attempts to balance departmental and university expectations for research, teaching, and service with additional (and often unacknowledged) diversity-related service demands. We willingly take on some of these additional service demands out of a sense of cultural duty while other culturally taxing (Padilla, 1994) service demands are imposed on us because of our race/ethnicity and gender (Harley, 2008). The final example that we share about our similar experiences working within white space provided the inspiration for this text. We have both experienced subtle and overt racial microaggressions (Smith, 2004) designed to "put us in our place" and these expressions of racial dominance have left us both with the lasting impression that predominantly White institutions of higher education are places where Black women social justice workers "don't quite belong" (Baszile, 2006, p. 206).

CONCEPTUAL ORIGINS OF *BEYOND RETENTION*

Dissatisfied with the status quo of not quite belonging, we envision *Beyond Retention* as a necessary step toward cultivating the spaces within PWIs where we and other women of color belong, where we are listened to and supported, and where we can thrive. The title of this introduction, "Where do We Begin?," acknowledges the audacious task we have undertaken with this book and frames our discussion of *Beyond Retention's* conceptual origins, including previous notable texts by and about women of color working within PWIs, and the themes of critical geography and intersectionality that inform this text. Our title also provides an entry point for discussing the organization of this book as well as the contributions we see *Beyond Retention* making to our respective fields of higher education administration and curriculum studies. Each of these components is discussed in the following sections.

Notable Texts By and About Women of Color in PWIs

Many exemplary texts written by and pertaining to the experiences of women of color working within PWIs helped to lay the conceptual foundation upon which *Beyond Retention* rests. Although space considerations prevent us from providing an exhaustive list of these texts, we recognize a few notable works below to highlight the diverse texts by other women of color in higher education that both inspired our work and provided important guidance on the landscapes and contexts of predominantly White higher education spaces that still need to be mapped. For example, *Spirit, Space, and Survival: African American Women in (White) Academe* edited by Joy James and Ruth Farmer (1993), is an anthology of African American women's experiences within PWIs. By bringing together the diverse experiences of African American women teachers, administrators, and artists in residence as they navigated academe, the publication of this text boldly inserted the experiences of women of color at PWIs into academic discourse, confirming for us that the issues we faced were indeed worthy of discussion and reflection. We were similarly inspired by *Women Faculty of Color in the White Classroom: Narratives on the Pedagogical Implications of Teacher Diversity* edited by Lucila Vargas (2002) and *Neither White Nor Male: Female Faculty of Color: New Directions for Teaching and Learning* edited by Katherine Grace Hendrix (2007). By focusing on the difficulties of teaching for social justice within predominantly White academic spaces, these texts highlight the very different learning environments women of color encounter at PWIs, while also providing strategies that we can use to more easily navigate this difficult terrain. Still other texts such as *From Oppression to Grace: Women of Color and Their Dilemmas Within the Academy* edited by Theodorea Regina Berry and Nathalie D. Mizelle (2006), *Tedious Journeys: Autoethnography by Women of Color in Academe* edited by Cynthia Cole Robinson and Pauline Clardy (2010), and *Women of Color in Higher Education: Turbulent Past, Promising Future* edited by Jean-Marie Gaetane and Brenda Loyd-Jones (2011) inspired us by sharing the candid narratives of women of color in faculty and administrative ranks at predominantly White institutions and confirming our belief that issues of race, gender, sexuality, and social class continue to influence the lived experiences women of color at PWIs despite the rhetoric of diversity commonly touted within these academic spaces. Finally, we were inspired by *Presumed Incompetent: The Intersections of Race and Class for Women in Academia* edited by Gabriella Gutierrez y Muhs, Yolanda Flores Niemann, Carmen G. Gonzalez, and Angela P. Harris (2012). Combining narratives about the campus climate, experiences with White allies, teaching experiences, and the paths to tenure and promotion for women of color in higher education, this text highlighted the need for comprehensive analysis of the multiplicity of paths women of color traverse within higher education spaces. Taken together, these texts validated our belief in the healing power of shared narratives, affirmed our assertions of the continued need to share and learn from the experiences and survival strategies of women of color working for social justice within PWIs, and also provided support for the multilayered approach to theorizing the experiences of women of color we engage in this book.

Significantly, the above-mentioned texts also highlight gaps in the literature on women of color working in predominantly White higher education contexts and point out needed directions for the focus of our text. Scholarship geared toward highlighting the experiences and improving the recruitment and retention of women faculty of color and other marginalized faculty groups is integral for altering the current terrain of higher education into generative landscapes capable of sustaining equity, fairness, and justice for women faculty of color. The significance of works such as those mentioned above cannot be overstated. Yet for all of its significance, such scholarship has yielded few changes to the status quo for women of color working within PWIs. The underrepresentation of women of color within faculty ranks, at senior faculty levels, and in administrative positions within PWIs continues to be widely chronicled (Baker, 2012; Castaneda & Isgro, 2013; Espenshade & Radford, 2009; Gutierrez y Muhs, 2012; Jones & Ebrary, 2012). Arguably, a different approach to work in this area that builds upon earlier exemplary texts and also addresses existing gaps is needed. Grounded in a framework of critical geography and intersectionality, our approach seeks new ways of understanding and responding to oppression within a presumably "postracial" era by enlisting a call and response format to present themes, issues, and strategies for resistance in this text. We explicate our approach and the organization of this text in the following sections.

Understanding and Resisting Oppression in the "Postracial" Era

With the election of the first African American U.S. president in 2008, and fueled by his subsequent reelection in 2012, the myth of a postracial era in U.S. history (where issues of race no longer determine life chances and outcomes) gained prominence. Yet Eduardo Bonilla-Silvia (2013) argues that, rather than the end of racism, the "post" in postracial era signifies new and more complicated expressions of racism that defy traditional approaches to understanding and resistance. Indeed, scholars have highlighted the many ways in which acts of racism and racial discrimination have persisted and even intensified within a U.S. society that is presumably postracial (e.g., Andrews & Tuitt, 2013).

Inspired by the work of Bonilla-Silvia (2013) and other critical scholars of race who have called for new ways of understanding and resisting racism and other related forms of oppression in the Obama era, we seek to foster both intellectual activism and genuine structural change within the academy through (1) personal narratives that speak truth to the power of the experiences of women faculty of color in higher education, and (2) accounts of strategies, policies, and practices by educational administrators that embrace the intersectionality of social justice leadership (Dantley, Beachum, & McCray, 2008) in order to actualize the rhetoric of diversity into institutionalized realities. *Beyond Retention: Cultivating Spaces of Equity, Fairness, and Justice for Women of Color in U.S. Higher Education* honors and extends previous work on the experiences of women faculty of color in PWIs by embracing the metaphor of call and response (Smitherman, 1977) as a means of documenting the need for the genuine incorporation of women faculty of color in PWIs while also offering strategies for developing academic spaces of equity, fairness, and justice.

Critical Geography

Critical geography is a field of study that is concerned with power dynamics that become manifest through interconnections of space, place, and various markers of identity. Like other critical projects, critical geography has an emancipatory goal of identifying and working to counter structures of oppression occurring within geographic spaces (Helfenbein, 2010). *Beyond Retention* is a critical geographic project intended to identify and mitigate structures of oppression that act as barriers to the full incorporation of women of color in predominantly White academic spaces. Our focus on critical geography acknowledges the "spatial turn" (Warf & Arias, 2008) in social science research and takes advantage of the usefulness of space and place based analyses in mapping out new geographies of possibility (Helfenbein 2006), for women of color working within PWIs.

Intersectionality

The theory of intersectionality was first articulated by Kimberlé Crenshaw (1993) as an exploration of the multiple ways that Black women experience oppression in society. This theory suggests that various culturally and socially constructed categories, such as race, gender, and class, interact on multiple and often simultaneous levels, contributing to systematic social inequality. Patricia Hill Collins (2000) enriches understandings of intersectionality by drawing connections between the personal experiences of women of color and social institutions by arguing that cultural patterns of oppression are not only interrelated, but are bound together and influenced by existing social systems (e.g., education, media, etc.). Intersectionality is an ambiguous and open-ended concept. Because of its vagueness and inherent open-endedness, it "initiates a process of discovery which not only is potentially interminable, but promises to yield new and more comprehensive and reflexively critical insights" (Davis, 2008, p. 78). Intersectionality is used in this text as a means of honoring the unique and interrelated forms of oppression experienced by women of color working within PWIs and as a framework of possibility that encourages new insights about and strategies to resist oppression.

Organization of the Chapters and Responses

Beyond Retention is organized around themes related to space and place and uses a call and response format to present narratives of women of color (i.e., calls) and the unique issues they face at PWIs and replies (i.e., responses) by women of color administrators working within PWIs. Call and response is a prominent feature of African American oral tradition, music, and dance (Smitherman, 1977). Call and response involves both verbal and nonverbal interactions between speakers and listeners. Each narrative in this book is a metaphorical call to women of color. This "call" serves as an invitation to connect and understand the varied intersections of race, class, gender, and sexuality that shape the consciousness of women of color as we navigate the racialized and microaggressive educational environments we struggle and thrive within. In this edited volume, we emphasize the subversive and libratory counternarratives of women faculty of color. The lived experiences of women of color in this book are positioned as counter in "an attempt to break that silence and bridge some of those differences between us, for it is not the difference which immobilizes us, but the silence" (Lorde, 1984, p. 44). We conceptualize these counternarratives as "calls" that identify racialized, gendered, sexualized, and class-based challenges within PWIs.

In the African American oral call and response tradition, expressive responses from listeners can serve as agreements, affirmations, and completions of the speaker's statements, or as new and spontaneous offerings (Smitherman, 1977). In *Beyond Retention*, responses to the chapters are provided by senior faculty and higher education administrators who are intersectional social justice leaders (Dantley et al., 2008) that share stories of successful incorporation of women faculty of color, lessons learned from unsuccessful attempts, and visions of creating equitable, fair, and just spaces for women faculty of color within academe. The calls and responses in *Beyond Retention* are divided into five interrelated sections that emphasize critical geographic themes of space and place; the author information and content of each of these sections is presented below.

Section I: Surveying the Landscape

Within the field of geography, land surveys are performed when there is a need for identifying, describing, and/or mapping spatial boundaries. The first section of this text is titled "Surveying the Landscape" in recognition of the ways that chapters and responses in this section identify, describe, and chart areas of danger and safety within the landscapes of predominantly White academic institutions. In Chapter 1, "Ripple Effects and Shockwaves: The Impact of a Black Female Faculty Member's Open Letter to Her Institution," JeffriAnne Wilder discusses the positive and negative reactions she received after penning an open letter to her university about her experiences within a predominantly White university in the South. Wilder's brave efforts to engage her university in discussions of diversity and her discussion of the consequences of that engagement function in this text as a roadmap that other women faculty of color can use to inform their own diversity efforts within PWIs.

Elena Flores responds to Wilder's call in "Courageous Actions: A Response to Ripple Effects and Shockwaves." Flores affirms Wilder's experiences by sharing her own experiences as an "Only" and explaining the psychological costs of constantly attending to the racial and cultural climate at PWIs. Significantly, the response provided by Flores builds on Wilder's chapter by outlining specific initiatives, policies, and resources administrators can engage to increase the numbers of women faculty of color coming through the academic pipeline and, just as importantly, to create spaces were diversity dialogues such as the one engaged by Wilder are welcomed and acted upon.

In Chapter 2, "Walking the Tightrope of Academe With No Net," Michelle Smith chronicles the difficult journey of Black women working within PWIs and the boundaries and spaces they must navigate to be retained and promoted. Smith offers four traits (i.e., tenacity, persistent focus, courage, and balance) that Black women can implement to ease their difficult journeys through the institution of higher education. Smith's traits operate in this text as thematic road markers that help Black women and other women of color stay on track toward tenure and promotion. Patricia Mitchell provides a response to Smith in "Lengthening Your Stride: Finding the Right Balance on the Tightrope." After discussing the use of tenacity, persistent focus, courage, and balance in her own successful navigation of predominantly White institutional landscapes, Mitchell discusses actions at The University of San Francisco to change diversity rhetoric into reality. Mitchell closes her response with tips from her book *Ten Stupid Things Women Do to Mess Up Their Careers*. Like the traits for success offered by Smith, Mitchell's tips are additional resources that can help women of color navigate the difficult terrain of PWIs.

Section II: Locating Safe Spaces

Safe spaces are physical and psychological spaces within which marginalized groups can break free of surveillance and the negative controlling images that seek to define them and keep them oppressed (Collins, 2000). "Section II: Locating Safe Spaces," includes calls and responses relating to themes of space and safety for women of color. Many graduate students of color experience graduate school, not as a safe space, but as a space of loneliness, marginalization, and exploitation (Daniel, 2007; Gay, 2004; Gildersleeve, Croom, & Vasquez, 2011; Williams, 2009). In Chapter 3, "I'd Rather Be Harriet: A Counterstory of Two Sister Scholars," Nadrea Njoku and Juhanna Rogers use the critical race theory method of counterstorytelling to illuminate the racist and sexist obstacles that Black women doctoral students experience within higher education settings. Additionally, their chapter sheds light on the ways in which the often conflicting roles of scholarship, marriage, and parenthood intersect with structures of race and gender to influence Black women's socialization into the professoriate. Through dialogues between fictional composite characters Chantelle and Ida, Njoku and Rogers identify friendship as a safe space wherein the negative controlling images of Black womanhood can be rejected in favor of empowering and revolutionary self-definitions.

In "Talking Back," Donyell Rosboro provides a response to Njoku and Rogers that reflects on the fluidity of multiple perceived boundaries between self and community, between past and present, between personal and political, and between public and private spheres. She highlights tensions in these boundaries that influence Black women's agency to choose, name, and place themselves. Roseboro contextualizes the fluidity of these boundaries and the importance of place by sharing aspects of her journey from a newly minted PhD in a tenure track position to a department chair and highlighting the processes of place-making she engaged along the way. Through her response, Roseboro speaks to both the unique challenges of Black women doctoral students and the broader struggles of Black women faculty in academia.

In Chapter 4, "Preparing to Lead: The Socialization of Black Women for Faculty and Administrative Careers Through Graduate School," Jennifer Johnson, Tykeia Robinson, Candice Staples, and Nina Daoud also discuss the experiences of Black women in doctoral programs. Chapter 4, along with Chapter 3, supplants existing literature on women of color in doctoral programs with stories that provide sociocultural context to existing empirical research. However, Chapter 4 differs from the previous chapter on Black women's experiences in doctoral programs by focusing on the ways that strong mentorship from faculty, administrators, and peers can create the safe spaces in which Black female doctoral students at

PWIs can thrive. By framing the PhD program as a critical point in the educational pipeline for women of color, Johnson et al. contribute invaluable information to the literature on retaining women of color in the professorate.

In her response titled "I Wish I Knew Then, What I Know Now: How to Build a Communal Pipeline," Tara Green discusses cultural communities that can be cultivated within PWIs, and emphasizes the importance of these communal pipelines (i.e., graduate organizations, peer networks, and advisors) in providing the knowledge and resources that faculty of color need for success in academia. In her response, Green shares her own experiences in graduate school, on the tenure track, and as a department chair. Her narrative demonstrates the cultural significance of the communal pipeline and the actions that she took to join and remain within this safe space.

Section III: Blurring Boundaries and Troubling Intersections

Boundaries and intersections control space and movement by defining physical limits and dictating acceptable crossings. This control of space and movement is never absolute, however, because both the space of the border and the space of the intersection are changeable (Massey, 1995). Section III is titled "Blurring Boundaries and Troubling Intersections" in acknowledgment of the ways that: (1) conceptualized boundaries of race, gender, class, and other cultural identity markers can limit how identities are understood and enacted; and (2) taken for granted understandings of intersecting cultural identity markers can be troubled, or rethought to facilitate new ways of thinking about and acting against oppression (Kumashiro, 2001).

In *Borderlands/La Frontera: The New Mestiza*, Gloria Anzuldua (2007) explores the intersections of various aspects of her identity (i.e., language, gender, sexuality, ethnicity, geography, etc.) and the empowerment gained through embracing the borderlands of physical and symbolic space. Throughout *Borderlands*, Anzuldua weaves various languages, modes of representation, and cultures together to illuminate the experiences of the "New Mestizas," those who claim various borderlands of identity. Anzuldua (2007) purposefully troubles taken for granted understandings of identity and culture through her writing. She shifts back and forth between poetry and prose, between self-reflection and social commentary, and between Spanish and English in ways that resist normative categorizations of her identity and her work. This resistance aids social justice by forcing readers to think about and respond to difference in new ways. Like Anzuldua, Yvania Garcia-Pusateri reflects on intersecting aspects of her identity formed through the inhabitation of various borderlands in Chapter 5: "Soy Latina, Donde Estas mi Gente?" Also like Anzuldua (2007), Garcia-Pusateri's work resists simple categorization; she writes her narrative in Spanish and English and engages in self-reflection that transcends linear time, circling back and forth from the past to the present. In this way, Garcia-Pusateri's work can be understood as a form of talking back (hooks, 1989) to the limiting stereotypes of what it means to be Latina within predominantly White academic spaces.

Titled "Mentoring and Encouraging Professional Development for Latinas and Other Women of Color," Ramona Ortega-Listen's response to Garcia-Pusateri also resists traditional categorization. Writing to both Garcia-Pusateri's specific narrative and a broader population of women of color in academia, Ortega-Listen recounts her own experiences of transgressing normative expectations while growing up as non-Catholic, Mexican American in Iowa. For individuals like herself, whose lived experiences and work bridge many geographic and/or symbolic boundaries, Ortega-Listen emphasizes the importance of knowing oneself and she shares the work of psychologist Erik Erikson as a helpful resource in that regard. Her response concludes with valuable lessons for new Latina/o scholars and women scholars of color.

Like other individuals who identify with multiple markers of identity that are marginalized by society, Black women identifying as LGBTQ engage in multiple and sometimes competing expressions of race/ethnicity and sexuality in order to survive within a society that devalues difference. Critical reflection on the interconnections among these multiple and marginalized aspects of identity can yield new insights about oppression as well as new strategies to resist it. In Chapter 6: "Triple Threat: Multiple Identities in the Academy," Lakeisha Meyer engages in reflection about the impact that she, as a "triple threat" (i.e., Black, female, and LGBTQ identifying), can have on social justice efforts in academia. Through a discussion of her educational experiences and career trajectory, and the influence that her triple threat status has had on each, Meyers adds visibility to the often unheard of experiences of queer Black women in academia. In doing so, she furthers intersectionality research and deepens understanding of mechanisms of oppression that operate within higher education spaces through markers of race, gender, and sexuality.

Nina Asher responds to Meyer in "Commonalities, Contrasts, Challenges, and Commitments." In her response, Asher, who also identifies as a queer women of color, discusses ways that her scholarship and pedagogy have been informed by her embrace of multiple identities. She shares excerpts of writings that she has penned over the years to underscore connections between identity, scholarship, and social justice praxis. Much of Asher's writing argues for a rethinking of taken for granted notions and a transgression of boundaries that thwart social justice. Like her other writings, Asher's response to Meyer also works to push problematic boundaries. Specifically, while praising the power and insight gained through Meyer's narrative, she also urges Meyer (and all of us) to question taken for granted assumptions related to identity and praxis. To do so, she argues, is to open ourselves to deeper "understandings of equity, justice, and representation." Insights gained from troubling intersections in this way allow new tools for fighting oppression to be revealed (Kumashiro, 2001).

Section IV: Geographies of Silence and Voice

A prevailing assumption of this text is that careful analysis and articulation of the ways that intersecting structures of race/ethnicity, gender, and class operate to suppress and silence women of color can provide information needed for resistance (hooks, 1989). For oppressed groups, finding one's voice is a crucial first step toward critical consciousness and liberation (Freire, 2000; hooks, 1989). Discussing the importance of coming to voice, hooks writes:

> Moving from silence into speech is for the oppressed, the colonized, the exploited, and those who stand and struggle side by side a gesture of defiance that heals, that makes new life and new growth possible. It is that act of speech, of "talking back," that is no mere gesture of empty words, that is the expression of our movement from object to subject—the liberated voice. (1989, p. 9)

In diverse ways, the chapters and responses in Section IV highlight themes of oppressive silence and the resistance associated with coming to voice. In Chapter 7, "Who Speaks for Me? Learning to Resist With Marginalized Statuses in the Academy," Jenelle Pitt discusses the invasions of privacy and violations of human rights she experienced when a "mentor" advised Pitt that her status as an unmarried mother should be concealed to protect her chances for promotion and tenure. From her initial acts of concealing her unmarried status to the confidence and pride she later displayed in revealing her truths within the PWI where she is employed, Pitt's narrative highlights movements from silence to speech that can inspire other women of color who have been impacted by negative controlling images (Collins, 2000) of womanhood.

Carol Henderson's response "Change Agents in the Academy: On Safe Spaces, Meaningful Advocacy, and Naming the Leak in the Academic

Pipeline" is remarkable in its simultaneous specificity and broad applicability. In her response, Henderson directly addresses the injustices and violations of human dignity experienced by Pitt. She commends Pitt's courageous act of coming to voice (hooks, 1989) and also places responsibility on university departments for cultivating "advocacy networks" to shield women faculty of color from negative experiences such as Pitt faced and to redress those negative experiences that occur. Though Henderson's response addresses the specific context of Pitt's experiences, it also holds broad applicability for all individuals interested in and genuinely working toward the development of safe spaces for women faculty of color. By sharing her own experiences of navigating academia as a single mother and detailing supportive practices that can be implemented to encourage the retention of women of color at PWIs, Henderson's response holds relevance for other women of color in academia and for their department chairs and administrators who embrace the needed work of making PWIs more equitable.

In situations of oppression, it is common for oppressed groups to adopt the mindset and actions of dominant groups (Freire, 2001). Though common, these forms of internalized oppression often go unacknowledged. Thus, work that breaks the silence on internalized oppression and its influence on the lives of women of color aids in liberation. Monica Burke engages in this form of silence breaking in Chapter 8: "Putting an End to Outside Looking In: It's Time for Women of Color in Higher Education to Create Social Capital" by discussing her own negative experiences with mentoring provided by a Black male supervisor. In this chapter, Burke discusses the importance of mentoring (which she sees as a means of attaining social capital), her negative mentoring experiences, and the successful mentoring experiences she ultimately found with White individuals. She also shares interviews from other women of color in higher education to support her arguments. Through the telling of her story, Burke breaks the silence about intraracial oppression and provides strategies other women of color can engage to gain social capital in spite of decreased mentorship opportunities within PWIs. In a similar manner, the response by Stacey Pearson-Wharton titled "We Cannot Do it Alone" breaks another silence around the topic of mentoring for persons of color. Pearson-Wharton shares her own successful mentoring experiences and the lessons that she learned from each of them. Importantly, she challenges the perception that an individual should share race-ethnic similarity with her/his mentor by offering reflections on the different trajectory her own life might have taken, had she not been open to the help of a White mentor.

Section V: Cultivating Homeplace

The concept of "home" has both material (i.e., physical structure) and symbolic (i.e., conveying a sense of belonging) significance (Dyck, 2005). Section five places emphasis on the symbolic significance of home through a focus on the place-making activities of women of color. By place-making activities, we refer to actions that women of color engage to cultivate spaces within PWIs where they feel a sense of belonging and where they are free to resist oppression. hooks (1999) refers to such spaces as sites of homeplace.

Like safe spaces, homeplaces are subversive—they enable Black women to proclaim their humanity within the context of a broader society that objectifies them. Yet homeplaces are also paradoxical. Within homeplaces, the primary means through which Black women exercise their humanity is service, yet forced servitude is also a primary means through which Black women's domination has been enforced (Collins, 2000, hooks, 1999). In ways similar to the creative reappropriation of Christianity that slaves utilized to extract messages of freedom from a religion contorted to keep them enslaved (Raboteau, 2004), Black women who cultivate homeplace reappropriate service in revolutionary ways that are linked to freedom. Describing Black women's radical process of reappropriating service hooks (1999) writes:

> Historically, Black women have resisted White supremacist domination by working to establish homeplace. It does not matter that sexism assigned them this role. It is more important that they took this conventional role and expanded it to include caring for one another, for children, for Black men, in ways that elevated our spirits, that kept us from despair, that taught some of us to be revolutionaries able to struggle for freedom. (p. 44)

Authors in both Chapter 9 and Chapter 10 of this section provide examples and offer strategies to help women of color cultivate homeplaces within predominantly White contexts through reappropriated acts of service at the local level. The authors' attention to the local is significant because this location provides a point of entry for thinking about and theorizing place-making activities at both micro and macro scales (Dyck, 2005).

Chapter 9: "Balancing the Call to Serve: The Costs and Benefits of Leaving a Legacy in the Academy" by Tamara Bertrand Jones, La'Tara Osborne-Lampkin, and JeffriAnne Wilder discusses cultural obligations to mentor and advise students of color and the psychological and career tolls the authors endure by meeting these obligations. In addition to providing readers with candid accounts of the everyday rewards and challenges of supporting students of color within PWIs, the authors offer strategies for managing cultural obligations to students of color that women of color working within various PWI contexts can adopt. Though Bertrand Jones, Osborne-Lampkin, and Wilder pay a price for their service, the strategies that they adopt to "work smarter" enable them to continue the revolutionary work of mentoring students of color at PWIs and, in doing so, to further efforts toward the accumulation of a critical mass (Collins, 2000) of people of color in academia.

In Chapter 10, Mahauganee Shaw invites opportunities for both micro and macro level political engagement in her chapter titled "Expressing Civic Virtue Inside a Crooked Room: A Call to Awareness for Women of Color at Predominantly White Institutions." While recounting the everyday activities of institutional activism she engages to align herself within the "crooked room" of predominantly White educational contexts and to simultaneously make that context a little straighter for other women of color, Shaw attends to the micro processes that make women of color feel out of place within PWIs and the activism women of color can engage to make places for themselves within academia. Shaw's chapter is daring in that it forgoes traditional calls for equity and inclusion by university personnel at various administrative levels in favor of action by women of color to remake predominantly White educational environments into spaces where they can thrive. Importantly, Shaw invites readers to join in practices of activist place-making within their respective PWIs. These united efforts at claiming and occupying space within PWIs are a necessary step toward the cultivation of sites of equity, fairness, and justice for women of color as envisioned in this text. Thus, while Shaw's chapter ends the sections of calls and responses in *Beyond Retention*, we perceive her work as a beginning and as an invitation for social justice-minded women of color working within various predominantly White educational contexts to join in this vital work of remaking PWIs into the homeplaces we need and deserve. Readers will notice that neither Chapter 9 nor Chapter 10 have responses from senior faculty or administrators. Instead, Brenda Marina follows Chapter 10 with "Answer the Call," which contains a number of insights and grounding questions (based on Chapters 9 and 10) for readers to reflect on. It is our hope that, in reflecting on these chapters, readers will be inspired to cultivate homeplaces within their respective institutions. Such work is crucial to transform the landscape of higher education in ways that are favorable for women of color. Chapter 12: "Where Do We Go From Here," concludes the text by summarizing important themes and identifying future directions.

Contributions to Higher Education Administration and Curriculum Studies

Within the field of higher education administration (including higher education leadership and student affairs), the landscape of higher education is changing before our eyes. As such, this text seeks to create a space to consider our practice and role in the changing higher education landscape while reinforcing our enduring values and professional growth. Intentionally developed with these fields in mind, we are challenged to think more broadly about our role as educators and change agents in higher education, to renew and expand our professional networks and partnerships, to examine the symbiotic relationship between inquiry and action, and to approach our work with fresh perspectives and energy. This text is an "experience" and offers a better understanding of institutional traditions by providing a glimpse into cultural landscapes, political landscapes and types of leadership that have influenced women in higher education (Masaoka, 2006). Each section gives voice to the inclusion and exclusion of women in leadership and administration. These reflections challenge and obligate women in higher education administration to *consider* how they will *collaborate* to *create* opportunities for other women of color. Moreover, *Beyond Retention* is a validation and affirmation which provides a space where women of color can both cultivate their talents and gain an appreciation of the value added by their presence in leadership roles in higher education (Johnson & Snider, 2015).

Within the field of curriculum studies, the term "text" takes on broad meaning and applicability; a text is anything that can be read, interpreted, theorized, or analyzed (Pinar, Reynolds, Slattery, & Taubman, 1995). The stories, strategies, and advice provided in *Beyond Retention* by women of color faculty and administrators employed within PWIs comprise rich, varied, and complicated texts that inform and extend the field of curriculum studies. Analysis of the intersecting experiences of women of color within PWIs and the ways that their experiences influence opportunities for incorporation, promotion, and tenure contribute to understandings of curriculum as racialized, gendered, and political texts (Pinar et al., 1995). Additionally, by privileging information by and about women of color in educational scholarship, *Beyond Retention* contributes to the necessary browning of curriculum studies (Gatzambide-Fernández, 2006). Finally, the focus on contexts of space and place and their influence on the experiences of women of color at PWIs continues a long line of emancipatory work in curriculum studies focused on the curricular significance of place (He & Ross, 2012; Kincheloe & Pinar, 1991; Reynolds, 2013).

REFERENCES

Andrews, D., & Tuitt, F. (2013). (Eds). *Contesting the myth of a 'post-racial' era: The continued significance of race in U.S. Education*. New York, NY: Peter Lang.

Anzaldúa, G. (2007). *Borderlands/La Frontera: The new Mestiza*. San Francisco, CA: Aunt Lute books.

Baker, M. (2012). *Academic careers and the gender gap*. Vancouver, British Columbia, Canada: UBC Press.

Barnett, B. M. (2006). Gender, race, and the Academic experience. *Conference Papers—American Sociological Association*, 1.

Baszile, D. (2006). In this place where I don't quite belong: Claiming the ontoepistemological in-between. In T. R. Berry & N. D. Mizelle (Eds.), *From oppression to grace: Women of color and their dilemmas within the academy* (pp. 195–208). Sterling, VA: Stylus.

Berry, T. R., & Mizelle, N. D. (Eds.). (2006). *From oppression to grace: Women of color and their dilemmas within the academy*. Sterling, VA: Stylus.

Bonilla-Silva, E. (2013). *Racism without racists: Color-blind racism and the persistence of racial inequality in America* (4th ed.). Lanham, MD: Rowman & Littlefield.

Castaneda, M., & Isgro, K. L. (2013). *Mothers in academia*. New York, NY: Columbia University Press.

Collins, P. H. (2000). *Black feminist thought: Knowledge, consciousness, and the politics of empowerment* (2nd ed.). New York, NY: Routledge.

Crenshaw, K. (1993). Mapping the margins: Intersectionality, identity politics and the violence against women of color. *Stanford Law Review, 43*, 1241–1299.

Daniel, C. (2007). Outsider-within: Critical race theory, graduate education and barriers to professionalization. *Journal of Sociology and Social Welfare, 34*, 25–42.

Dantley, M., Beachum, F., & McCray, C. (2008). Exploring the intersectionality of multiple centers within notions of social justice. *Journal of School Leadership, 18*, 124–131.

Davis, K. (2008). Intersectionality as buzzword: A sociology of science perspective on what makes a feminist theory successful, *Feminist Theory, 9*, 67–87.

Dyck, I. (2005). Feminist geography, the 'everyday', and local-global relations: Hidden spaces of place-making. *Canadian Geographer, 49*(3), 233–243. doi:10.1111/j.0008-3658.2005.00092.x

Espenshade, T. J., & Radford, A. W. (2009). *No longer separate, not yet equal: Race and class in elite college admission and campus life*. Princeton, NJ: Princeton University Press.

Freire, P. (2001). *Pedagogy of the oppressed* (30th anniversary ed.). New York, NY: Continuum.

Gay, G. (2004). Navigating marginality en route to the professoriate: Graduate students of color learning and living in academia. *International Journal of Qualitative Studies in Education, 17*, 265–288.

Gaztambide-Fernández, R. (2006). Regarding race: The necessary browning of our curriculum and pedagogy public project. *Journal of Curriculum and Pedagogy, 3*(1), 60–64.

Gildersleeve, R. E., Croom, N., & Vasquez, P. (2011). "Am I going crazy?!": A critical race analysis of doctoral education. *Equity & Excellence in Education, 44*, 93–114.

Glymph, T. (2008). *Out of the house of bondage: The transformation of the plantation household*. New York, NY: Cambridge University Press.

Gutierrez y Muhs, G., Niemann, Y. F., Gonzales, C. G., & Harris, A. P. (Eds.). (2012). *Presumed incompetent: The intersections of race and class for women in academia*. Boulder, CO: University Press of Colorado.

Harley, D. (2008). Maids of academe: African American women faculty at predominantly White institutions. *Journal of African American Studies, 12*(1) 19–36.

He, M. F., & Ross, S. (2012). Introduction to special issue: Narrative of curriculum in the South: Lives in-between contested race, gender, class, and power. *Journal of Curriculum Theorizing, 28*(3), 1–9.

Helfenbein, R. (2006). Thinking through scale: Critical geography and curriculum spaces. In E. Malewski (Ed.), *Curriculum studies handbook: The next moment* (pp. 304–317). New York, NY: Routledge.

Helfenbein, R. (2010). Thinking through scale: Critical Geography and curriculum spaces. In E. Malewski (Ed.), *Curriculum studies handbook: The next moment* (pp. 304–317). New York, NY: Routledge.

Hendrix, K. G. (Ed.). (2007). *Neither White nor male: Female faculty of color: New directions for teaching and learning*. San Francisco, CA: Wiley.

Hoelscher, S. (2003). Making place, making race: Performances of Whiteness in the Jim Crow South. *Annals of the Association of American Geographers, 93*(3), 657(630).

hooks, b. (1989). *Talking back: Thinking feminist, thinking Black*. Boston, MA: South End Press.

hooks, b. (1999). *Yearning: Race, gender, and cultural politics*. Boston, MA: South End Press.

Jackson II (1999). White space, White privilege: Mapping discursive inquiry into the self. *Quarterly Journal of Speech, 85*(1) 38–54. doi:10.1080/00335639909384240

James, J., & Farmer, R. (Eds.). (1993). *Spirit, space, and survival: African American women in (White) academe*. New York, NY: Routledge.

Jean-Marie, G., & Lloyd-Jones, B. (Eds.). (2011). *Women of color in higher education: Turbulent past, promising future*. Bingley, United Kingdom: Emerald.

Johnson, J., & Snider, J. (2015). PhorwarD progress: Moving ahead through mentorship in the academy. In B. Marina (Ed.), *Mentoring away the glass ceiling in academia: A cultured critique* (pp. 3–16). Lanham, MD: Lexington Books.

Jones, T. B., & Ebrary, I. (2012). *Pathways to higher education administration for African American women*. Sterling, VA: Stylus.

Kincheloe, J., & Pinar, W. (1991). *Curriculum as social psychoanalysis: The significance of place*. Albany, NY: State University of New York Press.

Kumashiro, K. (2001) Queer students of color and antiracist, antiheterosexist education: Paradoxes of identity and activism. In K. K. Kumashiro (Ed.), *Troubling intersections of race and sexuality* (pp. 1–26). Lanham, MD: Rowman & Littlefield.

Lorde, A. (1984). *Sister outsider*. Berkeley, CA: Crossing Press.

Masaoka, J. (2006). Ten things I learned about leadership from women executive directors of color. In F. Hesselbein & M. Goldsmith (Ed.), *The leader of the future 2* (pp. 55–60). San Francisco, CA: Jossey-Bass.

Massey, D. (1995). The conceptualization of place. In D. Massey & P. Jess (Eds.), *A place in the world?: Places, cultures, and globalization* (pp. 45–77). New York, NY: Oxford University Press.

Padilla, A. M. (1994). Ethnic minority scholars, research, and mentoring: Current and future issues. *Educational Researcher, 23*(4), 24–27.

Pinar, W., Reynolds, W., Slattery, P., & Taubman, P. (1995). *Understanding curriculum: An introduction to the study of historical and contemporary curriculum discourses.* New York, NY: Peter Lang.

Rebollo-Gil, G., & Moras, A. (2006). Defining an "anti" stance: Key pedagogical questions about engaging anti-racism in college classrooms. *Race, Ethnicity & Education, 9*(4), 381–394.

Reynolds, W. (Ed.). (2013). *A curriculum of place: Understandings emerging through the Southern mist.* New York, NY: Peter Lang.

Robinson, C. C., & Clardy, P. (Eds.). (2010). *Tedious journeys: Autoethnography by women of color in academe.* New York, NY: Peter Lang.

Smith, W. A. (2004). Black faculty coping with facial battle fatigue: The campus racial climate in a post-civil rights era. In D. Cleveland (Ed.), *A long way to go: Conversations about race by African American faculty and graduate students at predominantly White institutions* (pp. 171–190). New York, NY: Peter Lang.

Smitherman, G. (1977). *Talkin and testifyin: The language of Black America.* Detroit, MI: Wayne State University Press.

Thomas, G. D., & Hollenshead, C. (2001). Resisting from the margins: The coping strategies of Black women and other women of color faculty at a research university. *Journal of Negro Education, 70,* 166–175.

Vargas, L. (Ed.). (2002). *Women faculty of color in the White classroom: Narratives on the pedagogical implications of teacher diversity.* New York, NY: Peter Lang.

Warf, B., & Arias, S. (Eds.). (2009). *The spatial turn: Interdisciplinary perspectives.* New York, NY: Routledge.

Williams, D. (2009). Supervised by the majority: Understanding the cultural needs of graduate students of color. In D. Cleveland (Ed.), *When "minorities are strongly encouraged to apply": Diversity and affirmative action in higher education* (pp. 35–42). New York, NY: Peter Lang.

SECTION I

SURVEYING THE LANDSCAPE

CHAPTER 1

RIPPLE EFFECTS AND SHOCK WAVES

The Impact of a Black Female Faculty Member's Open Letter to Her Institution

JeffriAnne Wilder

Do you honestly believe that you have issues with race-based prejudice and discrimination here?

I haven't heard of any other faculty of color complaining; couldn't this just be your personal experience that has nothing to do with your race?

Instead of writing an open letter, why didn't you just talk to someone in private, over coffee?

These questions, posed to me by several colleagues, still send shock waves to my system. The seemingly innocent inquiries—and many variations of them—symbolize precisely why the dialogue surrounding diversity in the academy today is both difficult and stymied. Built within these questions is the (conscious and subconscious) denial of institutionalized racist practice that is still ubiquitous at many predominately White colleges and universities. Further inherent in these claims is the perception that underrepresented persons of color (inclusive of faculty and student populations) have the protected *space* and privileged *voice* to comfortably address racism and initiate "race talk" in the face of this widespread denial.

As a Black[1] female scholar who has experienced racism—in all of its forms[2]—I am keenly aware of the unique issues facing women faculty of color in academe. I have spent my entire undergraduate and graduate career at predominately White institutions in the Midwest, North, and Southern regions of the United States. Unfortunately, much of this time was spent as the only and/or one of the few people of color in my program/department. As a now tenured faculty member at a predominately White institution in the Southeast, I have grown accustomed to the formal and informal rules of the academy. Additionally, I have learned the critical strategies and tools faculty of color need to employ in order to manage the "race tax" and to be successful in their professional endeavors (see Rockquemore & Laszloffy, 2008). One of the more common "universal laws" graduate students and junior faculty (particularly faculty of color) learn early on is to *not* speak openly and publicly about your colleagues, department, and/or institution in a disparaging manner. Doing so can have costly implications for one's ability to acquire and secure social capital.

What happens when a Black female faculty member breaks the rules and pens a letter to her institution about her experiences with racism and the challenges of diversity and the myth of postracialism? Ripple effects and shockwaves. On January 20, 2014, the president of my university's faculty association (with my permission) disseminated my letter entitled, *My Experience as an "Only:" An Open Letter to My Department and SPU*[3] *Community* to the entire faculty community of roughly 570 full-time, tenured, and tenure-track individuals. What has ensued since the subsequent release of this document has been an institutional dialogue (inclusive of one-on-one, departmental, and organizational conversations and events) on race, racism, diversity, and postracialism. These formal and informal exchanges reflect the true challenges facing many colleges and universities across the nation that are making the effort to move beyond "mission and vision" statements of diversity to truly changing the institutional climate and culture for Black women faculty and other marginalized populations within the academy.

Guided by critical race theory (CRT) as a conceptual lens, I use my personal narrative as an entry point to describe the personal and institutional impact of sharing my story with my faculty colleagues and members of the administration. In this piece, I explore: What response(s) did I receive from my campus community regarding my letter? What specific events took place as a result of the public sharing of my experience? In what ways has this letter challenged and/or reinforced the institutional culture regarding race and diversity—specifically, faculty diversity strategies, policies, and accountability measures? How has sharing my experience changed my perspectives of my own experience at this institution, and the position of Black women faculty in general?

Specifically, the objectives of this essay aim to:

1. address the importance of Black women faculty exercising their voice within the academy, specifically those working at predominately White institutions;
2. describe the benefits and challenges associated with openly talking about one's experiences;
3. discuss the broader implications and "lessons learned" at my institution and how colleges and universities can be equipped to respond to and address the unique challenges of Black women in the academy.

I use my story—as narrated in my open letter—as a vehicle for debate, reflection and discussion on the nature of discrimination and inequality for Black women today.

Black Women in Academia

A primary goal of civil rights legislation was to improve access to education for underrepresented groups. While access has greatly improved for underrepresented minority students in the post-Civil Rights era, the ascension of racial and ethnic minorities into the professoriate has been a much slower climb. Currently, students of color make up slightly more than one third of the total U.S. college student population, yet faculty of color (African American, Hispanic, and Native American professors combined) comprise less than 10% of the faculty population in the United States (RYU, 2010). Many colleges and universities nationwide have attempted to redress this issue with the implementation of strategic diversity initiatives, but scholars of color remain underrepresented within the academy.

This is especially the case for Black female faculty. Today, Black women comprise 55% of all Black full-time faculty nationwide. There are many reasons to celebrate the recent achievements of Black women in academe, however they still face inequities within higher educational institutions (Wilder, Bertrand Jones, & Osborne-Lampkin, 2013). As scholars Patricia Hill Collins (1988) and Nellie McKay (1997) note, racism, sexism, and other interlocking oppressions can create a unique "outsider-within" status for African American women working specifically within predominately White institutions. Routinely, many Black female scholars have to contend with *"separation anxiety:"* separating who we are as distinctive, individuals from the negative, one-dimensional stereotypes and images that have constrained Black womanhood since slavery. These negative images of Black womanhood deem all Black women—regardless of their education, status, or position—as inferior, subservient, hostile, domineering, hypersexual, or overly masculine (Collins, 2000). Allen, Epps, Guillory, Suh, and Bonous-Hammarth (2000) and others (Collins, 1986, 2000; Evans, 2007; hooks, 1989) point out that because Black womanhood has long been devalued, Black women's intellectual capacity and production has been deemed inferior. As such, Black women often face questions of intelligence, competence, legitimacy, and overall "fit" in doctoral programs or in the professoriate (Allison, 2008; Collins, 1986; hooks, 1989; Johnson-Bailey & Cervero, 2004; Patton, 2004; Woods, 2001).

Critical Race Theory

In this essay, I am guided by CRT as a conceptual framework. CRT is particularly important in evaluating the experiences of African Americans in higher education, and offers a methodological guide to employing empirical research. CRT is a theoretical orientation and collective movement that at its core deconstructs mainstream (White) theory and practice and calls for the transformation of race, racism, and power (Delgado & Stefancic, 2000). Originating within the legal discipline, CRT has since been expanded to include a variety of interdisciplinary perspectives. According to Solorzano, Ceja, and Yosso (2000), CRT has five distinctive elements: "(a) the centrality of race and racism; (b) the challenge to the dominant ideology; (c) the commitment to social justice; (d) the centrality of experiential knowledge, and (e) the transdisciplinary perspective" (p. 63). Further, CRT is particularly useful in exploring race issues in education (Ladson-Billings & Tate, 1995). Of particular importance in this research are the first two elements—the evaluation of the continuing significance and the use of lived experiences (storytelling) as a tool for analysis. As Taylor (1999) notes, "stories can both challenge the status quo and help build consensus by creating a shared communal understanding" (p. 182). Given that the history and status of African Americans in academia has stemmed from racial discrimination, it is important to situate CRT as a starting point in this essay.

Feminist scholar bell hooks (1989) argues that for the oppressed, power originates in "moving from silence into speech" (p. 9). Patricia Hill Collins (1998) adds that when Black women come out of silence, they simultaneously come into voice *and* power. The voice and reach of Black female intellectuals is growing louder and stronger in the 21st century. A number of Black female scholars and other women of color have used their own stories to expose the continued struggle for justice in the academy. For instance, the recent work of Berry and Mizelle (2006), Bertrand Jones, Wilder, and Osborne-Lampkin (in press), and Gutierrez y Muhs, Flores Niemann, Gonzalez, and Harris (2012) employ the critical aspect of storytelling to disentangle the complex lives of women of color in higher education. As these scholars and others note, for academic women of color, speaking up is an empowering act of resistance and enrichment. More importantly, a keen awareness of women in academe is critical in ensuring the presence and growth of women faculty of color in higher education.

My University

Southeastern Public University (SPU) is a comprehensive, masters-level institution in the Southeast. With an enrollment of just over 16,000 students, SPU is a member of the state consortium of public universities. At SPU, Black scholars account for only 4% of the total faculty population.

Discussions of race relations are particularly challenging at my university in large part because we are located in Urbantown, a major metropolitan city in the south. Like many other southern areas, Urbantown[4] has a history of strained race relations and still faces challenges that prevent the city from complete advancement. A 2010 report on race-based disparities and perceptions of racism in the city revealed an increasing gap in perceptions and experiences of racism. In short, many White residents (who comprise roughly 70% of the city's population) do not believe that race is a problem is our city, while the vast majority of Black and other minority residents believe that race is a problem and report experiencing discrimination in many areas of their daily lives. As such, discussions of race on campus and in the broader Urbantown community can be polarizing.

Notwithstanding, diversity is a core feature of SPU's mission and strategic plan. One of SPU's key objectives is to "foster the intellectual and cultural growth and civic awareness of its students, preparing them to make significant contributions to their communities in the region and beyond" (SPU Strategic Plan). The university maintains an unreserved commitment to student success within a diverse, supportive campus culture. Of course, the gateway to a diverse student population begins with a diverse faculty population. As such, SPU established a diversity task force in 2006 to address faculty diversity efforts. In 2013, the president of SPU appointed a special advisor to examine how the university can improve the racial/ethnic diversity of the SPU professoriate. While SPU has been purposeful in articulating the importance of faculty diversity, recruiting and retaining a critical mass of underrepresented minority faculty remains a pressing concern.

My Experience

I am the only African American faculty member in my department of 18 full-time faculty. Since the start of my career at SPU in the fall of 2008, I have been the only underrepresented person of color in my department. Overall, I have had a successful career at SPU. I have established strong relationships with my students and colleagues, and have a reputation for being a passionate scholar committed to issues of diversity and inclusion. While I have experienced professional success at SPU, I work very hard to counter the negative stereotypes and preconceived notions others hold about Black people, and especially about Black women. The broader negative representations of Black women (angry, overly strong, uneducated, hypersexual, etc.) influence how many Black women experience, understand, and negotiate our racialized world. More importantly, they influence how people view me.

Let me offer an example here. On election night in 2008, I was invited to attend a gathering at a colleague's house to watch the return of the votes. I was a bit apprehensive about attending the get-together because I was still new to the university and did not know very many people outside of work. However, I recognized the importance of building social capital and fitting in (informal rule: make efforts to socialize with colleagues occasionally outside of work). When I arrived at my colleague's home that evening, I took the opportunity to meet and network with my some of my new colleagues.

In doing so, I struck up a conversation with another professor—an older, White gentleman. I introduced myself to him and mentioned that I was in the sociology department, although I did not explicitly identify myself as a professor or new to the university. [I assumed he knew that given that the majority of the individuals at the party that evening were fellow faculty]. We chatted for a few minutes about work when the election results came in.

Barack Obama had won the election, becoming the first Black president of the United States. Naturally, I was overjoyed. And so was everyone at the party, including this gentleman that I was conversing with.

However, I was totally blindsided by what he said to me next.

He leaned in close to me, shook his finger at me, and whispered, "No more excuses."

"Obama is president now," he continued. "So, no more excuses. Get your education. Tell your brothers, your cousins, everyone you know, to go get your education. No Excuses *now*."

I was stunned. I could not believe that this man, whom I had been casually chatting with for 15 minutes, did not realize that I was a professor—a PhD—just like he was. How could he assume that I did *not* have my education? Why did he further assume that my brother, cousins, family, and everyone I knew needed to run out and get an education, too? Why couldn't he tell that I was just like him?

As a new faculty member, especially as a young Black female, I did not have the voice and space to tell my "colleague" that he was an idiot. I was so hurt by his words that I politely excused myself and went home.

Over the next few days, I thought more and more about what this man said to me. I decided that if I wanted to be successful at SPU (and in life, for that matter) that I would have to put that incident behind me. Over the years at SPU, I have seen this same professor on campus, but he doesn't even remember me.

These kinds of racialized incidents have been a common feature of my educational experience since I was an undergraduate student. As a faculty member, race-based issues (gender and class, too) have followed me into the classroom and impacted my interactions with students—White and minority alike. Outside the classroom, in my interactions with colleagues and other members of the campus community, race appears at the most inconvenient times—in the form of (seemingly innocent) commentary about my hairstyle, inappropriate jokes about other minorities, and unfair standards and assumptions placed on students of color. The irony here is that I am a sociologist who works with many individuals who truly believe that they are committed to issues of equity and social justice. However, in the 21st century, minority group experiences of racism in the post-Civil Rights era are oftentimes covert, subconscious, and subdued (Bonilla-Silva, 2006; Feagin, 2010). Consequently, identifying racist practice and engaging in "race talk" is a complex and arduous task that involves a great deal of risk and low levels of validation (Rooks, 2014).

The Letter

I submitted my tenure dossier at the beginning of the 2013–2014 academic year. Coincidentally, I was growing more frustrated with the lack of Black and Brown faces in the faculty ranks. As a professor, I have served on several search committees and have a keen awareness of the hiring process at my institution. Like many other schools, SPU does not have a formalized action plan to consistently recruit and retain underrepresented faculty candidates at the university, college, or departmental levels. As such, when faculty of color are hired, it is generally happenstance or the luck of the draw.

In an effort to be more intentional, the president of my institution hired a special advisor to examine best practices associated with minority faculty recruitment and retention. This individual made a number of recommendations to the president about what our institution could do in the short term (i.e., the current academic year) to make small, yet meaningful changes. For instance, I, along with three other minority faculty members, was tapped to attend a large minority doctoral student conference for our region. We served as ambassadors for SPU to discuss our current faculty openings (we had almost 35 openings that year) and to develop a "pipeline" of top minority PhD students who could one day become candidates for future faculty openings. Additionally, our president sent a memo to the faculty and administration stating the importance of diversifying our faculty, and asked individual departments to share in this commitment.

That year, my department had two faculty openings, and I served on one of the search committees. Throughout the search process—which began with some intentionality toward racial diversity—I became increasingly nervous about the inclusion of qualified minorities in the final pool of top candidates. After a series of normal hiccups that can occur during a typical faculty search (e.g., individuals accepting other offers and dropping out of the pool), the final two candidates invited to campus for interviews were White males. At this point, I raised my concern over the pool (I want to point out here that both of these candidates were aptly qualified) and suggested that we "halt" the search. Due to the timing and other constraints, this did not happen and our search committee moved forward with those two candidates.

Frustrated at this outcome and the cumulative impact of my experiences at SPU, I sat down (as I oftentimes do) to journal about my feelings. It took me roughly 20 minutes to write what would become an open letter to my department and institution. Originally, my goal was not to share the letter publicly. After sharing it with two trusted colleagues at my institution, my letter was then shared with our president. He responded that the letter was difficult to read, but important for everyone to see. At that point, I was encouraged to consider "releasing" the letter to the entire faculty. As a way to offer support, I enlisted the assistance of 20 faculty supports—many individuals who were highly esteemed (and tenured) who could cosign on my call to action.

On January 20, 2014 (which also happened to be Martin Luther King, Jr. day), the following e-mail was distributed to the SPU faculty by the head of our faculty association:

Colleagues:

Greetings on this Martin Luther King Day.

Attached is an open letter to the University community that Dr. JeffriAnne Wilder has asked that I share with you. Along with JeffriAnne's letter is a list of faculty who support her call for action. It seems apt on this day for us to consider the issues and call for action that Dr. Wilder raises.

My Experience as an "Only:"
An Open Letter to My Department and SPU Community

I am writing this letter as a way to express my deep concern about the lack of a departmental plan to more thoughtfully and purposefully attract (and retain) faculty of color. I recognize that today, the term diversity has become a way to recognize, respect, and embrace all forms of difference within higher education. On all accounts, racial, ethnic, religious, sexual, and other diverse minorities truly make the landscape of higher education stronger. However, "diversity" does very little to redress the dismal numbers of people of color in the professoriate, including the few like myself who are at SPU. In 1960, Blacks represented only 3% of college/university faculty nationwide. Today—some 54 years later—that number only stands at 5%.

Yet, my concern goes far beyond these numbers. This is my life. As you know, I joined the SPU faculty in 2008. For 5 years, I was the only minority faculty member in our department. And for this entire time, I have been the only Black faculty member. At present, SPU has roughly 24 Black faculty out of 560. In relation to domestic, underrepresented minorities (Black, Hispanic, and Native American), Blacks make up the largest proportion of racial minority faculty at SPU. Although I have been surrounded by warm colleagues and a supportive university community, I am constantly reminded that I am an "only." There are times in which I grow physically and emotionally tired of being a minority in a predominately White department and university. Part of my fatigue is attributed to the fact that I do not feel totally comfortable to voice my "true" thoughts, concerns, and frustrations to others. I am also young, female, and untenured. And those identities—in conjunction with my Blackness—creates a fear and careful construction of "self" and "being" in a space that unconsciously privileges Whiteness, thereby marginalizing and silencing "onlys" like myself.

As a sociologist who studies the experiences of racial minorities in higher education, I know that SPU is not unique. I know that if I were at just about any other campus in the United States (save the HBCUs) the state of my workplace environment would look the same. However, other institutions have been successful in improving the numbers of racial minorities and achieving a critical mass of people of color in their faculty ranks.

My purpose in penning this letter is to implore our department, college, and university to move beyond the language of our mission, vision, and strategic plan. Our president has made faculty diversity a priority. But it takes much more than a commitment at the top. It requires departments who have never had formalized plans for faculty diversity to create them. That means that all members of the faculty—not just the "onlys"—should be vocal and intentional about truly wanting to make their department—and workplace—more reflective of the racially diverse world that we tell our students will be waiting for them once they leave SPU. Making diversity hires should not be mere happenstance. Nor, should they be just for diversity sake.

I also encourage my department (and institution) to consider minority faculty recruitment only a part of the problem. Retention is a much more insidious challenge. In my time at SPU, I have seen two of my best friends (both African American faculty) leave this institution for other universities. Both were in tenure-track positions, and one walked away from tenure here to an untenured assistant professor position somewhere else. The other left for an untenured research position. Unfortunately, neither one of them regrets their decision to leave. While they still speak fondly of their SPU colleagues and students, both of them speak to the culture of silence and apathy related to minority faculty satisfaction. And neither one of them can recall a concerted effort by SPU to keep them here once they announced their plans to leave.

Overall, I have been very successful as a faculty member at SPU. Yet, my success is cast against the backdrop of isolation, tokenism, and a "race tax" that at times is both palpable and inescapable.

We are in the midst of two faculty searches in our department, and given the timing, there is little that can be done at this point to be strategic and diversity-minded when filling these positions.

However, I would really like to hold the department and university accountable for truly "walking the walk" of improving faculty diversity in the future. Perhaps hearing from an only makes the concern more pressing and more real.

As we look toward assessing the racial climate on this campus this semester, I hope that this letter can be a starting point for reflection and discussion on the long road to making SPU a truly transformative place not just for students, but for the faculty who teach them.

Sincerely,

JeffriAnne Wilder, PhD
Assistant Professor of Sociology
Only since 2008

The Response: Ripple Effects

In the short time since the publication of my letter, the institutional impact can be described in two ways: ripple effects and shock waves. "*Ripple-effect*" events are inclusive of similar actions, events, and/or conversations **prompting further dialogue** about the institutional climate and campus culture. Perhaps the largest ripple effect I received was from the university president and chief of staff. Both of these individuals, who happen to be White males, were among the first to read my letter and the first to encourage an institutional dialogue on the issue. In particular, the chief of staff felt that although the repercussions could be personally uncomfortable for me, having as many faculty members read the letter was vital in dismantling the myth that SPU is devoid of racism. This support from "the top" was affirming and quite valuable for me.

The majority of the ripple effects of my letter were in the form of e-mails to me from individuals who were championing my efforts and expressed a desire to talk more about these issues. The following is a sampling of these exchanges:

> I just read your open letter, and I asked how I could join the list of supporters. I haven't met you—I haven't even met many of my colleagues in my own department yet (I am a first-year professor in English). I agree that SPU (and academe in general) needs a more diverse, robust professorate…. I am a young White woman, but I am also an ally. I just wanted to e-mail, introduce myself to you, to thank you for speaking out, and to let you know that I am happy to help in any way I might.

> Thank you for sharing your perspective with the SPU community. If I had been asked, my name would have appeared as a faculty supporter as well. I wonder if I may share your letter with some of my students at some point in the future? Thank you.

> Hi Dr. Wilder. I don't know if I should address you or Dr. XX on this issue, but I'd like you to add my name to the list of faculty supporters. Our department also has an "only" and we are lucky to have him. I don't know whether he feels silenced or not, but I know he gets tired of having to be involved in so much committee work such that we can meet the quota of having a minority representative. Anyway, I appreciated your letter and I hope that it makes a difference. I think it's important to make moves now since it is likely that we are going to be in a state of growth in faculty numbers over the next few years across the university. So if something happens now it might have an impact in a relatively short time frame.

> I will be retiring at the end of this spring term but I have been on the SPU faculty for over 31 years. Among my many dreams for change at SPU and in

our community, diversity has always been at the top of my list. I am trusting that all JeffriAnne is doing will move our university to "walking the walk." BTW I would also like to see more "walking the walk" support for student diversity so perhaps if we start with diversity among faculty ... the students will come!

My sentiments exactly! Thank you very much for having the courage to write this open letter. I am Asian American, a full professor in the dept. of Public Health, and have on many many occasions, tried to express the same sentiments you have.

Awesome letter JeffriAnne! I appreciate you writing it. And this is so timely for our department—we had a program meeting on Friday and struggled with how to define diversity as it relates to our program's goals/mission. Our discussion was on trying to determine what are we really talking about (re diversity) ... I forwarded this e-mail to my colleagues and strongly encouraged them to read it.

Thanks so much for writing your open letter, which just arrived in my inbox. SPU has the most racially diverse student body of any university I've worked for and the least racially diverse faculty. It makes no sense and needs to be changed. I want to talk more about what concrete steps we can take (or influence the administration to take) in order to recruit and maintain faculty of color; in the meantime, please add my name to the list of faculty supporters.

From the examples above, it became clear to me that many individuals who are a part of the SPU professoriate are committed to diversity, and would like to see the representations of racial/ethnic minority faculty increase just as much as I did. I was particularly moved by the number of faculty members expressing their support and allegiance that I had never met.

Beyond the e-mails, there were additional ripple-effect events that furthered the campus dialogue on race, diversity, and the recruitment and retention of minority faculty. In the spirit of my letter, another colleague penned an open letter to his department conveying his concern over a search for a dean. The search resulted in three finalists, all of whom were White men. This faculty member's letter caused so much controversy that the hiring for the position was delayed in order to attract more diverse candidates to the applicant pool.

In addition, the SPU office of faculty development hosted a faculty forum to encourage a broader platform for faculty to discuss race relations on our campus. I attended the event and had a chance to discuss my letter and to engage in a healthy dialogue about my experiences as a SPU faculty member.

Over the course of that semester, there were a host of other informal conversations and departmental workshops on issues of race and other aspects of diversity. Many individuals cited my letter as a launch point for dialogue and debate. All told, the ripple-effect events were transformative and assisted many members of the faculty community to better understand the differential experiences of individuals on our campus.

The Response: Shock Waves

While I derived a great deal of affirmation from many members of my SPU community, I also had to manage the negative reactions to my letter. I am defining these responses as "shock wave" events. These adverse reactions and responses worked to **stifle the dialogue**—and perhaps more importantly, deny the presence of racist and discriminatory practices against Black female faculty and other marginalized faculty populations. Unfortunately, there were some individuals in my department who strongly opposed my letter and took offense to its public dissemination. This was evidenced by avoidance, and perhaps more importantly silence about the issue in my department. A few of my colleagues explained that my actions cast our department in a negative light to the university community, and some were candid by saying that my words made them uncomfortable. This is not surprising, but rather symptomatic of race discussions (or the lack thereof) in the academy. As scholar Noliwe Rooks (2014) explains,

> We are simply uncomfortable talking about race. Because of that discomfort and because we haven't learned the skills necessary to engage in deep discussions on the topic, we avoid them at all costs.

The avoidance of race conversations were not limited to my White colleagues. Two African American female faculty at SPU shared with me their level of discomfort in raising awareness about their experiences of racism. One colleague shared with me in confidence that she would never speak publicly about her experience because she did not want to be perceived as a rebel or radical Black woman. Another woman of color explained her hesitation to sign her name on the list of faculty supporters in the following email:

> I commend your efforts and your courage in penning this letter. I pondered a response to your request for a few days, especially in light of my pretenure status. As you know, I have not been at SPU or in academia that long and have not been part of the wider diversity discussions on campus to attest to what the university has done or has not done to promote diversity. I am

more than willing to engage in discussion on this matter and investigating the issue further, but at this time given my status I cannot sign on.

While she has every right to decline my request to lend her public support of my letter (and I fully respect her decision to do so), the shock wave here is that her pretenure status does not allow this Black female faculty member the latitude to endorse political and controversial issues for fear of reprisal.

Perhaps the biggest shock waves I have experienced are the ones that I still cannot comfortably share with the readers of this essay. While I consider myself a risk taker, and someone who is not afraid to go against the grain, there are still very real consequences of full disclosure. I had several conversations with individuals at my institution who have shown me that my letter—and the call for action to deal with racism—or even accusations of them—can be viewed as offensive, painful, and ultimately detrimental to true coalition and relationship building across difference in the academy. Some folks were simply not ready to deal with race and racism. Frankly, I remain concerned about the new shock waves that the publication of this essay will bring. However, I am committed to serving as an agent for change, particularly for those women of color who cannot afford this same level of bravery—not because they do not want to be, but because they cannot be.

(THIS IS NOT THE) CONCLUSION: LESSONS LEARNED AND STILL LEARNING

In the time since I penned my open letter to my campus community, I have reflected on numerous occasions whether my actions were truly worth it in the end. Have the ripple effects outweighed the density of the shock waves? Sharing my personal experience in such a public way was certainly not easy. If I had the experience to do over again, I would. In many ways, my department and institution are better off now. Discussions surrounding race relations and the experiences of people of color are less difficult than they once were, yet there are some things about my experience as a Black female faculty member that will never change. I recognize that institutional transformation does not happen overnight, and that many more ripple-effect events need to take place in order for the culture of my institution—and academe, in general—to truly shift. How do we then, as women of color make it in the meantime? How shall we guide future generations of Black women in the professoriate? Slowly, with caution? Or, do we take up our collective and individual causes with a sense of urgency and fearlessness? I raise these important questions, but I do not have all the answers. What I am certain of is that my passion for teaching, learning, research, and service is far greater than any shock wave that I have experienced—in the past or presently. That passion is powerful.

NOTES

1. In this essay, I will be using the terms Black and African American interchangeably.
2. It is important to point out that there are many facets of racism, inclusive of interpersonal, institutional, and internalized domains. For a more detailed discussion of these dynamics, see Desmond and Emirbayer, 2009.
3. For the purpose of confidentiality, I will be referring to my institution as Southeastern Public University (SPU) in this essay.
4. In this essay, I will be referring to the city in which SPU is located as Urbantown.

REFERENCES

The Black academic: Faculty status among African Americans in U.S. higher education. *Journal of Negro Education, 69*(1/2), 112–127.

Allison, D. (2008). Free to be me? Black professors, White institutions. *Journal of Black Studies, 38*(4), 641–662.

Berry, T., & Mizelle, N. (Eds.). (2006). *From oppression to grace: Women of color and their dilemmas within the academy.* New York, NY: Stylus.

Bertrand Jones, T., Wilder, J., & Osborne-Lampkin, L. (in press). Beyond sisterhood: Using shared identities to build peer mentor networks and secure social capital in the academy. In B. Marina (Ed.). *Mentoring away the glass ceiling in academia: A global perspective.* Lanham, MD: Lexington Books.

Bonilla-Silva, E. (2006). *Racist America: Color-blind racism and the persistence of racial inequality in the United States* (2nd ed.). Lanham, MD: Rowman & Littlefield.

Collins, P. H. (1986). Learning from the outsider within: The sociological significance of Black feminist thought. *Social Problems, 33,* 514–532.

Collins, P. H. (1998). *Fighting words: Black women fighting for justice.* Minneapolis, MN: University of Minnesota Press.

Collins, P. H. (2000). *Black feminist thought: Knowledge, consciousness, and the politics of empowerment.* New York, NY: Routledge.

Delgado, R., & Stefancic, J. (2001). *Critical race theory: An introduction.* New York, NY: University Press.

Desmond, M., & Emirbayer, M. (2009). What is racial domination? *DuBois Review, 6*(2), 335–355.

Evans, S. Y. (2007, Fall). Women of color in American higher education. *Thought and Action,* 131–138.

Feagin, J. (2010). *Racist America: Roots, current realities, and future reparations* (2nd ed.). New York, NY: Routledge.

Gutierriez y Muhs, G., Flores Niemann, Y., Gonzalez, C. G., & Harris, A. P. (Eds.). (2012). *Presumed incompetent: The intersections of race and class for women in academia.* Boulder, CO: University Press of Colorado.

hooks, b. (1989). *Talking back: Thinking feminist, thinking Black.* Boston, MA: South End Press.

Johnson-Bailey, J., & Cervero, R. (2008). Different worlds and divergent paths: Academic careers defined by race and gender. *Harvard Educational Review, 78*(2), 311–322.

Ladson-Billings, G., & Tate, W. (1995). Toward a critical race theory of education. *Teachers College Record, 97*(1) 48–68.

McKay, N. (1997). A troubled peace: Black women in the halls of the White academy. In L. Benjamin. (Ed.). *Black women in the academy: Promises and perils* (pp. 11–22). Gainesville, FL: University of Florida Press.

Patton, T. O. (2004). Reflections of a Black woman professor: Racism and sexism in academia. *The Howard Journal of Communications, 15*, 185–200.

Rockquemore, K., & Laszloffy, T. (2008). *The Black academic's guide to winning tenure—Without losing your soul.* Boulder, CO: Lynne Reinner.

Rooks, N. (2014, April 11). This is what racial inequality looks like. *The Chronicle of Higher Education.* Retrieved http://chronicle.com/blogs/conversation/2014/04/11/this-is-what-racial-inequality-looks-like/

Ryu, M. (2010). *Minorities in higher education: Twenty-fourth status report.* Washington, DC: American Council on Education.

Solorzano, D., Ceja, M., & Yosso, T. (2000). Critical race theory, racial microaggressions, and campus racial climate: The experiences of African American college students. *Journal of Negro Education, 69*(1/2), 60–73.

Taylor, E. (1999). Critical race theory and interest convergence in the desegregation of higher education? In L. Parker, D. Deyhle, & S. Villenas (Eds.), *Race is … Race isn't: Critical race theory and qualitative studies in education* (pp. 181–204). Boulder, CO: Westview Press.

Wilder, J. A., Bertrand Jones, T., & Osborne-Lampkin, L. (2013). A profile of Black women in the 21st century academy: Still learning from the "outsider-within." *Journal of Research Initiatives, 1*(1), 27–38.

Woods, R. (2001). Invisible women: The experiences of Black female doctoral students at the University of Michigan. In R. O. Mabokela & A. L. Green (Eds.), *Sisters of the academy: Emergent Black women scholars in higher education* (pp. 94–116). Sterling, VA: Stylus.

RESPONSE

COURAGEOUS ACTIONS

A Response to Ripple Effects and Shock Waves

Elena Flores

As a Chicana clinical psychology professor for 19 years in the academy and now an associate dean in the school of education at a private university, I am honored to share my comments on JeffriAnne Wilder's courageous action. I share with her the experience of being "the only" or "one of a handful" of people of color in my doctoral program, in my predoctoral and postdoctoral clinical internships, in my research group, in my academic department, and now in higher education administration. It has been a very familiar and not always comfortable place for me, even though I have learned to navigate my way through the academic context and have been successful. I believe and feel deeply that this success has been at a psychological cost because I have always had to exert additional energy and attention to the cultural and racial climate of the department, the school, and the institution as a whole. As a woman of color, I bring my racial, cultural, class, gender identity experiences and perspective to everything I do; it is fundamentally who I am as an integrated whole person. It has been difficult to be who I am in an academic context that privileges a Eurocentric worldview, where predominantly White faculty and

Beyond Retention: Cultivating Spaces of Equity, Justice, and Fairness for Women of Color in U.S. Higher Education, pp. 19–24
Copyright © 2016 by Information Age Publishing

19

administrators are unaware of their prejudices and racism, and where there exists a lack of recognition and support for my cultural and racial reality. Similar to JeffriAnnes' experience at her institution, while I found and learned strategies for making it through the academic process in my institution, some of my fellow colleagues of color in the department and school did not survive and were not tenured. Given my experience, I believe it does take courageous action on the part of faulty of color to speak out and voice the realities of racial discrimination in university institutional practices and cultural climate. Like others, I commend her for stepping forward and sounding the alarm, it seems to have made a major contribution in raising awareness, opening up difficult conversations, and movement toward change.

We have moved into an era where touting the importance and virtues of diversity is now a part of many university mission statements. While university leadership may realize that recruitment and retention of faculty of color is central to this mission, there is a lack of understanding and sensitivity to the challenges this faculty face in the academic environment. It is common for faculty of color to experience some form of racial discrimination whether overt or subtle, especially daily microaggressions based on race, gender, or sexual orientation. Women of color frequently experience racial insults, disrespect, and indignities from White faculty and White students in the university. For example, based on personal experience and stories from my women of color colleagues, White colleagues often assume we are not as competent, interrupt and invalidate our ideas in meetings, ignore us in the department or at a reception, feel entitled to raise their voice or yell at us during a discussion, and deny their offensive behavior when it is pointed out to them, accusing us of being oversensitive to race. White students also question our competence, complain about our teaching (communication) style, comment on our accents, feel entitled to tell us directly they are not learning anything in our class, and write up detailed negative evaluations with racialized comments. These covert forms of racism reflect the internal stereotypes and prejudices that White colleagues and students hold about ethnic and racial groups whether consciously or unconsciously. The point is that these racial microaggressions are pervasive and exhausting, having a detrimental impact on women of color's psychological well-being, meaningful participation in the academy, and their ultimate retention and promotion. It is critical that the university leadership be intentional about raising awareness concerning racial microaggressions and discrimination impacting faculty of color, and creating spaces for dialogues to deconstruct the reality for faculty of color on a particular campus given the social, cultural, and political context. These conversations can lead to the development of initiatives, new policies, and additional resources for equitable hiring practices and support for retention of women faculty of color.

I believe that because race matters in this society and we have had centuries of cultural conditioning to racism, we need to speak openly and candidly about race for there to be any real consciousness raising or cultural change. For this reason, I think it often takes direct action, such as JeffriAnnes' open letter, to raise the issue and get the conversation started at the university community level. It was great that she had support from the president and several diverse senior colleagues to buffer the negative reactions she would inevitably receive. However, more sustained structural leadership is needed beyond the president that can channel the positive energy in constructive ways and harness the support of faculty. I think universities need a chief administrator for diversity, at the vice provost level, with the influence to address racial and cultural climate issues for faculty, staff, and students. I know this is happening in several universities, including at my institution. In addition, a diversity council of faculty and staff representatives from different schools or colleges and administrative units can draw upon the diverse experiences and expertise within the university to establish initiatives. As a member of the diversity council, I have been involved in several faculty generated ideas supported by the office of diversity for addressing issues of racism and developing an inclusive cultural climate. For example, I played a leadership role in developing an interdisciplinary panel on racism with a historian, sociologist, and psychologist, and then I facilitated a fishbowl discussion with faculty and students from the audience who volunteered to share their experiences and perspectives to guided questions. These types of campus community dialogues are very important and powerful to have because it brings together diverse voices in a safe, open space to learn from each other. A structured, thoughtful approach to having difficult dialogues on race and racism can happen, but it must be supported by not only the administration, but also faculty and students. Thus, a diversity council can garner the input and advice from different campus constituencies and promote the importance of a particular diversity initiative.

Yet, to achieve diversity is a matter of social justice action because changing institutional culture and climate is a gradual process that involves challenging dominant structures, policies, and ideologies. In JeffriAnnes' narrative we hear support from faculty who are clear allies and those who are clear adversaries to her open letter call for action. It is to be expected in a predominantly White institution that promotes diversity that some White faculty will agree with the need for a diverse professoriate, be sensitive to her experience, and want to be part of the movement forward. While other dominant group members will deny the existence of racist practices and structural inequality, and further marginalize her because they are uncomfortable. In reality, JeffriAnne is challenging the dominant group in general (both allies and deniers) to make their actions and practices consistent with the rhetoric of diversity, and this requires them to look at their own racism and White privilege. The oppressive and discriminatory practices that women of color experience in the academy occur within a structural system that affords advantages and privileges to White faculty because of a White supremacy ideology. White privilege is problematic for White people to understand because they often do not perceive they have advantages due to being White. It does not occur to them that they do not have to worry about being treated with indignities or deal with daily microaggressions because of the color of their skin. From a place of privilege, faculty can decide not to deal with race. When race or racism is raised, White deniers often turn racism into a problem of how White people feel making their needs and what's happening to them as the main issue in dealing with racism. Many White allies want to change oppressive institutional practices and are willing to own their privileged social and political locations in order to be committed to equality and justice. It is important that White allies use their awareness of racism and leverage their privileged position into action and activism to dismantle the structural inequality in the institution. There is a serious need for consciousness raising on White privilege, microaggressions, and various forms of racism (prejudice, implicit bias) at the institutional community, school, and departmental level. Creating learning opportunities to engage in antiracism reflection and discussion can be very powerful for diverse groups and for predominantly White groups. For example, our campus brought White antiracist activist Tim Wise to speak to the entire university community about White privilege. We then had subsequent workshops with faculty through our teaching cafes on microaggressions in the classroom, on inclusivity, and on identity-safe classrooms for diverse faculty and students. These efforts combined research, the literature, and the power of personal experiences to raise consciousness among faculty, to develop strategies collectively, and to influence practices in teaching.

JeffriAnnes' open letter is a great example of the power of voice using her own personal experience, which both challenges the dominant practice and develops awareness on diversity. Her lived experience becomes a catalyst for the university community to become engaged in a much-needed conversation on race and race relations. The power of shared stories in giving voice to realities that faculty of color experience in the academic environment is a meaningful approach for exposing the barriers, as well as developing action items for change. It is important that faculty of color have opportunities to come together in structured and supported ways to share common experiences and provide mutual support. For example, in our university we have had yearly ethnic minority faculty writing retreats where we also structure time for social contact and peer conversations. These retreats were invaluable for me to survive and become successful. It was a common space with other faculty of color that broke through my isolation and provided a community I could lean on at the university. We all have supported each other in various ways through our academic journey by sharing stories, discussing our work, peer mentoring, advocacy, and connections to resources. I believe that leadership needs to build community among faculty of color and provide the resources to support various gatherings, which can serve a major function for retention of faculty of color. Another example organized by our diversity office leadership is a 6-week discussion series that brings together female-identified faculty and women faculty of color across different ranks and statuses in the university. This discussion series focuses on stories of the women as they navigate the intersectionalities of race, class, gender/sexuality within the culture of academics in our institutional context. I was honored to attend a dialogue and to have facilitated another dialogue; thus, can attest to the power of diverse women sharing meaningful experiences about their struggles in the academy. This meaningful intercultural exchange deepened awareness of the centrality of race for women of color and opened alliances between White women and women of color.

In addition, as women gave voice to barriers, including discriminatory practices, they also empowered themselves to act by developing working groups on key areas for action. These working groups have proposed initiatives to the deans and provost to improve mentoring and strengthen allies for women of color. I believe more needs to be done on campus to build alliances between White women and women of color such that the power of the collective voice can challenge institutional practices and inspire the direction for climate change.

It is important that the collective voice, not only of women of color or faculty of color, but also White allies (women and men) speak out and recommend an action plan for the recruitment and retention of faculty of color. It does require more intentional practice in outreach and recruitment to diversify the faculty, but it is worth the effort because there are more and more amazing scholars of color that are highly qualified for academic positions. An aspect of recruitment must begin with developing position descriptions that attract diverse faculty because the academic programs themselves reflect issues of diversity, such as multicultural counseling, health disparities, urban education, and social justice. This may require some departments to revise their programs and course offerings by integrating diversity themes into standard and/or required course content. It is also essential that there be targeted recruitment for faculty of color through the distribution of position descriptions to diverse national and statewide professional associations and local professional networks. We could ask our current faculty of color for a list of diverse networks for professionals from underrepresented groups, and advertise new positions on these professional networks. I also believe departments need to be intentional in forming search committees such that ethnic/racial and gender composition are considered in order to obtain a diverse membership for selecting faculty.

Essential elements for the retention of women faculty of color are strong mentorships and the creation of community support across departments and even schools or colleges. Women faculty of color face unique difficulties in the academy, thus, they require mentors that can listen to their reality, provide advice on dealing with institutional bias and micro-aggressions, advocate on their behalf, and support their teaching and scholarship. Since there are few women faculty of color in positions to mentor other women, a good option is for institutions to develop peer mentoring programs and mentoring committees. While I was going through the process, I had an African American woman colleague who was a few years ahead of me as a mentor to discuss my struggles and receive advice and a White woman colleague with whom I collaborated on research projects from another university. Then I sought out a White woman faculty ally in my school that I could discuss my teaching with and receive sound pedagogical advice. I developed my own mentoring committee. Now in my leadership position, I am working to construct mentoring committees that draw not only on the diverse faculty in our school to mentor younger faculty of color, but that connects women of color and White women faculty allies across the university. As I indicated earlier, this is possible because the diversity office has created structured opportunities for women of color to gather and share stories for mutual support and collective action. JeffriAnnes' story and call to action has inspired many faculty to want to take action, including those at the top, but leadership for social justice requires action that creates equitable structures and processes for meaningful recruitment and retention of women faculty of color. It is my view that JeffriAnne exemplifies the new generation of women of color entering the academy who are using their voice in various ways to challenge dominant practices. While speaking out is always a risk, I believe this is often necessary due to the centrality of race in African American women's reality. It is also healthy to maintain ones identity and emotional well-being.

CHAPTER 2

WALKING THE TIGHTROPE OF ACADEME WITH NO NET

Michelle Smith

Metaphors are critical because they become a part of the landscape that ultimately compels change. Metaphor: In everyday use, an interpretive framework that guides social meaning and serves as a mental map for understanding the world. Metaphors work by showing how a set of relations that seems evident in one sphere might illuminate thinking and action in other spheres. Is there such a thing as a level playing field? In the world of sports, a level playing field is a concept about fairness; to create fair competition where no advantage is shown to either side; not that each player has an equal chance to succeed, but that they all play by the same set of rules. A metaphorical playing field is said to be level if no external interference affects the ability of the players to compete fairly. The level playing field is created and guaranteed by the implementation of rules and regulations ... building codes, material specifications, and zoning create a starting point/a minimum standard—a "level playing field."

Having diversity in the higher education setting is critical to the growth of all who are involved. It is a key ingredient of a quality education, scholarly discourse, and reflection. Faculty, staff, and students alike can benefit from learning within a setting that allows or demands that one adapt to the complex social structures of having to learn from, teach, or work with those who are not like oneself. Working with, or learning from or among

Beyond Retention: Cultivating Spaces of Equity, Justice, and Fairness
for Women of Color in U.S. Higher Education, pp. 25–45
Copyright © 2016 by Information Age Publishing
All rights of reproduction in any form reserved.

diverse groups of people is an education in itself. With increasing ethnic diversity in the United States it becomes even more critical to have faculty and staff of color who can support students and serve as role models. And with efforts aimed toward increasing diversity in the U.S. workforce, institutions of higher education must identify and undertake efforts that will help ensure a climate that is inclusive, embracing a wide array of differences that will be "value added" to the institution. Efforts of recruitment and retention are necessarily interdependent and work together toward the goal of diversifying faculty and staff. James and Farmer (1993) state, as more women faculty of color enter the professoriate, they are evaluating, clashing with, and challenging old practices while simultaneously articulating and establishing new ones. However, women of color are still underrepresented in the professoriate ranks of higher education. Only 7% of all faculty positions in higher education are held by African American women and the percentages of faculty positions held by Asian American women (6.7%), Latina women (4%), and American Indian women (0.6%) are also shamefully low (*The Chronicle of Higher Education*, 2010).

Traversing the tightrope of academe is a skillful journey with explicit and implicit rules and requirements. For example, predominately White institutions often view diversity as a free-standing policy, and the way that diversity is something that can be implemented without necessarily changing the underlying structure of the institution and its day-to-day operations. Many colleges and universities across the country see the faculty of color that they hire as a representation of their commitment to diversity. If colleges and universities are truly committed to the agenda of diversity they must refocus their commitment. Faculty of color and in particularly African American women, are required to implement diversity through service agendas and curricula that do not necessarily exist for their White counterparts. Faculty of color cannot be expected to be the only facilitators of service activities and implementing and teaching about issues of diversity in their courses. The effort of implementation takes time, physical and emotional energy, and a toll on untenured faculty of color. Ultimately, the time and energy needed to implement diversity may impede a faculty member's ability to meet her/his retention, promotion, and tenure requirements of writing and publishing (Brayboy, 2003).

Writing about pertinent issues, concerns, and understanding the experiences of African American women faculty at predominantly White institutions (PWIs) adds to the literature on women of color in education. This addition to the literature has implications for education in general and its communities, and is one way to unveil strategies for higher education institutions to implement support structures essential to the success of Black women and all women of color in academe.

Women professors, including those working within the feminized field of education, have often found themselves operating within narrow, predetermined institutional and organizational spaces. These boundaries were shaped by assumptions about who Black women were, what they were (and were not) capable of because of gender and race, and how they should fulfill their obligations to the community (Crocco & Waite, 2007). As African American women have progressed in the higher education arena, unfortunately, some assumptions about who they are and their capabilities have not progressed.

In this chapter, using the sports metaphors of "a level playing field" and "the art of funambulism (walking a tightrope/highwire)" we will explore the intersectionality of gender and race for African American women in academe and highlight how these two themes play a role in African American women's existence at PWI's. Special attention will be given to the following: (1) whether the tightrope is a level playing field, (2) how African American women artfully and skillfully use the props of tenacity, persistent focus, courage, and balance to traverse the tightrope of academe with no net, and (3) I will also identify key strategies for effective recruitment and retention of faculty women of color with specific emphasis on African American women.

The terms, Black and African American are utilized interchangeably in this chapter. This is done for two reasons. First it represents an ongoing struggle in and outside of the African American community over which term is most appropriate to define this group of people. Second, in much of the literature both words are used synonymously. In the context of this chapter, these terms are utilized to denote those persons of color who identify as Black, African American, African, Caribbean, or mixed-race persons who identify as Black and currently reside and work in the United States.

The Intersectionality of Race and Gender

Intersectionality (or intersectionalism) is the study of intersections between forms or systems of oppression, domination, or discrimination. The term is particularly prevalent in Black feminism, which argues that the experience of being a Black female cannot simply be understood in terms of being Black, and of being female, considered independently, but must include the interactions, which frequently reinforce each other. Kimberlé Crenshaw first coined the term intersectionality theory in 1989. Crenshaw stated that the intersectionality experience within Black women is more powerful than the sum of their race and sex alone, and that any observations that do not take intersectionality into consideration cannot accurately address the manner in which Black women are subordinated. Crenshaw (1993, 1995) distinguished among three ways in which race and gender intersect for women of color: structurally, representationally, and politically. The intersection of race and gender is particularly important for Black women because of the complex political and social context in which they live in the United States (Reid & Comas-Diaz, 1990). Structurally, "woman" and "Black person" are both considered to be lower status identities in the United States (Reid & Comas-Diaz, 1990). The low position that Black women occupy is related to the fact that they are in the position of being subjected to both racism and sexism (Crenshaw, 1993; King, 1988), sometimes even by members of their own social groups (i.e., they may experience sexism from within the Black community and racism from other women; Hurtado, 1989; King, 1988; Perkins, 1983; Reid & Comas-Diaz, 1990; Smith & Stewart, 1983). Representationally, Black women may be depicted by the media in ways that play on the unique negative, often sexualized, stereotypes of the Black woman (Collins, 1993), such as Jezebel, who is hypersexual and promiscuous; Mammy, who is asexual and nurturing; or Sapphire, who is domineering and emasculating (West, 1995, 2004). Politically, there has sometimes been a tension between the goals of Black people and women as groups, which leads to the possibility that individual Black women will feel torn between the potentially conflicting ideas, beliefs, and aims of the social and political groups that claim to represent women and those that claim to represent Blacks (King, 1988; Patterson et al., 1996; West & Fenstermaker, 1996).

When examining structural power relations, intersectionality functions better as a conceptual framework or heuristic device describing what kinds of things to consider than as one describing any actual patterns of social organization (P. H. Collins, 1998). Heuristic devices aim neither to prove things right or wrong nor to gather empirical data to test the existence of social phenomenon (P. H. Collins, 1998). The goal is not to prove intersectionality right or wrong, nor to gather empirical data to rest the existence of intersectionality. Rather, intersectionality provides an interpretive framework for thinking through how intersections of race and gender shape any group's experience across specific social contexts (P. H. Collins, 1998).

Despite increased numbers, Black faculty remains underrepresented as compared to their presence in the U.S. population and undergraduate education (Ryu, 2008). Unfortunately there has been little change in representation in the past 40 years, with Blacks representing 4% of the faculty in 1975 and 7% of the faculty in 2009 (U.S. Department of Education, 2011). While scholars have documented the challenges faced and noted the lack of change in representation among Black faculty in higher education, little attention has been paid to differences within this diverse group. For example, somewhat contrary to data and public discourses which suggest that Black women are represented in larger numbers and report higher levels of academic achievement relative to Black men in undergraduate and graduate education (e.g., Allen, Jayakumar, Griffin, Korn, & Hurtado, 2005; Cokley, 2001; Harvey & Anderson, 2005; Nettles & Perna, 1997), Black male faculty are more highly represented than their female counterparts, particularly at higher levels of academic rank (Harvey & Anderson, 2005; Ryu, 2008). In 2005, Black females outnumbered males at the instructor/lecturer level but were underrepresented among tenured faculty (44%) and full professors (36%) (Ryu, 2008). Further, there appear to be distinctions in the level of success that Black males and females experience in the academy. Thirty-nine percent of Black faculty overall had tenure in 2001, but the tenure rate was 43% for Black men and 34% for women (Harvey & Anderson, 2005). These statistics suggest that, in addition to racial differences in tenure and advancement, there are persistent disparities based on gender. Reflections published by female scholars of color (e.g., Berry & Mizelle, 2006; McKay, 1997; Vargas, 2002) and a growing body of empirical work (e.g., Chambers, 2011; Pittman, 2010; Thomas & Hollenshead, 2001; Turner, 2002) call attention to the unique challenges faced by female faculty of color as they navigate the success system in academia and try to distinguish the influence race and gender have on how they are perceived, treated, and evaluated as professors.

African American women face obstacles not experienced by their White colleagues. As a new faculty member, I find it disheartening and immediately enter into alert mode when I hear graduate students say on the first day of class, "Wow, you're the first African American woman that I have had as a professor." As we delve further into the course we find that this statement spans across the students' undergraduate career as well. Frequently, African American faculty participate in university meetings in which they are the only one or one of only a few. According to Wenniger and Conroy (2001),

> African American women are at once more visible and equally isolated due to racial and gender differences. The token woman often finds herself in situations where she is made aware of her unique status as the only African American female present, yet feels compelled to behave as though this difference did not exist. (p. 47)

An example is the opportunity to serve on search committees. In the span of a year at a new institution, I have served on three faculty search committees and on one administrator search committee. I believe it is an honor to serve; however, participating in service activities as defined by "cultural taxation" can take its toll and take over important time that should be devoted to research and scholarship that ultimately leads to progress toward tenure and promotion.

Extant literature suggests that the constructs of race and gender shape the academic roles of African American people in higher education (P. H. Collins, 1990; Miller & Vaughn, 1997; Thompson & Dey, 1998; Turner, Myers, & Creswell, 1999). A number of studies have attempted to explain the status of African American women in higher education. However, what generally occurs in many of these studies is that the experiences of Black women are compared to those of other women, usually White women, to verify whether or not they are meeting some arbitrary standard of normalcy in the academy (Miller & Vaughn, 1997). These studies are limited in their analysis because they do not take into account the legacy of race and gender relations in shaping the lives of African American women in society in general and in higher education more specifically (P. H. Collins, 1990; Gregory, 1995). These studies do not reveal how African American women interpret their experiences in PWIs, nor do they allow the women to discuss how sociocultural issues affect their overall academic citizenship.

There are many scholars who give voice to the question of activism in the forefront of academic discourse, challenging faculty members of all types to self-reflectively consider the nature of, and rationale for their work within the larger social world (Kuntz, 2006). As Ruddick (2004) claims, "activism requires academics … to cross boundaries of privilege and confront their personal stake in an issue, and the ways they are positioned differently from members of the organizations they work with" (p. 239). Self-reflective academic citizenship is a conscious movement beyond simply theorizing about social change, to actively participating in and advocating social transformation (Cloke, Crang, & Goodwin, 2004; D. Collins, 2005; Smith, 1987; Wilbert & Hoskyns, 2004).

Academic citizenship, then, requires faculty to acknowledge their role in society as a political one and that their daily practices as faculty—their "work"—has an effect on the students, faculty, administrators, and other citizens with whom they interact. Recognizing faculty work as political reframes faculty as civically engaged, countering the claim that higher education is distant from the real world. "All too often, civic-engagement is not rooted in the very heart of the academy: its courses, its research, its faculty work" (Musil, 2003, p. 4). The many practices which, together, produce conceptions of faculty work are multiple and dynamic. Hay (2001) indicates that the classroom itself serves as a nexus for several processes integral to academic citizenship: the material conditions in which faculty perform a central aspect of their work; an arena in which faculty may engage in the production and distribution of knowledge; the space in which faculty make "public" their work.

As an African American woman in the academy, as I teach my courses, establish my research and become civically engaged in service, I understand the dynamic of who I am and what I stand for versus who my colleagues think I am. I realize that daily I walk the tightrope of actively speaking up for social change and actively participating in and advocating for social transformation. But with that action comes the potential cost of reprisal from colleagues that I may work with.

As an already marginalized population, African American women faculty members are more often reprimanded by their dean and criticized by colleagues based on supposition, misperceptions, and on information without merit (Jarmon, 2001). Whenever such responses occur they compromise the professional integrity of African Americans, contaminate their professional experiences, and further highlight the politics of being an African American woman in higher education (Jarmon 2001).

Gay and Tate (1998) found that political and public policy attitudes were better predicted by Black women's level of racial identification than by their level of gender identification. They proposed that this may be due, in part, to more perceived experiences of racism than sexism, more awareness and dialogue about racism than sexism, and, correspondingly, more negative attitudes toward racism than sexism. This notion is somewhat supported by research that shows that Black women's expectation of general discrimination was predicted by perceived racial discrimination but not by perceived gender discrimination (Levin, Sinclair, Veniegas, & Taylor, 2002).

A Level Playing Field: Really?

Education has always been viewed as the great equalizer. However, what has not been taken into account is that increased education, strong work ethic, intelligence, drive, and aptitude does not necessarily translate into increased opportunity (i.e., a level playing field for advancement and success). The problems of inclusion and access continue to be prevalent for African American women as they pursue professional advancement in higher education institutions. What I would like to address is if the playing field is actually level. When we talk about everyone playing by the same set of rules, an underlying assumption is that everyone knows the rules and that those rules are explicitly stated. In actual practice, the rules of PWIs are often implicit, hidden and unspoken. For example, when a new untenured faculty member is hired, there is the expectation of research/scholarship, teaching, and service. However, what often remains unspoken in that dynamic is how much research/scholarship, how much teaching, and how much service is needed to ensure tenure and promotion. How exactly are these three areas evaluated and is there equal evaluation placed on each area? Researchers have noted that African American women at PWIs are often encouraged to participate in a number of campuswide service-type activities (Turner et al., 1999). Many African American faculty, especially women, are overwhelming burdened with service activities such that they become the resident advisor for ethnic underrepresented students on their campuses or they become the individuals that serve on several committees. This high visibility can be beneficial to them in some respects, but high visibility often leads to high levels of stress, as well as burnout and low levels of research productivity. Harley (2008) suggests that within the academy African American women simultaneously assume the roles of scholars, researchers, educators, mentors, service providers, and social change agents.

As African American women faculty members take the journey in the academy and move toward the tenure and promotion process with aspirations for advancement up the hierarchy of supervisory, management, and administrative goals, they are frequently "tagged as it" or the "go to person" for issues of diversity. In some ways their credibility and capital increases, but only within the realm of diversity. That is, not only do they perform the "expected" task and professional responsibilities of the professorate, they are also the advocates for Black issues, translators of Black culture, navigators of a patriarchal and racial minefields, community liaison, and conduits for others' problems. Yet, in these various formal and informal roles African American women are under surveillance to make sure that they do not pose a "threat" to the status quo (Harley, 2008). Unlike White male faculty members, women of color, especially African American women, are expected to handle minority and gender affairs, representing two constituencies. "Cultural taxation" is a term coined by Amado Padilla in 1994 as a way of describing the unique burden placed on ethnic minority faculty in carrying out their responsibility to service the university. He defined "cultural taxation" as the obligation to show good citizenship toward the institution by serving its needs for ethnic representation on committees, or to demonstrate knowledge and commitment to a cultural group, which, though it may bring accolades to the institution, is not usually rewarded by the institution on whose behalf the service was performed (Padilla, 1994). I believe this happens all too often and in these instances puts African American female faculty on the spot, to convince or persuade—to be the change agent. The faculty member feels the added pressure of being caught in a "Catch-22" because minority and gender issues are important to them.

Mitchell (1994) notes that the small numbers of women faculty of color compels them to serve simultaneously as a role model for their profession, race, and gender: "The accountability and time demands that the female ethnic professor encounters are especially pressing, given the fact that minority women occupy even fewer positions than minority men" (p. 387). In retrospect, this African American woman, who did not attain tenure in her first university states: "I am a female and African American.... I was doing a lot of things in terms of serving on this board, serving on that board, being faculty adviser for one of the professional fraternities." A Latina notes: "When you are one of three or four Latinos and being a woman, almost every committee wants you to be on it. It gives you opportunities, at the same time, I think, you are expected to do a lot of things not expected of other faculty."

These quotes bring attention to the contradiction and "double whammy" faced by women of color. On the one hand, there is too little opportunity and support for the work that is valued (research) (Fairweather, 1996); on the other hand, there is too much demand for work that is not rewarded (committee work, student club advisor, etc.). In most instances, service does not lead to tenure or to prestigious positions related to committee service, such as administration. Junior faculty members are particularly at risk. Institutional reward systems can deny tenure and security of employment to those who spend more time on service than on research and scholarship, even when the service is assigned to meet institutional needs. The invisible level playing field becomes this uneven seesaw of balancing research/scholarship, teaching, and service in route to tenure and promotion that unfortunately for some African American women becomes a locked door. An example of a locked door has been the opportunities to interview for positions of dean and associate dean respectively at two very different institutions. I can say without hesitation that my extensive time in higher education as an administrator has led to experiences that are vast and extensive, including coordinating a successful accreditation visit at one institution. These experiences speak to my ability to reach the final interview stage at both institutions. However, the sign that read "not enough" research and scholarship kept the door closed and locked. These two instances have played a significant role in changing the course of my career. After reflecting on my aspirations I sought out a new position at a different institution and am currently in a tenure track faculty position that also has some administrative duties attached.

Understanding the written and unwritten rules of academic life broadly, and departmental politics specifically, can help or hinder early career faculty during the tenure and promotion process. Thus, socialization is an important factor in the professional success of early career faculty (Clark & Corcoran, 1986; Johnson, 2001; Lucas & Murry, 2002). Clark and Corcoran (1986) defined socialization as "a mechanism through which new members learn the values, norms, knowledge, beliefs, and the interpersonal and other skills that facilitate role performance and further group goals" (p. 22). Early career faculty often have not received the proper prior training to become productive faculty members (La-Rocco & Bruns, 2006; Ortlieb, Biddix, & Doepker, 2010; Reynolds, 1992). Socialization activities for new faculty focus on the discipline-based knowl-edge and common skills required for academic and professional success. These areas, while important, fail to address many of the unwritten or unstated rules of academic culture that govern the academy (Johnson, 2001; LaRocco & Bruns, 2006; Reynolds, 1992). Successful socialization depends on many factors and often occurs prior to the first academic appointment. Previous exposure to academic culture in graduate school prepares faculty for assessing and evaluating their current (and future) departmental culture. Building upon the already challenging transition from student to professor, Black faculty often also experience isolation and alienation in departments (Johnsrud & DesJarlais, 1994; Phelps, 1995). Unfortunately, females are less likely than males to experience appreciation and support from colleagues (Bronstein & Farnsworth, 1998), while faculty of color receive less social support than White col-leagues (Ponjuan, Conley, & Trower, 2011). The lack of support is some-times a result of conflicting values that govern individual faculty members and the academy at large (Stanley, 2007).

Walking the Tightrope

Nik Wallenda is a very goal-oriented man who walked across the Little Grand Canyon Gorge in June, 2013. In 22 minutes, in high winds, he tra-versed 1,400 feet on a 2-inch cable 1,500 feet above ground without any safety apparatus. Nik Wallenda did not just wake up one morning and decide he was going to do this. He is a funambulist/aerialist who has trained all his life for these types of walks, Grand Canyon being the riski-est. His habits allowed him to achieve. But what's interesting, is that when it came time to perform, he ditched the encumbering harness and only used a balance rod. All his prior training kicked in and he simply focused on the walk. The core habits he developed over time, before the moment of performance, are what allow him to navigate life's challenge of walking a tightrope over the Grand Canyon with no net.

Tightrope walking (funambulism) is the art of walking along a thin ten-sioned wire or rope between two points, usually at a great height. It also is defined as a show especially of mental agility. Tightrope walkers some-times use balancing poles and may perform the feat without a safety net (The American Heritage Dictionary, 2009). Tightwire is also the art of maintaining balance while walking along a tensioned wire between two points. It can be done either using a balancing tool (umbrella, fan, balance pole, etc.) or "freehand," using only one's body to maintain balance.

According to Rossman (2000), barriers are variables that obstruct the progression of women into leadership positions. For change to occur, the barriers that have been identified must be deemed intolerable and something has to be done to remedy the situation. Schwarz and Hill (2010) purported that minority college educators affirm barriers such as student resistance and a difficult or biased administration as attributing to the underrepresentation of minority college professors. It is extremely imperative for administrators and educators on college campuses to be aware of how both race and gender produces inequities.

Kezar, Glenn, Lester, and Nakamota (2008) noted that challenging assumptions usually forms the foundational assertion for creating equity as it is unlikely that most people knowingly treat others in discriminatory ways. Therefore, higher education must first listen to the voices and challenge its own institutional system that creates barriers that hampers success and advancement among African American women who have historically been treated unfairly. Studies have shown that African American women have identified experiences within the academy through detailed accounts of counterstorytelling based on their perceptions of the unequal treatment they have received (Jackson & Harris, 2007; Patitu & Hinton, 2003; Williams, 1989). I too join them and add my voice.

The Props Used to Traverse the Tightrope of Academe With No Net

I equate walking the tightrope of academe with no net to those funambulists who courageously, artfully, and skillfully walk tightropes and highwires with no nets or safety harnesses. In June, 2013 Nik Wallenda walked a highwire across the Grand Canyon with no net and no safety apparatus. He merely used the prop of a balancing pole to traverse the 1,400 feet on a 2-inch cable 1,500 feet in the air. This reminds me of hooks's (1994) book *Teaching to Transgress*, in which hooks not only calls for a progressive, transformative-centered pedagogy, but also argues that African American faculty members must feel and be empowered, facilitated by a process of self-actualization, if they are to empower others.

In private and informal conversations, African American women have used several words (the props) that they have used to assist them in balancing as they traversed the tightrope of academe with no net. Here are four of the most used words/props that women have used.

Tenacity—tenacity is the quality displayed by someone who just will not quit— who keeps trying until they reach their goal; the quality or fact of being able to grip something firmly. Most people will tell you that tenacity is a great quality to have, especially if you are trying something challenging that takes a while to complete. Odds are the people you admire have shown real tenacity in achieving their goals. Anything really worth doing takes persistence, perseverance, and stubborn determination. Being a great baseball player requires real gifts, no doubt, but even the most gifted player won't make it to the big leagues without the tenacity required to make the long, hard journey up from the minors.

African American women in academe have had to be tenacious to endure the discriminatory tenants of sexism and racism. The proverbial, "we want you to teach the diversity course to undergraduate students who have never had a diversity course" was the beginning of my teaching career as an adjunct. I knew the material so what could possibly go wrong? My first semester I was challenged at every turn. The students had not had an African American woman as an instructor and they certainly had not had taken a diversity course, even though these were juniors in college preparing to become teacher educators. Their resistance to the material was overwhelming and at times their attitudes and responses were rude and inconsiderate. My goal after that semester was to come back with a stronger inner strength and different strategies to continue to work with students who were not open to issues of diversity.

Persistent Focus—continuing firmly or obstinately in a course of action in spite of difficulty or opposition; continuing to do something or to try to do something even though it is difficult or other people want you to stop; continuing beyond the usual, expected, or normal time; not stopping or going away. Focus: a main purpose or interest. As a former administrator at a large institution in the Midwest I was satisfied and quite happy with the work that I was doing in preparing high school students to enter the college or university of their choice. I reported to a talented, well-respected associate dean who one day during an annual review stated that in order for me to grow professionally, I needed to pursue a doctoral degree. I knew working full time and taking courses would not be an easy task and quite frankly I did not believe I needed a doctorate to continue to work and grow professionally in the higher education arena. After several conversations, I knew that I would have to travel the tightrope and have persistent focus in order to continue working full time and pursue a doctoral degree.

Courage—the ability to do something that you know is difficult or dangerous; mental or moral strength to venture, persevere, and withstand danger, fear, or difficulty. Courage in our conversations has been the fight to be part of the educational system that has always been viewed as the great equalizer. Courage is not a new phenomenon in my life. As a matter of fact during the spring of 2013 I knew that it was time for me to take charge of my professional career. This would take courage because I was excelling in my position as an administrator, but I knew I needed and wanted more. So in the fall of 2013, I accepted a new position as a tenure-track assistant professor, moving from the west coast to the Midwest. I then began the task of establishing my research and scholarship. My life is an example of walking the tightrope with no net.

Balance—the state of having your weight spread equally so that you do not fall; the ability to move or to remain in a position without losing control or falling. The balance of work and personal life has been a struggle for many. In academe one asks, how do I balance teaching, research, and service so that I am successful at obtaining tenure? A 2008 report coauthored by Sharpe, Darity, and Swinton suggests that Black women appear to be substantially less likely than other segments of the population to get on and stay on academe's tenure track. The researchers based their analysis on data from surveys that the National Science Foundation has administered to the same doctoral recipients repeatedly since the early 1990s, to track their progress over time. The fields covered by the surveys included engineering, mathematics, the sciences, and the social sciences. In crunching data derived from the surveys, the researchers found that Black women were about twice as likely to transfer from a tenure-track faculty position to an adjunct research path than members of other groups, including Black men. They were substantially less likely than other segments of the population to be retained in tenure-track faculty positions and more likely to go from having a postdoctoral fellowship to being unemployed. Reflecting on this study, I ask what throws one off balance and how do I keep from falling off the tightrope?

As an African American woman in the higher education arena, success for me comes at a high price. Walking the tightrope with no net, or in this case seeking tenure and promotion, is not an easy feat. There will be individuals along my journey who will try to upset the tightrope (prevent tenure and promotion) intentionally or unintentionally whether through their words and or actions. The significance of no net means there is little room for failure so I fight for a level playing field. I want the opportunity to be judged and evaluated fairly.

CONCLUDING THOUGHTS

The current era of higher education strategic planning signifies both a foundational and philosophical approach for improving and sustaining institutional accomplishments. As part of the vision for the future, many PWIs have identified diversity in faculty and the student body as one of many commitments. Many institutions focus on recruiting African American faculty, specifically women and then fail to have a plan in place for retention. Survival of African American women in the academy is contingent upon many variables, especially generating support networks inside and outside the university setting.

African American women will need to develop strong survival skills if they are to remain psychologically and physically healthy as members of PWIs. To assist African American women in becoming full participants in their academic departments and the community in general, department chairs and senior-level administrators may need to develop support programs for faculty of color. Support could be structured in the form of, professional development opportunities, and community support groups to help African American women in establishing professional as well as personal peer relations. Once established, the initiatives should be periodically evaluated.

Establishing Professional and Peer Relations

Colleges and universities can facilitate opportunities for women faculty of color to get together. For example, colleges can host social gatherings and academic activities targeted at promoting networking among its women faculty of color. Such activities could include: providing seed money for collaborative research of interest to women of color across disciplines, holding national or local conferences with the intent of bringing together women faculty of color, and host open forums that showcase research conducted by women faculty of color.

Mentoring networks are an effective means of supporting African American women faculty. Mentoring networks are vital support structures in a successful academic career, as emerging scholars seek to navigate the complex and protean racial and gender dynamics of academic institutions (Sorcinelli & Yun, 2007). Burgess (1997) contends that sponsorship is crucial to untenured junior faculty because senior faculty assist them in locating and securing research funding, developing research proposals, and introducing them to members of other networks, all of which are important for successful movement through the tenure process. The mentoring process is a two-way street. Extant literature has suggested a direct correlation between mentoring African American women in academe and their success in higher education (Crawford & Smith, 2005; Holmes, Land, & Hinton-Huston, 2007; Nichols & Tanksley, 2004; Patton, 2009). Conclusions were drawn from studies conducted by Mabokela and Green (2001), Holmes and Terrell (2004), and Danley (2003), attributing a major benefit of mentoring being career advancement and mobility (Holmes et al., 2007; Patton, 2009).

Professional Development Opportunities

Colleges and universities can provide professional development experiences that assist new women faculty of color to overcome challenges of multiple marginality. One example is the participation in a teaching development program. Participants in this program work in small groups guided by senior faculty members who were recipients of university teaching awards. The best mentor teachers grasped the need for faculty members to understand the technical side of teaching as well as the classroom dynamics. Mentor teachers can help newer faculty to see and address power relationships that may develop in a classroom that challenge the authority and credibility of a woman of color. Mentor teachers can also encourage new faculty members to accept their leadership role as the professor. Participating in such a program can foster understanding of group dynamics in the classroom. It can affirm different styles of teaching, such as fostering collaborative and small-group work. These programs can be used to inform not only women faculty of color but the rest of the campus community as well.

Assisting African American women in establishing professional and peer relationships and providing opportunities for engagement in professional development activities promotes a welcoming environment. Most women faculty of color contend that a healthy, supportive, rewarding, and inclusive environment is good for everyone. Kanter (1977) and others reveal that one crucial component in producing such an environment is to increase the representation of women of color across the campus—as students, administrators, and faculty. This representation must be reflected across student (undergraduate, graduate) and professional ranks (assistant, associate, and full professor). However, Harvey (1991) and others remind us of the critical importance of developing a campus culture that values and welcomes the contributions made by women faculty of color to the academic enterprise; that is, acknowledging that the inclusion of women faculty of color contributes to the academy as a whole. Cole (2000) emphasizes this point by stating that diversity—in the people, the ideas, the theories, the perspectives, experiences, and the pedagogy in American higher education—is crucial to a quality education (p. 2). Such support promotes a comfort level that can increase productivity at work and persistence on campus.

As faculty of color, we must assess the range of our individual needs, as well as identify multiple avenues for getting them met. It is also vital to ask without shame for the specific types of help that will meet our individual needs. Given the scale of needs, it is useful to proactively cultivate an ongoing, diverse, and ever-expanding mentoring network internally and externally, as well as institutionally and personally. One should seek faculty members and resources within one's department, but also within the general campus. Faculty of color have successfully developed affiliations in other departments, centers, institutes, and organizations across campus to foster intellectual development and make social connections with other faculty (Griffin, Pifer, Humphrey, & Hazelwood, 2011, p. 512). Significant barriers are often faced by African American faculty and administrators on predominantly White campuses (Crawford & Smith, 2005). The authors asserted that barriers such as "isolation, loneliness, and racially motivated victimization inhibit their academic success and tenure" (p. 52). Research has revealed that mentoring is a factor leading to advancement and mobility in personal development, employment, and success in education (Crawford & Smith, 2005; Holmes et al., 2007). However, it is not enough to just recruit more qualified African Americans in administrative positions without substantive programs in place to retain them.

Sotello Viernes Turner (2002) states that many women faculty of color see themselves as reflecting and projecting their realities in the work that they do. As professors they bring their experiences and knowledge into campus dialogues in the classroom, in the literature, and in their communities. Women faculty of color provide guidance and support for young women of color who are their students or their colleagues in the professoriate. They advocate for the admission of talented women of color into the student and faculty bodies. Their presence encourages others to pursue individual educational goals. Such contributions by women faculty of color are described in the following quote:

> The academy is shaped by many social forces. More women of color are defining and redefining their roles within it. New ways of thinking about teaching and research have provided spaces for women scholars to challenge old assumptions about what it means to be in the academy. While both the women's movement and Black [ethnic] studies movement have helped increase the parameters of academic work, new paradigms emerging from Black women's scholarship provide me with a liberatory lens through which to view and construct my scholarly life. The academy and my scholarly life need not be in conflict with the community and cultural work I do (and intend to do). (Ladson-Billings, 1997, p. 66)

REFERENCES

Allen, W. R., Jayakumar, U. M., Griffin, K. A., Korn, W. S., & Hurtado, S. (2005). *Black undergraduates from Bakke to Grutter: Freshmen status, trends, and prospects, 1971–2004.* Los Angeles, CA: Higher Education Research Institute.

The American Heritage Dictionary. (2009). Funambulism. Retrieved from http://www.thefreedictionary.com/funambulist

Berry, T. R., & Mizzelle, N. D. (2006). *From oppression to grace: Women of color and their dilemmas in the academy.* Sterling, VA: Stylus.

Brayboy, B. M. J. (2003). The implementation of diversity in predominantly White college and universities. *Journal of Black Studies, 34*(1), 72–86.

Bronstein, P., & Farnsworth, L. (1998). Gender differences in faculty experiences of interpersonal climate and processes for advancement. *Research in Higher Education, 39*(5), 557–585.

Burgess, N. J. (1997). Tenure and promotion among African American women in the academy: Issues and strategies. In L. Benjamin (Ed.), *Black women in the academy: Promises and perils* (pp. 227–234). Gainesville, FL: University Press of Florida.

Clark, S. M., & Corcoran, M. (1986). Perspectives of the professional socialization of women faculty: A case of accumulative disadvantage? *The Journal of Higher Education, 57*(1), 20–43.

Chambers, C. R. (2011). Candid reflections on the departure of Black women faculty from academe in the United States. *The Negro Educational Review, 62–63*(1–4), 233–261.

The Chronicle of Higher Education. (2010). Almanac of higher education 2012–2011. *The Chronicle of Higher Education, 57,* 20.

Cloke, P. J., Crang, P., & Goodwin, M. (2004). *Envisioning human geographies.* London, England: Oxford University Press.

Cokley, K. O. (2001). Gender differences among African American students in the impact of racial identity on academic psychosocial development. *Journal of College Student Development, 42*(5), 480–487.

Cole, J. (2000). Social change requires academic women's leadership. *Women in Higher Education, 9*(6), 1–2.

Collins, D. (2005, September–October). The ivory tower and scholar-activism. *Academe.* Retrieved from http://www.aaup.org/publications/Academe/2005/2005so/2005soactivism.htm

Collins, P. H. (1990). *Black feminist thought: Knowledge, consciousness, and the politics of empowerment.* New York, NY: Routledge.

Collins, P. H. (1993). The sexual politics of Black womanhood. In P. B. Bart & E. G. Moran (Eds.), *Violence against women: The bloody footprints* (pp. 85–104). Newbury Park, CA: SAGE.

Collins, P. H. (1998). *Fighting words: Black women & the search for justice.* Minneapolis, MN: University of Minnesota Press.

Crawford, K., & Smith, D. (2005). The we and the us: Mentoring African American women. *Journal of Black Studies, 36*(1), 52–67.

Crenshaw, K. (1989). *Demarginalizing the Intersection of race and sex: A Black feminist critique of antidiscrimination doctrine, feminist theory and antiracist politics.* University of Chicago Legal Forum 1989: 139–67. Retrieved May, 2014, http://allisonbolah.com/site_resources/reading_list/Demarginalizing_Crenshaw.pdf

Crenshaw, K. W. (1993). Beyond racism and misogyny: Black feminism and 2 Live Crew. In M. J. Matsuda, C. R. Lawrence III, R. Delgado, & K. W. Crenshaw

(Eds.), *Words that wound: Critical race theory, assaultive speech, and the first amendment* (pp. 111–132). Boulder, CO: Westview.

Crenshaw, K. W. (1995). The intersection of race and gender. In K. W. Crenshaw, N. Gotanda, G. Peller, & K. Thomas (Eds.), *Critical race theory: The key writings that formed the movement* (pp. 357–383). New York, NY: New Press.

Crocco, M. S., & Waite, C. L. (2007). Education and marginality: Race and gender in higher education, 1940–1955. *History of Education Quarterly, 47*(1), 69–91.

Danley, L. L. (2003). Truths about sojourner: African-American women and the professorship. Their struggles and their successes on negotiating promotion and tenure at a predominantly White institution. *Dissertation Abstracts International, 64*(3).

Fairweather, J. (1996). *Faculty work and the public trust.* Boston, MA: Allyn & Bacon.

Gay, C., & Tate, K. (1998). Doubly bound: The impact of gender and race on the politics of Black women. *Political Psychology, 19*, 169–184.

Gregory. S. T. (1995). *Black women in the academy: The secrets to success and achievement.* New York, NY: University Press of America.

Griffin, K. A., Bennett, J. C., & Harris, J. (2013). Marginalizing merit?: Gender differences in Black faculty d/discourses on tenure, advancement, and professional success. *The Review of Higher Education, 36*(4), 489–512.

Griffin, K. A., Pifer, J. M., Humphrey, J. R., & Hazelwood, A. M. (2011). (Re)defining departure: Exploring Black professors' experiences with and responses to racism and racial climate. *American Journal of Education, 117*(4), 495–526.

Hay, I. (2001). Critical geography and activism in higher education. *Journal of Geography in Higher Education, 25*(2), 141–146.

Harley, D. (2008). Maids of Academe: African American women faculty at predominantly White institutions. *Journal of African American Studies, 12*(1) 19–36.

Harvey, W. B. (1991). Faculty responsibility and tolerance. *Thought and Action, 7*, 115–136.

Harvey, W. B., & Anderson, E. L. (2005). *Minorities in higher education: Twenty-first annual status report.* Washington, DC: American Council on Education

Holmes, S. L., & Terrell, M. C. (Eds.) (2004). Lifting as we climb: Mentoring the next generation of African American student affairs administrators [Special issue]. *National Association of Student Affairs Professionals Journal, 6*(1), 1–134.

Holmes, S. L., Land, L. D., & Hinton-Huston, V. D. (2007). Race still matters: Considerations for mentoring Black women in academe. *The Negro Educational Review, 58*, 105–129.

hooks, b. (1994). *Teaching to transgress: Education as the practice of freedom.* New York, NY: Routledge.

Hurtado, A. (1989). Relating to privilege: Seduction and rejection in the subordination of White women and women of color. *Signs, 14*, 833–855.

Jackson, S., & Harris, S. (2007). African American female college and university presidents: Experiences and perceptions of barriers to the presidency. *Journal of Women in Educational Leadership, 5*(2), 119–137.

James, J., & Farmer R. (Eds.). (1993). *Spirit, space, and survival: African American women in (White) academe.* New York, NY: Routledge.

Jarmon, B. (2001). Unwritten rules of the game. In R. O. Mabokela & A. L. Green (Eds.), *Sisters of the academy: Emergent Black women scholars in higher education* (pp. 175–181). Sterling, VA: Stylus.

Johnsrud, L. K., & Des Jarlais, C. D. (1994). Barriers to tenure for women and minorities. *The Review of Higher Education, 17*(4), 335–353.

Johnson, B. J. (2001). Faculty socialization: Lessons learned from urban Black colleges. *Urban Education, 36*(5), 630–647. doi:10.1177/0042085901365007

Kanter, R. M. (1977). *Men and women of the corporation.* New York, NY: Basic Books.

Kezar, A., Glenn, W., Lester, J., & Nakamota, J. (2008). Examining organizational contextual features that affect implementation of equity initiatives. *The Journal of Higher Education, 79*(2), 125–138.

King, D. H. (1988). Multiple jeopardy, multiple consciousness: The context of a Black feminist ideology. *Signs, 15,* 42–72.

Kuntz, A. (2006). Academic citizenship: The risks and responsibilities of reframing faculty work. *Journal of College and Character, 7*(5). Retrieved May, 2014, from http://www.tandfonline.com/doi/pdf/10.2202/1940-1639.1197

Ladson-Billings, G. (1997). For colored girls who have considered suicide when the academy's not enough: Reflections of an African American woman scholar. In A. Neumann & P. L. Peterson (Eds.), *Learning from our lives: Women, research, and autobiography in education* (pp. 52–69). New York, NY: Teachers College Press.

LaRocco, D. J., & Bruns, D. A. (2006). Practitioner to professor: An examination of second career academics' entry into academia. *Education, 126*(4), 626–639.

Levin, S., Sinclair, S., Veniegas, R. C, & Taylor, P. L. (2002). Perceived discrimination in the context of multiple group memberships. *Psychological Science, 13,* 557–560.

Lucas, C. J., & Murry, J. W. (2002). *New faculty: A practical guide for academic beginners.* New York, NY: Palgrave Macmillan.

Mabokela, R. O., & Green, A. L. (2001). *Sisters of the academy: Emergent Black women scholars in higher education.* Sterling, VA: Stylus.

McGowan, J. M. (2000). African-American faculty classroom teaching experiences in predominantly White colleges and universities. *Multicultural Education, 8*(2), 19–22.

McKay, N. Y. (1997). A troubled peace: Black women in the halls of the White academy. In L. Benjamin (Ed.), *Black women in the academy: Promises and perils* (pp. 11–22). Gainesville, FL: University Press of Florida.

Miller, J. R., & Vaughn, G. G. (1997). African American women executives: Themes that bind. In L. Benjamin (Ed.), *Black women in the academy: Promises and perils* (pp. 179–188). Gainesville, FL: University Press of Florida.

Mitchell, J. (1994, January/February). Visible, vulnerable, and viable: Emerging perspectives of a minority professor. *The Journal of Higher Education, 73*(1), 74–93.

Musil, C. (2003). Educating for citizenship. *Peer Review, 5*(3), 4–8.

Nelson, C. (1997). *Manifesto of a tenured radical.* New York, NY: New York University Press.

Nettles, M. T., & Perna, L. W. (1997). *The African American education data book: Higher and adult education* (Vol. 1). Fairfax, VA: Frederick D. Patterson Research Institute of the College Fund/UNCF.

Nicolas, J. C., & Tanksley, C. B. (2004). Revelations of African American women with terminal degrees: Overcoming obstacles to success. *The Negro Educational Review, 55*(4), 175–185.

Ortlieb, E. T., Biddix, J. P., & Doepker, G. M. (2010). A collaborative approach to higher education induction. *Active Learning in Higher Education, 11*(2), 109–118. doi:10.1177/1469787410365655

Padilla, A. M. (1994). Ethnic minority scholars, research, and mentoring: Current and future issues. *Educational Researcher, 23*(4), 24–27

Patitu, C. L., & Hinton, K. G., (2003). The experiences of African American women faculty and administrators in higher education: Has anything changed? *New Directions for Student Services, 104,* 79–93.

Patterson, L. A., Cameron, J. E., & Lalonde, R. N. (1996). The intersection of race and gender: Examining the politics of identity in women's studies. *Canadian Journal of Behavioural Science, 28,* 229–239.

Patton, L. D. (2009). My sister's keeper: A qualitative examination of mentoring experiences among African American women in graduate and professional schools. *The Journal of Higher Education, 80*(5), 510–537.

Perkins, L. M. (1983). The impact of the "cult of true womanhood" on the education of Black women. *Journal of Social Issues, 39*(3), 17–28.

Phelps, R. E. (1995). What's in a number: Implications for African American female faculty at predominantly White colleges and universities. *Innovative Higher Education, 19*(4), 255–268.

Pittman, C. T. (2010). Race and gender oppression in the classroom: The experience of women faculty of color with White male students. *Teaching Sociology, 38*(3), 183–196.

Ponjuan, L., Conley, V. M., & Trower, C. (2011). Career stage differences in pre-tenure-track faculty perceptions of professional and personal relationships with colleagues. *The Journal of Higher Education, 82*(3), 319–346.

Reid, P. T., & Comas-Diaz, L. (1990). Gender and ethnicity: Perspectives on dual status. *Sex Roles, 22,* 397–408.

Reynolds, A. (1992). Charting changes in junior faculty: Relationships among socialization, acculturation, and gender. *The Journal of Higher Education, 63*(6), 637–652.

Rossman, E. M. (2000). A study of barriers affecting women in educational administration. *Dissertation Abstracts International, 64*(1), 40.

Ruddick, S. (2004). Activist geographies: Building possible worlds. In P. Cloke, P. Crang & M. Goodwin (Eds.), *Envisioning human geographies* (pp. 229–241). New York, NY: Oxford University Press.

Ryu, M. (2008). *Minorities in higher education 2008: Twenty-third status report.* Washington, DC: American Council on Education.

Schwarz, J., & Hill, K. L. (2010). Why so few minority professors in higher education? *Journal of Organizational Culture, Communications, and Conflict, 14*(2), 83–95.

Sharpe, R. V., Darity, Jr., W. A., & Swinton, O. A. (2008). *The state of Blacks in higher education* [Draft report]. Silver Spring, MD: National Association for Equal Opportunity in Higher Education.

Smith, A. & Stewart, A. J. (1983). Approaches to studying racism and sexism in Black women's lives. *Journal of Social Issues, 39*(3), 1–15.

Smith, D. E. (1987). *The everyday world as problematic: A feminist sociology.* Boston, MA: Northeastern University Press.

Sotello Viernes Turner, C. (2002). Women of color in academe: Living with multiple marginality. *The Journal of Higher Education, 73*(1), 74–93.

Sorcinelli, M. D., & Yun, J. H. (2007). From mentors to mentoring networks: Mentoring in the new academy. *Change Magazine, 39*(6), 58.

Stanley, C. A. (2007). When counter narratives meet master narratives in the journal editorial-review process. *Educational Researcher, 36*(1), 14–24.

Thomas, G. D., & Hollenshead, C. (2001). Resisting from the margins: The coping strategies of Black women and other women of color faculty members at a research university. *Journal of Negro Education, 70*(3), 166–175.

Thompson, C. J., & Dey, E. L. (1998). Pushed to the margins: Sources of stress for African American college and university faculty. *The Journal of Higher Education, 69,* 324–345.

Turner, C. V., Myers, S. L., & Creswell, J. W. (1999). Exploring underrepresentation: The case of faculty of color in the Midwest. *The Journal of Higher Education, 70,* 27–59.

U.S. Department of Education, National Center for Education Statistics. (2011). *Digest of education statistics*, 2010 (NCES 2011–015), Table 256.

Vargas, L. (2002). *Women faculty of color in the White classroom: Narratives on the pedagogical implications of teacher diversity.* New York, NY: Peter Lang.

Wenniger, M. D., & Conroy, M. H. (2001). *Gender equity or bust: On the road to campus leadership with women in higher education.* San Francisco, CA: Jossey-Bass.

West, C., & Fenstermaker, S. (1996). Doing difference. In E. N. Chow, D. Wilkinson, & M. B. Zinn (Eds.), *Race, class, & gender: Common bonds, different voices* (pp. 357–384). Thousand Oaks, CA: SAGE.

West, C. M. (1995). Mammy, Jezebel, and Sapphire: Historical images of Black women and their implications for psychotherapy. *Psychotherapy, 32,* 458–466.

West, C. M. (2004). Mammy, Jezebel, and Sapphire: Developing an "oppositional gaze" toward the images of Black women. In J. C. Chrisler, C. Golden, & P. D. Rozee (Eds.), *Lectures on the psychology of women* (3rd ed., pp. 237–252). Boston, MA: McGraw-Hill.

Wilbert, C., & Hoskyns, T. (2004). 'Say something constructive or say nothing at all': Being relevant and irrelevant in and beyond the academy today. In D. Fuller & R. Kitchin (Eds.), *Radical theory/critical praxis: Making a difference beyond the academy?* (pp. 57–67). Victoria, British Columbia, Canada: Praxis.

Williams, A. (1989). Research on Black women in college administrators: Descriptive and interview data. *Sex Roles, 21*(1-2), 99–112.

LENGTHENING YOUR STRIDE

Finding the Right Balance on the Tightrope

Patricia A. Mitchell

> I'll walk the tightrope that's been stretched for me,
> and though a wrinkled forehead, perplexed why,
> will accompany me, I'll delicately
> step along. For if I stop to sigh
> at the earth-propped stride
> of others, I will fall. I must balance high
> without a parasol to tide
> a faltering step, without a net below,
> without a balance stick to guide. (Danner, 1992, p. 87)

"Walking the Tightrope of Academe With No Net" explores the infrastructure of the academy and provides in great detail, a systematic account of many barriers impeding African American women from obtaining tenure and promotions at predominately White colleges and universities. The author draws on the lessons she learned while performing the balancing act and trying to walk the tightrope without falling. It was the late Dr. John Hope Franklin, a prolific scholar of African American history, who introduced the *"tightrope walking"* concept in his autobiography, *Mirror to America*. Franklin (2005) pointed out the struggles and

*Beyond Retention: Cultivating Spaces of Equity, Justice, and Fairness
for Women of Color in U.S. Higher Education*, pp. 47–53

47

discrimination he experienced throughout his trajectory in the academy
more than 60 years ago. He explained,

> While I set out to advance my professional career on the basis of the highest
> standards of scholarship, I also use scholarship to expose the hypocrisy
> underlying so much of the American social and race relations. It never
> ceased being a risky feast of tightrope walking. (p. 376)

Research findings reveal that instead of women and men being on
equal footing and their career trajectories gender-blind, inequality
remains embedded within the system (Aguirre, 2000; Pittman, 2010).
Even though women comprise over half of the students graduating from
colleges and universities, the picture still remains bleak for women in academe. As noted by the author, despite decades of efforts to create opportunities for women's advancement, deep inequities still exist for faculty of
color in the academy (Glazer-Raymo, 2008; Guinier & Torres, 2002; Ponjuan, 2005; Robinson & Clardy, 2010).

If nothing else, history has taught us that the climb up the ivory tower
for African American women is a very lonely climb with many other barriers impeding our trajectory (Salazar, 2009; Turner & Myers, 2000). There
is a preponderance of research discussing the experiences of faculty of
color at predominantly White universities (Combs, 2003; hooks, 2003;
Turner, Gonzalez, & Wood, 2008) that serves as a powerful reminder that
African American women faculty experience exclusion, isolation, alienation, and racism in these White universities (Aguirre, 2002; Allen et al.,
2002; Ladson-Billings, 1996; Pittman, 2010). In bell hooks's (1991) *Yearning: Race, Gender and Cultural Politics*, she writes:

> Folks may be comfortable with the presence of Black female academicians
> and may even desire their presence, but they are less welcoming of Black
> women who present themselves as committed intellectuals who need institu-
> tional support, time and space to pursue this dimension of their reality. (p.
> 152)

This chapter espoused "how predominately white institutions often
view diversity as a free-standing policy, and the way that diversity is something that can be implemented without necessarily changing the underlying structure of the institution and its day-to-day operations." While many
universities have been slow to truly embrace a diversity plan, others have
taken steps to put substance and real dollars behind a living plan. Accordingly, the *U.S. News and World Report* has ranked the university where I
work as one of top 20 universities and colleges for diversity. Over the last
5 years, the student population has become more diverse, but it has just
been since 2011 when the university created the office of diversity and

community outreach to define strategic institution goals in the area of diversity, inclusion, and equity. Since its inception, the office has moved swiftly to establish a council on diversity and to resurrect the president's advisory committee on the status of women. From an insider witnessing this changing university, I see a process driven by a commitment of a new president, its institutional mission, and its core values.

Even with universities institutionalizing diversity plans, Combs (2003) continues to reiterate how African American women experience lower promotion rates, more occupational job segregation, different predictors for advancement than African American men, and negative career expectancies due to racism and sexism. To counter this argument, this chapter contains a rich discussion of four props (tenacity, persistent focus, courage, and balance) used by African American women to traverse the tightrope of academe. Additionally, the author uses her own personal narratives to illustrate each prop. The narratives presented validate my own experiences, but it saddens me to know that I've spent almost 40 years in the academy, and so much still remains the same. I will add my perspective to each of the props by presenting a narrative from my trajectory in the academy.

Tenacity—As alluded to by the author of this chapter, White students underestimate the credentials and academic rank of female faculty of color. There is a body of research that shows White students are more apt to show less respect for African American women faculty than their White counterparts, and these students will challenge the women's authority as professors (Ladson-Billings, 1996; Stanley, 2006; Tuitt, 2003; Umbach, 2006). Speaking from personal knowledge, I can relate to being shown less respect by White students during my 38 years in the academy. Each semester when I designed my course syllabus, I would type my name followed by PhD, e-mail, and telephone number on the cover page. Early on in my career, there would be at least one student every semester asking, "What do you want us to call you?" My first thought was "What else would you call me, but Dr.?" But before I could answer, another student would say, "Can we call you by your first name?" I would politely remind the students to refer to me as Dr. … or Professor. Even in 2014, I still get the same questions and I am still responding the same way.

There is also another set of standards imposed on African American faculty women when it comes to assigning grades. Even though my grading policy has clear guidelines; clear explanations written in the course syllabus; rubrics being used to grade each assignment and graded papers returned with written comments, White students still appeal their grades more than students of color. It became so ridiculous one semester that when I submitted a final grade of (A−) for a White male student, you would have thought I had failed the student. He appealed the grade because he felt he deserved an A grade without the minus sign. At our university, even though the student can go through the appeal process, the instructor cannot be forced to change a grade. As a result, I had my documentation and the grade remained unchanged. So what was the lesson learned? Not much has changed over these many years. White students continue to ask what should they call me at the beginning of a new semester and they continue to appeal their grades.

Persistent Focus—As bell hooks (1991) espoused "the environment of the predominately White campus is not typically welcoming to Black women administrators or academicians who demonstrate commitment, competence, and integrity and above all, who are shown to be independent-thinkers" (p. 160). So many times, we will keep our thoughts about our career goals to ourselves. But not having an action plan can be career suicide. You need to have a defined plan that points you in the right direction toward your goals and aspirations. At my workplace, we meet once a year with our academic dean to discuss our academic career plan. This is a one-on-one opportunity to discuss our teaching, service, and research from the previous year; present an explanation of the three areas for the present school year and delineate what our plans are for the following year. The dean is there to give constructive feedback and provide guidance for those faculty preparing applications for tenure and promotion in the future. In addition to this academic career plan, you need to have short-term, intermediate and long-term goals.

Courage—I liked when the author talked about courage being the ability to do something that you know is difficult and dangerous and how she moved from the west coast to the Midwest to take a position. I did something similar 38 years ago, moving from the east coast to the west coast. I call it a "mid-life crisis." I was turning 30 when I quit my job as a school teacher in Maryland and moved to California. Having courage and faith sustained me until I found a job. That's exactly what happened. I interviewed for a position at my present workplace and 38 years later I am writing about that experience in this essay. If that did not take courage, I do not know what else you would call it.

Balance—Women often get in the trap of feeling like they are constantly burning the candle at both ends. The research shows that work/family policies are underutilized, as faculty perceive it may not be professionally prudent to use such policies (Friedman, Rimsky, & Johnson, 1996; Trower, 2003). The American Association of University Professors' efforts to address the special challenge of making academic careers more compatible with participation in family life proceed from their Statement of Principles on Family Responsibilities and Academic Work (2001). To encourage implementation of the policies and practices set forth in that document, the American Association of University Professors developed a website as a resource for both faculty and institutions. Our careers are demanding and in the final analysis, many women end up feeling exhausted, fatigued with no time of their own. Time management is a key aspect in finding personal time, along with the art of saying no or negotiating realistic deadlines to complete tasks. Your ability to perform at your best requires that you be realistic about what you can achieve in the time you have. It is possible for you to manage the expectations of teaching, service, and research in your faculty position.

At the end of the chapter, the author offers several recommendations to the institutions to help in the recruiting, promoting, and retention of African American women faculty. Certainly, this is an important resource for women and minorities seeking success in the academy. In addition to these wonderful suggestions, I would like to be frank with African American faculty women. What can we do on a personal level? Are we just turning our wheels day in and day out? In 2011, I wrote a book entitled, *Ten Stupid Things Women Do to Mess Up Their Careers*, after years of research and walking the tightrope, I concluded I was making these 10 mistakes over and over. I needed to open my eyes from being unaware to taking a bold stand in the management of my life and career. What about you? Those 10 mistakes are:

1. Lacking a mentor/advisor/coach.
2. Failing to have an action plan.
3. Underusing your communication skills.
4. Not tooting your own horn.
5. Having underdeveloped leadership skills.
6. Worrying about being like by everyone.
7. Neglecting the art of negotiation.
8. Not knowing how to guard your personal time.
9. Always putting others first instead of yourself.
10. Acting like a man (Mitchell & Parry, 2011).

Finally, let me again commend the author of this chapter, "Walking the Tightrope of Academe With No Net," for her analysis of how higher education has responded to faculty of color; its effect on gender equality; and identifying ingredients for promoting more representation of African American women at our predominately White universities. It is an indispensable source of information for academia, students, administrators, and policymakers who devote themselves to the question of how to effectively promote gender equality in higher education.

REFERENCES

American Association of University Professors. (2001). *Statement of principles on family responsibilities and academic work.* Washington: DC: Author.

Aguirre, A. (2000). Women and minority faculty in the academic workplace: Recruitment, retention, and academic culture. *ASHE-ERIC Higher Education Reports, 27*(6), 1–110.

Allen, W., Epps, E, Guillory, E., Suh, S., Bonous-Hammarth, M., & Stassen, M. (2002). Outsiders within: Race, gender, and faculty status in U.S. higher education. In W. Smith, P. G. Altbach, & K. Lomotey (Eds.), *The racial crisis in American higher education* (pp. 189–220). Albany, NY: State University of New York Press.

Combs, G. M. (2003). The duality of race and gender for managerial African American women: Implications of informal social networks on career advancement. *Human Resource Development Review, 2*(4), 385.

Danner, M. (1992). *I'll walk the tightrope.* In. B. W. Bell (Ed.), *Modern and contemporary Afro-American poetry* (p. 87). Boston, MA: Allyn & Bacon.

Friedman, D. E., Rimsky, C., & Johnson, A. (1996). *College and university reference guide to work-family programs.* New York, NY: Families and Work Institute.

Franklin, J. (2005). *Mirror to America: An autobiography of John Hope Franklin.* New York: NY: Farrar, Straus and Giroux.

Glazer-Raymo, J. (2008). *Unfinished agendas: New and continuing gender challenges in higher education.* Baltimore: MD: John Hopkins University Press.

Guinier, L., & Torres, G. (2002). *Miner's canary: Enlisting race, resisting power, transforming democracy.* Cambridge, MA: Harvard University Press.

hooks, b. (1991). *Yearning: Race, gender and cultural politics.* London, England: Turnaround Press.

Ladson-Billings, G. (1996). *Silences as weapons: Challenges of a Black professor teaching White students. Theory Into Practice, 35*(2), 79–85

Leon, D. J. (1993). *Mentoring minorities in higher education: Passing the torch.* Washington, DC: National Education Association.

Mitchell, P., & Parry, G. (2011). *Ten stupid things women do to mess up their careers.* Los Gatos: CA: Robertson.

Pittman, C. (2010). Race and gender oppression in the classroom: The experiences of women faculty of color with White male students. *Teaching Sociology, 38*(3), 183–196. Los Angeles, CA: SAGE.

Ponjuan, L. (2005). *Understanding the work lives of faculty of color.* Lansing, MI: University of Michigan Press.

Robinson, C., & Clardy, P. (2010). *Tedious journeys: Autoethnography by women of color in academe.* New York, NY: Peter Lang.

Salazar, C. F. (2009). Strategies to survive and thrive in academia: The collective voices of counseling faculty of color. *International Journal for the Advancement of Counseling, 31*(3), 181–198.

Stanley, C. A. (2006). Coloring the academic landscape: Faculty of color breaking the silence in predominantly White colleges and universities. *American Educational Research Journal, 43*(4), 701–736.

Trower, C. (2003). Leveling the field. *The Academic Workplace, 14*(2), 1–15.

Tuitt, F. (2003). Realizing a more inclusive pedagogy. In A. Howell & F. A. Tuitt (Eds.), *Race and higher education: Rethinking pedagogy in diverse college classrooms* (pp. 243–268). Cambridge, MA: Harvard Education Publishing Group.

Turner C., Gonzalez, J. C., & Wood, J. L (2008). Faculty of color in the academe. *Journal of Diversity in Higher Education*, *1*(3), 130–168.

Turner, C. S. V., & Myers, S. L. (2000). *Faculty of color in academe: Bittersweet success.* Needham Heights, MA: Allyn & Bacon.

Umbach, P. (2006). The contribution of faculty of color to undergraduate education. *Research in Higher Education*, *47*(3), 317–345.

SECTION II

LOCATING SAFE SPACES

CHAPTER 3

I'D RATHER BE HARRIET

A Counterstory of Two Sister Scholars

Nadrea R. Njoku and Juhanna N. Rogers

The history of African American women is full of figures that show what is possible to achieve in American[1] society. Likewise, we also have many stereotypical depictions of African American women—Mammy, Sapphire, Amazon, Welfare or Bad Mother, Video Vixen, and Angry Black Female (Collins, 2005; hooks, 1981; Wallace, 1990)—that dictate our limitations and inspire deficit thinking. Everyday Black women are faced with the decision on how to react to adversity. We could submit to these sexist and racist notions with our heads blooded and bowed, or we can protest the constant devaluation of Black womanhood and rise by rewriting historical and contemporary narratives of African American women.

The narratives of African American women in doctoral programs are understudied, in particular we know little about how the intersection of race and gender impact socialization to the professoriate (Feldner, Stevenson, & Gasman, 2014). What has been investigated tells a tale of insufficient access to mentorship (Morehouse & Dawkins, 2006; Patton & Harper, 2003) and a dehumanizing socializing experience (Gildersleeve, Croom, & Vazquez, 2011); however their research interests have strong ties to their racial experiences and social justice (Taylor & Anthony, 2000).

Beyond Retention: Cultivating Spaces of Equity, Justice, and Fairness for Women of Color in U.S. Higher Education, pp. 57–91

Through critical race theory and critical race feminism we use counter storytelling, in the form of a scripted play, to explore the gendered and raced experiences of African American female doctoral students in education.

AFRICAN AMERICAN WOMEN IN THE DOCTORAL PIPELINE

As higher education scholars, we explore history, sociology, and literature within the field of education, to establish an interdisciplinary understanding of the Black and gendered experiences. Existing literature suggests that students of color in academic spaces are often in defense of themselves and have to mentally prepare for hostile and chilly climates (Giles & Hughes, 2009; Harper, 2012; Solorzano, Ceja, & Yosso, 2000). Regardless of preparation, many students of color find the doctorial experience dehumanizing (Gildersleeve et al., 2011). Gildersleeve et al. found that Black and Latino students find themselves questioning their self-worth, self-censor as a defense mechanism toward racism, shift scholarly endeavors, and constantly question "Am I going crazy?!" For women of color, particularly Black women, the impact of doctoral studies becomes baggage filled with racially and sexually charged incidents that result in feelings of anger and internal ugliness (Griffin, 2012) coupled with racial battle fatigue (Smith, Allen, & Danley, 2007; Williams & Nichols, 2011). Collins (2000) argues that Black women need to unify in order to resist. Patton and Harper (2003) found that African American women with African American female mentors were able to establish rich and meaningful connections because they shared the intersecting identities of race and gender. These mentors were able to provide advice to "avoid professional pitfalls while being a sister and a friend," (p. 71) as well as assist in shaping positive self-concepts and encouraging them to reach their full potential within the academy. Some even described this sister-scholar relationship as a mothering one. However, students noted that there is a void in available African American female mentors because of their absence in their programs. Overly taxed schedules and poor reputation among other students also contribute in preventing mentoring relationships. Therefore, peer networks among African American women in doctoral programs play a role in filling the void of available sister-scholars by providing support, serve as a sounding board for grievances, and a reminder that they are not struggling alone (Patton & Harper, 2003).

THEORETICAL FRAMEWORK AND METHODOLOGY

Critical race feminism will be used to acknowledge the intersection of race and gender, distinguishing African American women from the experiences of White women and African American men in doctoral education. Critical race feminism has direct linkage to critical race theory (CRT) (Wing, 1999). Ladson-Billings and Tate (1995) posits that American education is plagued with racist cultural constructs. Accordingly, a work on African American women in education cannot ignore race as a central factor in their experience. CRT acknowledges the permanence of race in American society, challenging the structures of power, preference experiential knowledge or lived experiences, and an interdisciplinary use of sources (Delgado, R. & Stefancic, 2001; Ladson-Billings & Tate, 1995; Solórzano & Yosso, 2001). CRT assists in unpacking racialized experiences, specifically with the issues of Black women in higher education. However, one is not a White woman with color or a Black man with female gender issues (Wing, 1999). Thus, as Croom (2011) asserts, "[Critical race feminism] scholars challenge the monolithic woman or Black experience, to argue the interdependence of individuals' experience based on the multiple facets of their identity, to include race, gender, class, and sexual orientation" (p. 7). By using these theoretical frameworks we illuminate the unique experiences of African American women in the margins of the academy.

In the tradition of CRT we use counterstorytelling, in the form of a scripted play, to illustrate the experiences of African American women undertaking doctoral study. Counterstories serve the purpose of building community and helping others to realize that they are not struggling alone by giving a familiar face to empirical research. By giving voice to victims of racism and sexism, we also intend to disrupt the silence surrounding these unjust acts. Counterstories also assist in creating cultural wealth and create a historical record of the experiences of people of color. In the case of this text, a clear record of African American female experiences in doctoral education can serve as tools for dismantling systems of power. These narrative tools "move us to action and inform praxis" (Yosso, 2013, p. 15).

Counterstories are composed by drawing upon multiple sources of data. We interpret primary data collected from other research projects[2] through the use of existing literature and theoretical sensitivity (Strauss & Corbin, 1990). We also utilize cultural intuition for additional analysis. Cultural intuition, which has roots in Black feminist thought (Dillard, 2000), is of particular importance because it situates our experiences as African American women as an asset to interpret educational phenomenon. Delgado Bernal (1998) quotes Dillard as saying,

> While we will argue vehemently that Black women as a cultural group "theorize" and embody extensive life experiences which, while diverse, shape a coherent body, what we advance here is the notion that, in educational

research, such theoretical and conceptual standpoints are achieved; they are not inherent in one's race, class, sex, or other identities. (pp. 5–6)

Therefore, naturally, our own personal and professional experiences are also drawn upon as a data source. We have served as each other's' peer mentors since meeting in an introduction to CRT class 4 years ago. From the start of our friendship we have remained honest with one another in order to support and challenge our personal and professional development. We are also both mothers who find it necessary to obtain a PhD not only for ourselves, but for the young Black men we are raising. We use all of our experiences as scholars and African American women to bring life to this counternarrative through a sensitivity and responsibility to all of the sister-scholars working to obtain a doctoral degree. Once all of the data was compiled and analyzed two composite characters, Chantelle and Ida, were created.

Through conversations between these two women, over the course of several years in a doctoral program, we aim to demonstrate how African American women utilize peer support networks to cope with raced and gendered experiences, as well as provide support for career goals. In this instance, their decision on whether or not to pursue a career as a faculty member or an administrator is a central theme. You will find that these women utilize a method talking back and forth, repeating concepts without fully fleshing out that particular concept. This "back and forth" method is used as a method between the two women to flesh these ideas out.

We highlight the utilization of historical role modeling to combat dehumanization that occurs in doctoral education (Gildersleeve et al., 2011) and deficit thinking. This role modeling also highlights how these two women use the lived experiences of an historical figure to craft their decision making in the face of adversity. In the tradition of CRT counter-stories, notes are utilized throughout the text to extend arguments and cite appropriate research (Yosso, 2013).

A COUNTERSTORY OF THE BLACK FEMALE DOCTORIAL EXPERIENCE: A THREE ACT PLAY

ACT 1: THE MEETING

IT'S SUMMER 2011 AND OVER COFFEE, CHANTELLE AND IDA MEET FOR THE FIRST TIME OUTSIDE OF CLASS. THEY GET TOGETHER TO FINISH A PAPER FOR A CLASS THAT ENDED THE PREVIOUS SEMESTER.

IDA

I am so glad we have a chance to get to know each other. I remember you from when I interviewed for the master's program, but you graduated soon after.

CHANTELLE

Oh really? That was years ago, I guess. How time flies?! Now here we are in a PhD program together; exploring race and gender. By the way, I thought your comments in class were really thoughtful. I am glad we are getting together to work on this project.

IDA

Where are you from?

CHANTELLE

I am from Philly. You?

IDA

Atlanta

CHANTELLE

Cool. I always wanted to go to Spelman!

IDA

Girl, everybody! I went to Dolliole, tho. So I got the AUC experience.[3]

CHANTELLE

Really?! How was that?

IDA

It was awesome. I loved college. But I was from Atlanta, so I stayed at home. I didn't get the dorm experience. But I got my Different World experience, Mr. Gains, Dwayne Wayne, and all.[4]

CHANTELLE

(Laughing)
So are you Whitley?

IDA

(Recoils at the thought)
No! I knew Whitleys tho. I was more of a Freddie.[5] I studied art, lead pro-test, and stayed in a pair of painted jeans.
(Laughs)

Those were the days. What about you? You went to an HBCU?

CHANTELLE

Oh no, Chile. [pronounced with a long I and silent e] I went to Waldorf. I studied English and African Studies.

IDA

Oh! Fancy.

CHANTELLE

Not fancy at all. Hard. Lonely, but worth it. It prepared me for this.

IDA

Well that's good. Perhaps you are grappling better than I am. Some days I want to just go home. I could have never come here for undergrad.

CHANTELLE

Oh, I never said I didn't want to go home. Who said that? I hate it here too, but I am not shocked by what I see or what's put in front of me. You don't think your HBCU prepared you?

IDA

Oh, Dolliole prepared me academically! It's just the environment. It's been a bit of a culture shock to me. Too many people! Too many White people. I feel like' I would have gotten lost. I don't think any Black woman, HBCU grad or not, would find this environment welcoming. I say women because I am a woman, I can't speak for the male experience. However, I will take my HBCU experience over what I see the undergraduate students go through here, any day. That place helped to mold me in ways I wouldn't have been molded here. In my most salient and developmental moments I never thought about race. I mean we were all Black, so clearly race was present, but it wasn't something we considered stood between us and our goals or dreams. I mean we had White and Asian students on our campus. Never once did I think: Is it my color? Do they think I'm stupid? Why did they say that? Nor did I question the motives of the professors. And more than half of my professors were White.[7]

CHANTELLE

Really? Your professors were White?

IDA

Yep. Shocking, right? My art classes were dominated by Black faculty, but your degree is more than your major. All the hard sciences, English, history, or philosophy classes were taught by White faculty.[8] I never had an issue with them.

CHANTELLE

Wow. That's interesting. A Different World didn't prepare me for that! I can understand your assumption that you would feel lost. Even though I went to a PWI, I see how students of color get lost in the cracks, here and there. I struggle here in different ways than I did at Waldorf.

IDA

Really?

CHANTELLE

Yeah! I was the cat's meow at Waldorf. People loved me. They raised me up on a pedestal. I was involved, president of the Black Student Union, and went abroad three times. I even sat on the President's cabinet.

IDA

Cool. That must have been nice. I know the president is a Black woman there.

CHANTELLE

Oh yeah. I love Syilvia.

IDA

Do yall have a relationship?

CHANTELLE

Yeah, we talk by e-mail. She wrote my letter of recommendation to get in here. She encouraged me to get my PhD, but she never told me how the process of getting the PhD would make me feel.[9]

IDA

Your parents went to college?

CHANTELLE

No. They just graduated from high school. My mom works for the state and my dad is a postman. My grandparents went to college though. Your parents?

IDA

My mom did when I was in grade school. My dad didn't. So theoretically I am not a first generation student, but I feel like one lots of the time.

CHANTELLE

Yeah. That definition needs revising, I think. It's a spectrum, really. Not black or white, yes or no.

IDA

I have a question for you. It may be a bit personal. Do you want to be a faculty member?

CHANTELLE

Oh yeah. That's what I want to do. I want to teach and I want to write.
    (Sips Coffee)
You?

IDA

I don't know. I think it might be nice to be able to set my own schedule, read good books, and write, but that's not really why I came here. I came to be an administrator. When I was recruited to grad school I was told that I should walk away from my alma mater where I was working to solidify myself. And that's what I am doing, but I fully intend to go back.

CHANTELLE

I think all of us in some ways want to go back to the place that inspired us to do this work. So, that makes sense.

IDA

But sometimes I think about being faculty too. And then there are times when I don't think I will be able to stomach it.[10]

CHANTELLE

I think there are many of us that have that same fear and reservation, especially those of us that are women of color. I worry about my ability to become faculty.[11]

IDA

If faculty life is anything like this process, they can have that. Its sooo competitive and people will just stab you in the back to get ahead. They will hug you, smile and when those arms get fully wrapped around your back, they will stab you. Will that be faculty life? Does that come with it? No thank you.

CHANTELLE

Hmmmmmmmm. Maybe it does, but that hasn't really been my experience. So I guess I can't say if it is or not. But I've seen older Black women in the faculty go through things that trouble me.

                              IDA
Really, like what?

                           CHANTELLE
Just things. I think that's a different conversation for a different day. Too
much for right now.[12]

                              IDA
       (Gives skeptical look.)
Oh well I guess we should change the subject then.

                           CHANTELLE
       (Trying to dismiss the topic and obligation to expand on what she's
       seen she is relived to change the topic.)
Sure, lets.

                              IDA
       (Searching for where to take the conversation next, she fishes for a
       new topic to peak Chantelle's interest.)
Soooo, you have kids? Married? Work for the CIA?

                           CHANTELLE
       (Laughs)
I don't work for the CIA, just trying to keep some things in confidence.

                              IDA
Alright, I gotcha.

                           CHANTELLE
I do have a son. I am not married.

                              IDA
Awwww, what's your son's name?

                           CHANTELLE
Donald.

                              IDA
How old is he?

                           CHANTELLE
He's 5. You? Have children? Married?

IDA

I am married, no children. I want children though. My husband wants children now. I want to wait until after I finish my dissertation.

CHANTELLE

You think you will give in?

IDA

I don't know. I feel like my biological clock is ticking, I am just worried about a baby's impact on my goals. I need to finish this.[13]

CHANTELLE

That's real. It's hard to balance being a mom, doing it alone, although I do coparent, and getting this degree. Especially with no family in this city.

IDA

Exactly. I think I would rather be closer to family. But he wants them now! I'm not convinced.

CHANTELLE

Well having children is hard work, and very hard work for Black women in college in general,[14] but it can be done. I had my son before my master's program. Being a working mom is night and day from being a student mom. But, hey I always say live your life. The work will be here, do what makes you happy.

IDA

That's true. I just imagine writing my dissertation with a screaming toddler running back and forth, turning the house upside down. I already don't like to clean.

CHANTELLE
(Wide eyed and amused, she chuckles and shakes her head.)
I get it. Totally get it. I am sure I would have more time to clean, write, and read for class if I didn't have my son, but I would never trade him for the world. He motivates me and is part of the reason I came back to school. These degrees are as much his degrees as they are mine.[15]
(Pauses to sip coffee.)
Did you get any of those departmental fellowships they announced yesterday?

IDA

(Shaking head)
Oh no! I don't apply for those.

CHANTELLE

Why not?

IDA

I applied one year and it was a terrible experience. First, I couldn't get in touch with my major professor to write my letter. So I had to have another professor write my letter. Then I waited and waited. An older student said that I would get a letter in the mail, so after I heard people talking about their awards I still held onto the fact that I would get the big award. I waited and waited for the letter to come. It never came. Then I was home visiting my mom and I got an e-mail stating I didn't get an award. I don't know why it hurt so much, but it did. I cried and cried.

(Laughs)

My mom came in and saw me crying and asked why? I was able to get the words out between tears to say "I didn't get a fellowship." She was so disturbed by my state of mind that she went out the room and talked with my husband. He came into the room

(Laughs)

and said "are you okay? Please clean yourself up. Your mom is very disturbed. She said you are crying uncontrollably and she doesn't even understand what a fellowship means." Well besides explaining in depth why these fellowships meant so much, I had to convince her to not come to Indiana and beat the faculty up. When I got back from home my mom called to check on me. She scolded me for being too caught up in others validation. All I remember her saying was "Look, fuck those people! They don't know your worth. Don't kill yourself over stuff that don't matter. Fuck a scholarship, fuck a fellowship, fuck a ship!"

CHANTELLE

(Laughs)

Oh my gosh! That sounds like my mom. She has no clue what I am going through and why problems that are little to her matter to me in such big ways.

IDA

Yeah they don't understand, but they know things. They have lived life, and she was right. I was taking it all too seriously. So to avoid being obsessive and overindulging judging myself by others standards, I don't apply anymore.[16] Maybe later on, but not now.

CHANTELLE

Do you have many female friends in the program? I know there are a significant amount of Black girls here, on campus and in our program.

IDA

Yeah, I have a few girlfriends. But I think I am closer to the guys than the girls. Those are just the students who I have found the most in common with. I was the only Black girl in my cohort, so that's just how it worked out. But now I have you!

CHANTELLE

(Smiling)
Yes! Now we have each other!

ACT 2: TO BE YOUNG, GIFTED, AND A BLACK WOMAN

EXT. A TABLE OUTSIDE OF A RESTAURANT THEY ARE EATING. IT'S SUMMER 2012, IT IS A YEAR SINCE THE TWO FIRST MET. THE CHARACTERS ARE SITTING ACROSS FROM EACH OTHER. A WAIT-RESS, ATTENDING TO THEM, TRAVELS IN AND OUTSIDE OF THE RESTURANT. THEY HAVE GATHERED SO IDA CAN UPDATE CHANTELLE ON HER MEETING WITH A MAJOR PROFESSOR.

CHANTELLE

So you have to tell me about your meeting with Dr. Smith. Y'all were supposed to meet last Thursday, Yes?

IDA

Yes. We met.

CHANTELLE

Well, what did he say? Is he going to let you be an author on the article?

IDA

Yeah he agreed to put me on as last author, but my place in authorship is really my issue. I did all the work with collecting and analyzing the data. Then this boy comes in and does some writing and edits and he's second author. I conceived the idea and followed that through from research to rough draft with Dr. Smith. He said the draft I composed wasn't up to standard so he brought Jamal in to edit it. Now Jamal gets billing over me. At this point I don't think Smith will continue to be my advisor. He certainly won't be my dissertation chair.

CHANTELLE

Oh this is terrible. Why would Dr. Smith do this? You talked to Jamal about the authorship issue?

IDA

Yes! I did. I called and asked what happened. I asked him to also tell Dr. Smith that this was my idea and that it wasn't right.

CHANTELLE

What did he say?

IDA

He called me angry.[17] He said I should give him this pass because he's graduating soon, that I am being selfish. Excuse me, but that this is my work! This is the topic I wanted to continue to develop for my dissertation. It doesn't even matter. I probably won't get that far. I think I am just going to quit and start working after this semester. We need the money with the baby on the way.

CHANTELLE

What? I can't believe he said that. And no, you are not going to leave. You're the smartest person I know! You have too many loans to quit now!

IDA

(Cracks a smile, but goes back to sullenly playing with food)
I know I do, but that's not the point. I am not good enough.[18] Smith said I'll never finish at this rate. He said my writing is bad and I work too slow. He said that it took me too long to work on this article and he was disappointed with the outcome. He was disappointed with a lot of things. Ultimately he said he didn't know how I would finish a dissertation. "You'll never finish at this rate."

CHANTELLE

(Mouth wide open and in shock)
What did you say when he said that? I know you put him in his place.

IDA

I didn't say anything. I just kept the goal of why I came. I had to focus on what I came to do, get on that article. I contributed too much and put in too much work to not be included. Plus I am 6 months pregnant. I couldn't lose my composure and risk hurting my baby. Chile, I would have gone into labor. When I go off it's a point of no return. I would have never gotten credit for my work and gotten too riled up. At the end of the day, this baby is my priority. I was hurt by what he said, but I couldn't get fixated on that one comment.

CHANTELLE

Well then what changed between then and now? You seem to be hurt by what he said, no?

IDA

Of course, I'm devastated. On one hand my brain is screaming: What does he mean I can't finish? Who does he think he is? But on the other hand, I wonder if it's worth the stress. I have a lot going for me. I have this baby, my husband, and a master's degree. I am tired of being hurt and abused by these people! I don't have to stay here and take this. I am done with this PhD program, it's not worth my life.

CHANTELLE

Don't say that. I need you here.[19]

IDA

No you don't! You have mentors to support you. You don't need me.

CHANTELLE

Yes, I do.

IDA

(Dramatic pause)

Chantelle, I am being eaten alive. They are eating me alive.[20] I just can't. I didn't come here for this. I came because I wanted to make a difference. I wanted to come get this degree and go back home. Home seems so far away. The reasons I came seem so far away. If I leave now I can salvage what's left of me and start over.[21]

(Pause)

I can't believe I trusted him. He convinced me to stay here and study with him. He said he was going to guide me. Help me. Support me. But he hasn't. I get pregnant, miss a deadline, and now I am worthless to him. I almost lost this baby. I was in this hospital fighting for my life. That's why he didn't get the draft when it was due. He can't understand that?! I refuse to let him or anyone else eat me alive. I am gone.

(Starts crying.)

I'm going to have this baby. I don't need a PhD. I don't need it. I don't need it.

Chantelle reaches for Ida's hands to comfort her.

CHANTELLE

You have to stop crying, Ida. Please don't cry. You are so much better that you are giving yourself credit for.

Chantelle moves next to Ida, hugs her and starts to sing. Ida continues to cry.

To be young, gifted and Black,
Oh what a lovely precious dream
To be young, gifted and Black,
Open your heart to what I mean
In the whole world you know
There are billion boys and girls
Who are young, gifted and Black,
And that's a fact!
You are young, gifted and Black
You must begin to tell yourself
There's a world waiting for you
Your's is a quest that's just begun
(With humor)
When you feel really low
They both chuckle
Yeah, there's a great truth you should know
When you're young, gifted and Black
Your soul's intact[22]

Singing stops.

Don't let him get in your head, he doesn't belong there. But you do belong here and I Don't want to hear no mo' about it.

IDA

I know, but it's so hard. For the last week and half he's been playing on a loop in my head. In my head all I can think about are his words. His judgments. When my baby kicks and my husband brings me flowers, all I can think about is how I can't write an article, more less a dissertation.

CHANTELLE

I think that he's wrong, but I think you need to do better about choosing where you place your expectations. You need mentors that look and feel like you do. Sometimes you need a Black woman to guide you through this. Smith can't understand your situation because he's never been in your shoes.

IDA

But there are no Black women that teach in our program.

CHANTELLE

But there are Black women who teach for this university. Just because they don't teach in the department doesn't mean they can't be supportive. There are allies throughout the academy, but sometimes a Black girl needs another Black girl who's been her shoes. They will be a breath of fresh air. They will understand the feelings you are having. They can encourage you with your best interest at heart.[23] I'll share some of my mentors with you.

IDA

Will you? Really?

CHANTELLE

Of course! Now please go dry your eyes. We are in this restaurant crying and singing Nina Simone. It's a lot.

They both laugh.

ACT 3: I'D RATHER BE HARRIET

IN THE SPRING 2013 BOTH IDA AND CHANTELLE HAVE REACHED THE END OF THEIR STUDIES IN THE DOCTORAL PROGRAM. THEY HAVE PROPOSED THEIR DISSERTATIONS AND ARE DECIDING THE NEXT STEPS BEYOND GRADUATION.

CHANTELLE

Dr. Nadrea Rogers[24] said that she's been hearing a lot from you lately. Has she been helpful to you?

IDA

Oh my God, yes! She has been so helpful. After you introduced us we have really hit it off. She's been extremely supportive and inspirational. Thank you, Chantelle. That relationship has been a lifesaver. She really gets me.

CHANTELLE

I am glad. I feel the same way about her. I've been in love with her since I started the program. She's like a surrogate mother to me.

IDA

That's awesome. I only wish I'd know her earlier. You hear more about the faculty job?

CHANTELLE

Yeah they are reopening the search. They want someone whose research interest is a bit different. I gather it's not race studies or qualitative work. I think they are more interested in a number cruncher.

IDA

Yeah, you told me that! But, they knew you did race and gender studies when they met you, right?

CHANTELLE

Yeah, they know that. They also know I don't do quantitative work primarily. But, I'm like ok. When I got there they made it clear that they wanted someone who does statistical analysis, but I was clear to them that my strength is qualitative analysis.

IDA

How does that make you feel about the process in general, going forward applying for faculty jobs?

CHANTELLE

Ummm, good. I want to do more.

IDA

It doesn't discourage you at all?

CHANTELLE

No. I absolutely want to do more.

She starts to text. Dialogue stops momentarily.

IDA

Huh?

Continues to text. There is a long pause. Continues to look at Chantelle, waiting for her to finish. Chantelle never looks up and continues to text.

IDA

What's going on with the phone?

CHANTELLE

Ummm, my friend sent me this long e-mail this morning. I took the time to send her a response this morning and then I got dressed to come meet you. I don't know if the e-mail got deleted or I forgot to press send! So, I am responding to her e-mail again, please give me a second.

Chantelle continues to play with her phone and Ida continues to eat having given up on the prospect of a conversation for the moment.

CHANTELLE

One second.
    (Long Pause)
That was just strange. But I guess universities do all kinds of things for all kinds of reasons. I do know I want to do more interviews. I haven't interviewed for a professional job since 2005/06. So regardless I need to brush up on interviewing skills and the new ins and outs of job searches. Interviewing virtually is a new thing for me.

IDA

So, you're certain you are staying through the fall? I know you talked about moving home after you propose.

CHANTELLE

Ummmmmm

Continues to play with food

IDA

    (With frustration and urgency.)
So you are staying?

CHANTELLE

Here? For another year?

IDA

Yeah.

CHANTELLE

I don't know. No, I think I am certain about staying. Right now I don't have any other options and I haven't applied for more stuff. So as far as I know there is nothing coming down the pipeline to pull me away. I do feel like I need a change of

IDA

Scenery?

CHANTELLE

Change of scenery. A change of environment. Ummm, I am ready to have like, a life.

IDA

Yeah, I agree. Anything, but here. I was looking jobs up yesterday. I kinda don't know where to start. I haven't interviewed for a professional job in years. I just wonder how attractive of a candidate I will be? I am over edu-cated for everything and not "experienced" in much of anything. The reason I was asking you about jobs and the process was because ... well, I am trying to love and accept myself exactly as I am.[25] See, if I would've been invited to interview for a job, like you were, and then for them to call me up, the way they did you to say, "we decided to go another way" ... I am not as resilient as you. It would have taken me much longer to bounce back and say "I got to keep going." I would have had to sort my feelings out. It takes me much longer to get over rejection. To say "we want you, come visit our campus. You are top choice." Then to visit and have them call and say "you're not a good match." That's like lying to me! I would be stuck on what went wrong rather than plotting my next move. I would still be recovering from the loss.

CHANTELLE

I think I have developed, over time, to not spend so much time

IDA

Processing?

CHANTELLE

Yes

Looks down at her food.

I want some sauce. I feel like at one time there was some sauce and today there is no sauce.

IDA

You can't eat this gravy like sauce?

CHANTELLE

Hot sauce! That's what I need hot sauce!

Reaches over to another table and grabs hot sauce bottle.

I think over time I got use to moving on. I don't know if that has anything to do with several failed engagements, disappointments, having to manage the emotional side effects of grad school alone … I think it may be all of these things together that has heightened my ability to be okay with other people telling me "You're not a good fit." I went in being me and they want something else and that is ok with me.

IDA

Hmm, maybe it is the life things. Those disappointments in life that help you rebound.

CHANTELLE

Yeah, just life things. I've developed a thick skin. There is not a whole lot that can knock me off my horse. I stay focused on the goal, the bigger picture. The picture could get ripped right off the page, but the story still moves for me. And then sometimes, no matter how much you prepare, or whatever, it just doesn't work out. And then sometimes it ain't all about you.

IDA

That's real.

CHANTELLE

As far as the faculty opportunity, I didn't have much to lose. It would have been ideal for my situation. My son would have thrived in that environment, it would have been a steady income, and a new environment, but we are doing alright here. We can manage until I finish this degree. But they weren't checking for me and the work I do.

IDA

Right. You're not going to settle

CHANTELLE

Shaking her head.

Exactly, I am not going to settle. I am not going to show up and pretend, like oh …

IDA

(Seamlessly finishes sentence)

I can be exactly who y'all want me to be.

CHANTELLE

Exactly. One thing that Dr. Rogers says: When you show up for an interview, you show up exactly as you are. So, when they hire you

IDA

(Seamlessly finishes sentence)

They know what they getting.

CHANTELLE

They know what they getting. Don't go in being someone you're not and put on airs, or whatever the case may be. I am not saying go in and wild out! But, be you. Nothing more and surely nothing less.

IDA

You know, there are moments, though, when Black women are authentic. I've watched them achieve an authentic balance in their jobs, making change and calling the shots, but they get kicked to the curb as soon as the powers that be get a chance to pull the rug out from under them.[26] And that's when I want to say "I don't want to be in the academy," faculty or administrator. I just know that, I remember in undergrad, a guy asked me why I was an art major. I told him it was because I wanted to make a living as an artist. I can't work for nobody. I want to be my own boss. You can't fire yourself! Now, I remember going to get my master's degree in education and telling him about it. He was like: "What?! I thought you said you never wanted to work for anyone or have a boss. Why are you changing your mind?" I just remember there was a moment when I realized I needed a steady job and in this system that meant I needed to get more education and get a good paying job.[27]

CHANTELLE

(Whispers)
Is your rice hard and cold?

IDA

No, but it's kinda cold.

Chantelle shrugs her shoulders and moves on to eating again.

IDA

I just feel like … I lost my train of thought. It's not that I don't want a boss. But I am impacted by a regular job in so many ways. I feel like it's my physical appearance. Being that I am a woman, being that I am Black, makes it easier for a boss to tell me what I am and not going to do.[28] Shut up and take it. And I feel like it would take nothing less than a revolution for change to occur. I mean why does it take a revolution for you to understand that I am worth the space I am taking up? I see the advantages of being a faculty member, but when it comes down to being up for tenure I feel like it's going to come back down to my body and whether or not my body is worth the office space.

CHANTELLE

That might be different though. I mean who's going to do this work if we don't do the work?

IDA

Yeah, but am I going to die doing this work under someone else's terms?

CHANTELLE

Well, that's true too. Both of us have become ill during this process at some point.

IDA

And not just with the sniffles or a head cold. There are people dying to get a PhD, literally.

CHANTELLE

But, I wouldn't say this is just this city, this is happening all over the country. Black women are sacrificing a lot, including their health, to obtain degrees. This could be anywhere.

IDA

I know! That's what is so scary to me. I could go back home, the most comfortable place I know, and still be tormented by the same injustices I have faced in this academic space.

CHANTELLE

I think we are all looking for that space.

IDA

A comfortable home. A creative place.

CHANTELLE

I think we are looking for that space, but I also recognize that space may not exist in totality. Or how we dreamed it. And while I agree with everything you're saying I would have so say that maybe in the mist of trauma, as a way to protect ourselves, we over generalize. I mean I know your story. But, you are not alone. So with that being said, you can't run because you think the boogie monster is hiding under the desk of every faculty member's office in all the colleges and universities in this country.

IDA

I just think in the case of the faculty job you were invited to interview for, they wanted you to be an expert on this one particular topic with no flexibility or consideration for your standpoint. That's the cotton they wanted you to pick. I am not trying to pick no one's cotton. Or fit into a boxed definition of what I am supposed to be doing. No! I would rather be Harriet than be Patsy.[29]

CHANTELLE

You trying to call me Patsy? I ain't no Patsy, or no one's backbreaking super woman, amazon, black woman![30]

IDA

I am not calling you Patsy! I am saying that's who they want you to be. Picking cotton. Cotton is the trite topics that are hegemonic or always praised by the White patriarchal society as important topics of study.

CHANTELLE

Girl, you have been reading way too much bell hooks.[31] You are super imposing these slave stereotypes on this situation.
 (Laughs)
 And since I like that type of thing, I am going to take it there, too. Yes, I would much rather to be Harriet too. That's what I am saying when I mean "who else will do the work?" I mean to be Harriet in every way. I am going to lead my people right out of slavery and into the Promised Land. Nevertheless, you need to ask yourself what will be your cause? What form of bondage do you see your people being shackled by? And where will you be leading them? I know what is going to free me. Do you? You can't be scared to go back, several times, and get those who need your help.

IDA

I am not scared.

CHANTELLE

 (With sensitivity in her voice)
Well that's what it sounds like to me. You sound scared of being hurt. Of being told no. You sound terrified to confront the system, like you're surprised it's not working totally in your favor. Duh. You knew that when the

boy asked you why you were going to be an artist. And there is nothing wrong with being your own boss. I have an entrepreneurial spirit too, but I know some of the things I want to accomplish are better served within the academy. Many people don't get paid to travel the world studying the nuances of higher education, race, and gender, but faculty do.

                                    IDA

(Chuckles)
Ok, maybe I am scared. But don't I have a right to be?

                                 CHANTELLE

Sure, but don't let it immobilize you. And personally, I don't think it's funny. You are using humor or laughing to cope, but it's no laughing matter. This is serious. And wouldn't be a sister if I didn't tell you the truth.

                                    IDA

And I appreciate that. But Harriet wouldn't keep putting up with the same thing would she? Allowing people to hurt her over and over again. I have a choice on how I face this world; how I face the academy! And I choose Harriet!

                                 CHANTELLE

Uhhh, but I don't think Harriet saw it that way. I think she saw a goal, had a purpose, and chose to not flee from the cause. While she left the bondage of slavery, she returned time after time, in the face of danger, to conquer slavery on her own terms. Her terms were the Underground Railroad, freedom. Although, she knew one woman could not free them all, she knew she could free some. And she did.
    (Laughs)
Now, to be honest, you're the one who sound like Patsy to me. Wasn't Patsy was the one who asked Solomon to drown her? She wanted to die and couldn't even do it on her own. She was faced with pain day after day and the only way she saw out was through death. That's doom and gloom. But there was no problem solving on her part. Harriet is one hell of a problem solver. And so are you! I think we both have traits we envy in each other. You envy the way I bounce back?

                                    IDA

Yeah, I wish I could hit a wall and get up without crying.

                                 CHANTELLE

Well, I wouldn't say I don't cry, but I don't waste much time doing so. I envy the way you speak. You speak with so much authority. When you are in meetings you speak as if you are an expert on what you are talking about. You're very sure of yourself, I wish I could speak like that. I am always in the middle … It could be this way or it could be that way. But never on spot like you are.

IDA

Well I have to be sure about something. I believe everything I am saying, but I just don't want to be wasting my energy trying to please a system that wasn't built for me.

CHANTELLE

None of the systems were built for us, except being the help. Or picking the cotton.

IDA

Right. So then how do I buck against that without, like you said earlier, sacrificing my life?

CHANTELLE

Is a dream worth anything unless you want to sacrifice your life for it? I mean metaphorically, but also in reality

IDA

I'm not losing my sanity trying to fight someone's boxed idea of what a faculty member should be. I'd rather bow out now. All these conversations we have, when I look back, I sound so tragic!
    (With emphasis)
I am not trying to be a tragic mulatto for the rest of my life.

CHANTELLE

We all have our moments, our days.

IDA

Right. I don't want my story to end here, or at graduation when I cross the stage. I don't want them to say "she was a good writer, great ideas, too bad she isn't in the field anymore."

CHANTELLE

"Do y'all know what she does now?"

IDA

Right! I just don't want to believe that this is all there is for me. A life full of emotional eating and debriefing on how to go back to work. Moments crying in the bathroom stall after someone turned me down for a job, a fellowship, an award, or told me that I won't have a job next year. Moments when I found out, by looking through a conference booklet, that the idea I shared with a friend turned into their conference presentation! Or publication. Or going home and neglecting myself. Nor neglecting my son who needs to be fed and my husband needs a wife, not a Black feminist scholar. Hell no! That's not going to be my life. But that is my life now. How do I recover, regroup, remake myself into the woman I romanticized about when I applied to this program?

CHANTELLE

Damn.

Shakes head

See I told you. You speak with authority.
    (With humor and sarcasm)
I am about to cry.

IDA

Weren't you the one that said this wasn't a laughing matter?

CHANTELLE

Yeah, but we can't go back to work with red blood shot eyes. I mean all the things you are saying are true. I feel it, I do. That's the way I feel most of the time. But what else should we feel? If we felt great about all our days, which we do sometimes …

IDA

We do.

CHANTELLE

We wouldn't feel like there was a reason to fight. A reason to stay here and do the work. This is all more the reason why you should become a faculty member.

Looks at IDA with a grin.

IDA

    (Laughs)
No one can be serious with you. You the one who should stop playing and coping with humor.

CHANTELLE

(Laughs)

I was being harsh when I called you out, but you were being tragic. I hate when you do that.

Calls waitress over for check.

Can we have our checks please?

WAITRESS

Together or separate?

IDA and CHANTELLE

Separate.

IDA

I told you, I ain't no tragic mulatto.

CHANTELLE

Ummmmmhmmmmmmm.

IDA

For real.

CHANTELLE

You think we should stop coming to this place? My food is always cold. I told you we should have gotten Indian.

Waitress comes over and delivers checks.

WAITRESS

You pay up front.

IDA and CHANTELLE

Thank you.

IDA

Starts to gather her things

We need to find a new way of talking things out. Maybe next time we should walk and talk, because I am getting fat.

CHANTELLE

Me too!!!

                                    IDA
Thanks for checking me. Thanks for encouraging me.

                                CHANTELLE
Sure thing. I only do for you what you do for me. And every time you're
being tragic, I am going to tell you.

They get up and start to leave.

                                    IDA
It's my truth, don't judge me.

                                CHANTELLE
So now you admit it?

                                    IDA
Whatever!

DISCUSSION AND CONCLUSION

Traveling through the academy, pursuing terminal degrees, solidifying
career plans, and seeking intellectual validity, African American women
are met with pushback on our research interest and tremendous roadblocks to degree completion. These obstacles, more often than not, come
in the form of racist and sexist acts interpreted through layers of identity
that are unique to each individual. Chantelle and Ida are two uniquely
different African American women experiencing their doctoral programs
from similar, but separate vantage points. Stereotypical images of Black
women haunt Ida throughout her graduate school experiences. In Acts 1
and 2, ghosts constantly rattle shackles of low self-esteem, impossibilities,
and intellectual objectification. She interprets her experiences as setting
her up to be an academic work mule. While she had a jovial undergraduate experience, surrounded by the prospects of African American success,
the dehumanization she experiences as doctoral student seems to strip
her of the tools she gained at her HBCU. The trauma of being both Black
and female crystallizes with Ida's experience with Dr. Smith and Jamal.
Dr. Smith violates her intellectuality and trust as her mentor. Jamal violates her existing trust in the Black male network she has built in the program. While scholarly circles of unity and trust among African Americans
exists in many academic spaces, competition frequently causes acts of
betrayal by African American women and men to members of their own
race. The conversation between Jamal and Ida is just one example.

Unlike Ida, Chantelle benefits from early mentorship by Black female professors. Although they hold appointments outside of her doctoral program, she is able to harness her relationship with them to benefit her professional and personal outlook. After Chantelle introduces Ida to some of these women to Ida we see her gain a stronger voice. Although she is still unsure of her career path, she and Chantelle are able to utilize stereotypical images of African American women, such as the tragic mulatto, as a means to interpret their present emotions. They collectively decide to not take the tragic approach to their futures. As a testament to Ida's newfound strength and support from Chantelle as peer mentor, Ida is able to move from "tragic" feelings or deficit thinking to aspiring to be like an historical African American female figure she admires. Through references to Black feminist text we also see both women take on a revolutionary consciousness.

Throughout the text we see them grapple with how they react to their circumstances and environment. In Act 3 we observe both women use historical role modeling—the utilization of historical figures and their lived experiences as knowledge of what is possible—to redefine their career goals and challenge each other's perspectives. By contrasting the depiction of Patsy and the history of Harriet Tubman they began to formulate career goals that will transcend their own common notions of what is possible. They both wish to use their educations to free others. We, the authors, see Patsy's desire to end her life, comparable to dropping out of school or deciding not to pursue a degree because it will be "hard" or "difficult." We do not wish to inadvertently make a judgment on those who make those choices for their lives. Or condemn women in the past that chose death as a protest to their circumstances. However, we would like to make a statement to women in the academy about choosing to preserver by completing their academic goals.

Many times students like Chantelle and Ida face choices between motherhood, wifehood, and career. It can take a toll on a student's desires to persist. Ida's dialogue about choosing her family over her degree serves as an example. Thankfully, however, these two students rely on historical examples of resilience to anchor their Black bodies securely to the goals they have set, rather than feed into deficient stereotypes that eat away at their dreams. These dreams, as acts of resistance, do not support the metanarrative or benefit hegemonic cultural structures. It is through self-redefining that these two women look to historically African American figures for validation. Therefore they productively evaluate and evolve; they rise. In order to combat discrimination in the dominant society and self-define, Black women must employ direct testimony by or through dialogue between these women. Lorde (1984) posits, "if I didn't define myself for myself, I would be crunched into other people's fantasies for me and eaten alive" (p. 137). We have found that through dialogue with ancestors and ourselves we are redefining what it means to be an academic. We are also combating the matrix of dominance—the social construction of oppression that is created by the intersections of race, gender, and class (Collins, 1991)—that wants to confine us to the boundaries of boxes and academic label.

NOTES

1. The term African American has been used synonymously with Black, and we utilize it here to refer to women and men of African descent who reside in the United States and have antebellum ancestry from the Continent of Africa.

2. Data is being drawn from two previous research studies. One study collected the narratives of 10 African American women in doctoral programs and specifically explored salient racial and gender experiences in their education. The second study explores the experiences of reentry African American mothers at an urban Midwestern university.

3. Dolliole is a fictional university located in the Atlanta University Center (AUC). In reality the AUC is a consortium of four historically Black colleges and universities [HBCUs]: Spelman College, which is referenced above, Morehouse College, Clark Atlanta University, and Morehouse School of Medicine. Morris Brown College, also a HBCU, is a former member of the AUC. For many prospective, current, and alumni the AUC symbolizes the urban HBCU culture experience.

4. "A Different World" a spin-off of "The Cosby Show" ran on network television from 1987–1993. Set at the fictional Hillman College, the characters of a Different World projected an image of HBCU student culture. At the height of its popularity it was the second most viewed Black sitcoms. Empirical research on its impact on popular perceptions of HBCUs, but for critiques and commentaries on the show see Parrott-Sheffer (2008) and Hobbs (2008)

5. Whitley Gilbert and Winifred "Freddie" Brooks were two female characters of "A Different World." Juxtaposed to each other they serve as opposite depictions of African American women. Whitley, a native of Richmond, Virginia and a third generation Hillmanite, is upper class and receives enormous financial support from her parents. On the other hand, Freddie is a native of New Mexico and biracial. She is much more socially conscious, artistic, and lacks the financial support afforded to Whitley. On the show they often clash over their philosophical and class-related differences.

6. Wardolf is a fictional Northeastern Ivy League university.

7. See Brown and Davis (2001), Gallien (2005), Palmer and Young (2010) and Sutton and Kimbrough (2001) on the social and cultural benefits of African American student attending HBCUs.

8. See Foster (2001) on White faculty at HBCUs.

9. See Gilersleeve et al. (2011) on dehumanizing socialization process experienced by Black and Latino students in doctoral programs.

10. See Croom (2011), Hughes (2012), and Patton and Catching (2009), for accounts of African American female professors.

11. See Gildersleeve et al. (2011) on doctoral student self-doubt and shifting scholarly endeavors.

12. In a Meaningful Mentorship: A CRT Perspective on Mentoring Students and Faculty of Color, Horace et al. (2013) reveal the commandments of being a good mentee. One of the commandments was to protect your mentor and keep their personal stories in confidence. Another aspect of protecting a mentor was to defend that mentor when other students make defamatory remarks about the mentor.

13. See Castañeda and Isgro (2013), Reed (2011) and Ward and Wolf-Wendel (2004) on the experiences of mothers in the academy and the professoriate.

14. See Njoku (2014), Sealey-Ruiz (2007), (2013), and Thomas (2001) on the experiences of African American mothers in college.

15. See Njoku (2014), Sealey-Ruiz (2007), (2013), and Thomas (2001) on the experiences of African American mothers in college.

16. See Gildersleeve et al. (2011) on doctoral student questioning one's self-worth on self-destructive and invalidating thinking.

17. See Collins (2005) and Walker (1983) on issues of sexism in the African American community and within the African American academic community, respectively.

18. See Gildersleeve et al. (2011) on doctoral student questioning one's self-worth on self-destructive and invalidating thinking.

19. See Patton (2009) and Patton and Harper (2003) on the need of peer networks for African American women in graduate and professional school.

20. Ida's despair in this situation is a reference to Lorde's (1984) quote "If I didn't define myself for myself, I would be crunched into other people's fantasies for me and eaten alive." Here we see her depending on her White male professor's definition of her instead of her own.

21. See Gildersleeve et al. (2011) on shifting scholarly endeavors.

22. The song "To Be Young, Gifted, and Black," written by Nina Simone and Weldon Irvine (1969) was inspired by her friend Lorraine Hansberry during the postmortem run of Hansberry's play by the same name. As the songs performer, Simone speaks about Hansberry's spirit speaking to her and inspiring the song. This moment speaks to the power of sisterhood or peer networking and spirit of using the art of African American women to inspire strength and courage.

23. See Horace et al. (2013), Patton and Harper (2003) and Patton (2009) on benefits of same-sex and race mentors for African American women.

24. Dr. Nadrea Rogers is inspired by both our mentor Dr. Robin L. Hughes and named after each of us as a protest against all of the naysayers in our past.

25. Here we find that while Ida participates in deficit language, she is trying to accept herself. According the Gildersleeve et al. (2011) the "Am I going crazy?!" narrative is strife with personal contradictions that may result in students beneficially centering race. "The narrative is not neutral, but contradictory. It is overwhelmingly constraining, but some consequences from this constraint are not necessarily bad. The narrative is rife with tensions and contradictions in it constitution, consequences, and instantiation" (p. 100).

26. See Patton and Catching (2009) on a counter narrative of African American education faculty.

27. See Bennett (2009) and Throsby and Zednik (2011) career decision making and job holdings of artist.

28. See Roberts (1997) on the legal assault on the African American female body.

29. Ida is comparing and contrasting herself to two historical notions of the African American female slave. One is Harriet Tubman, a general on the Underground Railroad. The other is the interpretation of Patsey, the non-fictional character in Solomon Northup's memoir *Twelve Years a Slave* (1853), in the 2013 film of the same name.

30. See Collins (2000), hooks (1981), and Wallace (1990) on stereotypes of African

31. American women, in particular the notion of the unfeminine Black superwoman.

32. This a specific reference to hooks (1981) and her extended reference to the history of African American women in America and the devaluation of African American womanhood.

REFERENCES

Bennett, D. (2009). Academy and the real world developing realistic notions of career in the performing arts. *Arts and Humanities in Higher Education, 8*(3), 309–327.

Bernal, D. D. (1998). Using a Chicana feminist epistemology in educational research. *Harvard Educational Review, 68*(4), 555–583.

Brown, M. C., & Davis, J. E. (2001). The historically Black college as social contract, social capital, and social equalizer. *Peabody Journal of Education, 76*(1), 31–49.

Castañeda, M., & Isgro, K. (Eds.). (2013). *Mothers in academia.* New York, NY: Columbia University Press.

Collins, P. H. (1991). *Black feminist thought: Knowledge, consciousness, and the politics of empowerment.* New York, NY: Routledge.

Collins, P. H. (2000). *Black feminist thought: Knowledge, consciousness, and the politics of empowerment.* New York, NY: Routledge.

Collins, P. H. (2005). *Black sexual politics: African Americans, gender, and the new racism.* New York, NY: Routledge.

Croom, N. N. (2011). *Finding rainbows in the clouds: Learning about the full professorship from the stories of Black female full professors* (Unpublished doctoral dissertation). Iowa State.

Delgado, R., & Stefancic, J. (2001). *Critical race theory: An introduction.* New York, NY: New York University Press.

Dillard, C. (2000). The substance of things hoped for, the evidence of things not seen: Examining an endarkened feminist epistemology in educational research and leadership. *Qualitative Studies in Education, 13*(6) 661–681.

Felder, P. P., Stevenson, H. C., & Gasman, M. (2014). Understanding race in doctoral student socialization. *International Journal of Doctoral Studies, 9,* 21–42. Retrieved from http://ijds.org/Volume9/IJDSv9p021-042Felder0323.pdf

Foster, L. (2001). The not-so-invisible professors White faculty at the Black college. *Urban Education, 36*(5), 611–629.

Gallien, L. B (2005). The historical and cultural context of education African American college students. In M. S. Peterson (Ed.), *Instructing and mentoring the African American college student* (pp. 3–14). Boston, MA: Pearson Education.

Gildersleeve, R. E., Croom, N. N., & Vasquez, P. L. (2011). "Am I going crazy?!": A critical race analysis of doctoral education. *Equity & Excellence in Education, 44*(1), 93–114.

Griffin, R. A. (2012). I AM an angry Black woman: Black feminist autoethnography, voice, and resistance. *Women's Studies in Communication, 35*(2), 138–157.

Harper, S. R. (2012). Race without racism: How higher education researchers minimize racist institutional norms. *The Review of Higher Education, 36*(1), 9–29.

Hobbs, L. (2008, February). Higher learning. *Vibe Magazine,*111.

hooks, b. (1981). *Ain't I a woman: Black women and feminism.* Boston, MA: South End Press.

Horace, J., Rogers, J., Hughes, R. L., Davis Patton, L., Howard-Hamilton, M., Davis, J.E, & Njoku, N. (2013, January). *Meaningful mentorship: A CRT perspective on mentoring students and faculty of color.* Symposium presented at the annual meeting of the Association for the Study of Higher Education, St. Louis, MO.

Hughes, R., & Giles, M. (2010). CRiT walking in higher education: Activating critical race theory in the academy. *Race Ethnicity and Education, 13*(1), 41–57.

Hughes, R. L. (2012, February 27). 'The help': Let them eat pie [Web blog]. Retrieved from http://diverseeducation.com/article/31380/

Ladson-Billings, G., & Tate, W., IV. (1995). Toward a critical race theory of education. *The Teachers College Record, 97*(1), 47–68.

Lorde, A. (Ed.). (1984). Learning from the 60s. In *Sister outsider: Essays and speeches* (pp. 134–144). New York, NY: Crossing Press.

Wallace, M. (1990). *Black macho and the myth of the superwoman.* New York, NY: Verso.

Morehouse, L., & Dawkins, M.P. (2006). The McKnight Doctoral Fellowship Program: Toward and seamless approach to the production of African American doctorates. *Journal of Negro Education, 75,* 563–571.

Njoku, N. (2014). *Watering our mothers' gardens: Best practices for supporting African American re-entry mothers in college.* Paper presented at the annual meeting of the American College Personnel Association, Indianapolis, IN.

Northup, S. (1853). *Twelve years a slave: Narrative of Solomon Northup, citizen of New York.* Auburn, AL: Derby and Miller.

Palmer, R., & Young, E. (2010). The uniqueness of an HBCU environment: How a supportive campus climate promotes student success. In T. L. Strayhorn & M. C. Terrell (Eds.), *The evolving challenges facing Black college students: New insights for practice and research* (pp. 138–161). Sterling, VA: Stylus.

Parrott-Sheffer, A. (2008). Not a laughing matter: The portrayals of Black colleges on television. In M. Gasman & C. L. Tudico (Eds.), *Historically Black colleges and universities: Triumphs, troubles, and taboos* (pp. 207–222). New York, NY: Pelgrave McMillan.

Patton, L. D. (2009). My sister's keeper: A qualitative examination of mentoring experiences among African American women in graduate and professional schools. *The Journal of Higher Education, 80*(5), 510–537.

Patton, L. D., & Catching, C. (2009). 'Teaching while Black': Narratives of African American student affairs faculty. *International Journal of Qualitative Studies in Education, 22*(6), 713–728.

Patton, L. D., & Harper, S. R. (2003). Mentoring relationships among African American women in graduate and professional schools. *New Directions for Student Services, 104*, 67–78.

Reed, L. C. (2011). Star light, star bright: A Black female scholar seeks to find "voice" in the academy. In G. Jean-Marie & B. Lloyd-Jones (Eds.), *Women of color in higher education: Changing directions and new perspectives* (pp. 283-301). Bingley, United Kingdom: Emerald.

Roberts, D. (1997). *Killing the Black body.* New York, NY: Pantheon.

Sealey-Ruiz, Y. (2007). Rising above reality: The voices of reentry Black mothers and their daughters. *The Journal of Negro Education, 76*(2), 141–153.

Sealey-Ruiz, Y. (2013). Learning to resist: Educational counter-narratives of Black college reentry mothers. *Teachers College Record, 115*(4), 1–31.

Simone, N. & Irvine, W. (1969) *To be young, gifted and Black* [Recorded by Nina Simone]. On Black Gold Album. New York, NY: RCA Records.

Smith, W. A., Allen, W. R., & Danley, L. L. (2007). "Assume the position ... You fit the description" psychosocial experiences and racial battle fatigue among African American male college students. *American Behavioral Scientist, 51*(4), 551–578.

Solorzano, D., Ceja, M., & Yosso, T. (2000). Critical race theory, racial microaggressions, and campus racial climate: The experiences of African American college students. *Journal of Negro Education, 69*(1/2) 60–73.

Solórzano, D., & Yosso, T. (2001). Critical race and LatCrit theory and method: Counterstorytelling. *Qualitative Studies in Education, 14*(4), 471–495.

Strauss, A. L., & Corbin, J. M. (1990). *Basics of qualitative research* (Vol. 15). Newbury Park, CA: SAGE.

Sutton, E. M., & Kimbrough, W. M. (2001). Trends in Black student involvement. *NASPA Journal, 39*(1), 30–40.

Taylor, E., & Antony, J. S. (2000). Stereotype threat reduction and wise schooling: Towards the successful socialization of African American doctoral students in education. *The Journal of Negro Education, 69*(3), 184–198.

Thomas, V. G. (2001). Educational experiences and transitions of reentry college women: Special considerations for African American female students. *Journal of Negro Education, 70*(3), 139–155.

Throsby, D., & Zednik, A. (2011). Multiple job-holding and artistic careers: Some empirical evidence. *Cultural Trends, 20*(1), 9–24.

Walker, A. (1983). To the Black scholar. In *In search of our mothers' garden: Womanist prose* (pp. 320–325). New York, NY: Harcourt Brace Jovanovich.

Wallace, M. (1990). *Black macho and the myth of the superwoman.* New York, NY: Verso.

Ward, K., & Wolf-Wendel, L. (2004). Academic motherhood: Managing complex roles in research universities. *The Review of Higher Education, 27*(2), 233–257.

Williams, J. L., & Nichols, T. M. (2011). Black women's experiences with racial microaggressions in college: Making meaning at the crossroads of race and gender. In C. R. Chambers & R. V. Sharpe (Eds.), *Black American female undergraduates on campus: Successes and challenges* (pp. 75–95). New York, NY: Emerald.

Wing, A. K. (1999). Race and gender issues: Critical race feminism. *Journal of Intergroup Relations, 26*(3), 14–25.

Yosso, T. J. (2013). *Critical race counterstories along the Chicana/Chicano educational pipeline.* New York, NY: Routledge.

RESPONSE

TALKING BACK

Donyell L. Roseboro

Responding to any work that interrogates the lived experiences of Black women at predominantly White institutions (PWIs) requires "talking back" (hooks, 2004) to history with a discursive currency that captures past and present. Such a response inevitably assumes an individual stance relative to collective consciousness, the intersection of which frames the ways we author and/or are authored by the world. Though there is no singular Black woman consciousness, there are experiences as Black women that give rise to predictable pivot points in our lives. These pivot points are what make us laugh and cry together across time, space, and multilayered otherness. They are what make possible a sense of collective solidarity in this particular "imagined community" (Anderson, 2006). Perhaps most important, the pivot points that mark boundaries, that return us from whence we came, that pull us away from the unseen, are those that resurrect collective memories from our foremothers. In this resurrection, we witness their complicated resiliency and historical trauma (Danzer, 2012; Wiechelt, Grycznski, Johnson, & Caldwell, 2012). My response to Njoku and Rogers thus embraces the specificity with which they speak in their counterstory and the larger interior struggle faced by Black women in academia.

From their narratives, three themes emerge—choosing, naming, and placing—each of these situated theoretically by critical scholars who deconstruct the normalizing epistemologies that have privileged certain

Beyond Retention: Cultivating Spaces of Equity, Justice, and Fairness
for Women of Color in U.S. Higher Education, pp. 93–103
Copyright © 2016 by Information Age Publishing

definitions over others. Although we work against assumptions that unlimited choice exists for anyone, critical theorists have for decades argued that Black women live with multiple oppressive histories (Wing, 1997), have historically been treated as property (Spillers, 1997), and continue to face hypersexualized images of themselves in the media (Collins, 2005). In our grappling with and struggle against these experiences, we operate within a framework for transcendence based on a "strong Black woman" identity that further complicates our psychological responses to the world (Beauboeuf-Lafontant, 2007). Although what we can or cannot choose is constrained/shaped by history, traditional definitions of choice reinforce an individualistic perspective of failure that ignores the structural ramifications of oppression. In this respect, choice never represents a singular or individual decision. At best, our definitions of choice represents a way of understanding how lives are mapped, how agency is assumed and/or denied, and how those of us with intersecting identities struggle within such binaries. In this sense, choice moves beyond its typical associative definitions with democracy and, by extension, freedom. Instead, defining choice in its historicized and cultural complexity can illuminate the borders we cross daily to exist.

Border crossing is no easy task. Indeed, it represents a way of being and moving in the world that demands attention to how we define ourselves and how we are defined by others. Such crossings occur at the interstices of identities (Anzaldúa, 1997; Cummins, 2013), disciplines (Linkon & Russo, 2012), and physical structures (Duffield, Olsen, & Kerzman, 2013). The journey represents an interior movement (Spillers, 1998) with external and tangible implications (Sternberg & Barry, 2011). To live with these tangible implications requires a coming to consciousness that forces us to privilege certain identities—even as we exist with multiplicity, certain identities demand more attention at times than others. The danger for us is to not rank oppressions (Moraga, 1981) and, by implication, oppressive identities. Doing so would potentially negate the complicated ways that intersecting identities create us in the world. Perhaps more important, and for the purposes of this paper, we must consider the ways that identities, privilege, and border crossing come imbued with assumptions about choice. So even though I may be born with certain identities, that birth does not mean that I will assume that stereotypical identity. It does not mean that I live with a consciousness of the collective history of that identity group nor does it mean that I equate my lived experiences to other members of that group. When and where I enter (Cooper, 1892/ 1988), is determined by my circumstances of birth, the sociopolitical expectations of the era, and my own agency. So while choice has come to superficially mean we can just make a selection, my sense of agency "refers to perceived causality of the self, [that is,] the feeling of causing something to happen" (Dewey & Knoblich, 2014, p. 1). While I may not be able to choose without regard to whom the world expects me to be, I can claim a different space, an alternate path, an unexpected outcome.

As we traverse borders, we learn to name experience and, in that naming, confront the stigmas associated with some identities. The stigmas associated to certain identities shape our responses—whether we attempt to ignore, embrace, or hide the stigma reflects an interior struggle (Goffman, 1963), one that inevitably affects our construction of the particular identity. How we name ourselves in relationship to the world thus becomes a complex social construction dependent on collective definitions and individual responses. Black women's recognition of and response to microaggressions (Lewis, Mendenhall, Harwood, & Browne Huntt, 2012), refutation of stereotypical media scripts (French, 2012), and persistent resilience (Mendenhall, Bowman, & Zhang, 2012) serve as reminders of how Black women have renamed their collective narrative. It is a renaming that is both personal and political, as much about who we are as it is about the discourses we seek to define us. When, for example, we (along with other women of color) embrace womanist epistemology rather than feminist, we claim other ways of theorizing our existence (Jain & Turner, 2012). In fact, renaming represents an interrogation of predetermined identities and a conscious becoming of others. We are not born Black women, we become so (Roseboro, 2006; Wittig, 1993).

Naming, as a response to oppression, signifies a dimension of intellectual activism. If such activism is, as Collins (2012) argues, "speaking the truth to power" and "speaking the truth to people," then it is inevitably tied to discourse(s), the assumptions that shape discourse(s), and the ways we respond to words (p. xiii). In this sense, activism also takes place in relationship—between the individual and the collective, between an idea and an action. It is shaped by, and shapes, systems and processes simultaneously. Given that renaming involves the speaking of previously unspoken truths, then the act of renaming denotes a shifting of traditional discourse, history, and/or power. These truth-telling shifts challenge traditional master narratives and in so doing, illuminate counterstories that present alternative ways of perceiving, experiencing, and interpreting the world. And, perhaps equally important, when this renaming occurs in tandem with an oppositional gaze, it "opens up the possibility of agency" (hooks, 2003, p. 94). This agency of Black women, their counterstories, and public works convey a spirit of activism born from othered spaces— spaces marked by difference and to which their lived experience responds.

Space, for Black women, has come wrought with complicated meaning. On one hand, space can act as a vehicle for building solidarity, for the nurturing of collective action toward a common good (Mohanty, 2003).

On the other hand, space can Other and, in that othering, erase particular identities, and create factions between individuals or groups. And perhaps more troubling, given the passage of time, the same space can do both—build solidarity and erase. Navigating these possibilities, particularly when the function of a space can change unpredictably over time, requires a constant negotiation of one's selves in relation. Black women in search of solidarity embrace those spaces that foster the familial but learn quickly that most spaces cannot and do not serve that function (Lorde, 2007). Claiming a home of any space is more likely when we come to realize that home is not necessarily tied to the physical, not always bound by geography. Rather, as Anzaldúa (1987) suggests, "I am a turtle. Wherever I go, I carry 'home' on my back" (p. 43). Finding home in any space thus becomes an act of self-discovery, one that captures the agency inherent in such exploration.

For Black women struggling to find home, the epistemological journey they must make centers more on how, why, when, and in what manner they situate themselves or find themselves placed. In either case, the act of situating or being placed speaks to the intersecting of identity, space, and representation. To be oneself in a space one claims and to be seen as belonging in that space is the quintessential dilemma. Black women's history of being othered, placed, and misrepresented (Alexander, 2011) complicates our attempts to find spaces that nurture and love just as they challenge and question. Finding spaces that allow us to be us while we form the language to talk back to those assumptions, traditions, histories, and master narratives that undo us is the challenge. This kind of talking back demands a way of knowing and being the world that accepts ambiguity, multiple truths, and nonlinear perspectives. It is a talking back that lives with the tension that stems from working the pivot points of multiple identities in disparate spaces. It is a tension that can connect Black women across generation and space. Yet in this tension, we continue to talk back, to listen, to breathe, to place ourselves.

I'D RATHER BE HARRIET

When Njoku and Rogers title their chapter, they purposefully evoke a narrative that begins with slavery in the United States. This beginning situates their lived tapestries and by so doing, it places them in relation to ancestors, institutions, and time. Perhaps more important, their juxtaposition of Maya Angelou's *Still I Rise* (1978) poem to slavery as an institution and to Harriet Tubman's particular narrative connects survival and transcendence to going back and leading forward. In both instances, the journey is a collective one framed by the ideology that to rise, to transcend such unspeakable inhumanity, serves as a testament to the unpar-ralleled humanity of Black people. It is a testament made possible through witnessing, being with the world in deeply contested and mean-ingful ways (Dillard, Abdur-Rashid, & Tyson, 2000). Such witnessing illus-trates the layered identities of Black women, the ways in which they must "lean in' (Sandberg, 2013) when desperately wanting to retreat, and the interior struggles that persist long after the witnessing.

It is, perhaps, these interior struggles that Black people in the United States still contend with despite being centuries removed from enslave-ment. Historical trauma is a type of trauma that is not based on individual experience but, rather, stems from a collective history of loss, destruction, and abuse (Danzer, 2012; Wiechelt et al., 2012). Collective memory and loss, passed on through generations evoke particular responses that may seem disconnected from the individual's experiences. Yet such trauma can manifest itself in tangible ways (i.e., substance abuse). If this trauma gets examined as individual behavior absent any attention to the role of histor-ical trauma, then clinical treatments are often ineffective (Morgan & Free-man, 2009). The individual behavior can only be understood and/or explained with respect to the collective history with and within that trauma. When Njoku and Rogers privilege Harriet's experience over their own, it is not necessarily to say that her condition was any better. Instead, it suggests that her condition, at least, could be understood given the parameters of her time. To feel as enslaved as Harriet in a time when slav-ery does not exist is, in contrast, a more perplexing condition, one that forces us to distinguish between enslavement and slavery. Enslavement is a specific circumstance that lacks the finality that the term slavery con-notes. Slavery, however, was an institution, replete with complex regula-tory systems (i.e., slave codes).

To be physically enslaved demands that one understand the con-straints, the consequences of attempting to escape those constraints, and the behavioral expectations associated with one's position as enslaved. To feel enslaved without the physical conditions of that slavery seems contra-dictory, at best. At worst, it means that one's psychological experiences do not mirror one's physical conditions and, without such mirroring, articu-lating a coherent external identity becomes more difficult. How do I express interior turmoil in any kind of convincing way when, by all outer appearances, I am perfectly positioned? How do I express the duality without being recommended for psychiatric evaluation? Dubois (1903/1996) captured this duality when he said

> It is a peculiar sensation, this double-consciousness, this sense of always looking at one's self through the eyes of others, of measuring one's soul by the tape of a twoness—an American, a Negro; two souls, two thoughts, two

unreconciled strivings; two warring ideals in one dark body, whose dogged
strength alone keeps it from being torn asunder. (p. 102)

Much later work that attempts to theorize the lived experiences of people
of color uses Dubois' framework. In hindsight, he put forward a belief
that there did exist some particular strength to Black people that made
possible the transcendence of (or living with) this duality.

Njoku and Rogers use the voice of Ida in their counterstory script to
suggest that, for Black women, the ability to choose exists despite the
countervailing ways those choices are limited. Because we are often forced
to privilege some identities over others, these choices can illustrate
extended interior conversations that take place between our respective
selves. Just as the counterstory attempts to capture the difficulty inherent
in these conversations, the dialogue elevates Black women as resilient,
able to resist, persist, and evolve. And so, when Ida exclaims "But Harriet
wouldn't keep putting up with the same thing would she? Allowing people
to hurt her over and over again. I have a choice on how I face this world;
how I face the academy! And I choose Harriet" (p. 80), she recognizes
that her experiences are always positioned in relation to other Black
women. And in this positioning, she can claim some sense of agency—if
other Black women can rise, so can she.

I AM SO GLAD WE HAVE A CHANCE
TO GET TO KNOW EACH OTHER

Black people in the United States have long operated with extended kinship networks. Indeed, understanding the importance of "fictive" kin
(Stack, 1996) to Black people in the United States allows us to expand our
definitions of the familial. It allows us to reimagine ancestry and lineage,
to reconsider how one comes to belong. In Njoku and Rogers' counterstory, they are in search of belonging but find it elusive at PWIs of higher
education. Although the numbers of African Americans in colleges and
universities has increased from 1990–2012 between Blacks and Whites, we
still remain a rather small percentage of the college going population,
particularly at the doctoral level. From 1990 to 2012, the percentage of
25- to 29-year-olds who attained a bachelor's degree or higher increased
from 26 to 40% for Whites, and from 13 to 23% for Blacks (Aud, Wilkinson-Flicker, Kristapovich, Wang, & Zhang, 2013). In 2009–10, there were
48,069 doctoral degrees awarded. Of those, 6.3% were Black (Statistical
Profile, 2012). In 2011 just 6% of faculty members nationwide were Black.
Clearly, we are few in number. Given this, loneliness seems unavoidable.
But while the narrators in the counterstory discuss the loneliness, they

also describe it as "lonely, but worth it" (p. 8). Indeed, Chantelle says to Ida, "Don't say that, I need you here" when Ida is considering leaving the program. There is a clear sense that they are familial and, in this extended kinship network, they have discovered a place. To belong, to feel at home, to maintain some sense of sanity, it seems clear that they must sustain this space together.

Chantelle's exclamation, "I need you" also suggests that her success is dependent on Ida's, that theirs is a reciprocal way of being in the world. It reveals her inner panic when faced with the possibility of increasing isolation and loneliness. Perhaps more telling, Chantelle voices the inner struggle she faces by saying of a faculty member, "but she never told me how the process of getting the PhD would make me feel" (p. 63). It is a feeling marked by the questioning of themselves and their abilities, of their preparedness, intellect, and persistence. The doctoral journey is a process with boundaries and gateway markers along the way. It is a process that interrogates one's commitment to the collective, to the dream (of higher education), and to the possibilities. At one point Ida says "I could go back home, the most comfortable place I know, and still be tormented by the same injustices I have faced in this academic space" (p. 78). In this moment, Ida constructs a binary between home (comfort) and the academy (injustice). To choose to remain in the academy thus represents a conscious decision to forego home for an exclusionary and oppressive space, one that may never shift in its cultural framework.

OF HOPE

I completed my doctoral program in 2005 and set off into the sunset for Southern Illinois University Edwardville. When I left, I felt prepared to face the unknown. In my doctoral experience, I had the fortune to meet several other Black women. We traveled the journey together, nourished by the academic debates, challenged by our professors, questioned by our White classmates, yet we remained steadfastly supportive of each other. When I landed at Southern Illinois University Edwardville I realized quickly that I had no understanding of the politics of academia from the faculty standpoint. Fortunately, I was mentored well by a White woman who spoke openly about what it meant to achieve in an institution designed to eliminate. Nonetheless, I struggled those 2 years, mostly because I felt so far removed from home. Though I loved my institution and colleagues, I never felt as if I had a place in the Midwest—even the racism felt strangely different.

When I arrived at UNCW in the fall of 2007, I came with a much more comprehensive and textured understanding of academia at PWIs. I learned to question in ways that would unravel motives and manipulative behavior. Perhaps most important, I had learned to embrace my distrust—it was clear that I would always operate with a hermeneutic of suspicion and it was equally clear that this suspicion had strengthened my steps and made my journey more purposefully directed. Although I was not a research extensive institution, I published steadily, knowing that tenure could still be unattainable. And when I went up for tenure, I remember people staring at me in disbelief wondering why I remained skeptical with 13 publications. I wanted to scream "Because I'm Black and White America has historically not judged us fairly." Instead, I remained quiet, taught my classes, and waited. When the word came that my tenure vote was positive, I closed the door to my office to be alone. Minutes later I was embraced by a Black woman colleague who knew and who shared that moment with me.

Three and a half years later, I am now a department chair, and I find myself informally mentoring other women of color who are newer to the academy. The one question that persists about PWIs is "What is the place and where do I belong?" In the past, I have fought to prove to newer women of color in the academy that we need to teach at PWIs. This message has been a part of my mentoring narrative forever. Our success here means something—it proves that our ancestors who endured the hoses, the dogs, the bombings, died with dignity and in hope. It proves that those who assumed we were inferior, unintelligent, and controllable misread us. It proves that we are always a "we", bound across generations and through time. And, in our persistence at PWIs, we can change the culture of the institutions.

Now, I question that mentoring narrative. Though academia has become more inclusive, there is and will always be, an elitist core, a philosophy that teaching at a university is not for everyone, it distinguishes some from others, and elevates us when we finish … that will remain. Instead I believe that, for Black women working at PWIs, the work is important in that it requires us to know ourselves. Njoku and Rogers began their piece with reference to Maya Angelou and I will end this chapter with a return to her. On May 28, 2014 she closed her eyes, put down her pen, and moved on. I am still struggling with what that loss means for us as a people. I attended Wake Forest as a graduate student while she was still teaching. Though I never had her in class, I was able to witness, to share the same space with her on multiple occasions. Maya said of herself, "I'm not a writer who teaches. I'm a teacher who writes. But I had to work at Wake Forest to know that'" (as cited in King, 2014, p. 74). In so many ways, she taught all of us who we could be. She remembered, she knew, she loved us, and she expected better of us.

In her 32 years at Wake Forest (a PWI), she taught hundreds of students how to claim, author, and present themselves. Students paid tribute to her and in those tributes, one theme emerged as central to her epistemology of teaching—naming. Nicole Little (class of 2013) said,

> In class Dr. Angelou made us learn each other's names. She wanted us to understand how you feel when someone calls your name across the room. She wanted us to experience what it meant to have your chest swell with pride because someone remembered your name. (Wilson, 2014, p. 79)

And, Tycely Williams (class of 1997) recalled,

> One semester, she gifted each of us with a leather briefcase with our full name etched in gold script. I remember her saying, 'I want you to go into the world feeling like somebody, I want you to go into the world with your heads high, but your hearts higher. Remember, you have a name" (Wilson, 2014, p. 79)

We can find a home in PWIs, but not in the typical way we consider home. Home is not the institution, its traditions, or its history. Home, for Black women teaching at PWIs is in relationship. Ours is a tapestry of belonging, cultivated by centuries of struggle and love. Though we may be held together by disparate threads, we are fortified by each other. Let us not forget.

REFERENCES

Alexander, S. A. J. (2011). M/othering the nation: Women's bodies as nationalist trope in Edwide Danticat's "Brath, eyes, and memory." *African American Review, 44*(3), 373–390.

Anderson, B. (2006). *Imagined communities: Reflections on the origin and spread of nationalism* (Rev. ed.). New York, NY: Verso.

Angelou, M. (1978) Still I rise. In *And still I rise.* New York, NY: Random House.

Anzaldúa, G. (1987). La concienza de la mestiza: Towards a new consciousness. In R. R. Warhol & D. P. Herndl (Eds.), *Feminisms: An anthology of literary theory and criticism* (pp. 765–775). New Brunswick, NJ: Rutgers University Press.

Aud, S., Wilkinson-Flicker, S., Kristapovich, P., Wang, X., & Zhang, J. (2013). The condition of education. *Institute of Education Sciences.* Retrieved from http://nces.ed.gov/pubs2013/2013037.pdf

Beauboeuf-Lafontant, T. (2007). You have to show strength: An exploration of gender, race, and depression. *Gender & Society, 21*(1), 28–51.

Collins, P. H. (2005). *Black sexual politics: African Americans, gender, and the new racism.* New York, NY: Routledge.

Collins, P.H. (2012). *On intellectual activism.* Philadelphia, PA: Temple University Press.

Cooper, A. (1988). *A voice from the South*. New York, NY: Oxford University Press. (Original work published in 1892)

Cummins, A. (2013). Border crossings: Undocumented migration between Mexico and the United States in contemporary young adult literature. *Children's Literature in Education, 44*(1), 57–73.

Danzer, G. (2012). African Americans' historical trauma: Manifestations in and outside of therapy. *Journal of Theory Construction & Testing, 16*(1), 16–21.

Dewey, J. A., & Knoblich, G. (2014). Do implicit and explicit measures of the sense of agency measure the same thing? *PLoS ONE, 9*(10), 1–9.

Dillard, C., Abdur-Rashid, D., & Tyson, C. (2000). My soul is a witness: Affirming pedagogies of the spirit. *International Journal of Qualitative Studies in Education, 13*(5), 447–462.

DuBois, W. E. B. (1996). The souls of Black folk. In E. J. Sundquist (Ed.), *The Oxford W. E. B. Dubois reader* (pp. 97–240). Oxford, England: Oxford University Press. (Original work published in 1903)

Duffield, S., Olsen, A., & Kerzman, R. (2013). Crossing borders, breaking boundaries: Collaboration among higher education institutions. *Innovative Higher Education, 48*(3), 237–250.

French, B. (2013). More than Jezebels and freaks: Exploring how Black girls navigate sexual coercion and sexual scripts. *Journal of African American Studies, 17*(1), 35–50.

Goffman, E. (1963). *Stigma: Notes on the management of spoiled identity*. New York, NY: J. Aronson.

hooks, b. (2003). The oppositional gaze: Black female spectators. In A. Jones (Ed.), *The feminism and visual culture reader* (pp. 94–105). New York, NY: Routledge.

Jain, D., & Turner, C. (2012). Purple is to lavender: Womanism, resistance, and the politics of naming. *Negro Educational Review, 62/63*(1-4), 67–88.

King, K. M. (2014, Fall). Maya Angelou: Reynolds Professor of American Studies. *Wake Forest Magazine*, p. 73.

Lewis, J., Mendenhall, R., Harwood, S., & Browne Huntt, M. (2013). Coping with gendered racial microaggressions among Black Women college students. *Journal of American Studies, 17*(1), 51–73).

Linkon, S. L., & Russo, J. (2012). Border crossings: Interdisciplinarity in new working–class studies. *Labor History, 53*(3), 373–387.

Lorde, A. (2007). *Sister outsider: Essays and speeches* (Rev. ed.). New York, NY: Crown.

Mendenhall, R., Bowman, P., & Zhang, L. (2013). Single Black mothers' role strain and adaptation across the life course. *Journal of African American Studies, 17*(1), 74–98.

Mohanty, C. T. (2003). *Feminism without borders*. Durham, NC: Duke University Press.

Moraga, C. (1997). La Güera. In R. Delgado & Stefancic (Eds.). *Critical White studies: Looking behind the mirror* (pp.471–474). Philadelphia, PA; Temple University Press.

Morgan, R., & Freeman, L. (2009). The healing of our people: Substance abuse and historical trauma. *Substance Use & Misuse, 44*(1), 84–98.

Roseboro, D. (2006). Coming out Black: The student movement for the Sonja Haynes Stone Black Cultural Center at UNC-Chapel Hill. *NASAP 9*(1), 67–82.

Sandberg, S. (2013). *Lean in: Women, work, and the will to lead.* New York, NY: Alfred A. Knopf.

Spillers, H. J. (1998). Interview. In T. Haslett (Ed.), *Black cultural studies website collective.* Retrieved January 3, 2005, from http://www.blackculturalstudies.org/spillers/spillers_intvw.html.

Stack, C. (1996). *Call to home: African Americans reclaim the rural south.* New York, NY: Basic Books.

Statistical Profile. (2013). Retrieved from http://nces.ed.gov/programs/digest/d13/tables/dt13_324.80.asp

Sternberg, R. M., & Barry, C. (2011). Transnational mothers crossing the border and bringing their health care needs. *Journal of Nursing Scholarship, 43*(1), 64–71.

Wielchelt, S., Gryczynski, J., Johnson, J., & Caldwell, D. (2012). Historical trauma among urban Indians: Impact on substance abuse and family cohesion. *Journal of Loss & Trauma, 17*(4), 319–336.

Wilson, E. (2014, Fall). Maya Angelou: Reynolds Professor of American Studies. *Wake Forest Magazine*, pp. 78–79.

Wing, A. (Ed.). (1997). Brief reflections toward a multiplicative theory and praxis of being. In *Critical race feminism: A reader* (pp. 27–34). New York, NY: New York University Press.

Wittig, M. (1993). One is not born a woman. In A. M. Jaggar & P. S. Rothenberg (Eds.), *Feminist frameworks: Alternative theoretical accounts of the relations between men and women* (3rd ed., pp. 178–181). Boston, MA: McGraw-Hill.

CHAPTER 4

PREPARING TO LEAD

The Socialization of Black Women for Faculty and Administrative Careers Through Graduate School

Jennifer M. Johnson, Tykeia N. Robinson,
Candice L. Staples, and Nina Daoud

Despite gains in college access and completion among women across the educational pipeline, Black[1] women continue to be underrepresented in tenure-track faculty positions and senior leadership roles (e.g., college president, provost) in higher education. Research suggests that the scarcity of Black women in these roles can be attributed to a leaky academic pipeline (Espinal, Munoz, & Kiyama, 2010; Turner & Myers, 2001). Negative experiences during graduate school, for example, can diminish interests and aspirations to continue along the academic career track by otherwise qualified potential candidates (Austin & McDaniels, 2006). Compared to their peers, Black female graduate students report having few role models (Blake-Beard, Bayne, Crosby, & Muller, 2011; Fries-Britt & Turner-Kelly, 2005), less support of their scholarly interests (Gay, 2004; Gildersleeve, Croom, & Vasquez, 2011; Turner & Thompson, 2003), and fewer opportunities to actively engage in research with members of their

Beyond Retention: Cultivating Spaces of Equity, Justice, and Fairness
for Women of Color in U.S. Higher Education, pp. 105–126
Copyright © 2016 by Information Age Publishing
All rights of reproduction in any form reserved.

department (Gasman, Gerstl-Pepin, Anderson-Tompkins, Rasheed, & Hathaway, 2004). Additionally, students of color describe the physical, cultural, intellectual, and professional isolation experienced throughout graduate school (Duncan, 1976; Gay, 2004).

Black women enrolled in programs where they have the opportunity to work with faculty and senior campus leaders from their own racial/ethnic group, whether male or female, may have a unique vantage point to glean a sense of what a career in academe would be like for them (Ellis, 2001; Fries-Britt & Turner-Kelly, 2005). Current literature, however, highlights the challenges faced by women early on while navigating higher education such as a chilly climate (Maranto & Griffin, 2010), marginalization of their research (Griffin, Pifer, Humphrey, & Hazelwood, 2011; Maranto & Griffin, 2010; Smith, Turner, Osei-Kofi, & Richards, 2004), and gender discrimination (Maranto & Griffin, 2010). Race and gender stereotypes can create double obstacles for Black women in leadership roles, who are called upon disproportionately to serve as the "diversity expert" for campus matters as well as attend to both the academic and personal needs of all students of color within their departments or on campus (Griffin & Reddick, 2011; Moses, 1989).

Other potential barriers to pursuing advanced careers in the academy are more personal in nature. In exploring sources of stress for Black faculty at predominantly White institutions, Thompson and Dey (1998) found that the most salient sources of stress for both male and female faculty were time constraints and promotion concerns. Black women, however, reported more overall stress than their male counterparts. In Thompson and Dey's study, the women were less likely to be married or living with a partner, less likely to have a family, and more likely to spend time on household chores. All of these factors placed strain on the time women had to engage in the behaviors linked to promotion. Witnessing firsthand the experiences of these advisors and mentors, especially women of color, may inspire some, but may also squelch the desires for students to follow in those footsteps upon degree completion (Fries-Britt & Turner-Kelly, 2005; Trower & Chait, 2002; Turner & Myers, 2001). In other words, the ways Black women are socialized through graduate school may have distinct implications for their short-term and long-term career trajectory.

As Black women continue to be underrepresented in faculty and senior leadership positions across colleges and universities, it is important to understand the experiences, issues, and obstacles faced by these individuals as they attempt to navigate academe. This chapter takes a look at a critical junction in the educational pipeline, the doctoral program, to expand our understandings of the underrepresentation of Black female faculty and senior administrators in higher education. Drawing on socialization theory (Antony, 2002; Austin & McDaniel, 2006; Gopaul, 2011; Thornton & Nardi, 1975), this autoethnography explores the graduate school experiences of four Black women, outlining the conditions, contexts, and communities that shaped our progression through our master's and doctoral degree programs. Specifically, this study is guided by the following question: "What experiences as graduate students in the academy facilitate or diminish interest in pursuing an academic career?"

We begin with an overview of autoethnography (Ellis & Boenher, 2004) as the methodology for sharing our stories. Following the scholarly narrative tradition, we collectively share our motivations for pursuing the PhD, our early experiences navigating our programs, and the ways that our socialization process continues to be shaped by our identities, personal aspirations, and professional experiences in the field. We conclude with a critique of the prevailing literature in these areas and offer recommendations for ways to not only increase the opportunity structures leading to the ranks of full professorship and senior administration, but that may also make these roles more attractive to Black women.

SOCIALIZATION THEORY

Students' desires for training and professional development are shown to be key motivating factors influencing the decision to pursue graduate study to reach career goals (Golde, 1998; Golde & Dore, 2001). Socialization theory is most often used to frame studies that explore and illuminate the process of graduate education (specifically doctoral education), its impacts, and implications for student persistence and degree completion (Gopaul, 2011; Sweitzer, 2009). This theory is also used to understand more broadly the various structures, norms, policies, and contexts of graduate degree programs (Austin & McDaniels, 2006; Weidman, Twale, & Stein, 2001). Merton, Reader, and Kendall (1957) define socialization as "the processes through which [a person] develops [a sense of] professional self, with its characteristic values, attitudes, knowledge, and skills … which govern [his or her] behavior in a wide variety of professional situations" (as cited by Gopaul, 2011, p. 287). With respect to this definition, one's behavior (as well as their knowledge, values, and attitudes) is important in establishing membership within specific professional groups. Given this definition, socialization theory serves as a useful conceptual framework to structure our understanding of the various contexts, mechanisms, and structures that contribute to the training of graduate students. This conceptual framework also guides our exploration of the specific ways that graduate programs encourage students to pursue a professorial career or discourage them from it.

Thornton and Nardi (1975) proposed a four-staged socialization model, transforming novices to professionals: anticipatory, formal, informal, and personal. The process of gaining awareness of the various traits, components, values, and expected behaviors of the group that one aims to join characterizes the "anticipatory stage." As students enter the "formal stage" they are considered "veteran newcomers" with some sense of the expected and appropriate behaviors of their field. While students have yet to learn all of the group norms and standards, they continue to gain this information through observation, interactions with mentors and peers, and engagement with the existing group culture and mechanisms of support. Upon entering the "informal stage," novices learn the unspoken expectations associated with their role within a particular profession. They also develop an understanding of how much flexibility they have within their new socialized role. The final stage, the "personal stage," is described as the period when one internalizes and integrates her new role and identity with an existing self-concept (Austin & McDaniels, 2006; Gopaul, 2011; Thornton & Nardi, 1975).

When socialization theories are applied to educational settings, the process through which doctoral students gain the knowledge, skills, and competencies needed in their field can be better understood. Braxton and Baird (2001) adapt socialization theory to understand the "beginning, middle, and dissertation" stages of the graduate school experience. Components of the "beginning stage" include identifying a faculty mentor, securing financial assistance and support, establishing a peer network, and becoming familiar with the perspectives, jargon, and focus of the field and the specific graduate program (Austin & McDaniels, 2006; Braxton & Baird, 2001). The "middle stage" takes place between the completion of coursework and sitting for qualifying or comprehensive examinations. A student achieving a relative competence of the norms and practices of her discipline characterizes this stage. At this stage a student focuses on her research interests and identifies (oftentimes under the direction of a primary advisor) a committee of faculty to guide her in completing the third and final process, the "dissertation stage." Students working on their dissertation often rely heavily on their committee for advice, support, encouragement, and feedback on their research. Weidman et al. (2001) posit that the process of doctoral student socialization is nonlinear, dynamic, and interactive as students acquire professional skills and subject matter knowledge through academic learning and direct engagement with peers and faculty (Gopaul, 2011; Weidman et al., 2001).

Weidman et al. (2001) argue that graduate students acquire professional skills and subject matter knowledge through academic learning and direct interaction and engagement with peers and faculty. Theory places special emphasis on the impact of the faculty relationships in the socialization and training of graduate students, especially at the doctoral level (Austin & McDaniels, 2006; Weidman et al., 2001). Throughout the socialization process, doctoral students may obtain a substantial amount of counsel and direction from faculty who nurture and support students in understanding the culture, norms, and values of graduate study and academic life (Weidman et. al., 2001). This guidance is especially important for doctoral students who have intentions to continue in academic careers. Unfortunately, scholars have shown that many graduate students are underprepared for the professoriate due to a lack of "systematic guidance" in learning the expected roles, norms, and values of academic life (Austin & McDaniels, 2006). Being socialized into academic roles during graduate study is critical to one's professional success in the professoriate.

Some critics of socialization theory posit that conventional adaptations fail to consider the nuanced ways in which women and students of color experience graduate school (Antony, 2002; Austin & McDaniels, 2006; Gopaul, 2011). Socialization is often viewed as a "teacher to pupil" phenomenon, implying that faculty are the holders of knowledge needed to successfully navigate graduate study, which must be passed down to students. This paradigm fails to recognize that students enter graduate school from diverse backgrounds and experiences that can impact the faculty/student dynamic. In an environment where students are not allowed to bring their values and perspectives into their study, students may lose the motivation to complete their graduate degree program. Moreover, this prevents traditional practices to be examined, critiqued, and transformed. Antony (2002) critiques this "assimilation" approach to socialization, arguing that interactions should be more bidirectional in nature, allowing for the perspectives and experiences of students from diverse backgrounds to shape the academy. He challenges faculty members to develop and employ practices that acknowledge the unique experiences and contributions of all scholars. Consistent with his perception, studies have shown that Black scholars who successfully transitioned into faculty positions understood the norms and expectations of the faculty career but were intentional about not compromising their own personal values and beliefs (Antony & Taylor, 2004; Taylor & Antony, 2000). Conversely, those who fully adopted and assimilated into the professional norms of faculty careers without retaining their own personal perspectives reported being less satisfied in their positions; many left the professoriate for other career opportunities (Antony & Taylor, 2004; Taylor & Anthony, 2000).

An understanding of the ways Black women are socialized throughout graduate school is useful for framing our discussion of the ways our experiences in the academy shape our decisions to consider careers in academia. It also illuminates how one's multiple levels of identity, such as race/ethnicity, class, gender, age, family role, and professional identity, influence the socialization process. The themes highlighted in this chapter reflect some of the conditions, contexts, and communities that shape students' progression through their graduate degree program. These themes also afford a deeper understanding of the graduate school experience for students more broadly by identifying the various components that lead to a realized professional identity.

METHODOLOGY

As an autoethnography, this chapter allows us as authors to utilize our personal experiences as the primary source of data. According to Ellis and Boenher (2004), autoethnography is "an autobiographical genre of writing and research that displays multiple layers of consciousness, connecting the personal to the cultural" (p. 733). Due to the nascent nature of this topic within the field of higher education, this method is particularly useful for illuminating the nuanced experiences of Black women in graduate programs. Furthermore, the "researcher as subject" aspect of autoethnography allows coresearchers to effectively communicate our narrative, thus avoiding the misrepresentations of our experiences by others (Denzin & Lincoln, 2000). By using this method, we hope to present "evocative stories" (Ellis & Bochner, 2000, p. 744) in a manner that allows readers to "relive the events emotionally, with the writers" (Denzin & Lincoln, 2000, p. 931).

Data Collection

This chapter highlights our experiences from the perspective of four Black women affiliated with the same doctoral program in "higher education" at a large public research-intensive university. This program is directed by a small, ethnically diverse faculty, many of who investigate issues of race, class, equity, gender, and social justice in their scholarship and teaching. Having been in existence for over 30 years, graduates of the master's and doctoral programs have pursed options in a diverse array of careers across academia (e.g., student affairs practitioners and tenure-track faculty) and senior administration (e.g., directors, deans, provosts) as well as advanced careers in higher education policy through state-affiliated and nonprofit organizations. Accordingly, students in this program have a wide range of postgraduation career options and, as evidenced by our narratives below, feel that they have adequate support to pursue careers across a diverse array of professions.

As colleagues and peers in the program, we have had several informal conversations about our experiences in graduate school and thoughts about careers, however, this project provided an opportunity for us to have a more formal discussion about our experiences, critically engage in the literature, and share our stories with a wider audience. After individually reviewing the literature, we came together and engaged in a 2-hour focus group interview to discuss the socialization of graduate students and the extent to which the prevailing theories resonated with own experiences. This lead to a deeper reflection on not only our initial motivations for earning a doctorate, but also the ways that our personal identities and experiences interacting with peers and faculty in our program shaped our perceptions of viable career options upon graduation.

The Participants

Although we each identify as Black women, we acknowledge that we come from diverse ethnic, socioeconomic, and educational backgrounds with multiple points of intersectionality. Three of us, Candice, Tykeia, and Nina, entered the PhD program in 2012, while Jennifer began in 2009 and completed her degree in 2013. We each decided to begin doctoral study at different points in our lives. Nina moved continuously through school, entering the PhD program immediately after completing her master's program. Both Tykeia and Jennifer worked full time in education and college access programs after earning their bachelor's degrees, and completed their master's degrees as part-time students before enrolling in the doctoral program full time. Candice enjoyed several years of progressive administrative experience in higher education advocacy prior to entering a master's program, and then transitioned to the doctoral program a year later. Our identities, coupled with our personal, academic, and professional experiences leading up to our enrollment in the doctoral program, undoubtedly shaped our experiences therein.

Next, we share our reflections on our experiences and socialization as graduate students, connecting these experiences with prevailing literature, to highlight the diverse and complex nature of our experiences in academe as we contemplate career options. We end with recommendations for strategies to intercept messages and interrupt experiences that may occur in graduate school that make qualified candidates for faculty and senior administrative roles feel isolated, alienated, unfit, or unwelcome in the academy.

Reflected in our narratives, our experiences prior to beginning doctoral study, as well as our experiences in the program, strongly influence our perceptions of our futures within the academy. Initially interested in exploring the socialization process of doctoral programs and implications for career trajectories, we began by discussing our motivations for attending graduate school and the role of mentorship in our experiences. We then describe the nature of our interactions with faculty and peers in the doctoral program thus far, our early socialization experiences as doctoral students, and finally our vision for the future in terms of our own career trajectories.

Making a Difference in the Field: Motivations for Obtaining a Doctoral Degree

Several themes emerged in relation to our motivations for pursuing a PhD. Consistent with previous research, our interests in pursuing a graduate degree was driven by questions about "how higher education works" coupled with an intrinsic desire to "make a difference" (Carlone & Johnson, 2007). This was largely spurred by our early career experiences as well as our experiences in our undergraduate and master's programs. Jennifer and Tykeia each held administrative roles in higher education prior to beginning the PhD program. We each shared instances where we recognized that we are naturally inquisitive individuals and we were not satisfied with the "status quo" in terms of the ways things were done in our professional lives. As a counselor for a college access program, Jennifer was responsible for encouraging first generation college students to pursue higher education. Early on in this role, she became dissatisfied with the seemingly antiquated policies and practices utilized by her colleagues in the program. With the support of her supervisor, she began to integrate the knowledge of student affairs "best practices" learned through enrollment in a master's program focused on higher education management. Making an impact on this small scale was satisfying, but she was driven to do more. By furthering her studies in a doctoral program, she hoped to gain the knowledge base and credentials needed to make a large-scale change. She shared,

> We were making okay decisions, but it felt like we were just going along with the status quo without knowing why or why not to do things and that was really frustrating.... Once we started to really make informed decisions, I could see the program grow and flourish. With that stability, I started thinking about being in the position to make change not just to impact a single program, but all programs on either an institutional or system level. In order to do that, and have that level of influence, I knew I needed a PhD.

Similarly, Tykeia shared how she wanted to know more about the underlying policies and practices that guided the decisions made related to her job. Through her studies in a higher education graduate program, she became aware of the gaps between the scholarly literature and her experiences as a practitioner. With several years of progressive experience coordinating academic success and retention programs for students in science, technology, engineering, and math (STEM) fields she shared,

> While I was in undergrad, I was a part of an opportunity program for students studying STEM fields or licensed professions. The program targeted populations that are underrepresented in those fields within the state of New York, which is where I'm from.... As an administrator in these types of programs, I had a lot of questions about how the program was run and I didn't really feel like the work [of the programs or program administrators] was represented in the [academic] literature.

A drive to be in a position to not only learn more, but to effect change prompted her to consider applying to EdD and PhD programs. In both of our experiences, as practitioners and students in higher education programs, our motivations to continue our education was driven by a desire to effect change and provide leadership in the programs we served in order to positively impact our students.

Candice was engaged in higher education work directly after completing her bachelor's degree, working with students, such as herself, who were enrolled at historically Black colleges and universities. She eventually decided to pursue a master's degree in higher education after years of working with these colleges preparing their students for leadership opportunities and careers. She shared,

> I was always very interested in higher education, I just didn't know it was called higher education as a field ... I was curious to know why the programs I worked with were resistant to adopting the programs and initiatives we proposed.

Candice initially began the master's program as a way to move up in her professional career with no plans to pursue a doctorate. During the program, however, she was inspired to continue by a desire to see more Black women in leadership roles driving these types of decisions in the field. She shared,

> Upon receiving my master's, I realized I had more questions than answers, but my questions were [now] more focused on women who looked like me pursuing a role that I could potentially have one day ... as a college dean or provost. That's what encouraged me to pursue a PhD.

Although our experiences working in higher education shaped our interests, as students in master's programs we began to explore specific areas more closely, raising additional questions for us to explore. Reflecting on her graduate experience and thoughts about the PhD, Nina shared,

> I didn't really know what "faculty" entailed coming into the master's program since my undergrad, master's, and PhD were all stacked so closely together. When I got to [the master's program] and really enjoyed the research, I realized that I had a ton of questions ... and I could craft an entire research agenda around them. So, I think that was the catalyst for applying for the PhD—knowing I had an area of research I was interested in enough to pursue for a faculty career.

Across our experiences we wanted to have the opportunity to make a difference or see a change in our field. Moreover, exposure to new ideas, experiences, and research through the master's program propelled interest in pursuing a PhD even after returning to midlevel administrative careers in higher education. The PhD was viewed as a credential necessary not simply for career advancement, but to propel us into positions to enact change and make a lasting difference in the educational opportunity structure for the next generation of students.

That Extra Boost:
Mentorship and Mattering in the Academy

Once the seed and inspiration for pursuing doctoral study had been planted for each of us, our interests transformed into an action plan. The initial motivation for pursuing an advanced graduate degree was nurtured through encouragement and mentorship from faculty, administrators, and peers (many of whom were doctoral students). Engagement with faculty members as master's students was particularly critical during this transition. Whether through classroom interaction, graduate assistantship experiences, involvement with research projects, or one-on-one advising, faculty interaction influenced the process of identifying and prioritizing our individual academic interests and career goals. Nina credits a couple of key faculty members for helping her not only gain a better understanding of "faculty life," but also guiding her during the application process. She shared,

> I came into the master's program knowing I wanted to get a PhD ... with no idea of what a PhD really meant ... I didn't think I would have the tools or the skills or the mentoring to be able to do it right after. So, I came in thinking "okay, I'll just use this master's program to build relationships, understand higher ed, [and] get some work experience under my belt." ... I talked to some [professors] and they said, "No, you don't have to do that. Why

wait?" I didn't really know what the steps were, but [faculty mentors] helped simplify the process.

While Nina didn't know "what a PhD really meant" as a master's student, early on she was able to speak with faculty and engage in topics through her coursework that became the beginning of her research agenda. These burgeoning interests were encouraged and as a result, she immediately applied for PhD programs in the field.

Tykeia talked about how her work supervisor, a female faculty member, helped convince her that given her interests, she needed to earn her doctorate. She shared,

> I was in a [master's] program that trains administrators, and that is what I wanted to be. [Given] the questions I was interested in, I began to recognize the limitations of working with my faculty advisor. It wasn't her area, and she couldn't guide me in the way I wanted to be guided at that time. I developed a different relationship with my [work] supervisor, who was a faculty member in engineering; [she] was very vocal in her desire for me to pursue a PhD. She recognized my positionality and potential impact, that what I wanted to study was worth studying, and that the master's wouldn't be enough to effect the changes I wanted to see. She would tell me, "If you want to sit at the table with faculty, you need to bring the credential that they have."

These examples highlight the ways that faculty members recognized our potential as academics and future leaders in higher education, and were supportive of our burgeoning scholarly interests. The questions that we were interested in exploring not only "mattered," but *we* could be, and *should* be the ones leading these discussions in the field. Thus, early doubts about our readiness to pursue the PhD were diminished by encouragement and support from faculty members through their formal and informal actions that demonstrated their belief in our potential.

Mentorship and support through the PhD application process also came from other graduate students pursuing the PhD and those who had recently completed their doctoral degree. These individuals helped to demystify the process of applying to a doctoral program for us as master's students. They also went out of their way to connect us with other students and recent graduates to assist us in gaining perspective about various programs, faculty, and the potential challenges of pursuing a doctorate. For example, when Candice mentioned she wanted to pursue a PhD at a particular program to a classmate within her master's program, this classmate introduced her to a PhD in that program the same day. Tykeia also talked about having several peers and colleagues within her master's program who gave her advice and insight on doctoral study. In fact, an advanced doctoral student took her to lunch one day and helped her identify potential EdD and PhD programs and faculty with research that aligned with her specific interests at the time. These are just a few instances where we were able to learn from peers about the process, and help find a program that would help us maximize our potential. Through these conversations, it was impressed upon us that there were certain things we should look for in potential doctoral programs: a strong faculty mentor, financial support, and a community (whether academic or personal) to help sustain us to graduation.

The Socialization Process: Interactions With Faculty and Peers

We each applied and were admitted to a variety of programs but our individual decisions to attend the same PhD program were shaped by its geographic location, the reputation of the program, and early interactions with faculty, current students, and graduates of the program. Given our experiences prior to making this decision, we each felt it would be important to select a program that not only was supportive of our burgeoning interests, but also allowed us to cultivate meaningful relationships with both faculty and peers. Jennifer shared,

> I put a lot of thought into the type of environment I wanted to be in as a doctoral student. I knew I wanted an environment that was supportive and not competitive and one where I could work collaboratively with my peers. I immediately sensed that when I met the faculty and students in the program; they seemed generally interested in my interests. Fortunately, those expectations I had about collaboration and support was met in abundance as a student.

The extent to which Jennifer's statement reflects the experiences of Nina, Candice, and Tykeia is shaped by the context of our time in the program. As doctoral students, we have had different types of interactions with faculty in our department given our individual scholarly interests, and have had diverse opportunities to work with administrators through graduate assistantships on campus. Additionally, Jennifer entered the program during a "rebuilding time" with several students from diverse educational and professional backgrounds, while Nina, Candice, and Tykeia entered with a smaller, less diverse group. Within this context we reflected on our overall "socialization" in the program through interactions with various members of the campus and higher education community.

Over the first 2 years of our program, we have cultivated different types of relationships with faculty, some in a formal "student-advisor" capacity, while others were more informal in nature. These relationships provided opportunities to be actively involved on research teams and projects, learning the process and protocol for engaging in academic research from the bottom-up. We have been able to carry these skills into completing our own research projects. As Candice shared, during her first year she worked as a member on a research team, and by her fourth semester in the program, she was able to complete her own project. She reflected, "this semester has been the first semester where I've really be able to conduct my own research and I think that has also made me reconsider my thoughts about faculty, that maybe that is something that I can do." We continued to expand our networks and experiences on campus as well, engaging in summer employment opportunities and various internships in higher education policy. Again, through these experiences we strengthened our skills and gained a better understanding of the direction we wanted to take our careers postgraduation.

Overall, we agreed that we had largely positive interactions with faculty and found them to be supportive of us as scholars and individuals. Jennifer shared,

> I know people who have complained about not being able to work with, or even talk to their faculty members. Not having to go through those issues is a blessing.... They already see me as a faculty member … they've already stirred up that aspiration; I think that's what's helping me with this transition.

Additionally, we talked about having at least one female faculty member who we considered to be role models who we could go to for both academic and personal questions. We also recognize the balancing act these women have to engage in as they navigate their careers and personal lives. Observing their experiences has raised some concerns about our own ability to navigate personal and professional relationships beyond graduate school. We at times struggled with competing personal, academic, and professional responsibilities, striving to maintain a sense of balance. At times, we have felt that this balance is unrealistic. Reflecting on making time for social relationships and progressing in the field, Jennifer shared,

> I don't want "work" to be all that I am, but I know you have to make time to do the things that will get you tenure and promotion. Why do I feel like it's one or the other? I can't excel in all those areas at once?

This sparked a wider discussion on the ways that women in general, and Black women in particular are expected to make a lot of compromises in relationships, which may result in limiting our career opportunities. We reaffirmed one another in our decisions to pursue a terminal degree, and praised one another for our commitment to moving forward. Candice shared,

> We have to, as Black women who are up and coming, and mentoring those who are coming up, we have a responsibility to push back against that narrative.... We are very fortunate to see examples of people doing it, we see it in action, and we should be empowered to do the same.

As evident from the aforementioned quote, while we shared the ways we have interacted with faculty, our relationships with peers and one another became central in our conversation. We recognize that as doctoral students, given the size and scope of the program, our peer relationships are more selective in nature. Thus, peer relationships tend to be either "academic" or "personal." We reached out to advanced students for guidance on how to navigate courses and writing expectations, and worked with faculty to hone our research and presentation skills. Working with one another as peers in the program has been a balancing act, but an important resource when attempting to navigate the PhD program. Candice shared,

> I would say the peer support is extremely important to me ... I need to know that we're all doing work ... even if I'm in my house by myself, I need to be on "gchat" and know that someone else is writing, and is irritated that it's nice outside and we're writing.

Similarly, Nina shared,

> There are things you absolutely cannot get from people who are not in a PhD program ... I almost never talk about negative things that happen in school outside of the people who are in the program with me, and I think that it's necessary ... I really appreciate the opportunity that we have amongst each other to have that space to say "I hate this" or "I don't feel like going to class today" ... if you say these things outside, it's like, "well no one told you to be in a PhD program, get over it." I think it's a really an important part of my experience and I definitely appreciate it, it's made this a lot easier than if I had these feeling bottled up.

This support system was also important, given we were relocating from family. Tykeia shared, "Coming here not knowing anyone, not having any family in the area, I have built strong friendships with my peers here and I have come to rely on those relationships to get me through." In addition to our relationships with one another, we recognize the importance of having diverse types of relationships that can sustain us personally, spiritually, and professionally. Recognizing that socialization is an ongoing process, we understand that we will continue to expand our network of support as our academic and professional interests change over time.

Preparing to Lead: Visions for the Future

The original question guiding our investigation was: "What experiences as graduate students in the academy facilitate or diminish interest in pursuing an academic career?" Our conversation began with an assessment of whether or not the traditional faculty tenure-track career fit into our plans. Our discussion expanded to include the recognition of the diverse array of professional options and opportunities that are available to us upon earning our doctoral degrees. Through our reflection, we continue to acknowledge the advantages of being socialized in a graduate program with a rich history of preparing students for a diverse array of professional careers. Nina shared that her experiences thus far has helped her think of various possibilities upon graduation, she shared,

> I came in thinking faculty... I think by my third (policy) internship... I had a better understanding of policy and I know I would have felt restless having to wait for an assignment to come your way based on an external agenda. My naturally inquisitive nature lends itself to faculty, and working with students in an academic setting, is pretty exciting to me. I really enjoy the writing, and like submitting publications, and submitting to conferences ... it's one of the things I would really like the most.

One somewhat unique advantage in our program is having the opportunity to work directly with two tenured Black female professors. Tykeia shared that one way she learns how to navigate the process, and see which path is for her, is through observing various individuals. She shares,

> There are days where I feel like a tenure-track position is feasible, and there are days when I don't think it's feasible at all. I've been intentional about observing other people at different parts of the process ... quietly observing ... I've watched students start out the search ... and then on the flip side of that I've watched [my advisor], at this point of her career, going up for full. I've talked to [department faculty] and other people about their experience and what kind of motivation or prompted them, and I'm just kind of gathering information at this point.

While working as an administrator at an historically Black colleges and university, Jennifer shared she feels she has grown a new appreciation for the diversity of options for Black women to lead. She shares,

I think it's helpful to see faculty in a new light. In my head I had a perception of what it meant to be a "tenure-track" professor, but I realize that that model has been limited by my graduate experiences. Now, I not only see faculty members who look like me, but I have a better appreciation of the diverse array of perspectives that faculty of color bring to higher education. I feel confident that I can find my place in the academy.

Whether we are planning to pursue faculty careers or take on leading roles as administrators in policy, our socialization through graduate school has exposed us to many of the knowledge and skills sets needed to pursue the futures that we want. Despite grim reports of the opposite, we are confident in our ability to learn from one another and lift each other up in the pursuit of our dreams. To that end, we recognize that it's important for us to remember the following when it comes to socialization through graduate school, it's critical to have multiple reference points when navigating academe. Tykeia sums it up by sharing,

They're all doing it in their own way ... as Black women ... or even as academics, it's easy to fall into that "you have to go about this process THIS way." And I think that ... "they've all gone about the process their own way; the way that worked for them." We have to realize that even in navigating this PhD process, I'm not doing it like Nina is doing it, and I'm not doing it like Candice is doing it, I have to do what's best for Tykeia.

No matter which direction we choose, it is clear that we plan to be a leading voice in the field and we recognize the importance of supporting one another along the path.

CONCLUSION

Taken together, our early socialization through graduate school has been shaped by both our experiences with faculty in our program, and by our peer interactions. Central to the ways we understood our experiences was recognition of the motivations for pursuing the PhD in the first place. While prevailing theories emphasize the importance of faculty interactions during the PhD program, it is evident from our experiences that professional experiences and interactions as master's students provided us with the support to pursue in the PhD. While we have been fortunate in having few barriers along the way, we outline some of the prevailing areas that tend to prohibit aspirations for future careers in faculty and senior administration.

Navigating a Chilly Climate

Although in our experience we were enrolled in programs where faculty members and fellow peers were engaged in the types of research and activities that reflected our own interests, the literature is replete with examples of where this is not the experience of many Black women in graduate school. Maranto and Griffin (2011) defined a "chilly climate" as an academic department where individuals feel excluded, devalued, and marginalized. In a lot of ways, the professoriate continues to be dominated by White males, and to successfully produce publications, faculty must forge alliances with each other. Women may suspect that they are not welcomed in the "old boy's network," or have access to meetings where decisions on teaching, research, and promotions are made. Men, who indirectly perpetuate this chilly climate by not collaborating with their female colleagues, directly hinder the success of their female colleagues (Maranto & Griffin, 2011). For Black women, chilly campus climates can cause enough frustration and fatigue from dealing with racist situations, that they consider leaving their institution (Griffin et al., 2011).

We essentially avoided this chilly climate by being very intentional in our selection process for a PhD program. From our experience in graduate school, we learned the importance of being socialized in an environment of faculty collegiality and respect, regardless of individual backgrounds and scholarly interests. Therefore, we believe that in order to combat a chilly climate, colleges and departments must continue efforts to diversify their campus community in the broadest sense of the word. Recruitment of strong candidates from the diverse backgrounds along with opportunities for tenured and junior faculty to interact can help build opportunities for collaboration. From the perspective of graduate students, seeing the shifting tide in terms of new partnerships forging across programs and departments may build confidence that they too will be able to work across difference and have professional relationships as newcomers with seasoned scholars and leaders in the field.

Mattering in the Academy

Based on our motivations for attending, and tendency to study race and gender issues, Black women often live in the academy with an "outsider within" status (Jayakumar, Howard, Allen, & Han, 2009). Black women who are housed in departments that marginalize or question the legitimacy of their research, however, face implications that extend beyond the institution. For example, journals require submissions to undergo a peer-review process before articles are accepted. If institutional peers question the legitimacy of research conducted by women of color, and the academy is primarily White and male, who are the peers responsible for reviewing article submissions in mainstream journals? Not women of color. This conundrum leaves faculty of color to publish in journals that are not considered top tier or mainstream, and journals that specialize in topics of race and gender, which are not viewed as favorably by tenure committees (Maranto & Griffin, 2011). Within administrative roles, Black women often complain of the disproportional requests for service on committees or request to advise students of color. This too takes away from time that can be devoted to expanding their vision for their program and the institution.

However, Stanley (2006a) argued there are advantages to living on the margins, and that by occupying space as an outsider-within means African American women have the ability to accurately gauge the strengths and weaknesses of the dominant culture as faculty. Faculty of color are more likely to employ innovative teaching strategies to improve student learning and to promote student cross-racial interactions than White faculty (Griffin & Reddick, 2011; Jayakumar et al., 2009; Turner et al., 1999). These strengths should be seen as valuable contributions to the field and, when recognized, have the potential to help transform the culture of a program to reflect the needs of higher education in the 21st century.

Revising Socialization Theory

In his work, Antony (2002) questions theory that asserts that socialization is achieved by way of assimilation and challenges academia to develop and employ theories of socialization that acknowledge the unique experiences and contributions of the all scholars. He proposes:

> This type of socialization recognizes that an individual can master content and develop the acumen to work with the traditional norms, values, and standard of a profession without having to internalize, or accept as one's own, those norms, values and standards. (pp. 373–374)

These approaches seem most appropriate when considering the diverse motivations for pursuing graduate education in the first place. One interesting takeaway from our narrative is the uncovering of the limited scholarship available to understand the motivations of students of color to pursue doctoral degrees. The dominant narrative assumes that doctoral students at research-intensive institutions hope to secure a "tenure-track faculty position" at a "research-intensive institution." This assumption is fueled by scholarship that almost exclusively focuses on understanding how students are socialized into the academic practices of a discipline. Twenty-first century doctorates are called upon to lend their expertise in a diverse array of areas. Thus, it is important to consider this when thinking not only about how students experience graduate school, but whether graduate schools are structured in ways that adequately prepare graduates to work in a diverse landscape. Dynamic and bidirectional approaches to graduate student training and socialization recognize that faculty also learn from their students in this process, which then transforms the academy from the inside out.

Given the current trends in higher education, where Black women in the educational pipeline are outpacing men in nearly all academic areas, it is surprising to see a disparity when it comes to faculty and senior ranks in administration. This suggests that there remains either a glass ceiling that Black women are not able to overcome, or there is something innate in the culture of the academy that dissuades women from moving up the ladder. Is there something about the culture of the academy that dissuades women from continuing in what could be a very promising career trajectory? Moreover, do we really know what Black women want out of academic careers in the 21st century? These questions should be explored in future research that cuts across both academic disciplines and institutional contexts.

As we discussed our experiences and reviewed the literature, we noticed that few scholars discuss the power that women of color possess despite the challenges they face in the academy (Turner, 2003). We assert that if faculty and administrators of color were encouraged to embrace their power on the margins, the retention of these groups would increase. In addition to power on the margins, Turner, Myers, and Creswell (1999, p. 40) identified four pieces that are essential in the retention of faculty of color to combat a potentially chilly climate: "satisfaction with teaching, supportive administrative leadership, a sense of accomplishment, collegiality, and interacting with other faculty of color." Each piece underscores the importance of an inclusive environment on a macro level, and positive professional relationships on a micro level.

Our narrative emphasizes the power of peer support and mentoring among Black women as we attempt to make sense of the academic and professional expectations of higher education. It's important to note that although we share certain social identities (e.g., race and gender), the ways that our identities shape our experiences provide uniqueness in our lived experience. To advance this work, future studies must highlight the importance of gaining a better understanding of the within-group differences of Black women in the pipeline, to understand how these differences influence experiences in the academy. Moreover, we feel that structural diversity on all levels has the potential to positively impact the educational and professional aspirations of Black women by shattering the notion that there is a single "prototype" when it comes to being successful in the academy.

NOTE

1.   Black is used throughout this piece an umbrella racial term to refer to individuals who have African ancestry. Under this umbrella term fall African American (i.e., native-born Blacks) and Black immigrants (i.e., born outside of the United States or second generation Blacks). This chapter is focused on the experiences of Black doctoral women, some of whom are African American, and others who are Black immigrant.

REFERENCES

Antony, J. S. (2002). Reexamining doctoral student socialization and professional development: Moving beyond the congruence and assimilation orientation. In J. C. Smart (Ed.), *Higher education: Handbook of theory and research* (Vol. 17, pp. 349–380). New York, NY: Agathon Press.

Antony, J. S., & Taylor, E. (2004). Theories and strategies of academic career socialization: Improving paths to the professoriate for Black graduate students. In D. H. Wulff & A. E. Austin (Eds.), *Paths to the Professoriate: Strategies for enriching the preparation of future faculty* (pp. 92–114). San Francisco, CA: Jossey-Bass.

Austin, A. E., & McDaniels, M. (2006). Preparing the professoriate for the future: Graduate student socialization for faculty roles. In J. C. Smart (Ed.), *Higher education: Handbook of theory and research* (Vol. 21, pp. 397–456). Dordrecht, The Netherlands: Springer.

Blake-Beard, S., Bayne, M. L., Crosby, F. J., & Muller, C. B. (2011). Matching by race and gender in mentoring relationships: Keeping our eyes on the prize. *Journal of Social Issues, 67*(3), 622–643.

Braxton, J. M., & Baird, L. L. (2001). Preparation for professional self-regulation. *Science and Engineering Ethics, 7,* 593–610.

Carlone, H. B., & Johnson, A. (2007). Understanding the science experiences of successful women of color: Science identity as an analytic lens. *Journal of Research in Science Teaching, 44*(8), 1187–1218.

Denzin, N. K., & Lincoln, Y. S. (2011). *The SAGE handbook of qualitative research.* Thousand Oaks, CA: SAGE.

Duncan, B. L. (1976). Differential social perception and attribution of intergroup violence: Testing the lower limits of stereotyping blacks. *Journal of Personality and Social Behavior, 34,* 590–598.

Ellis, E. M. (2001). The impact of race and gender on graduate school socialization, satisfaction with doctoral study and commitment to degree completion. *The Western Journal of Black Studies, 25*(1), 30–45.

Ellis, C., & Bochner, A. P. (2000). Autoethnography, personal narrative, reflexivity: Researcher as subject. In N. K. Denzin & Y. S. Lincoln (Eds.), *Handbook of qualitative research* (2nd ed., pp. 733–768). Thousand Oaks, CA: SAGE.

Espinal, M. M., Munoz, S. M., & Kiyama, J. M. (2010). Transitioning from doctoral study to the academy: Theorizing trenzas of identity for Latina sister scholars. *Qualitative Inquiry, 16*(10), 804–818.

Fries-Britt, S., & Turner-Kelly, B. (2005). Retaining each other: Narratives of two African American women in the academy. *The Urban Review, 37*(3), 221–242.

Gasman, M., Gerstl-Pepin, C., Anderson-Tompkins, S., Rasheed, L., & Hathaway, K. (2004). Negotiating power, developing trust: Transgressing race and status in the academy. *Teachers College Record, 106*, 689–715.

Gay, G. (2004). Navigating marginality en route to the professoriate: Graduate students of color learning and living in academia. *International Journal of Qualitative Studies in Education, 17*(2), 265–288.

Gildersleeve, R. E., Croom, N. N., & Vasquez, P. L. (2011). "Am I going crazy?!": A critical race analysis of doctoral education. *Equity & Excellence in Education, 44*(1), 93–114.

Golde, C. M. (1998). Beginning graduate school: Explaining first year doctoral attrition. *New Directions for Higher Education, 101*, 55–64.

Golde, C. M., & Dore, T. M. (2001). *At cross purposes: What the experiences of today's doctoral students reveal about doctoral education.* Philadelphia, PA: Pew Charitable Trusts.

Gopaul, B. (2011). Distinction in doctoral education: Using Bourdieu's tools to assess the socialization of doctoral students. *Equity & Excellence in Education, 44*(1), 10–21.

Griffin, K. A., & Reddick, R. J. (2011). Surveillance and sacrifice gender differences in the mentoring patterns of Black professors at predominantly White research universities. *American Educational Research Journal, 48*(5), 1032–1057.

Griffin, K. A., Pifer, M. J., Humphrey, J. R., & Hazelwood, A. M. (2011). (Re)defining departure: Exploring Black professors' experiences with and responses to racism and racial climate. *American Journal of Education, 117*(4), 495–526.

Jayakumar, U. M., Howard, T. C., Allen, W. R., & Han, J. C. (2009). Racial privilege in the professoriate: An exploration of campus climate, retention, and satisfaction. *The Journal of Higher Education, 80*(5), 538–563.

Maranto, C. L., & Griffin, A. E. (2011). The antecedents of a 'chilly climate' for women faculty in higher education. *Human Relations, 64*(2), 139–159.

Merton, R. K., Rader G. G., & Kendall, P. L. (1957). *The student physician: Introduction studies in the sociology of medical education.* Cambridge, MA: Harvard University Press.

Moses, Y. T. (1989). *Black women in academe: Issues and strategies.* Washington, DC: Association of American Colleges, Project on the Status and Education of Women.

Smith, D. G., Turner, C. S. V., Osei-Kofi, N., & Richards, S. (2004). Interrupting the usual: Successful strategies for hiring diverse faculty. *The Journal of Higher Education*, *75*(2), 133–160.

Stanley, C. A. (2006). Coloring the academic landscape: Faculty of color breaking the silence in predominantly white colleges and universities. *American Educational Research Journal*, *43*, 701–736

Sweitzer, V. (2009). Towards a theory of doctoral student professional identity development: A developmental networks approach. *The Journal of Higher Education*, *80*(1), 1–33.

Taylor, E., & Antony, J. S. (2000). Stereotype threat reduction and wise schooling: Towards the successful socialization of Africa America doctoral students in education. *The Journal of Negro Education*, *69*(3), 184–198.

Thompson, C. J., & Dey, E. L. (1998). Pushed to the margins: Sources of stress for African American college and university faculty. *The Journal of Higher Education*, *69*(3), 324–345.

Thornton, R., & Nardi, P. M. (1975). The dynamics of role acquisition. *American Journal of Sociology*, *80*(4), 870–885.

Trower, C., & Chait, R. (2002, March-April). Faculty diversity: Too little for too long. *Harvard Magazine*, *104*(4), 33–37, 98

Turner, C., & Myers, S. (2001). *Faculty of color in academe: Bittersweet success.* Needham Heights, MA: Allyn & Bacon.

Turner C., & Thompson, J. (1993). Socializing women doctoral students: Minority and majority experiences. *Review of Higher Education*, *163*(3), 355–370.

Turner, C. S. (2003). Incorporation and marginalization in the academy from border toward center for faculty of color. *Journal of Black Studies*, *34*(1), 112–125.

Turner, C. S., Meyers, S., & Creswell, J. (1999). Exploring underrepresentation: The case of faculty of color in the Midwest. *The Journal of Higher Education*, *70*, 27–59.

Weidman, J. C., Twale, D. J., & Stein, E. L. (2001). *Socialization of graduate and professional students in higher education: A perilous passage?* San Francisco, CA: Jossey-Bass.

RESPONSE

I WISH I KNEW THEN, WHAT I KNOW NOW

How to Build a Communal Pipeline

Tara T. Green

In their essay, "Prepared to Lead: Black Women for Faculty and Administrative Careers Through Graduate School," Jennifer M. Johnson, Tykeia N. Robinson, Candice Staples, and Nina Daoud pose a question that, if seriously considered, can help provide guidance to graduate students at critical junctures in their career: "Specifically, this study is guided by the following question: 'What experiences as graduate students in the academy facilitate or diminish interest in pursuing an academic career?'" As I look back on my career, I admit that I enjoyed the experience I had when I was a graduate student at Louisiana State University (LSU). I was not expecting it. In fact, I find it hard to believe, even today. But to be sure, I benefited greatly from the community that provided me with the tools to establish and reach my career goals. My goal here is to share what I learned, with hopes that these lessons will encourage and empower readers in pursuit of an academic career.

I thought I was destined to save the world by becoming a lawyer. But I was wrong. I graduated with a degree in English from Dillard University, a

Beyond Retention: Cultivating Spaces of Equity, Justice, and Fairness for Women of Color in U.S. Higher Education, pp. 127–133
Copyright © 2016 by Information Age Publishing

127

historically Black university (HBCU) in New Orleans. Near the end of my sophomore year, I was accepted into a predoctoral program hosted at a private research institution and that experience led me to make two conclusions. The first was that I would not apply for admission into that school because my faculty mentor told me I would never graduate from there if I was somehow let in. His words, in fact his treatment of me, convinced me that I should stay away from major predominantly White private institutions. However, I realized that my calling was academia; therefore, I further concluded that I should pursue a doctorate at a university that would welcome me. Several of my English professors had been enrolled in the English graduate program at LSU and although they were not full-time graduate students who were engaged in the life of the department and campus, they were pleased with their choice. As they discussed their dissertation projects, I noticed how their eyes lit up. Their enthusiasm inspired my decision to attend LSU. Going to graduate school was a historical event for me, to say the least. Graduating with a degree from Dillard made me a first-generation college graduate and the first in my family poised to earn a graduate degree. I was determined, that even though I had gotten into graduate school on academic probation, that I would not leave LSU until I had a doctorate in hand. It was my plan to accomplish the goal in 5 years.

Although I had graduated with honors, in fact had been an honor student since kindergarten, LSU placed me on provisional admission because of my low GRE scores. I am a Black woman. Therefore, I saw this merely as one more challenge to prove that I belonged. "You mean I have to work harder." Nothing new. As far as I knew, this was the mantra I had recited along with the Jack and Jill poem in preschool. When I entered LSU, there was a cohort of other Black students in the department, many of whom were being funded by a fellowship for African American students. This was the 90s. LSU was under a desegregation order, and such financial aid provisions were made to attract the grandchildren of those African Americans who had been denied an education at LSU and campuses that shared its racial demographics. It was not until I graduated with my MA and entered the doctoral program that I received a tuition waiver and a teaching assistant appointment. My parents, loans, and menial jobs funded the first 2 years.

My purpose here is to share the ways in which I learned—by taking serendipitous steps—how to rely on my community to uplift myself. I want to qualify an earlier statement that I made. I enjoyed my experience at LSU because I was part of a cohort—African American students in English and chemistry, as well as one here and there in several other departments. We were part of the Black Graduate and Professional Student Organization, of which I served as president one year, which was supported with funds by the provost's office. Participating in this organization led us to affiliate with the National Black Graduate Student Association and to attend its annual conference, as well as host a conference on our campus. These conferences gave me insight that I otherwise would not have had. I learned from presenters how to write a résumé, the importance of seeking a mentor, how to write a dissertation, how to negotiate for a job, et cetera. Although I did not know it then, these kinds of professional meetings filled in gaps that some of my peers were undoubtedly receiving from their dissertation advisors and in some cases, their relatives who were also in academia. Our cohort relied on one another to find out tidbits and to share the information as we advised one another how to deal with challenges associated with the graduate school politics.

In some ways, we filled in the gap for the lack of mentors and African American faculty. My department had only one African American woman, but many if not most of us opted to work with the other professors as we found them a better personality fit. It is important to note that there is a difference between a dissertation advisor and a mentor, as I learned at the conference. On one hand, a mentor is a person who could provide advice on career-related matters. On the other hand, a dissertation advisor is a person who advises on how to meet the standards of writing a dissertation and may provide advice about the job process. I set out to have both.

My dissertation advisor was a middle-aged Southern White man who had a reputation for moving his advisees from graduate students to alumni. Because of his reputation, I chose him and he graciously accepted. There were several times when he watched out for me—by being a strong voice behind the door where decisions were made. It was he who made the case for me to advance to the doctoral program after I completed my Masters and he who made the case for me to receive a teaching assistantship. I had done the work, and at some point, someone had to pay attention. By sharing his observations with others, he served as my advocate. I understood the importance of this relationship and worked to build it. I would go to his office often to talk about books I had read, criticism I was pondering, and of course, to discuss the departmental political issues of the day. My discussions with him and other faculty revealed the importance of knowing which faculty worked best with whom for not knowing could (and for some of my friends did) lead to assembling a dysfunctional thesis or dissertation committee. From our discussions, I learned how to negotiate the fine line between disaster and success.

During my time as a graduate student, I also presented my work at four national conferences. I took several lessons from these. One, I learned how to respond to questions about my work. This would come in handy when I went on the job market several years later. To be sure, some people want to engage with a level of professionalism while others want to use graduate students to make themselves look and feel good. I was then and remain less interested in participating in the latter part. From these experiences, I learned the importance of presenting myself with dignity and grace as it takes just a few seconds to establish and/or ruin a reputation. Second, I was able to meet people in the field who have watched me grow from graduate student to full professor. These women and men have given me advice, based on their own experiences, on more topics than I can count over the past 15 years. But, what has been most helpful has been to see how they conduct themselves as presenters and how they have carved out their own power through their reputation as respected scholars in the field.

In fact, two of them—both men, have been my number one supporters. The authors are correct when they state, "The learning within this stage and the subsequent stage is facilitated through observation, interactions with mentors and peers, and engagement with existing group culture and mechanisms of support." One of these mentors, has written numerous letters of recommendations, made phone calls on my behalf, helped me to negotiate jobs, and given me valuable advice. As he moves toward retirement, I cannot help but wonder what African American literary studies would have been like without his presence, but I do understand that much of what I do to help others has been inspired by what he has done to help me. Second, my "Dad," whom I met at a conference in 2001 that was held in the city where I now reside, has been on active duty, almost since we met. He too has given me valuable guidance about my career, but like a dad, has given me advice about all sorts of other subjects.

Developing relationships with my mentors could not have happened had I not been open to them. When these men introduced themselves to me, and it was clear that they wanted to act as mentors, with no strings attached, I followed through after the initial meetings. I sent emails to the men thanking them for taking the time to talk with me at the conference and expressing my hope that we would stay in touch. Before the next conference, I contacted them and asked if we could meet to discuss questions I had regarding my research interests. I was genuine and they were receptive. While some may see conference attendance as a way to simply network; I see these as opportunities to meet new people and to build relationships. Networking can result in nothing more than a collection of cards. Relationships can lead to career and character building.

Being open to what is available is the most important lesson I have learned. By extension, this means the willingness to take risks. I entered the profession as an assistant professor of English at a state HBCU in Louisiana. During my first year, I realized that I loved my students and loved being a part of their educational journeys, but that I was not pleased with the amount of energy I was putting into surviving at the institution. I had a 4-4 teaching load, and taught an extra course during the fall and the summer to supplement my salary of $35,000/year. I knew public school teachers who were making much more than me. I had gone to a research institution with the expectation that I would carve out a career as a teacher-scholar, but I was on the fast track to becoming a teacher only, and a very tired one at that. Publishing was simply not more important than teaching and service at the institution. In graduate school, no one had taught me the differences between the universities—the various kinds of profiles, the importance of reputations associated with certain kinds of institutions. I was a first-generation college graduate, after all. As far as I knew, research could be done and was expected to occur for those teaching at an ivy league, an HBCU with a graduate program, and large predominantly White institutions. Those were the only categories as far as I knew. There were no variations.

I learned at my HBCU that there were other categories as I struggled to grade papers and to write an article or two for publication in a journal. One of the mentors that I mentioned above entered at the right time. It was he who asked me just what was I doing at that university and encouraged me to leave or that I would become trapped under a pile of students' papers and a long list of service appointments. It was almost too late. I had been at the institution for 2 years, but I was still in my twenties—full of energy, ambition, and a healthy dose of naiveté. When I went on the market, I got only two invitations to interview. My feelings and spirit were crushed. I expected much more. But one of the phone interviews turned into a campus interview and an offer.

I was ready to leave Louisiana and the South. My joint position in English and ethnic studies at a university in Arizona was a major challenge. No one knew how taxing it would be to have two deans, one in two different colleges. No one knew how to write my memorandum of understanding. In fact, when I was preparing my dossier for tenure review 4 years later my "Dad" asked me what was my tenure home. No one knew. "Dad" also told me what to keep in mind when choosing my external reviewers. He advised me to submit a list of people at reputable institutions or at least internationally known scholars in my field. Let no one have an opportunity to question the validity of the reviewers, he cautioned. He was right.

My willingness to leave the comfort of my home state gave me a wealth of experience. For 5 years I dealt with a yearly change in deans, chairs, and program directors. As they moved, this meant that I had to learn the art of navigation. I had to become bilingual. What was the culture of one part of the institution was not necessarily the culture of the other part. The expectations, the points of views, the means by which people commu-

nicated varied significantly from one room to the next or one meeting to
the next. I had to learn how to adjust. Further, I learned how to write promotion and tenure documents for a new program, how to make a case for
support to upper administration, and how to develop new courses.

Five years later I was more than ready to leave. Mentally I was ready to
get back to an institution where I was not the only African American and
not the only African American woman with a doctorate. In short, I was
ready to rejoin a Black studies community. More importantly, I had done
the work to become a chair of a department or program. I knew what
needed to be done and was more than certain that I knew how to get it
done. After 8 years, the skills that I developed at the first two institutions
have now resulted in a respected program at my current institution.

Such an experience helped me to greatly understand who I am as a
scholar and as a person. I am a Southern Black feminist woman most of
the time and not always in that order. My accent marks me in some
respects, at least it did in Arizona. Every time I would open my mouth and
a person would ask me where I was from, the statement told me that I was
different, a foreigner. As a scholar, I know that an African American
Southerner has a set of identifiers—survival of racially motivated violence, the presence of Africa through the slave trade, the Civil Rights
Movement, and Negro Spirituals. Surely it is this history that drew me to
my work as a Black women's literary scholar, but it took me a long time to
realize how much of that history informed my work. For me, my willingness to leave the South and to live as a "foreigner" in the Southwest
helped me to embrace my identity, thus empowering me to build a relationship with myself first and to advance my career second.

What is most important while carving out a career is knowing that we
do have the power of choice. I left Arizona, a university where I came to
realize that I was not valued as a member of the academic community no
matter how much I contributed. I was criticized harshly by my peers and
rarely rewarded for my work. There were times when I was ignored, even
to the point where my bodily safety was compromised, and other times
when I was exploited for my diversity status. My "Dad" prepared me to
move forward by telling me to write my ideas in a notebook and take it
with me when the next door opens. It occurred to me one day, in a
moment of deep reflection, that my ancestors would not be pleased with
me if I tolerated my situation any longer. I had achieved what my grandparents and parents could only dream, and *I* was letting others ruin the
experience. I wrote a letter of resignation the year I was under review for
tenure, fully expecting to leave that summer. In February I received a call
to visit my current institution. It was as much a process by which I was
interviewing them as they were interviewing me for I had no intention to
seek shelter in North Carolina. I knew the difference between running

from a place and running to one. I preferred the latter. They passed my test and I apparently passed theirs. Happiness, I have learned, is much more important than dying slowly in an abusive situation.

What have I learned? To be receptive to what the community within the academic community has to offer. There are many people in academia who enjoy mentoring or at least giving advice to folks who seek to learn and elevate themselves. Not all scholars are interested in such relationships; in fact, some are overwhelmed by a lifetime of mentoring. But sometimes it takes only a couple of minutes to learn a lesson. I fondly recall the experience of asking one question of a major African American female literary scholar at a social gathering that resulted in me learning life-changing ways of being. It is up to the individual to seek these opportunities, understand and respect their worth, and carry them forward. That's the meaning of power.

SECTION III

**BLURRING BOUNDARIES
AND TROUBLING INTERSECTIONS**

CHAPTER 5

SOY LATINA,
DONDE ESTAS MI GENTE?[1]

Yvania Garcia-Pusateri

I know who I am. I have always known, yet I am constantly told who I am.
I am Latina; however, I do not meet the standards of my own *gente* (people). As a light-skinned nonfluent Latina, my *orgullo* (pride) ceases to
exist. Who am I if I'm not what I was born? As a woman of color, society
forces me to subject myself to its standards, yet I must endure segregation
of my gente. Am I responsible for my *padres'* (parents) choice to assimilate? Assimilation achieved a better life for my siblings and me. Assimilation was survival in my *padres'* eyes. Even though they yearned for the
American Dream, their orgullo could not be forgotten, causing me to be
confused about who I was supposed to be, American or Garcia.

I was born in Glendale, California to immigrant parents, Rigoberto
and Sandra Garcia. My *padre* (father) was from Guatemala and my *madre*
(mother) was from Ecuador both respectively different cultures, but
Latino nonetheless. Both came to the United States when they were
young adolescents with the driving notion from their parents that America symbolized a better life, and they passed on this same notion to my
siblings and me, which impacted my self-awareness and cultural identity.
This ideal—that America was the end-all, be-all was more than just the
common American Dream for which many new Americans strive when
they get here; it was an identity my *padres* wanted to incorporate into rais-

Beyond Retention: Cultivating Spaces of Equity, Justice, and Fairness
for Women of Color in U.S. Higher Education, pp. 137–152
Copyright © 2016 by Information Age Publishing

ing us, which at times conflicted with the cultural identity they passed onto us. This clashing of identities was a battle that affected me then and continues to impact me today. Am I the *hija* (daughter) of Latino culture? Am I the *hija* of America, or am I both? Can I be both? My life experiences have led me to ask these questions time after time. One would say that the beauty of America is that you can be both, or whatever you choose to be. But the difficulty with race is that it is not only how society sees you, but also how your own *gente* sees you, that categorizes you.

My earliest memories are set in the house where I grew up, a house that had a Jacuzzi and a swing set and a lot of room to run around, and was located in a nice, quiet suburban neighborhood. While this place played host to my earlier memories, this was not the house that first greeted me. My *padres* lived in many places during the early years of their marriage, and when I came along, they were living in a little house—their first home together—in El Monte, a small suburb with a large Latino population in Los Angeles County. While they first brought me home to this house, they had already planned to move out of this neighborhood as they continued to build their family, so that my siblings and I could have a better life, a better house, a better school district, and anything else that would translate into a better life. My *madre* said that if the move was not possible, she and my *padre* would enroll me in a school in another district, about 45 minutes to an hour away. As they raised me, my *padres* were constantly focusing on the future, which largely centered on education. The schools in our first neighborhood would not provide the life they wanted or envisioned for me. The new house my *padres* eventually bought—my childhood home—represented the life they wished for not only my siblings and me, but for them.

The move away from El Monte not only took me away from my extended family (at that time both sides of my family lived within a 30-minute commute of each other), but it also took me away from my cultural community. A *comunidad* (community) in Latino culture raises and shapes the identity of its *hijos* (children). The *comunidad* teaches what it means to be Latino and the history of our *gente*. While I was only 2 years old when we made the move, this shift in location caused me to be displaced from my *comunidad* and has impacted my place and relationship with my own *gente*. As I reflect on this displacement, I wonder if my connection to my *gente* would be different, if I had remained in El Monte. Would it be better, or would it be what it is today?

Growing up, I always wondered why I was different; while I had similar physical features to my cousins, there were subtle differences between us. They spoke Spanish fluently, and while I understood the language, I did not. They spoke with accents, and I did not. Yet, I also knew I was different than my White friends because it was made very clear to me by my *madre*. "You're not White, so you can't do what they do" or "It's because they are White." These were common responses she offered me if I asked her permission to do something that my White classmates did, or if I asked her a general question about them. It was confusing to me because she dressed me like them, enrolled me in a school with a predominately White student body, and chose to live in a neighborhood that was mostly White, except for the occasional African American or Asian/Asian American family that would move in every now and then.

While aspects of Whiteness infiltrated my upbringing, it was always certain that we were a Latino family; there was no escaping that. My *padres* took great pride in who they were and wanted to transfer that same pride to my siblings and me.

Spanish music was not foreign to me, and it was very common to hear it played in the house or in a car ride. Latin American food was common as well. While my *madre* did not cook it all the time, there were a couple of dishes she consistently made. My *padres* taught me to simultaneously speak English and Spanish as I learned how to talk. They eventually stopped, and I lost my fluency, though I could always understand the language.

When I was really young, my *hermana* (sister) and I would spend most of the week with our *abuelita* (grandmother) and *primos* (cousins) from my *madre's* side. I began to notice the differences between my *hermana* and I and my *primos* and *abuelita* the more I spent time with them. We only spoke Spanish at my *abuelita's* house; she did not speak very much English, nor did she choose to do so. My *primos* all spoke fluent Spanish, and while I did then, too, I could still sense a difference between myself and my *primos* at the mere age of 5. We dressed differently, and my *madre* would always ensure that my *hermana* and I wore the latest fashions that young children could wear in the late 1980s and 1990s and refused to shop at common department stores like K-Mart. Margaret E. Montoya (1998) writes of a similar experience. "My *trenzas* [hair braids] announced that I was clean and well-cared for at home, my *trenzas* and school uniform blurred the differences between my family's economic and cultural circumstances and those of the more economically comfortable Anglo students" (p. 436). While many family members suggest that my siblings and I were my *abuelita's* favorite grandchildren, I could see then that my *hermana* and I were treated differently. The dynamic between my *madre* and her *hermanas* played a role; however, the way we were raised, with a strong infusion of American culture in our upbringing, silently impacted our identities.

Now that I am older and in a place that is vastly different from where I was raised, the immersion of American culture enables me to adapt to my current surroundings in my place of work as well as my doctoral program.

As much as I wish that my cultural heritage had a greater presence in my upbringing, the immersive aspect of American culture helps me to not only navigate White spaces at greater ease but also allows me to explore my identity at greater lengths. My work permits me to be in a space in which race and identity are a fixture of my day; I not only discuss it, but I advocate for these concepts to have a place in a historically White institution. While I am a full-time employee, my program allows me to be veiled as a student and a student alone. While working with race and identity form the heart of my daily duties, it also is the vessel to my education that allows me to explore who I am and what being Latina means through my scholarship. Navigating White spaces all my life has not only prepared me to be the only Brown face in the classroom, but it allows me to understand how to utilize the aspects of White culture that make me who I am. At a historically White institution, I am not afraid to navigate the system, and I am not afraid to penetrate White culture and make my case for inclusion.

Although our cultural upbringing was strong, my *padres* felt it was important that we saw ourselves as, and were seen as, Americans. Sometimes I felt like my *padres* wanted us to only see our American identities. In addition to Spanish music, the only other music that I grew up listening to was oldies or Motown. This was only music that existed in my world at the time that was not Spanish. My *madre* would also make hamburgers, steak, chicken, and mashed potatoes, as well as other "American" dishes. I eventually learned about other American dishes that my *madre* never made when I was in high school and college which surprised many of my friends. For the longest time, casseroles were foreign to me (and still continue to be).

Even the toys we received contained mostly American characteristics. My first Barbie was the traditional White doll with blonde hair and blue eyes. For the most part, all dolls I owned were White, and my Cabbage Patch Kid doll had brown hair, but had a White name, "Mindy." I did not get an ethnic Barbie, which was African American, for a long time. I owned a Latina Barbie much later. Disney was a huge part of my childhood. My *padre* recorded all types of Disney cartoons and shows before I was born that I would watch repeatedly. I would always get a Disney Princess Barbie, and while I would be excited to have the doll, I would subconsciously wish I could look like them. I wished I could have their white pale skin and, their blue- or green-colored eyes. Inherently these dolls made me want to be something that I was not—and could never be.

Even the church that my *padres* attended embodied Whiteness, and while they tried to blend into the background, it was evident that my *hermana* and I stuck out. Our dark hair did not match the blonde, red, and light brown hair that surrounded us; the name Yvania was hard to pronounce and was not the same as Sarah or Katie. Garcia did not match

Smith or White, and our pronunciation of words segregated us from the other children in our Sunday school class. Because we did not fit into the Whiteness in our congregation, we were seen as "different" and therefore, we were unsuitable to befriend. We did make friends in our church, some life-long ones. Still, the differences in race have brought on challenges that have been beneficial, but still difficult to manage.

This fusion of Latino and American culture defined my childhood and identity. However, this clash of cultures disrupted my development. While much of this conflict was needed and has made me the woman I am today, it was hard to understand or embrace this disruption. It was important to be an American, but just as important to be a Garcia. My *padres* would always say I was different, but in the same breath say I am no different than any American. It is confusing to read between the lines as a child and even during adulthood. I still have trouble processing what this means today. My challenge today is dealing with the reality that my network of relationships consists of more White bodies than Black and Brown. While I am comfortable with this and know that I do my best to find community in those that are diverse, the real challenge for me is answering those who question and wish to critique my network.

I attended a private Lutheran school from kindergarten to third grade, and while there was at least one African American and Asian American student, along with some biracial students, I was the only Latina in my class. I knew I was different, and my classmates knew I was different. Even in kindergarten I subconsciously felt the tension, and when it came time to choose where I sat, I gravitated toward a South Asian girl whose parents were from India. Subconsciously I went to her because even though she was lighter than me, she seemed like she was Latina because her skin was just a couple shades darker than my sister's. Even my *hermana* came over and sat with us. This gravitation resulted in me making my first friend, and while she only stayed for half the year, this clear memory serves as a defining moment in my life in which race subconsciously made its mark.

Race also made its mark on the soccer field. When we were very young, my *padre* always coached my *hermana* and I, as well as my other *hermanos*. I loved to play soccer and enjoyed having my *padres* at my games. Things changed, though, when I was in middle school and we started to play teams that were from different cities near the suburban neighborhood in which I lived. Many of these cities had large Latino populations, and the first time we played one of these teams, I received an instant dose of reality of how I was perceived by my gente. My opponents were all Latina and constantly taunted me on field, calling me a sell-out and other inappropriate names. They "played dirty" with me, treating me more roughly than my White teammates. I had no idea why they were being mean to me and my *hermana*, and while in the middle of a battle, my *madre* was yelling and screaming at my *padre* to get my *hermana* and I off the field. She even got into it with other the team's supporters—a lot of Spanish was being spoken. After that first game, my *padres* told me not to worry about the other team and said they were jealous of us. They talked to us a little about race, but they mostly explained that the other team's behaviors stemmed from their being in a different class than us.

During these years I understood that people viewed me as "different" and I began to grapple with what it meant to be American and Garcia. Even when my *padres* were planning simple events like birthday parties, they made sure that both American and Latino culture were represented. Starting on my fifth or sixth birthday, my *padres* had two separate birthday parties for me. In the morning, we would have a party that my classmates and their parents attended, and in the evening both sides of my family would come. Each party was different: the early party with my friends was always associated with a Disney film, and the music was from a Disney soundtrack. My family ordered food from the market, like sandwiches or chicken. The piñatas and birthday cakes served as the only Latino elements. The cake always had strawberries on top and contained almonds on the side, and my classmates tended to dislike it because it did not instantly taste like sugar. They enjoyed the piñata because of the free candy.

The early party would start sometime in the late morning and end in the early afternoon. After it ended my *madre* would change and begin cooking, and sometimes my *tias* (aunts) would come over to help. My *padre* would leave to get the beer and other needed items. The dynamic of my evening parties was drastically different. The music switched from Disney to salsa or cumbia, and the food was homemade and completely Latin American. There were always more than enough Coronas and Tecate, and all you could hear was the sound of my family speaking Spanish. A new, unbroken piñata appeared, as well as a new birthday cake. While the party was still for me, another purpose of the party was to bring the family together. When it came time to sing happy birthday, we sang two versions, one in English and the other in Spanish.

Judging from the video footage that my *padre* or *tio* (uncle) captured at my parties, my family would sometimes arrive early for the evening party, which meant that they were present during the end of my morning parties. Both they and my friends' parents would look uncomfortable, because my family would speak Spanish or the music would suddenly change to salsa or cumbia. Or if the situation was flipped and my friends' parents' or my *padre's* friends from church would stay for the evening party, they would not be able to fully adapt to the new setting. While I thought it was normal to have two birthday parties, I could sense little differences in the changing atmosphere or the way my *padres* carried themselves between parties.

After my first friend left halfway through kindergarten, I made another friend who became my childhood best friend. She looked exactly like my Barbie dolls—blonde hair and blue eyes. We got along right away and were inseparable. However, I picked up on the subtle differences between us, and that would influence my own behavior at home, which my padre would quickly observe. Sometimes the behaviors I picked up from my friend were negative and would spark lectures regarding how I was different because she was White and I was not.

Even though my friend and I were children, the way she would act or speak to her *madre* and the way her *madre* communicated with her was odd to me. Sometimes she was very strict, and at other times she was not. It seemed that she could stay all day at my house and her mother would not call; sometimes my *madre* would call to remind her she was still at our house. At other times she would not be able to visit because she was on restriction.

When I visited her house, the dynamic of the house was different from my mine. Both parents worked, so sometimes a babysitter watched us, or if her mom was there I do not remember her being around very much, which allowed us to create our own adventures (sometimes resulting in negative situations). Her family always ordered food, particularly pizza. Sometimes when her sister was around, my friend would not let her play with us. When I would treat my *hermana* similarly when my friend was over, I would get a strong talking to from my padre. He always made sure to explain that the *familia* (family) was the most important thing, and that friends come and go but *hermanas* are forever.

While my *padres* adored my friend and saw her as an extension of the family, they made sure I did not spend all my time at her house, which worked in my friend's favor because she preferred my house over hers. This way my *padres* were able to ensure my *hermana* was always included. Having friendships like this one continued to reflect the different cultures I continuously navigated. I frequently questioned why I had to be different and why I could not do the same things as my White friends. I experienced or saw subtle things in elementary school that reminded me that I stood out, but I did not completely observe the differences between my White and Latino classmates until high school.

The different interactions I had with my *gente* and with the dominant culture created an interest in race for me. At first this interest was subtle, and when I would bring it up, my *padres* tried to steer me away from it and insist that I was American, Ecuadorian, Guatemalan, and nothing else mattered. My lack of fluency in Spanish was a consequence of a decision and their way of protecting me. I would always ask why they stopped teaching me to speak Spanish. They would always say they did not want it to affect my learning in school like it did my *primos*, who were put into English as a second language courses, and they did not want me to have an accent and be teased for it like my *primos*. It is only now that I finally understand their motives and have come to peace with it.

Navigating college was an intense experience, and this experience shaped how I viewed myself and what it meant to be Latina. My cultural lens strengthened during this time, along with my understanding of the world, and my identity began to shift and, at times, collided with itself. Like the environments of high school and other schools I attended, the largest racial population at my undergraduate institution was White. While this was not new to me, I was dealing with something that was different. This was the first time I was in the company of individuals that came from privileged backgrounds. I was not used to being in conversations that centered on money or leisurely activities that not even my *padres* had experienced. While I was not used to this, the collision of identity and self did not take place until the conversation turned into a battle of race and religion as well as politics. I did not know how to respond to questions regarding my racial identity and its connection to my faith or how my political beliefs could never meet with teachings of the faith I was supposed to be practicing.

I understood that society viewed me based on the friendships I had and my interactions with others. I realized that I could not hide my racial identity from the dominant culture, and that the accompanying preconceived notions were projected onto me. To the Latino *comunidad*, I was seen as "racially ambiguous" and able to blend into White culture. My lack of fluency in my native tongue, my skin tone, my dress, and my other characteristics suggested that I did not acknowledge my culture and would rather live in a White world and assimilate. Many of my peers called this to my attention, mostly in brash and unfriendly ways.

I deepened my journey with race as part of my college experience. Race spoke to me during this time, and similar to Margaret E. Montoya (1998), I began to develop an "understanding of myself in relation to Anglo society" (p. 435). I attended college at a small, predominately White private religious institution; however, the university was located in a highly Latino-populated neighborhood. It was here where I, like Montoya (1998), "began to think about myself in relation to my classmates and their families" (p. 435). The majority of my friends were White and very conservative, meaning that they came from homogenous and sometimes privileged backgrounds. For the most part they only had White friends and went to White churches and only saw culture as an opportunity to try new restaurants. Conservative also meant that they lived their lives completely different my family. In addition to these groups, I had few friends of color. I shared a special kinship with the friends of color I did have. While we may have had different cultural backgrounds, we were able to bond through our experiences and discuss things that I could not speak about with my White friends. Some of them could not understand the perils of being the only brown face in the classroom, and being a Garcia in a Smith world was as foreign to them as Spanish was to me. While race was haunting me, I often put my journey to the side, swimming with the tide and assimilating into the White culture. The more I did, the more questions I had. However, it seemed like each question was again met with my *madre's* answer: "It's because they are White...."

A private religious institution was no cheap venture for a first-generation student like myself, so I had loans as well as scholarships. A scholarship geared toward first-generation Central American students from Los Angeles County was one of my main sources of financial aid. The organization that awarded the scholarship not only provided aid but also professional development and a sense of community. Attending monthly professional development seminars in East Los Angeles was one of the requirements for receiving the scholarship. My *padre* picked me up and drove me down, and he would always encourage me to learn as much as possible and apply it to my studies.

I remember my first seminar like it was yesterday. I came dressed casually (somewhat preppy) and was a little nervous because I did not know anyone, and my cohort clearly knew each other well. I later discovered that many of them went to high school together in addition to attending the same colleges. Even though I was nervous, I was excited about being around Latinos that were not related to me. I was hopeful that this experience would teach me to be Latino. While I was around other students of color at my undergrad institution, I was missing Latinos. Yosso, Smith, Ceja, and Solórzano (2009) write, "Latinas/os foster academic and social counterspaces in which they build a culturally supportive community and develop skills to critically navigate between their worlds of school and home" (p. 660). I was hoping that I could find that supportive community in this opportunity.

Although I came seeking a sense of belonging among my own gente, I experienced more push back than welcome. While my racially ambiguous appearance suggested that I was Latina, my gente saw me as "Whitewashed." I grew up in the suburbs and chose to assimilate into Whiteness, I did not speak Spanish fluently, which not only deterred me from carrying on a conversation but also from understanding the lingo or slang. I was attending a "White institution" and dressed like I was White. While I somewhat successfully tried to make friends, my attempts to integrate myself into the blending of *cultura* (culture) and *comunidad* served as *chistes* (jokes) more than nods to my legitimacy. Even though the joking was rationalized as friendly humor, I knew where my *gente* drew the line and where I stood.

I tried so hard to appear Latina. I would come home with an accent and use the slang I learned from my counterparts. Of course my *padres* caught on real quick and questioned my new ways of speech, instructing me to stop at once, stating I "was American and not Mexican." They would tell me that I was there to learn and not pick up new habits. While I tried to explain my strategies and my desire to appear more Latina in order to be accepted, they insisted that I was Ecuadorian, Guatemalan, American and different from my counterparts (again, this "different" response—the bane of my existence). I did not want to be different; I just wanted to be Latina and to be seen as one. During my time with the scholarship program, I did make friends but had to also accept my place. Dhruvarajan and Vickers (2002) write, "Our focus is on developing an approach in which all of us learn to situate ourselves in relation to others who are differently situated" (p. 15). While my approach was to accept where I fell short, I still felt the need to fight for a place among my own *gente*, a fight I still continue today. While sometimes the battlefield is internal, the fight has seeped its way into the communities of my work. Working at a historically White institution is exhausting, with the constant juggling of rationalizing the importance of services for students of color and strategizing ways to ensure that our programs and services receive funding that not only keeps them but expands as well. While navigating White space is second nature to me, I do feel replenished when I am around my *gente*. However, cultivating these relationships with my *gente* is challenging when there are entrance criteria; because of who I am, my presence in these spaces has not always been welcomed. While the words are not said, the feelings of invisibility demonstrate where I stand with my *gente*. As a doctoral student, I am the only Latina in my program. This reality has allowed me to find solace in the Black community. While I feel accepted there, there are challenges that come with this acceptance that lead me to have to explain certain White relationships I have and have chosen to have.

I am Latina, yet my community sees me as "racially ambiguous" and as being able to blend into White culture. My light complexion allows me to enter a world that was never meant for me, where my "racially ambiguous" appearance positions me to represent a historically silenced voice. My existence in White culture humanizes narratives that are often silenced and ignored. Experiences of my fellow Black and Brown brethren become real and legitimate. I am able to speak to their importance and demonstrate that White culture not only needs to listen to them but accept them as part of our history. While my "light" complexion allows me to blend into Whiteness, it does not change the fact that I'm not White.

Society sees me for what they allow my brown face to be. For many, I am an immigrant and intruder on this stolen land. I am the one that stole their place in college or that took away their job. I am also the one who is not really American. While these harsh realities are every day experiences for me, the treatment of my *gente* cuts me deeper. My seamless assimilation into Whiteness was not my choice but the result of my *padres'* decision, a decision that was not meant to ensure their survival, but to enhance the likelihood that my siblings and I could experience the American dream.

Pursuing the dream came at a price, though, when my gente perceived me to be rejecting them and embracing Whiteness. Jiwani (2006) writes of

> Internalized racism wherein they reject their own cultural communities in favor of what they perceive to be the freedom afforded to them by the dominant society" as well as frictions of assimilation, [the] illusory promise that suggest to them that if they behave in particular ways, if they become more like girls and young women in the dominant society, they too can share the rewards of such privileged membership in the sense of being accepted and being more like their White counterparts. (p. 75)

While it may have seemed that these were my actions, assimilation was my lot in life and the staple of my American identity.

Many would have thrown in the towel and accepted assimilation as their reality, never looking back, but this focus on assimilation led me to a haunting examination of my race. While I yearned to be accepted, my own naïveté could not shield me from the internal warfare between myself and my gente. Jiwani et al. (2006) provide a great description of my experience: "Intraethnic violence is one example of internalized racism and the different values that are attached to assimilation" (p. 75).

Pyke and Dang (2003)

> observed the existence of an inner hierarchy within these Asian American groups. At the pinnacle of the hierarchy were the "white-washed"—those who were seen as having "sold out" to the dominant culture by emulating its preferred and valued behaviors and lifestyles" (as cited in Jiwani et al., 2006, p. 75)

I am Latina, and while my *comunidad* may utilize this "intraethnic violence" to other me, I am not deterred nor am I indifferent toward my *gente*. They are still my *gente*. My fight will just be different. I just wonder why the act of "othering" takes place within our own *gente*. We speak of *familia* and *comunidad* when it comes to the advocacy of our dreams, and ourselves, but we racialize our own when we have fought for so many years to be accepted as people rather than to be seen as stereotypes. This makes me question what the point of *comunidad* is when we cannot even accept the vast diversities of our own *gente*. If we come from all over, why must there be certain criteria to demonstrate before we are accepted as one of the *gente*? If it is to be accepted that my country of origin will not accept me then how can my own gente not only accept me but recognize me as one of their own?

During my graduate school experience, which was at the same institution where I began my journey with race, I discovered the powerful concept of "intersectionality." A term coined by legal scholar Kimberle Crenshaw (1989), intersectionality is the "multidimensionality of Black women's experience with the single-axis analysis that distorts these experiences" (p. 139). I not only found its concentration on race and gender interesting, but I was also intrigued by the concept's fusion of multiple identities, which allowed me to view my own multiple identities differently. Yes, I was Latina, but I had an American identity that for the longest time only communicated Whiteness and did not make room for both to be represented. I could not be me if both were not present. Intersectionality helped me see that both these identities were salient.

Intersectionality also helped me see that the intraethnic violence I was enduring was a form of identity politics and provided me with a thicker shield with which I could do battle. Crenshaw (1991) argues that

> the real problem of identity politics is that it elides intragroup difference, a problem that intersectionality purports to solve by exposing differences within the broad categories of "women" and "Blacks," and serving as a force for ... mediating the tension between assertions of multiple identity and the ongoing necessity of group politics. (as cited in Nash, 2008, p. 2)

Finally, having an opportunity to see my identities blend together provided me the courage and language to engage in identity politics and fight for my place within my *gente*. The intersectionalities within my identities were not a weakness but an enhancement and an opportunity to infiltrate into Whiteness and advocate not only for my gente, but for others as well.

Graduate school not only brought me to the intersections of my identity but also allowed me to encounter the real question of race and why it continued to haunt me. For the longest time race was the road on which I found myself traveling off and on, but once I allowed myself to travel freely, race became more contextual to me. Trucios-Haynes (2001) writes, "a broader conception of racial identity—one that includes the critical aspects of Latina/o identity—is a step toward recognizing the histories of all communities of color in the United States and their interrelatedness" (p. 5).

Embracing my journey with race allowed me to explore my own intersectionalities and position in relation to with my *comunidad* as well other communities of color. With my assistantship in the multicultural center of my graduate institution, I was well-equipped on my journey to self-discovery. While I visited the center a couple times during undergrad, I immersed myself in multiculturalism during this internship. Within my position, I mentored students of color and supervised the programs that my student staff coordinated. I also took part in cultural celebrations, as well as dialogues centered on race. I saw the intersections of race at play. Within this position I had the opportunity to see communities of color come together and create a coalition.

While I found refuge in other communities of color, I did not think about the community seeing me as their own, their *hija*. But when I was there I was more than welcomed; I was accepted. This seamless acceptance motivated me to reflect this approach, which strengthened my rapport with students. While I was not the same color as them and while I perhaps did not share the same culture, I recognized that our experiences could bring us together, allowing for my validation of their experiences to carry the same weight as someone that looked like them. Trucios-Haynes (2001) writes, "The Black-White paradigm is so dominant that it shapes our understanding of what race and racism mean and the nature of our discussion about race" (p. 9). Providing a sense of care and authenticity has allowed me to move past this Black-White paradigm with my students, demonstrating that the struggle is a common lived experience for many which can be fought together.

As a woman of color in higher education, my work focuses on equity and inclusion. I am an advocate for my students and for institutional change. As a Latina in my field, my intersecting identities influence my role as an administrator and lead me to negotiate relationships and find refuge in other communities of color. In these various spaces, my physical appearance demonstrates my legitimacy as a fellow person of color, and I never feel the need to explain how and what makes me Latina. These communities welcome me as I am and provide me a sense of support. While most people of color experience their own community as their family, I view the diverse communities with whom I work as my family.

As a new professional in the Midwest at a historically White institution, I thought the Latino community would be different. I recognized that the Latino population would be small, and I was prepared to see that reality, but I was hoping that a small community would not be disappointed with me but would welcome me with open arms. At my first Latino staff and faculty meeting, I recognized that I would meet my old fate and, again, not be Latino enough; answering in English as they spoke to me in Spanish unveiled my shortcomings.

While I encountered this before, this experience complicated my relationship with my *gente* even more. As a small *comunidad* within a larger homogenous community, I believed things would be different and that this would be the *comunidad* that could replicate what I had been searching for. Not only was I looking for a familial dynamic, but I was also grasping for mentorship and guidance that could prepare me for this transition, both as a young professional and a Latina from the city who had moved to the cornfield. This short interaction spurred strong emotions and led me to make a decision. Race was never going to stop haunting me, and I was never going to stop asking questions and searching for answers. I was never going to stop asking what makes one Latina and how White immersion takes away your racial identity. While I did not have the ideal relationship with my *gente*, it was not going to stop me from embracing who I am and acknowledging that, while assimilation played a role in my upbringing, it was my culture nonetheless. My *padres* were proud of their heritages and made sure to enrich our lives and instill that pride within us. Even though my gente did not see it or chose not to acknowledge it, I was not going to stop seeing myself as Latina. Yuval-Davis (2006) writes, "Identities are individual and collective narratives that answer the question 'who and/are I/we?'" (p. 197). The identity politics I had to navigate were challenging—very challenging—but this process taught me how to build a welcoming and inclusive community. I was learning how to combat a force that colonizes racial communities and designates a set of norms that define what it means to be Latino, African American, Asian and so on. Identity is not dictated, but lived. A true *comunidad* lets you "[live] your life as you see fit and therefore presupposes that self-appointed groups not impose their identity on you against your will" (Gutmann, 2003, p. 8).

The world was not going to stop seeing me as Latina, so why should I? While I had my challenges with my *gente*, I learned how to not run away from White space and, instead, how to embrace my seat at the table within higher education as well as academia, a seat that historically has been out of reach for so many. My seat at the table allows me to represent those without a voice. My positionality allows me to dialogue with my White colleagues and discuss the complications as well as the intersectionalities of race, which helps them see that race is not only skin deep but a plethora of stories that students as well as my fellow staff, administrators, and faculty bring to our campuses, and that every day the dominant culture constantly challenges them about who they are and who they are supposed to be.

While identity is intersectional, it is also a hybridity. Coined as a defining feature of Chicana womanism, Nuñez, (2013) describes hybridity as "[identity], perspective, thought" (p. 9). My hybridity allows me to negotiate and embrace my intersecting Latina and American identities. Nuñez writes, "The Chicana is the cultural hybrid of two distinct hybrids. And she is a woman—with all of the fluidity and chaos of the archetypal feminine (p. 9). As a Latina, I am a child of America and it is with this lens that I carry myself and approach my work in higher education.

I am Latina, yet my community sees me as "racially ambiguous" and able to blend into White culture. My light complexion allows me to enter a world that was never meant for me, where my racially ambiguous appearance positions me to represent a historically silenced voice. My existence in White culture humanizes narratives that are often neglected and ignored. I am Latina, and while my community may "other" me, I am not deterred nor am I indifferent toward my people. They are still my people ... but so are those in various cultural communities that see me as their *hija* and their *hermana*. These experiences drive my work with students, and inspire me teach them that their identity is theirs and only they can truly know and declare who they are. In their eyes, I am one of them. I am Latina.

NOTE

1.   The chapter title is translated as "I am Latina, Where Are My People?"

REFERENCES

Crenshaw, K. (1989). Demarginalizing the intersection of race and sex: A Black feminist critique of antidiscrimination doctrine, feminist theory, and antiracist politics. *University of Chicago Legal Forum*, 138–167.

Dhruvarajan, V., & Vickers, J. (2002). *Gender, race, and nation: A global perspective*. Toronto, Ontario, Canada: University of Toronto Press.

Gutmann, A. (2003) Introduction. In *Identity in democracy* (pp. 1–37). Princeton, NJ: Princeton University Press.

Jiwani, Y. (2006). Radicalized violence and girls and young women of color. In Y. Jiwani, C. Mirchell, & C. Steenbergen (Eds.), *Girlhood: Redefining the limits* (pp. 70–89). Montreal, Quebec, Canada: Black Rose Books.

Montoya, M. E. (1998). Masks and ccculturation. In R. Delgado & J. Stefancic (Eds.), *The Latino/a condition: A critical reader* (pp. 435–441). New York, NY: York University Press.

Nash, J. C. (2008). Re-thinking intersectionality. *Feminist Review, 89*(1), 1–15.

Nuñez, I. (2014, April). Chicana womanist perspectives on curriculum. In S. Ross, C. Mikell, S. Janis, M. F. He, & E. Tuck (Eds.), *Womanist curriculum perspectives and possibilities*. Paper presented at the annual meeting of the American Educational Research Association annual meeting, Philadelphia, PA.

Trucios-Haynes, E. (2001). Why "race matters:" LatCrit theory and Latina/o racial identity. *La Raza Law Journal, 12*, 1–42.

Yosso, T., Smith, W., Ceja, M., & Solórzano, D. (2009). Critical race theory, racial microaggressions, and campus racial climate for Latina/o undergraduates. *Harvard Educational Review, 79*, 659–690.

Yuval-Davis, N. (2006). Intersectionality and feminist politics. *European Journal of Women's Studies, 13*(3), 193–209.

MENTORING AND ENCOURAGING PROFESSIONAL DEVELOPMENT FOR LATINAS AND OTHER WOMEN OF COLOR

Ramona Ortega-Liston

The purpose of this message is to encourage women to share their career experiences. I want to encourage all women of color to find appropriate mentors and take advantage of opportunities for professional development whenever opportunities arise. I have learned through my own research about the value of mentoring and that Hispanics have made efforts to address the need for mentoring by developing intergenerational and ethnic specific programs (Castillo-Montoya & Torres-Guzmán, 2012; Villaseñor, Reyes, & Muñoz, 2013). One example of this kind of ethnic-specific program is *mujerista* mentoring, which focuses on the significance of cultural capital and does not require that the mentee be assimilated into the dominant culture. Instead, the mentee may embrace and use her diversity to thrive (Mkandawire-Valhmu, Kako, & Stevens, 2010; Villaseñor, Reyes, & Muñoz, 2013). All ethnic groups have valuable attributes to share with others in their organizations, including possessing the cultural competence needed to relate to the inherent diversity in ethnic sub-cultures. In this response, I addresses both the specifics of issues

Beyond Retention: Cultivating Spaces of Equity, Justice, and Fairness
for Women of Color in U.S. Higher Education, pp. 153–163

addressed in Yvania Garcia-Pusateri's chapter and the broader issue of mentoring and professional development for women in academia.

Yvania, I am fascinated by your narrative—the story of how you grew up in Glendale, California and the conflicting societal and professional challenges you have faced and currently are facing. I have no doubt that other women of color have experienced or are currently experiencing similar issues. Our stories have similar undercurrents about being Latina in a world where we are the minority; however, there are a few important differences. I grew up in a large Mexican American family in Iowa with parents who had been migrants and who spoke Spanish to each other, but rarely spoke Spanish to us, and we were raised as Methodists; we were not Catholic. I grew up in the 1950s speaking only English, as Spanish was discouraged by educators in those days. Much to my chagrin, not speaking Spanish caused and still causes other Latinos to see me as not one of them. In the 1950s, the dominant education philosophy was that speaking Spanish, and not learning English, would hinder a child's ability to succeed. This was a belief, you indicate, that was held by your parents too.

It may give you comfort to know that I understand your early youthful feelings and the feelings you have now as a young Latina in academia. What strikes me the most about you is that you are confident in who you are. Just knowing who you are and having amazing poise and self-confidence will propel you to great heights—experiences that up to now, you likely have barely glimpsed. In your narrative, you wrote that you *know* who you are and that you have always known who you are despite conflicting ideas arising from opinions of some family, friends, colleagues, and other Latinos.

Your comments about your strong sense of self resonate deeply with me, evoking memories about significant events in my own life and how my social experiences at different stages of my development enabled me to gain a strong self of self. I view my own knowledge of who I am as a vital component of my success. Because of my background in counseling and psychology, I relate the development of a strong sense of self to the work of the prominent psychoanalyst, Erik Erikson. Erikson (1902-1994), who developed the concept of identity crisis, established an eight-stage theory of human development that explained the influence of social experiences on identity. I learned about Erikson and his theory when I was a graduate student at Harvard University studying counseling and consulting psychology.

My road to Harvard was long and perilous, but I made it despite being a single mother at 17. My migrant worker parents were in no position to help me financially and, besides, I had violated society's precept by being an unwed mother. Nor did I receive needed moral support from the man I later married. He never went to college and my education threatened him. In spite of great odds, I managed to complete a doctorate late in life (55) and went on to be appointed by two different presidents to three prestigious presidential commissions and volunteered at the White House. I had a brief stint as a congressional staffer for a prominent politician and a position as an investment banker where I made more money than I make now. I am now a tenured associate professor with some advice to give you that builds on your strong sense of self.

Erikson (1968) argued that a healthy or unhealthy sense of who we are (ego) develops in the age of adolescence, between the ages of 13-20. This he calls the fifth stage of human development. Adults who enter and exit this stage knowing who they are normally do not suffer an identity crisis and will most likely mature into healthy, productive adults. It is clear to me that you know who you are, what you want, and where you are going. I encourage you to keep traveling the road you are on and to read Erikson, not only for what his work will teach you, but because it will help you become a better person and teacher of young people. Knowing yourself will help you understand your students and where they are developmentally. This applies to all students of every ethnicity and culture and to other adults with whom you work. For the same reasons, I also recommend the writings of retired Harvard professor and psychologist, Jerome Kagan; I was mesmerized by his teachings.

As I mentioned earlier in my narrative, you and I share a few similarities and a few differences in how we grew up in Latino households in different parts of the country—you in California and I in Iowa. The first similarity is that we both had parents who came to the United States hoping for better lives for themselves and the children they eventually would have. All of those children were born in this country and, therefore, think of themselves as Americans first - Americans who just happen to be Latin.

I have a fair complexion and easily drift back and forth between the Midwestern White culture and whatever else I am. I say, "Whatever else I am," because I view myself as a Midwesterner to a greater extent than I do Latina or Mexican American. I grew up with Methodist church potlucks and casseroles and quilting bees. Yes, mom and dad cooked Mexican food that I loved to eat and I still cook their prize dishes today—hot tamales, tacos, and tortillas from scratch. I tend to think of myself as an American first and foremost. This has to do with being born, in my opinion, in the state of Iowa and not in Texas, California, or Florida where there are large populations of Hispanic/Latino subcultures. Those of us born in Des Moines, Iowa had far too few others who "looked like us." Therefore, although I have always known who I am, and possess a confidence of unknown origins. I, like you, have always been comfortable in my own skin. Importantly, I have never wanted to be someone else. I was not the typical teenager who wanted to look like or be like someone else. I was just me—the girl with only one name, Ramona. My parents had so many children (nine survived childhood) that I was not given a middle name.

In your narrative you wrote that you were not named a Sarah or Katie. Well, neither was I. My girlfriends had short names like Ann, Sue, and Mary. I was the only Ramona. I felt put upon that I had to learn to write and spell R-A-M-O-N-A O-R-T-E-G-A, not Ann, Sue, or Mary. In the long run perhaps it was good training to be forced from the beginning to deal with life's challenges, large and small. Not having a middle name made me feel different, but it was the same kind of difference as being a Midwestern girl of Mexican descent; I was just different. I felt I was different, and I liked it! Not having a middle name was ancillary to who I was. The point I want to make is having confidence and being comfortable in your own skin is what will help you succeed. The primary difference I felt from other girls my age was because of my clearly identifiable Latino last name. Or, as you have so cleverly put it: being "Garcia in a Smith world." In my case, I may not have looked all that different from other girls with whom I grew up, but I *was different because of my last* name. There were five girls in my family. I am the only one who has never changed her name.

I use my father's Latino surname. To my students I am Dr. Ortega. All four of my sisters use their Anglo/American husbands' last names; not I. I was proud of, and remain proud of, my Latino roots. Being a Latina is an important part of my identity, but it is not a thing I dwell on. Nor was it anything my parents dwelled on. This may be another difference between the two of us; my parents never told me to remember my Mexican heritage. We were taught to assimilate with the White culture and I accepted it. My ethnicity is just a fact. It just is. It is who I am and it is like breathing. I rarely think about my cultural heritage. It just is. It is not a negative or a positive; it's just a fact—a positive fact.

The house you described growing up in is distinctly different from the house where I grew up. My family was poor. My dad built our house with his own hands and my older brothers told me they helped. It was a tarpaper shack. It was home. In the early years, it did not have running water or an indoor toilet. I learned to pump water from an outside pump at an early age, chop wood to make a fire to heat enough water to take a bath by the time I was 6 years old. As each new child was born, an extra room was added to the house. Eventually, our house looked like a long, lime green caterpillar. Our house was built in the Des Moines River flood plain and rampant flood waters flooded us out nearly every year. FEMA was not there to help flood victims then. Instead, my mom and dad and all my brothers and sisters "pitched in" (that's a farming phrase) and shoveled the mud out of the house, washed down the walls with a garden hose, and measured how high flood waters had risen to the ceiling.

Together we mixed water and paste and hung wall paper on the walls and laid down new linoleum. Not fancy, just new.

Few toys or Christmas presents were purchased for us and certainly not a Barbie doll of any description. I had one doll. She was a gift from a White woman leader in our Methodist church that I consider a childhood mentor; she believed in me because I had a good memory. I acted in the church Christmas play and my reward was that one, lovely doll. Being poor also meant that few new clothes were bought and those that were came from Montgomery Wards or Sears Roebuck Company. K-Mart was not around then, but had it been, Mom and Dad would have gravitated to it. Most of my clothes were hand-me-downs and came from the church rummage sale. My sisters and I were quite clever at mixing and matching odds and ends and ended up looking respectable and presentable, if not quite chic. Other girls often offered compliments on our clothing.

When I was 16, I entered high school and Mom luckily found a job at a department store. She then bought a few "nice" clothes for my sisters and me from time-to-time. I now believe that poverty is a common denominator among ethnic groups. Many other former migrant and Black and White families growing up in the same neighborhood were equally poor. Being poor was the rule—not the exception. Poverty was a common denominator, but not the only one. Everyone in my family was and is hard working and industrious. It is a family trait. No matter how poor we were, my brothers and sisters and I were popular kids. We were attractive and clean with the good manners that mom insisted on. We never cursed and my brothers were high school athletes of some renown. I was popular enough to be elected to student council and as secretary of the junior high school photography club. These experiences of being hardworking and industrious, like my experience as an unmarried mother, my experience of being married to an unsupportive spouse, and my experience of poverty shaped who I am.

You write that your parents were aware of the value of a good education and sought the best schools for you. This was not the case for me. Mom, in broken English, urged my brothers and sisters and me to "get a good education and make something of yourselves." By a "good education" she meant graduating from high school. College was nothing anyone dreamed of or even discussed. Dad, on the other hand, thought we were destined for blue collar jobs and taught me and my brothers and sisters to drive a tractor, plant and harvest crops, butcher in the springtime, clean menudo with lye and water that burned our small hands, milk the cow, and gather eggs from the hen house. As a teenager in high school, I was conscious of smelling faintly of cow as I sat in the classroom. Dad thought school was a "waste of time" and he threatened to burn our schoolbooks if he caught us studying or doing homework. He was not like your dad in any respect. I rarely risked my dad's ire; he was a brutal man. If I could memorize what was said in the classroom, I did well enough, but mathematics was something that I could not easily memorize. I did manage to memorize the times table and I was often a finalist in the school spelling bee. Both accomplishments gave me a sense that maybe, just maybe, I was smart—sort of. I took great pride in both abilities.

Another area where we differ is your discussion of having an extended family and moving away from them. Our relatives lived in Texas, not in Iowa. Aunts, uncles, and cousins visited occasionally during summers. When they did visit, they seemed different—they were Texans. I am sure we seemed different to them too. They spoke fluent Spanish; I did not. They spoke with a Texas accent. I spoke with a Midwestern accent; if I speak Spanish, it is with an English/Midwestern accent. I never experienced a sense of living in a Latino community, nor did I have a sense of living in an extended family. We were a nuclear family—on our own. Strength, resilience, and courage sometimes can stem from being raised in a nuclear family. One result is that my brothers and sisters and I developed strong bonds that sustain us to this day. These strong bonds emanate from shared childhood experiences. No one else lived the experiences we shared, some painful, some poignant and wonderful because they were rare. My brothers and sisters and I like to say that the hardships we endured made us strong and developed our character.

Together, we learned the value of education. One of my oldest brothers served in the Marines during the Korean conflict and used the G.I. Bill to go to college to eventually become a lawyer. He was the first of us to go to college and served as an exemplary "role model." Out of the nine children who lived to adulthood, five have multiple college degrees. Our degrees total 13 different graduate and undergraduate degrees including teaching, nursing, law, political science, and aircraft design. I doubt that any of our early schoolteachers could have foreseen our success. None encouraged us to go to college. Simply put, teachers and counselors did not consider us "college material." We proved them wrong. They must be astonished that I was named to the High School Hall of Fame. My brothers and sisters and I view our collective successes as emanating from tenacity and perseverance. Luck had nothing to do with our success. I like to quote Oprah who says that when she is told how lucky she is, she replies, "Luck is when opportunity meets preparation." Amen. It is here, Yvania, that I reiterate my earlier message that you continue to nurture your strong sense of self. Like my own social experiences shared in this response, your social experiences, both positive and negative, have made you who your are—a strong, confident, Latina woman who knows herself and who uses that knowledge to successfully navigate the different spheres of your life. Knowing yourself will enable you to take advantage of the many opportunities that being "Garcia in a Smith world" will afford you.

The remainder of this response is for up and coming Latina scholars and other women scholars of color and relates to the topics of mentoring and professional development. Research by many scholars clearly illustrates that Latinos lag behind all other ethnic groups in terms of high school and college graduation rates, underscoring just how extraordinary my siblings' and my degree accomplishments were. Delgado-Romero, Manlove, Manlove, and Hernandez (2007) pointed out that, "despite the fact that Latinos/as make up the largest ethnic minority group in the country … fewer obtain a bachelor's degree or higher … and [fewer] become faculty in university settings (2.9%) than do Whites and other minority individuals" (p. 37). This research has been supported more recently by Ortega-Liston and Rodriguez (2014).

Much contemporaneous discussion has occurred in higher education circles that focus on issues of recruiting, retaining, and promoting Latinos. Concerns raised have been published and discussed at length (Ibarra, 2003; Guanipa, Santa-Cruz, & Chao, 2003). However, despite the growing interest shown by Latino high school, college, and graduate students in becoming professors, some encounter hurdles on their way toward graduation, such as low numbers of Latino/a faculty available to serve as role models. I urge all Latinos to seek out and gravitate to other Latinos and different ethnic minorities to find suitable mentors and role models. I find other women of color to be the best source for *trusted* friendships and collegiality. Unfortunately, none of my ethnic minority friends and colleagues have been in a position to mentor me. Far too few of my colleagues have advanced to higher level positions; we are collectively struggling together to reach the top. This is an important point; as women of color we must recognize that we are in this *together*. I am firmly convinced that an important *sisterhood* exists because of skin color and cultural backgrounds. Relationships with other women of color are invaluable because of our shared experiences (Marina, 2014). Collectively we are all aspiring scholars.

LESSONS I WANT TO TEACH
UP AND COMING SCHOLARS OF COLOR

The first lesson I have to offer is that you seek respected mentors for yourself from those around you. Studies about mentoring programs designed for minorities and/or women have yielded limited, but insightful, observations. For example, mentoring can be a way for women and minorities to gain a foothold in organizations. With respect to women in the workplace, Fox and Schuhmann (2001), emphasized, "One important variable in women's continued entry into the administrative professions is access to high-quality mentoring experiences" (p. 382). But while mentoring may provide initial entry, race can be a barrier against forming mentoring relationships. For example, in a survey of African Americans in public accounting, a scant 40% reported involvement in a mentoring relationship (Annisette, Ross, & Wells, 2005). However, I urge women of color to remember that White male mentors are in positions of power and influence and that they are often the first to agree to mentor women and minorities. Ethnic minorities are far too rare in the public and private sectors; however, when available, it is wise to seek them out and ask them to mentor you.

Research shows that women of color often relate to other women of color because of common experiences (Marina, 2014). Whether your mentor is White, Black, or Latino, make sure to let him/her know what you have to contribute to the relationship (i.e., as a researcher). Do you have data analysis skills? Remember the answer is always "no" unless you ask. A lesson I teach my own students is to never say "no" to yourself. Others may say no to you, but if you do not ask you have said no to yourself. Always ask. The second lesson I have to offer is to seek the society of others who are like you in and outside of your organization. Men and women who are "like" you often relate to you better than others who have not shared the same experiences. Do not avoid others who are not like you because everyone has something to contribute to your development even if they provide examples of what not to do. Third, build your resume by accepting work assignments that make you more marketable. Choose assignments that work to your advantage in terms of building skills that you do not possess or wish to improve. Do not choose assignments that have little "pay back." The literature reveals (Mitchell & Heslie, 2013; Ortega-Liston & Rodriguez Soto, 2014) that minorities often are given assignments that are time consuming and tedious, but have few benefits to their own tenure track careers. Supervisors look favorably upon employees who are team players and pitch in and help when needed. Be a good team player, but avoid being burdened to the detriment of your career development.

Fourth, network with peer groups and national associations. Networking is a skill that can be developed and will more than likely help build socializing skills and valuable associations. Focus on building friendships/ associations that will last over time. Having someone you can voice concerns to in order to "get things off your chest" comes in handy from time-to-time. Networking early on is advantageous to new hires. Attend national conferences in your discipline to gain peer recognition. Many universities offer travel funds to offset registration fees and costs of attending out-of-state and out-of-country conferences. If available at your institutions, take advantage of these funds.

Conference participation often requires paper presentations. Do not avoid writing conference papers. Some conference papers may lead to future publication and publishing should be a primary goal for everyone seeking tenured positions. Submit your own panel ideas to conferences. Members can be close associates and friends with whom you share common values and ideas. You can also save money by sharing hotel rooms with friends. Related to my advice on conference participation, the fifth lesson I have to offer is to conduct your own original research. The best advice I can give my mentees is to develop research interests from which original data can be gathered and published. If quantitative analyses is not your strength, data analysis companies exist to help you make sense of the data you collect.

The sixth lesson I have to offer is to engage in community service that enhances your resume. Find public and private sector agencies and foundations that have broad appeal and serve on their boards. This is a great way to enhance a resume. While there are many places where you can volunteer your time, be choosy. Choose service opportunities with the greatest cache. Do not wait for organizations to seek you out; be assertive and give them a call, asking how you can help.

Lesson seven is that you should endeavor, when given the choice, to teach courses that interest you and that support your research agenda. When you are given a choice of what to teach, choose subjects/topics that hold the promise of writing in that specific area or conducting research in it. Publish articles based on your original research. All those who wish to become professors must publish; the old "publish or perish" doctrine still holds.

The eighth lesson is to follow the 20 minute rule of writing the first thing in the morning. Before you have your coffee or orange juice, before you take the dog for a walk, before you go for a run, before you take a shower, before you do anything—sit at your computer and write your ideas for 20 minutes. Also, follow the two page a day writing rule. Every day you should complete two edited manuscript pages. I offer this advice because my university invited a speaker who discussed how to get published; I learned these rules from that speaker and scrupulously follow them because *they work*.

Lesson nine is to expand your publications by coauthoring articles and books with others who have similar research interests. Minorities and women professionals do not look to each other sufficiently enough as possible sources for joint publications. I have begun to co-author articles with other Latinas and women of color. It has proved highly beneficial and rewarding. Not publishing with other women and/or ethnic minorities is a d opportunity. It is also important to reference and cite other ority researchers. A review of the literature shows that minorities and nen do not often cite their own research, that men are cited more ten than women, and that men tend to cite themselves and the work of ther men (Maliniak, Powers, & Walter, 2013).

The tenth lesson is to mentor other up-and-coming minority scholars. Mentoring others behind you is rewarding—especially if it is another someone who "looks" like you. Be generous, but not too generous, with your time, energy, and talent. This final lesson brings me to one of Erik Erikson's stages of healthy human development. Stage eight is one that he terms *Integrity vs. Despair*. In this stage, the healthy adult reaches down and lifts up other younger people by assisting them, coaching them, and mentoring them. In other words, healthy adults feel a responsibility of passing on to the next generation information and guidance ensuring that future generations will benefit from their own experiences, knowledge, successes, and failures. I hope that I have passed on advice that will make the lives of future scholars easier, happier, more fruitful and more prosperous so that I, in turn, may view myself as having made a positive contribution to future generations of Latino, Black, and Asian women scholars and leaders. I urge all women of color in academia to think of yourselves as a scholar first and foremost in order to live out your professional dreams and to travel the roads that you seek.

REFERENCES

Annisette, M., Ross, F., & Wells, J. (2005). *The professional experiences of African-American accountants: Analysis of survey results*. Washington, DC: Howard University Center for Accounting Education.

Castillo-Montoya, M., & Torres-Guzmán, M. E. (2012). Thriving in our identity and in the academy: Latina epistemology as a core resource. *Harvard Educational Review, 82*(4), 540–558.

Delgado-Romero, E. A., Manlove, A. N., Manlove, J. D., & Hernandez, C. A. (2007). Controversial issues in the recruitment and retention of Latino/a faculty. *Journal of Hispanic Higher Education, 6*(1), 34–51.

Erikson, E. (1968). *Identity: Youth and crisis*. New York, NY: Norton.

Fox, R. L., & Schuhmann, R. A. (2001). Mentoring experiences of women city managers: Are women disadvantaged? *American Review of Public Administration, 31*(4), 381–392.

Guanipa, C., Santa-Cruz, R. M., & Chao, G. (2003). Retention, tenure, and promotion of Hispanic faculty in colleges of education: Working towards success within the higher education system. *Journal of Higher Education, 2*, 187–202.

Ibarra, R. A. (2003). Latino/a faculty and the tenure process in cultural context. In L. Jones & J. Castellanos (Eds.), *The majority in the minority: Retaining Latino/o faculty, administrators, and students in the 21st century* (pp. 207–219). Sterling, VA: Stylus Books.

Marina, B. L. H. (2014). A cultural connection to identity development for graduate female students of color. In F. K. Kochan (Series Ed.) & F. Kochan, A. Kent, & A. Green (Volume Eds.), *Perspectives on Mentoring: Vol. 4. Uncovering the hidden cultural dynamics in mentoring programs and relationships: Managing the complexities* (pp. 63–78). Charlotte, NC: Information Age.

Maliniak, D., Powers, R. M., & Walter, B. F. (2013). *The gender citation gap.* Retrieved September 23, 2013, from http://papers.ssrn.com/sol3/papers.cfm?abstract_id=2303311

Mitchell, S. M., & Heslie, V. L. (2013, April). The profession: Bargaining and service in the political science profession. *Political Science*, 355–369.

Mkandawire-Valhmu, L., Kako, P. M., & Stevens, P. E. (2010). Mentoring women faculty of color in nursing academia: Creating an environment that supports scholarly growth and retention. *Nursing Outlook, 58*(3), 135–141. doi:http://dx.doi.org.ezproxy1.lib.asu.edu/10.1016/j.outlook.2010.02.001

Ortega-Liston, R., & Rodriguez Soto, I. (2014). Challenges, choices, and decisions of women in higher education: A discourse on the future of Hispanic, Black, and Asian members of the professoriate. *Journal of Hispanic Higher Education* doi:10.1177/1538192714540531

Villaseñor, M. J., Reyes, M. E., & Muñoz, I. (2013). Mujerista mentoring for Chicanas/Latinas in higher education. *Journal of College Student Retention: Research, Theory and Practice, 15*(1), 49–64.

CHAPTER 6

TRIPLE THREAT

Multiple Identities in the Academy

Lakeisha D. Meyer

Every person's story is unique. This inherent distinctiveness means each narrative enriches our understanding of the world around us. My story, like yours, has components that are shared with the narratives of others. As a Black woman in academia, I am part of a group with shared struggles and accomplishments. There are other aspects of my concept of self that intersect with my identity as a Black woman. I am also a member of the LGBTQ community and a first-generation college student from a rural, working class background. All of these identities impact my professional life. Based on what I consider my three main identities or group membership identifications, I am a "triple threat." I identify as a woman, Black, and a member of the LGBTQ community. This has positive and negative implications depending on the context.

The relationship between my personal identities and the personal and professional realms of my life is complex. This chapter will address how multiple identities impact life in academia through the application of personal narrative. According to Nash (2004), "Scholarly personal narrative is the unabashed, up-front admission that your 'own life signifies,' ... that is to say that your own life has meaning, both for you and others" (p. 23).

Beyond Retention: Cultivating Spaces of Equity, Justice, and Fairness
for Women of Color in U.S. Higher Education, pp. 165–179
Copyright © 2016 by Information Age Publishing

Our personal stories are significant; they have value. Our stories do not only have implications for us, but others. Sharing our personal narratives is important if we are to understand others and ourselves; however, we must also be willing to hear the stories of others. All of our stories have meaning and consequences for various aspects of our lives. In this piece, I will focus on how my narrative relates to my educational experiences and my professional life in higher education and explore how my personal identities have influenced this narrative.

The connection between narrative and scholarly work is an important one. It is necessary for me to be able to connect who I am and my story to some of the work I do in academia. This is a relatively recent realization for me. When it comes to critical scholarly work, it is important to consider how our personal experiences have impacted our construction of knowledge related to that area. Our academic work can reflect our personal and professional interests. Linking personal and professional pursuits can enhance the work we do in our fields, leading us to critically examine topics through the lenses of our own experiences (Holvino, 2010). Even though I have believed this to be true, I had not ventured to apply it to my own work until recently. I had been telling myself that I would transition into new research areas once I received tenure. I wanted to do some research informed by my personal experiences with identity development. Then I realized that I used to say that I would transition to those interests once I finished my dissertation. The result of me not pursuing scholarly activities, in which I was personally invested, was a research agenda and trajectory that did not adequately fulfill my need to have a personal connection to my scholarly work. Now, I have incorporated narratives related to identity development and providing services to underserved populations into my scholarly work. Narrative has a particularly important role in the lives of women of color. And like Holvino, my personal identities are related to my professional ones. As I have become more secure in my personal identity, I have been more willing and able to incorporate my interests in these topics into my work in higher education.

My narrative is of particular importance because of my work in an institution of higher education. Institutions of higher education are organizational systems. It is critical that these institutions be inclusive. It is also important to recognize that there are many stories missing if we only consider the narratives of the majority or those that are conventional.

> Telling the stories and articulating the narratives of organizational actors across different axes of power and identity practices is an important intervention for changing dominant organizational discourses because it brings to light alternative narratives that seldom find their way into mainstream accounts and organizational mythologies. (Holvino, 2010, p. 263)

The Black woman occupies multiple identities that result in us not fitting the prototypes of gender and race (Collins, 1990; Crenshaw, 1989; hooks, 1989). According to sociologists Ridgeway and Kricheli-Katz (2013),

> It is literally harder to be "seen," for your perspective to be heard, or your contributions credited when you don't fit easily with people's automatic lenses for noticing, making sense of, and understanding others, lenses that are institutionalized as well as held by individuals. (p. 307)

In addition to the invisibility faced by Black women, there are other identities that may be considered "invisible" because there are not sufficient visual cues for someone to assign group membership (i.e., sexual orientation). The invisibility of Black women and other aspects of identity support the notion that our narratives must be shared.

Background

I grew up in a very small farming community in rural Kentucky. My family was one of few Black families in the town. My household included my father, mother, and younger brother. Most of my family lived in the area and we were all very close. I grew up living right next to my maternal grandparents, on their farm. My parents, who are still married, both worked factory jobs, as did most of my family. It is important to point out here that when I speak of family, I include my grandparents, aunts, uncles, and cousins. For many people, when they use the term family, they seem to refer only to their immediate family (parents and siblings). This is an important distinction for me as I examine my experiences in higher education. I see myself not only as an individual, but a member of a close communal group of relatives. My accomplishments are not mine alone. This communal view extends to my professional life as well and has had an impact on my life in academia. I value working together and collaboration; I believe I can succeed while also helping others to do the same. My individual success is not determined by competition and who I "beat," but my own standards and those of the communities to which I belong.

Unifying My Identities

The intersection of my identities has impacted my experiences in academia in a number of ways. Even though I have worked within a variety of institutions, I have only worked at predominantly White institutions (PWIs). Because of my multiple, intersecting identities I often feel divided in terms of my alliances and commitment to the various groups. I do not experience the feeling of division when the groups that I work with identify common goals and find ways to work together toward the same end, but this does not always happen. I have participated in groups and committees that were able to work collaboratively toward common goals related to policy. An issue related to this has come up for me in the context of developing campus policies. I was a member of a special interest group that took on the task of developing policies and procedures for reporting and responding to incidents of bias related to sexual orientation and gender expression.

At that same institution, I was a member of a group that was developing specific procedures for reporting incidents of racial bias. It seemed that multiple policies were being developed for addressing issues of bias depending on group membership. Having multiple policies and procedures based on group membership is problematic. It dismisses the importance and even the existence of multiple, or intersecting, identities. To whom would I report an incident of bias if I were targeted simultaneously due to my race and my gender? Fortunately, this is not a decision that I had to make. I do not know what came of those policies. Perhaps the groups ultimately came together. It is possible that each group was not aware of what the other was doing. This is one example of how we may overlook the implications of multiple group memberships and the intersection of identities is vitally important.

I cannot separate my "Black-ness" from my "woman-ness." Which one is most salient varies from situation to situation and depends on which of those identities stands out most at a given time. In the context of academia, it is most often my "Blackness" of which I am most aware. This is particularly the case in the classroom. Most of the classes that I have taught have included no Black students. I was generally the only Black person in the classroom when I was a student, but the implications for me as a professor are quite different. Although the courses I teach do not have an overt cultural component, culture and diversity are topics that are covered in each class that I teach because of their relevance. When discussing issues of race, I am particularly aware that I am the only one, or one of a few Blacks in the room. This has had an effect on how I have approached certain topics in class, particularly those related to race and sexual orientation. I pay close attention to my tone and often withhold my personal opinion, but rather ask questions that bring out a variety of views. I openly discuss some of my educational experiences related to my racial identity. It is generally easy for me to disclose this type of information because I know that my skin pigmentation suggests that I am Black and there is the natural assumption that I identify as Black; this is not the case regarding sexual orientation. When addressing this topic, I do not self-disclose to the same degree or in the same manner. This topic is not as safe for me. There still is not a level of acceptance that makes me comfortable enough to always share this information about myself in professional environments. However, it is an important part of my identity.

Taking a stand on some issues may create a sense of isolation within the institution. Sometimes events occur that make race a significant issue across the country (e.g., the O.J. Simpson trial, the election of President Obama, etc.). A relatively recent event that holds this status in my mind was the Trayvon Martin case. Trayvon was a 17-year-old Black boy who was shot and killed by a Floridian man, who was ultimately acquitted of manslaughter and second-degree murder charges. About a month after Trayvon Martin's murder, I posted a sign on my door in support of Trayvon. At the top, it had a picture of Skittles in the shape of a heart and on the bottom it said, "Trayvon Martin, you will not be forgotten. We must let our children know that we love them to LIFE." Someone (we never found out who) left a note on my door written in red marker. It said, "Trayvon Martin attacked George Zimmerman before he was shot in self-defense. Check your facts please." I saw the note on my door just before going to teach a class. By the time I arrived to the classroom, I was in tears. My note was an attempt to express the deep sadness I was feeling due to the loss of life of a young Black boy. I did not say anything about Zimmerman and didn't even comment on the circumstances of Trayvon's murder. I couldn't understand how my sign could have prompted someone to write such a note and leave it on my door. I desperately wanted to know who left the note and wondered if it might be possible for us to have a conversation about why they believed their note was an appropriate response to my sign. I left both my sign and the response on my door and added the following statement to the bottom of the response: "He may have attacked him. I just want to make sure it's fully investigated and the process started too late ... in my opinion. Sincerely, Lakeisha." I was left shaken by the incident. I felt attacked for my views and was disturbed by the fact the person left an anonymous note and did not attempt to engage in a dialogue about the issue. I decided to take my issue to campus public safety, but there was very little they could do. After the incident, I was nervous on campus. It had an impact on me that I could not have imagined. I was suddenly uncomfortable walking to my car alone at night. Was it a student, faculty, or staff? I had no way of knowing. I did not understand why my reaction to the note was so strong. I just know that I changed how I experienced being on campus for some time after the incident.

In hindsight, much of my reaction to the incident was mediated by how I thought I would be perceived for my views. I even went so far as to present an idea that I did not believe at all: that Trayvon "may" have attacked this Floridian man. I wanted to make it clear that the sentiment expressed in the first note I placed on my door had nothing to do with this Floridian man or why Trayvon was shot. My note was one of mourning. It did not feel comfortable broadcasting my specific views about the case to most of my colleagues and students.

Intersectionality Theory

This essay will explore the impact of my personal identity intersections on my professional life through the discussion of issues related to stereotypes, status and privilege, organizational systems (e.g., institutions of higher education), representation in institutions of higher education and institutional change. My background is in school psychology. However, when considering the relationship between my personal identity and my life in academia I draw from several fields. When addressing the intersection of my identities, I consider the interdisciplinary concept of intersectionality. Intersectionality has three primary themes. First, every person belongs to multiple societal classifications at one time and these categories are "mutually constitutive." Second, identities existing at the intersection of gender and race are unique and are more than the sum of each separate identity. And third, these categories or identities reflect inequalities that substantially impact life (Cole, 2009; Cole & Zucker, 2007; Ghavami & Peplau, 2013; Peplau, Veniegas, Taylor, & DeBro, 1999). There are multiple studies that provide evidence to validate the themes of intersectionality (e.g., Brewer, Conrad, & King, 2002; Ghavami & Peplau, 2013; Harnois, 2005; Harvey, 2005; Holvino, 2010; Weber, 2001; Zinn, Hondagneu-Sotelo, & Messner, 2005). Such research also supports the notion that an understanding of intersectionality will result in more effective approaches to institutional change. Institutions of higher education are environments that foster intellectual freedom and critical thought. They are complex organizational systems. How they function is impacted by factors at multiple levels of the system. Change at the institutional level requires the work at all levels. A fuller understanding of the experiences of women of color in higher education is necessary in order for institutions to better meet our needs.

STEREOTYPES AND STEREOTYPE THREAT

Most research examining stereotypes has addressed one aspect of identity, such as race or gender, but has not looked at the intersection of those identities. The results of a study by Ghavami and Peplau (2013) provide evidence to support this intersectionality hypothesis. They found that each ethnicity-by-gender group had stereotypes that included unique features. Features were considered unique if the feature appeared only on the "ethnicity by gender" list, but not the ethnicity or gender list alone. The groups examined in the study were Blacks, Middle Easterners, Latinos, Whites, and Asian American. The stereotypes of each group were also examined by sex. The stereotypes of men in general and women in general were included as well. The group with the highest proportion of qualities that were unique was Black women. When people identified stereotypes for Blacks, women, and Black women, there were stereotypes listed for Black women that were not identified as being characteristic of Blacks or women separately. The group with the lowest proportion of unique qualities was White women.

Stereotypes are pervasive and can impact our personal interactions. Studies examining stereotypes indicate that there are widely held beliefs about the attributes that characterize various groups. Ghavami and Peplau (2013) found that the attributes listed for Black women contained attributes that were unique to Black women. Only five attributes overlapped with those listed for Blacks. It is interesting to note that none of the listed characteristics for Black women overlapped with those for women in general. Regarding stereotypes of Whites, White women only had two attributes listed that were unique and not characteristic of White males or Whites in general. These were "ditsy" and "sexually liberal." There are a few stereotypes that may have direct implications for the workplace. Some of the stereotypes listed for Whites, White men, and White women included "high status," "intelligent," "successful," and "educated."

Ridgeway and Kricheli-Katz (2013) state that the more salient race or gender is in a particular situation, the more the person perceiving the woman of color will respond to her in a way that reflects racial and gender stereotypes. The only stereotype listed for Black women that is related to these is "unintelligent." There was one attribute listed for Black women that may have positive workplace implications, "confident" (Ghavami & Peplau, 2013). However, this potential benefit is not likely enough to counter the disadvantages associated with the experiences of Black women (Ridgeway & Kricheli-Katz, 2013). People respond to Black women differently than they do women or Black people in general based on stereotypes (Purdie-Vaughns & Eibach, 2008).

Stereotypes about class, gender, and race are widely believed by individuals but also indicated, to the point of institutionalization, in the media, and in the structures of systems and organizations (Acker, 2006; Ridgeway, 2011; Ridgeway & Kricheli-Katz, 2013). This is the case in institutions of higher education as well. These stereotypes often lead those around us to respond to us in a manner that is biased (Ridgeway &

Kricheli-Katz, 2013). People respond to us specifically based on the stereotypes of Black women. These stereotypes include things like "big butt," "overweight," "confident," dark-skinned," "hair weave," and "assertive" (Ghavami & Peplau, 2013). The stereotypes associated with Black women can have a significant influence on the experiences of Black women in academia. These stereotypes, and the resulting stereotype threat, have contributed to my experience of impostor syndrome, which can lead to the sense that one must work twice as hard to get the same recognition.

Stereotype threat refers to the tendency to perform poorly due to an awareness of assumptions about competency, generally in the form of low expectations (Amoroso, Loyd, & Hoobler, 2010; Steele & Aronson, 1995). It is when one expects their *personal identity*, as it relates to minority group membership, will be evaluated instead of your capabilities. This especially occurs when there is a negative stereotype about that group (Block, Koch, Liberman, Merriweather, & Roberson, 2011; Roberson & Kulik, 2007). The negative effects of stereotype threat occur whether or not the person believes the stereotype and irrespective of how accurate the stereotype is. There is evidence to support that stereotype threat may be stronger in work environments where people of color and women are the minority (Block et al., 2011). Institutions must also be careful not to place women and minorities in the position of being a token. Tokenism is the minimal effort to include a minority to create the appearance of inclusive hiring practices in the work environment (Hogue & Yoder, 2006). Tokenism reinforces stereotypes and encourages stereotyping (Block et al., 2011; Ely, 1995). There is also a relationship between stereotypes, stereotype threat, and impostor syndrome. Impostor syndrome is "an internalized, reproducing, negative influence in the professional lives of scholars of color" (Dancy & Brown, 2011, p. 615). "The research literature describes the feelings of inadequacy that define impostor syndrome and supports the presence of this condition in oppressive contexts" (Dancy & Brown, 2011, p. 621).

Impostor syndrome is a common experience for many, regardless of personal identity. My feelings related to impostor syndrome are especially associated with my identities as a Black woman and as someone from a working class background who was the first person in my family to go to college. I also feel like I do not fit in because I am from a rural background and am the first person in my family to experience the educational advantages that I have. As a result of these aspects of my identity there is an "academic," upper-middle class language that I was not exposed to when I was young. Many people experience impostor syndrome. But impostor syndrome cannot be fully understood without taking into consideration race, gender, sexuality, and class (Leonard, 2014).

Factors like these play a role in determining who must deal with the lack of confidence associated with impostor syndrome.

I understand what impostor syndrome is and I have experienced it. At times I have thought that I do not deserve to be in my position, that I am just a token. When I start to think in that way I begin to believe that I have to work harder to make up for my deficiencies, even though those inadequacies are imagined. At times I have even started to think that my multiple, intersecting identities were not a strength, but a burden instead. When I am performing optimally at work, overextending myself only intensifies the degree to which I experience anxiety. I noticed that I felt more capable and sure of myself after updating my vita. So now I update my vita often. It is also helpful for me to look at it periodically, so I place my vita somewhere where it is visible to me. It may seem like a small thing, but it serves as a reminder of my achievements. As Black women, we do not need to overwork in academia as compensation for imagined inadequacies (Meyer, 2014).

STATUS AND PRIVILEGE

Understanding the relationship between stereotypes, status, and identity intersections is important for Black women in academia. It has an impact on how we, and those around us, construct knowledge. Status is also related to privilege. Privilege refers to the advantages experienced by someone based purely on the basis of some identified characteristic. As a Black woman, my experience with privilege is quite limited. However, I may be considered educationally privileged, which will be discussed in the following section. Privilege can be related to the status hierarchies that often exist in organizational systems. Amoroso et al. (2010) define a status hierarchy as a ranking of individuals according to certain qualities. "Status is less an attribute of individuals than an aspect of occupying a particular location in the social structure and is determined by shared beliefs about the value of particular characteristics and the individuals possessing such characteristics" (Amoroso et al., 2010, p. 799). The status hierarchy within the academy is influenced by educational privilege, particularly since educational attainment in part determines one's position in the academy.

Educational Privilege

Someone can be privileged in one area and marginalized in another. Clearly, there is an important relationship between privilege and multiple identities. It can be difficult for someone to acknowledge his or her own privilege. I believe it is easier to acknowledge privilege in a particular area when we understand that privilege in one area does not mean privilege in all areas. This is particularly important when it comes to understanding privilege related to race. If a White woman acknowledges that she has experienced privilege as a result of being White, it does not negate the marginalization she experiences as a woman. Throughout all of my educational experiences, at every grade level, including college and graduate school, I was generally the only Black person in the classroom. At times, it was difficult for me to navigate those experiences. I felt like I was invisible and under a microscope at the same time. Privilege can mean a number of different things. Here I focus on one of the many subtle ways privilege manifests.

In 1973 Motown Records released "A Motown Christmas." I was born one year later and it has and will likely always be my favorite Christmas album. It was the epitome of Christmas music and was full of renditions of favorites in a way that turned them into true holiday classics for me. One year during elementary school, students were allowed to bring in two Christmas songs to play at various times during the school day right before Christmas break. I was beyond excited and could hardly wait to bring in my album. I knew which two songs I wanted to play. When the day came and it was time for me to play my songs, I decided to save the best for last and played "Give Love on Christmas Day" by the Jackson 5 first. The music had barely begun when I heard the mumbling begin. Then I heard someone say, "That ain't Christmas music." The students talked among themselves and seemed to pay no more attention to the song. At first I could not understand what he meant. Then I realized that all of the other music that had been played was by White artists and the songs were generally standard Christmas carols. During all of the other songs, the class sang along. I chose two holiday classics that were only holiday classics to me. I never played the second song and I do not think anyone noticed. This is an example of one of my early experiences with privilege. At least that is how I identify it now. I did not have the privilege of my music being considered true Christmas music. It was an example of how the experience of the minority can be negated by the privilege of the majority.

In spite of my early experiences with discrimination, I have come to be a member of an elite group in that I have my PhD and am a professor at a university. Much of my success can be attributed to the various ways that I experienced privilege in my educational experiences. This is in spite of representing multiple groups who sometimes have little educational privilege and poor educational outcomes. Beginning in the fourth grade, I participated in a gifted and talented program in my school district. One day a week, I and the other students identified as gifted and talented went to a different school in the district for the day. I was exposed to material that was not present in my general education classroom. For example, I learned how to use a computer and learned about Greek mythology. One day a week I experienced a classroom that was engaging and sufficiently challenging; this is where my educational privilege began. I was exposed to concepts that were not part of my typical classroom and they enriched my educational experience.

As a result of my positive school experiences, I became the first person in my family to go to college. I then continued on to graduate school and ultimately earned my PhD. This enriching aspect of my educational background did not preclude me from experiencing educational disadvantage, particularly as I climbed the academic ladder through college and graduate school. Even though I had experienced some forms of educational privilege, there were still aspects of the academic world that I did not understand. There was a language that I did not speak. I was socialized academically to some extent but any academic socialization was limited by the fact that I was in a poor, rural school district and this socialization was not reinforced at home or in my social interactions outside of the academy. I must point out, though, that my family also contributed to my education privilege by ensuring that I had access to books. Not only did I have access to books, but also I was encouraged to read and my family modeled regular reading habits. Still, I did not quite fit in. When I started graduate school I had very little understanding of what was involved in completing a dissertation. I still remember being told how to pronounce "doctoral" correctly. There seemed to literally be a language that I was not well equipped to speak.

REPRESENTATION IN INSTITUTIONS AND SOCIAL SYSTEMS

According to Ghavami and Peplau (2013), social systems are generally organized as hierarchies of power and status within institutions of higher education, hierarchies exist at multiple levels. For example, there may be a hierarchy composed of staff, faculty, and administrators. Within the faculty ranks there may be visiting, assistant, associate, and full professors. Women of color are significantly underrepresented at PWI's, particularly at higher levels of the hierarchies (Berger & Webster, 2006; Correll & Ridgeway, 2003, Ridgeway, 2013).

The three pillars of being a professor are teaching, research, and service. This is generally the case regardless of the institution of higher education, although schools vary in their expectations in each of those areas. One area significantly impacted by my status as a woman of color is service. When I refer to service I mean participation in activities at the program, departmental, and institutional levels such as committee membership and service on boards. My service is most impacted by my experience as a Black woman. Race is generally salient for women of color at PWI's. We are often the only person of color at the table and are, therefore, placed in the role of being perceived as the token. The value of our representation at every level is minimized and relegates us to feeling like we are the victims of tokenism. This is significant because at institutions where people of color are expected to be represented at every level of service, this places faculty of color, particularly those with multiple marginalized identities, under undue burden.

There can also be an impact on teaching demands. Faculty of color consider teaching responsibilities to include experiences outside of class and emotional development to be more important than White faculty (Antonio, 2002; Dancy & Brown, 2011). In addition to required service to the university and a commitment to supporting students outside of class, members of marginalized groups also have a deep commitment to service related to social justice and social change. Balancing commitment to the university and personal commitment to personally relevant causes can be difficult.

SUCCESS AND INSTITUTIONAL CHANGE

From the human services perspective, systems change efforts include the modification of fundamental structures and procedures, such as values and policies (Foster-Fishman, 2007). The nature of academia means that individuals have accomplished certain things in order to gain their positions in the academy. According to Jackson (2008) there are seven themes that characterize the experiences of faculty of color: lack of support, revolving door syndrome, tokenism, typecasting, one-minority-per-pot, and brown-on-brown taboo. Some of these themes have been addressed in some form in this chapter. Although I have not personally had experiences associated with each of these themes, they may provide a framework for conceptualizing how we might improve the environments of institutions of higher education to better support women of color.

Women and people of color are underrepresented in numerous disciplines and lines of work (Block et al., 2011). As a Black woman I am in a unique position to facilitate change in the environments in which I work because of my identity intersections. As has been stated previously, Black women are perceived as having specific qualities unique to them that are not associated with stereotypes of Blacks or women. Some people respond to Black women like they are the prototypical or stereotypical Black woman. Of course, Black women are not their stereotypes. There are plenty of women who have characteristics different from the ones identified as stereotypes. These Black women may be referred to as "off diagonal" (Ridgeway & Kricheli-Katz, 2013).

> Over time, encounters with "off diagonal," unprototypical people who are still categorized as members of their group (even if exceptional ones), but are freer to behave in atypical, nonstereotypical ways, may gradually create "openings"—opportunities for change in our beliefs regarding the behavior of prototypical members. As a result, our beliefs about how prototypical members of a group behave may gradually change as a result of repeated interactions with nonprototypical members. Encounters with 'off diagonal' people—like successful Black women—however, are likely to affect our beliefs about race, gender, and class only when such encounters reach a critical mass and visibility is impossible to dismiss. (p. 312)

Holvino (2010) also addresses the issue of change, with a particular emphasis on the role of narrative. Ensuring that women of color are free to articulate their stories within hierarchical systems such as higher education is crucial if the "dominant organizational discourses" are going to change. These stories, my stories, must work their way into mainstream narratives and institutional traditions (Ely & Meyerson, 2000; Holvino, 2010).

CONCLUDING THOUGHTS

The intersecting identities of women of color impacts many aspects of our lives. This is evident in research on issues from stereotypes to institutional change. My experiences in academia have generally been positive. However, there are many areas that can be improved to ensure the success and retention of women of color. My work in higher education is intricately linked to my experiences as a Black woman. My story is also influenced by identification as a member of the LGBTQ community and someone who is a first-generation college student from a poor, rural background. My story is unique, but many aspects are shared with those who identify in some of the same ways that I do. My personal stories related to stereotypes, status, and privilege impact how I view my role in the academy.

REFERENCES

Acker, J. (2006). *Class questions*. Lanham, MD: Rowman & Littlefield.

roso, L. M., Loyd, D. L., & Hoobler, J. M. (2010). The diversity education dilemma: Exposing status hierarchies without reinforcing them. *Journal of Management Education, 34*(6), 795–822.

ntonio, A. (2002). Faculty of color reconsidered: Reassessing contributions to scholarship. *Review of Higher Education, 73*(5), 582–602.

Berger, J., & Webster, M. (2006). Expectations, status, and behavior. In P. Burke (Ed.), *Contemporary social psychological theories* (pp. 268–300). Stanford, CA: Stanford University Press.

Block, C. J., Koch, S. M., Liberman, B. E., Merriweather, T. J., & Roberson, L. (2011). Contending with stereotype threat at work: A model of long-term responses. *The Counseling Psychologist, 39*(4), 570–600.

Brewer, R. M., Conrad, C. A., & King, M. C. (2002). The complexities and potential of theorizing gender, caste, race, and class. *Feminist Economics, 8*, 3–18.

Cole, E. R. (2009). Intersectionality and research in psychology. *American Psychologist, 64*, 170–180.

Cole, E. R., & Zucker, A. N. (2007). Black and White women's perspectives on femininity. *Cultural Diversity and Ethnic Minority Psychology, 13*, 1–9.

Collins, P. H. (1990). *Black feminist thought*. Boston, MA: Unwin Hyman.

Correll, S. J., & Ridgeway, C. L. (2003). Expectation states theory. In J. Delamater (ed.), *The handbook of social psychology* (pp. 29–51). New York, NY: Kluwer Academic/Plenum.

Crenshaw, K. W. (1989). Demarginalizing the intersection of race and sex: A Black feminist critique of antidiscrimination doctrine, feminist theory and antiracist politics. *University of Chicago Legal Forum, 1*, 139–167.

Dancy, T. E., & Brown, M. C. (2011). The mentoring and induction of educators of color: Addressing the impostor syndrome in academe. *Journal of School Leadership, 21*, 607–634.

Ely, R. (1995). The power of demography: Women's social constructions of gender identity at work. *Academy of Management Journal, 38*, 589–634.

Ely, R., & Meyerson, D. E. (2000). Theories of gender in organizations: A new approach to organizational analysis and change. In B. M. Staw & R. I. Sutton (Eds.), *Research in organizational behavior* (Vol. 222, pp. 105–153). New York, NY: Elsevier Science/JAI.

Foster-Fishman, P. G., Nowell, B., &Yang, H. (2007). Putting the system back into systems change: A framework for understanding and changing organizational and community systems. *American Journal of Community Psychology, 39*, 197–215.

Ghavami, N., & Peplau, L. A. (2013). An intersectional analysis of gender and ethnic stereotypes: Testing three hypotheses. *Psychology of Women Quarterly, 37*, 112–127.

Harnois, C. E. (2005). Different paths to different feminism? Bridging multiracial feminist theory and quantitative sociological gender research. *Gender & Society, 19*(6), 809–828.

Harvey, A. M. (2005). Becoming entrepreneurs: intersections of race, class, and gender at the Black beauty salon. *Gender & Society, 19*(6), 789–808.

Hogue, B., & Yoder, J. (2006). Tokenism theory: What happens when few women work with many men. In M. Karsten (Eds.), *Gender, race, and ethnicity in the workplace: Legal, psychological, and power issues affecting women and minorities in business* (pp. 199–261). Westport, CT: Praeger.

Holvino, E. (2010). Intersections: The simultaneity of race, gender and class in organization studies. *Gender, Work and Organization, 17*, 248–277.

hooks, b. (1989). *Talking back*. Boston, MA: South End Press.

Jackson, J. F. (2008). Race segregation across the academic workforce: Exploring factors that may contribute to the disparate representation of African American men. *American Behavioral Scientist, 51*(7), 1004–1029.

Leonard, D. J. (2014, February 5). *Impostor syndrome: Academic identity under siege?* Retrieved from http://chronicle.com/blogs/conversation/2014/02/05/impostor-syndrome-academic-identity-under-siege/

Meyer, L. D. (2014, February 19). *Impostor syndrome and working harder*. Retrieved from http://www.psychologytoday.com/blog/identity-intersections/201402/impostor-syndrome-and-working-harder

Nash, R. J. (2004). *Liberating scholarly writing: The power of personal narrative*. New York, NY: Teachers College Press.

Peplau, L. A., Veniegas, R. C., Taylor, P. L., & DeBro, S. C. (1999). Sociocultural perspectives on the lives of women and men. In L. A. Peplau, S. C. DeBro, R. C. Veniegas, & P. L. Taylor (Eds.), *Gender, culture, and ethnicity: Current research about women and men* (pp. 23–37). Mountain View, CA: Mayfield.

Purdie-Vaughns, V. J., & Eibach, R. P. (2008). Intersectional invisibility. *Sex Roles, 59*, 377–391

Ridgeway, C. L. (2011). *Framed by gender*. New York, NY: Oxford University Press.

Ridgeway, C. L. (2013). Why status matters for inequality. *American Sociological Review, 79*, 1–16.

Ridgeway, C. L., & Kricheli-Katz, T. (2013). Intersecting cultural beliefs in social relations: Gender, race, and class binds and freedoms. *Gender and Society, 27*, 294–318.

Roberson, L., & Kulik, C. T. (2007). Stereotype threat at work. *Academy of Management Perspectives, 21*, 24–40.

Steele, C. M., & Aronson, J. (1995). Stereotype threat and the intellectual test performance of African-Americans. *Journal of Personality and Social Psychology, 69*, 797–811.

Weber, L. (2001). *Understanding race, class, gender, and sexuality: A conceptual framework*. New York, NY: McGraw-Hill.

Zinn, M. B., Hondagneu-Sotelo, P., & Messner, M. A. (2005). *Gender through the prism of difference* (3rd ed.) New York, NY: Oxford University Press.

RESPONSE

COMMONALITIES, CONTRASTS, CHALLENGES, AND COMMITMENTS

Nina Asher

Behind the story I tell is the one I don't.
Behind the story you hear is the one I wish I could make you hear.

—Dorothy Allison (1996), *Two or Three Things I Know for Sure*

Stories are powerful. Stories are transformative. Stories reclaim. Stories heal. And they can be helpful in rethinking and redefining discourses and fields of study in insightful, generative, enriching ways. We know this from feminist scholarship—and especially from the writings of women of color and queer women over the past 3 decades (Allison, 1996; Anzaldúa, 1987; hooks, 1990; Mohanty, 1991; Pratt, 1984; Trinh, 1989). Therefore, when we contextualize our stories in self-reflexive, thought-provoking ways, in relation to our discourses, pedagogies, and service-related activities in the academy, we take a step toward not only self-representation but also critical transformation. Dr. Lakeisha D. Meyer does so in her essay, "Triple Threat: Multiple Identities in the Academy." In this invited "response" to Dr. Meyer's "call," I speak to both commonalities and contrasts across her narrative and mine as well as key considerations and commitments in terms of addressing issues of race, gender, culture, socio-

Beyond Retention: Cultivating Spaces of Equity, Justice, and Fairness
for Women of Color in U.S. Higher Education, pp. 181–186
Copyright © 2016 by Information Age Publishing

economic status, and nation and the related implications for theory, research, and practice in education.

Like Dr. Meyer, I am a queer woman academic of color and have navigated the academy as an untenured assistant professor, learning the written and unwritten rules and modes of operation in the U.S. academy. *Unlike* Dr. Meyer, I am an immigrant woman who is now a naturalized U.S. citizen. I grew up in a large metropolis in another country (Bombay—now Mumbai—in postcolonial India) and each of my parents had earned a bachelor's degree. Like Dr. Meyer, I received my doctorate in the United States and have engaged race, culture, gender, class, and nation in my work to date in the areas of teaching, research/scholarship, and service. While Dr. Meyer's work is in school psychology, mine—informed by postcolonialism, feminism, globalization, and critical perspectives on multiculturalism—is in curriculum theory and curriculum studies. At this time I am a tenured full professor in the Department of Curriculum and Instruction at the University of Minnesota-Twin Cities, where I served as department chair from 2011–2014. Like Dr. Meyer—I have worked at primarily White institutions throughout my career as a full-time faculty member—at a branch campus of Penn State University for 2 years, then at Louisiana State University for 12 years prior to my current job. All of these are major, public, research universities.

Dr. Meyer speaks poignantly to multiplicities and intersectionalities in terms of identity, tensions of (in)visibility in educational and work contexts, and the significance of relating across differences—being "willing to hear the stories of others" as Dr. Meyer thoughtfully phrases it. She reminds us too of the need to have these commitments inform, enrich, and shape one's research agenda in vital ways. I agree—as a scholar, a woman of color in the academy, and a citizen in a context of increasing global interdependence. Indeed, my own research, scholarship, teaching, and service to the field have been informed by these considerations. For instance, in an article ("Beyond 'Cool' and 'Hip:' Engaging the Question of Research and Writing as Academic Self—Woman of Color Other") published early in my academic career (Asher, 2001) I wrote:

> In terms of my day-to-day lived experiences, I find that I engage with/in the academy as both—academic Self *and* woman of color Other—as I research, write, and teach. Or, more accurately, I find that I am compelled to do so: for me, critique is not a choice. I do not have the option of visiting marginality solely as a researcher. I live there. And I am reminded of it in innumerable ways (a parent of a prospective student asking me where I am from originally; hints about how I might be filling a "minority" faculty slot; rejection of my statement of a hybrid, academic identity in exchange for a given cultural and ethnic "Indian" identity) which are as manifest as they are subtle in a hard-to-document way. I find that if I am to continue conducting

research and writing with integrity, I cannot ignore professionally what I experience personally as an educator of color. (p. 2)

As I continued to develop my scholarship at the intersections of postcolonialism, feminism, and education, I also sought to examine how colonialism influenced my personal, educational, and professional journeys, the stories that have shaped my consciousness, my commitments. For instance, in "Writing Home/Decolonizing Text(s)" (Asher, 2009), I cited bell hooks' beautiful, powerful essay, on "homeplace" as a "site of resistance," where hooks writes about how the homeplace belonged to the women, who, in the face of terrible hardship and poverty under slavery and racial apartheid, resisted by "making homes where all Black people could strive to be subjects, not objects" (hooks, 1990, p. 42). I wrote about the strength of the women who came before me and survived the ravages of colonialism and also the contradictions I experienced in the postcolonial context in which I grew up.

> Although born in postcolonial India, I grew up listening to the stories of my mother describing the terror she experienced as a little girl, seeing the British soldiers running children over in their tanks, leaving them for dead in the streets of Bombay. As a little girl my mother saw her home burning when there was a massive explosion at the docks nearby.... My mother also talks about her mother's courage and strength of character in gathering her children and a few items of clothing and getting them out safely, before the building was consumed by flames. These horrific and painful images her stories evoked are etched in my mind, as are the utterly delightful settings and events sketched in the scores of children's books, written by English author, Enid Blyton, which friends and I devoured insatiably, as children. Yes, for me, home and elsewhere, colonized and colonizer, past and present, oppression and resistance are necessarily intertwined. (Asher, 2009, p. 6)

Little wonder then that over 2 decades now, informed by postcolonial and feminist theories and critical discourses of multiculturalism, I have written consistently on issues of identity and culture in relation to curriculum, teaching, and teacher education. Paying attention to individual narratives, context-specificities and contradictions, I have pushed for "rethinking multiculturalism as relevant to all—White students and those of color" (Asher, 2005, p. 1079) and also for "those who see themselves as 'multiculturally open' (or 'progressive' or 'liberal' and so on) to confront squarely their own assumptions and the limits of their vision" (Asher, 2007, p. 72). Arguing that "the self, regardless of its location, is never exempt" (Asher, 2007, p. 72), I acknowledged that I too need to continue to do my work (e.g., teaching, conducting research)—in a critical, self-reflexive manner.

Indeed, at the time of writing, I am engaged in a qualitative research project on globalization and education in India (thanks to a Fulbright research award and a sabbatical leave from my employer, University of Minnesota-Twin Cities). After over two-and-half decades in the U.S. academy—first as a graduate student and then as a faculty member—I have returned to my country of origin for an extended period. I recognize that I have returned to India—a "globalized" and "economically liberalized" India—as an expatriate, a U.S. citizen, and an educational researcher whose career is based in the U.S. academy.

In addition to new learnings through the research project itself, there are also the learnings that come out of the critical, self-reflexive process of engaging my own situatedness and intentionally interrogating the frames of culture, difference, and privilege that I hold even as I engage those that I encounter through my research and interactions with students, colleagues, and others (e.g., shopkeepers, bankers, taxi drivers) in 21st century India. It is a stimulating exercise, pushing me to grow once again, as a scholar and a researcher and expand my own knowledge base and skills. At the same time it is also a somewhat daunting challenge and a humbling experience—I have so much to (un)learn! I am recognizing, for instance, that with my years of academic experience and accomplishments notwithstanding, I occasionally miss critical cultural cues and become aware of the assumptions underlying my own framing of a particular situation or interchange. For example, in the initial meeting with prospective participants (students enrolled in a master of arts in elementary education program at a leading higher education institution in a major Indian metropolis), I passed around sign-up sheets for scheduling interviews and also gave each student a consent form, an information sheet about the project itself, and a demographic questionnaire. A week or so into the project, when attending a class during which students made presentations based on their fieldwork, I made a brief announcement that there was still time for students to schedule an interview—because many who had signed up at the initial meeting had not yet set up interviews. A few students came up to me looking rather apologetic and said that they wanted to schedule an interview but could not because they had either misplaced the papers handed out at the initial meeting or not collected them at all in the first place. Of course, I immediately gave them the documents and scheduled interviews. At the same time, I recognized that it never occurred to me that the students would not feel free to touch base with me to get the documents. I became aware of my own unexamined "American" cultural frame according to which students would simply ask professors/researchers for materials that they missed. So, yet once again, I recursively reminded myself of what I had written several years ago: "The self, regardless of its location, is never exempt."

Now, I return again to Dr. Meyer's experiences, accomplishments, and struggles. Dr. Meyer writes eloquently, feelingly about her (in)visibility at the intersection of race (being a Black woman) and gender (being a member of the LGBTQ community) and the constraints and challenges she therefore encounters in the academy. The insights and concerns that she shares regarding external and internal pressures (e.g., stereotype threat and imposter syndrome) are, indeed, widely experienced by fellow scholars situated in the margins. At the same time, I would also push for a further examination of her cultural framing. For instance, Dr. Meyer's description of her elementary school classmates' disappointing response to her selection of Christmas music does indeed evoke empathy and sympathy. However, when she writes "the experience of the minority can be negated by the privilege of the majority," it would be fruitful also for her to render visible and examine the apparent centering of Christianity in this narrative. How did Dr. Meyer's elementary school create space for students from various religious/spiritual traditions to share the same? For students from atheist backgrounds to represent the same? If not then what lacunae do we—school psychologists, educators—need to address? What are some of the insights that emerge for Dr. Meyer at the intersection of race (in terms of which she is on the margins) and religion (in terms of which she is at the center)? And perhaps most importantly, as a result of such critical, self-reflexive examination, what new learnings can she/we also bring to her/our students to help them expand and deepen their own understandings of equity, justice, and representation?

We are indebted to myriad women of color—queer and heterosexual—across national borders on whose shoulders we stand today. Sharing those stories and also our own—with a rigorous, thoughtful engagement with the intersectionalities we encounter—will allow us and our students to continue to commit to working toward equity and justice.

REFERENCES

Allison, D. (1996). *Two or three things I know for sure*. New York, NY: Penguin.

Anzaldúa, G. (1987). *Borderlands/la frontera*. San Francisco, CA: Aunt Lute.

Asher, N. (2001). Beyond "cool" and "hip": Engaging the question of research and writing as academic self-woman of color other. *International Journal of Qualitative Studies in Education*, *14*(1), 1–12.

Asher, N. (2005). At the interstices: Engaging postcolonial and feminist perspectives for a multicultural education pedagogy in the South. *The Teachers College Record*, *107*(5), 1079–1106.

Asher, N. (2007). Made in the (multicultural) U.S.A.: Unpacking tensions of race, culture, gender, and sexuality in education. *Educational Researcher*, *36*(2), 65–73.

Asher, N. (2009). Writing home/decolonizing text(s). *Discourse: Studies in the Cultural Politics of Education, 30*(1), 1–13.

hooks, b. (1990). *Yearning: Race, gender, and cultural politics.* Boston, MA: South End Press.

Mohanty, C. T. (1991). Under western eyes: Feminist scholarship and colonial discourse. In C. Mohanty, A. Russo, & L. Torres (Eds.), *Third world women and the politics of feminism* (pp. 51–80). Bloomington, IN: Indiana University Press.

Pratt, M. B. (1984). Identity: Skin, blood, heart. In E. Bulkin, M. B. Pratt, & B. Smith (Eds.), *Yours in struggle: Three feminist perspectives on anti-Semitism and racism* (pp. 11–63). Brooklyn, NY: Long Haul.

Trinh, T. M. (1989). *Woman, native, other: Writing postcoloniality and feminism.* Bloomington, IN: Indiana University Press.

SECTION IV

GEOGRAPHIES OF SILENCE AND VOICE

CHAPTER 7

WHO SPEAKS FOR ME?

Learning to Resist With Marginalized Statuses in the Academy

Jenelle S. Pitt

I am Black. I was born in Canada, raised in Los Angeles, and proudly claim my West Indian roots. I have a beautiful 5-year-old son. Looking back, never would I have imagined that the first bit of mentoring I would have received about having a child while also being tenure-seeking would move me into such a place of guilt, shame, and mental lassitude. I remember the day I arrived at my mentor's office for our appointment. After being congratulated on my pregnancy, I was asked, "*'How serious is your relationship with your child's father?' We're in a committed relationship,*" is how I responded. What followed next would eventually start me down a path of insanity. It was suggested that I set up a meeting with my dean to discuss how serious I was about my job and share that I was in a committed relationship because being Black and a single mom in a city like [name withheld] … "[would] not go over well for promotion and tenure" (Pitt, Vaughn, Shamburger-Rosseau, & Harris, 2015).

These are words I will never forget from a person who took an interest in my success and was a *mentor*—someone I trusted, hands down. What had been communicated to me was that I was indeed the *Other*, and that I

Beyond Retention: Cultivating Spaces of Equity, Justice, and Fairness for Women of Color in U.S. Higher Education, pp. 189–211

was not just different, but fundamentally opposed to what was *right* (Hill Collins, 2000, 2009). My embodiment and soon-to-be family structure were perceived as wrong, not as an intentional choice (Mannis, 1999). As I took the elevator downstairs to exit the building, I dragged those damned controlling images (e.g., jezebel and welfare queen) (Benjamin, 1997; Harris-Perry, 2011; Hill Collins, 2009) with me. It did not matter that I had a PhD from a research-intensive university—a status that I thought would afford a degree of protection, status, and privilege (Orelus, 2013). What about my long, straight hair? Would that not somehow give me a *boost*, as Hill Collins (2005) notes "some … claim that hair texture has long been more important than skin color in racial politics" (p. 195). As I walked to my car and those statuses faded further into the background, it was still, somehow, not readily apparent that all that really mattered was that I was birthing a child as a single mom—one of the most branded experiences of motherhood, particularly for Black women, especially when we do not practice speaking for ourselves (Mannis, 1999; T. Stanley, 2005).

Wanting to thwart the danger that lurked ahead, I executed the strategy set before me. It was suggested that I purchase a ring and wear it. The next week, I went out and bought a 2-carat cubic zirconia ring, so that my committed relationship would be elevated to the status of being engaged and bring with it positive stereotypes. The strategy worked well. Hell, some people even thought I was married. What I should have realized is that "it [made] little sense in the long run for [this Black woman] to exchange one set of controlling images for another, even if positive stereotypes [brought] better treatment in the short run" (Hill Collins, 2009, p. 125). Not being fully awakened to my power as a Black woman and Black mother, I set up a meeting with my dean, as instructed, to express my commitment to the university and inform him that I looked forward to making continued contributions. Vacillating between shame and empowerment, I balanced moments of happiness as I prepared for the baby—while simultaneously, contributing a high level of teaching, research, and service which left me feeling exhausted. Leaving the dean's office, I thought, "Who knew academia would bring with it so much drama?" I was so naïve.

It is without question that Black women in the academy experience interlocking systems of oppression based on race, gender, and class bound by a matrix of domination (Crenshaw, 1989; Hill Collins, 2009). Black women are made to feel invisible and isolated (Wilder, Bertrand Jones, & Osborne-Lampkin, 2013) due to marginalization that is institutionalized in academia and situated in differently applied policies and procedures (Odhiambo & Charoenpantikul, 2011). This is evidenced by us comprising 3% of full-time teaching faculty (*Chronicle of Higher Educa-*

tion, 2010). Moreover, Black women also tend to be concentrated in lower ranks, with 4% serving in the position of associate or full professors (Ryu, 2010), revealing *outsider-within* status (Hill Collins, 1986), where we are considered "part of the whole but outside the main body" (hooks, 1990, p. 341). I wish, several years ago, when my counterstory of being a Black, single mom on the tenure track became a point of interest during a mentoring interaction, I would have resisted nice but negative advice. Likewise, I wish my mentor would have viewed my experience of living on the periphery not from a place of dispossession, but from "the site of radical possibility" and instead, "nourishe[d] my capacity to resist" (hooks, 1990, p. 341). What a powerful meeting that would have been instead of one that prepared me to maintain the status quo.

This is a story about one woman's journey in academia. Counterstorytelling moves experiences of being on the margin to the center. Counterstories emerge from within and interrogate dominant narratives that have been put forth as *truth* used to exert control and minimize or erase voice (Delgado & Stefancic, 2012; C. Stanley, 2007). Thus, I will utilize much of my personal narrative of being a Black, single mom, who is tenure seeking, as a context by which to explore critical incidents related to mentoring, spaces of resistance, and finding voice. By choosing to write about my experiences, I am continuing to heal and finding it cathartic as I draw strength from the discovery of self-knowledge and self-definition (Hill Collins, 2009). It is also my hope that by sharing what I have learned that my story (a) in some way supports others who are discovering ways to speak their truth, wherever they are in the process, and (b) offers institutions of higher learning examples of opportunities that can be leveraged to reposition mentoring as a powerful tool in academe, especially for those of us who live on the margins.

MENTORING

Mentoring for women in academia has been cited as a factor that contributes to professional success and career advancement (Gibson, 2004; Paludi, Martin, Stern, & DeFour, 2010). Yet, for Black women, access to and quality of mentoring still remain an issue (Edwards, Beverly, & Alexander-Snow, 2011), particularly for those who are on the tenure track (Holmes, Land, & Hinton-Hudson, 2007). While mentoring has various definitions, many would agree it involves a nurturing relationship between a senior and junior person, in which the senior ranked individual offers professional and psychosocial support to facilitate academic, personal, and career development via informal and formal means (Rowley, 1999; Thomas, 1990; Tillman, 2001). Senior colleagues who mentor can also serve in the capacity of role model, ally, and sponsor. A role model may not know that he/she is serving in this capacity, but nevertheless, offers an example for the junior person to follow, relative to achieving success (Crosby, 1999; Williams, 1994). An ally advocates for the individual or for a group of individuals to which he/she may not belong and takes on a social justice-vested role (Kendall, 2006). A sponsor is one who can offer support by using his/her position of privilege, power, and influence to help the junior colleague navigate politics and bureaucracy, gain power, and become situated differently in the university where recognition, promotion, and tangible rewards manifest (Ibarra, Carter, & Silva, 2010; Thomas, 2001).

Traditional narratives can be interrupted when more mentors serve in the role of ally and sponsor (Crawford & Smith, 2005; Dace, 2012; Tillman, 2001). Ntozake Shange notes, "being Black and a woman and an academic is a metaphysical dilemma" (Reid, 2012, p. 6). Accordingly, mentoring must be situated in such a way that it takes into account our lived experiences (Berry & Mizelle, 2006; Bova, 2002; C. Stanley & Lincoln, 2005). For example, Black, female faculty receive disproportionate amount of requests for service (Davis, Reynolds & Jones, 2011; Harley, 2008). I am no exception. The manifestation of good mentoring on behalf of the institution includes advocacy prior to the request being initiated as a way of minimizing stress and continuing to protect time for research and support work/life balance (Tindall & Williams, 2011). Ideally, institutional members would be able to clearly articulate why a particular Black, female faculty is being asked to serve. Does the request align with her strengths and interests? Has the institution created the type of environment that supports her in feeling empowered in her "no" (Griffin, 2013) regardless of who is asking (e.g., senior-level university administrator)?

Some mentoring relationships are assigned when one enters the academy, which may or not be helpful, as the presence of mentoring programs does not automatically equal support or successful outcomes, particularly for diverse faculty (Greene et al., 2008; C. Stanley, 2006). In fact, institutions are encouraged to be more intentional when exercising formal mentoring programs with the expectation that tenure-seeking faculty of color will participate. Pairing a more senior colleague with a (Black) female junior faculty member, for example, who does not understand or demonstrates disinterest in her lived experiences and scholarship, will not only prove to be detrimental, but can also lead to dissatisfaction, turnover intent or actual institutional departure (Odhiambo & Charoenpantikul, 2011; Patitu & Hinton, 2003). Likewise, assigning (Black, female) tenure-seeking faculty to senior colleagues who are not publishing is a set up for failure (Davis et al., 2011; Ortlieb, Biddix, & Doepker, 2010; Tillman, 2001).

It is crucial for Black, female academics to work a variety of mentoring arrangements (Wilson, 2012), including establishing relationships and maintaining networks outside of their respective departments or home institutions (Thomas & Hollenshead, 2001). Some of these outside arrangements may entail e-mentoring (Bierema & Merriam, 2002) via the use of e-mail, text, Skype, or other technological means. External mentoring can be particularly important when vulnerable faculty encounter microaggressions that occur in university settings (Pittman, 2010), especially when the offender is located at the faculty members' home institution. For me, outside mentoring with senior colleagues, e-mentoring, and peer mentoring have been ways to cope with the mundane extreme environmental stress (Carroll, 1998; Pierce, 1975) of working in academia, while remaining productive.

Peer Mentoring: Taking Off the Ring

Though mentoring in various forms is critical to advancement, Black, women faculty often employ peer mentoring as a success strategy (Edwards et al., 2011; Myers, 2002). Peer mentors serve in the role of mentor and protégé and tend to emerge from a like group where support is offered, technical information is shared, and feedback is given relative to career advancement (Kram & Isabella, 1985; Mullen, 2005). Sometimes, shifting "away from a hierarchical power relationship and traditional models of mentoring, we are ... able to regroup, resist, and change our expectations and behaviors via the supportive tool of peer mentoring" (Henderson, Hunter, & Hildreth, 2010, p. 34). This was particularly vital for me, as I had not revealed to any of my outside senior mentors the *strategy* that had been employed at my home institution. Out of fear, I hid the negative perceptions of my Black, single-motherhood experience in the academy on mentors who could have supported me through the process. I was locked in silence for a very long time—the type of silence bell hooks (1990, 2000) reminds us is unique and multifaceted.

About 3 years ago, I attended a conference and was speaking with one of my peer mentors about some of my struggles. I shared how beaten down I felt at work, the bullying that was occurring as a result of an unhealthy mentoring relationship at my home institution, as well as the turbulence I was encountering in my personal life—feeling ashamed to tell family and friends the extent I thought I had to go to in order to achieve tenure. I was mostly embarrassed and upset that I somehow convinced myself this was the only way. While marriage was always on the table, remembering that I was told that my situation would "not go over well for promotion and tenure," I forced myself to keep up a façade that outlasted the real commitment with my son's father. It is no surprise that when my peer mentor asked, "What's going on … you seem like you got a lot on your plate," everything poured out of me. Before I knew it, I did not care who was around as the tears started to flow, and I gave voice to what I was experiencing.

What my peer mentor helped me realize is that I was imprisoned, and if I wanted to move toward a place of radical resistance and begin practicing a stronger orientation toward freedom, I had to change my script, including what I was telling myself, and of course, take off the ring. The thought of it scared me. Yet, I knew the burden of the "bling" and what it represented had gotten to be too much to bear and my very soul was grieving the loss of who I was and wanted to become (Rockquemore & Laszloffy, 2008). Feeling empowered outside the walls of the conference as we waited for the poster presentations to begin, my peer mentor helped me resist by taking off the ring and preparing a packaged response that I could use when colleagues approached me about my relationship. "Circumstances have changed," is all I would say, accompanied with a look that conveyed, "I dare you to ask me something else."

I am learning that my marginalized living "offers [to me] the possibility of radical perspective from which to see and create, to imagine alternatives, new worlds" (hooks, 1990, p. 341). My peer mentor not only blessed me with advice on that day (e.g., important to live my truth) and offered emotional support, but also "nourished," in that moment, my ability to resist. I continue to utilize my peer mentors, as they have served as connectors to broader networks, sounding boards regarding my scholarship, collaborative partners on manuscripts and conference presentations, consultants regarding how to respond to microaggressions, and as friends, which appears to be consistent with peer mentor utilization in the literature (Diggs, Garrison-Wade, Estrada, & Galindo, 2009; Holmes et al., 2007).

MOTHERING

It was not until after the birth of my son and I returned to the academy, that I began to notice the depth of mothering responsibilities I was also taking on in service to the institution. Additionally, I was strapped with figuring out how to carve out quality time with my son while juggling productivity and my overall spiritual, mental, physical, emotional, and financial well-being (Thompson & Dey, 1998; Tindall & McWilliams, 2011). "You must publish," is what a mentor outside of my institution told me.

"No matter what you have going on … You have to find the time." While I believed this was true, especially if I decided to remain in academia, the burden of protecting my time mostly fell on me (Clardy, 2010)—the one who was, and is, still trying to find voice. The shifting that occurs as a result of moving between states of high visibility and tokenism to marginalization and invisibility (Gregory, 2001; Jones & Shorter-Gooden, 2003; Orelus, 2013), "is the uncomfortable nexus inhabited by Black women, which positions us as outsiders within the academy" (Henderson et al., 2010, p. 29). My mentor helped me develop strategies such as (a) writing away from the office, (b) having regularly scheduled check-ins to discuss my scholarship progress, (c) supporting me in assessing which service requests to accept and decline (Rockquemore & Laszloffy, 2008), particularly if they did not relate to my research, and (d) standing firm as I learned how to move from an oppressed "yes" to a graceful "no" (Berry & Mizelle, 2006; Griffin, 2013). Yet, she was outside of my home institution. Therefore, her ability to speak for me in a sponsorship role and influence changes in my backyard (e.g., number of service requests I was getting in the first place and level of administrative responsibilities I was being asked to take on without increased pay) was limited.

Students of color more often seek out faculty of color for academic advising, mentoring, and general support (Griffin & Reddick, 2011; Turner, 2002), and even refer to Black, female faculty as *second moms* (Carroll, 1998; Nzinga-Johnson, 2013a). While I feel a responsibility to supporting students, I have also found that when colleagues do not have the same type of service load and feel perfectly fine closing their door to focus on other commitments, these situations leave a *sistah* feeling drained. I am still figuring out how to more effectively incorporate my efforts into the tenure and promotion consideration process, which is problematic as these types of activities are usually not given credit through formal means in university settings (Diggs et al., 2009; Evans, 2007). As a way of practicing resistance, I have begun to give voice to my lived experiences in the narrative sections of the tenure and promotion materials I submit for review. While administration has at least acknowledged this conundrum for faculty of color and Black, female faculty, no formal policies or procedures have been institutionalized to address the issue. In situations like these, sponsorship is critical to thriving in academia (Thomas, 2001).

I have also started to embrace community mothering and *othermothering* as essential for survival and as a means of strength (Hill Collins, 1991; Hinton-Johnson, 2006). James (1993) denotes othermothering as the formal or informal acceptance of caring for another's offspring. Community mothering, which stems from othermothering, can be traced to African ideals of caring for the whole guided by respect for the collective and rooted in interdependence, social activism, and empowerment (Gilkes,

1980; Hill Collins, 1991; O'Reilly, 2004). "Motherhood can serve as a site where Black women express and learn the power of self-definition" (Hill Collins, 2009, p. 191). It is because of othermothering arrangements that I have felt that it is possible to bridge my roles as (single) bloodmother and academician (Hinton-Johnson, 2006) without adhering to the Strong Black Woman or Black Super Mom myth (Hill Collins, 2005, 2009). As I have become stronger in this belief, I have also turned my attention to maintaining balance between home and work (Gregory, 2001; Tindall & McWilliams, 2011).

So much of how my son has been raised while I have been on the tenure-track has been embedded in community mothering. For instance, when my son was an infant and my mom was mostly in Los Angeles taking care of her brother who had a stroke, a trusted colleague of mine, who was also tenure seeking, would mother my son on days that I had to go to campus for meetings that were outside of the 3-days a week childcare plan I had already budgeted for the month. She would step in when I needed to attend work meetings and events (often service related) that were scheduled at 7 A.M., after 6 P.M., or on the weekends, as the cost of drop-in care was nearly $50 each time. When she was not available, I would ask one of my son's teachers, another community mother, to intercede until I finished teaching at 7 P.M. Accommodations in teaching and meeting schedules, while simultaneously attacking dominant norms in the academy, are ways to support junior female faculty of color mothering on the tenure track, especially when they do not feel safe giving voice to their circumstances (Bushouse, 2013).

As the situation with my uncle has changed, my parents have become the primary othermothers for my son. It has been a blessing for Jaidon to receive care from his grandparents and teaching about our Caribbean roots and traditions, as well as for me to learn about motherwork directly from my mom. This has also strengthened our mother-daughter relationship. When colleagues say, "I don't know how you do it," relating to balancing the roles of academician and mom, I resist by saying, "Well, if it weren't for the support of my mom and dad who provide care and pour into my son so I can be on campus for 12 hours on a Saturday and Sunday working on a grant or a manuscript, for example, I don't know how I would do it either," paired with a smile. Thank God for empowered, packaged responses.

Othermothers and community mothers are not "babysitters," but instead, take on a critical role in transmitting culture, values, identity, and education to children (Hill Collins, 1994, 2009). While I could offer a flat response of, "I don't know how I do it either" or "It's not easy," and leave it at that, part of it boils down to the business of speaking my truth. The other part of it is continuing to practice breaking free of packaging responses in a way that makes others, even administrators, feel comfortable. When comments are made which gives rise to the image that I somehow magically accomplish all of my work and home responsibilities in isolation (i.e., Strong Black Woman or Black Super Mom myth), I resist by giving voice. Yet, even in my new found moments of truth speaking, when I am constantly "bombarded with warped images of [my] humanity" (Harris-Perry, 2011, p. 29), I still struggle with resisting the elements that allow my "[tilting] and [bending] … to fit the distortion" (p. 29) in academia.

FROM MAMA TO MAMMY

Many of the experiences of Black women in academia have been likened to "maids" (Harley, 2008), "work mules" (Harley, 2008), and "mammies" (Benjamin, 1997). While the mammy stereotype was dominant during slavery, it still persists in the academy today. "[The] primary role of Mammy was to provide domestic service, characterized by long work hours with little or no financial compensation" (Bryant et al., 2005, p. 314), where "subordination, nurturance, and constant self-sacrifice were expected" (p. 314). I agreed to chair a search, which I did not know also meant being strapped with the burden of paying for candidate meals. When I inquired about support upfront, I was told I would be reimbursed. Having personal funds when one candidate came to campus did not mean that I would have money when the remaining candidates arrived. Remembering I was told that the process needed to be as consistent as possible, I feared that if everyone was not taken to the same amount of meals that this would somehow potentially result in a failed search. A successful search held the possibility of bringing relief. No longer would I be the sole full-time faculty member in a very large program, while also serving as program coordinator. I needed the search to be successful. So, I took a birthday card my parents had given me that contained a $100 bill and took remaining candidates to various meals. When that money ran out, I moved on to the Valentine's Day card that my parents had given me, which contained $50.

Here I was—the mule, maid, and the mammy—keeping the institutional household intact by any means necessary, even if that meant not having enough resources for my own home. I felt prostituted, in a sense (Lugo-Lugo, 2012), and the institution was my pimp. As I turned inward and began to understand how I was situated, I sought ways to resist. I used feigned subservience (Rockquemore & Laszloffy, 2008) as one way of existing on the margins, which entails masking ways to challenge dominant norms. As the search was in progress and I sought reimbursement, I made sure to send emails to the appropriate personnel:

> Hi [name omitted]. I hope all is well. I am writing to inquire about the reimbursement paperwork that was submitted … Just trying to gauge when they might be making their way to [name omitted], as the monies spent in support of the search were for bills.

As the process moved along, I sent friendly follow-up inquiries noting, "As the monies used in support of the search were actually set aside to pay bills, I am wondering about the time frame for receipt as I still have outstanding expenses that were not paid last month."

NO MORE MAMMY: WHERE'S MY MONEY?

When the search ended, which resulted in not one, but two, full-time tenure-track faculty members being hired, I gave voice to my lived experience when I went in to speak with an administrator in the chain of command. I went regarding a salary increase, given that I was doing the work of the three full-time faculty members who were no longer at the institution. To my surprise, the person told me that my initiation of conversation regarding salary increase was interpreted as a lack of support directed at him/her. My outside mentor was right when I spoke with her the day before the meeting: "Now, listen to me carefully. Be sure to tell him, 'I know that you support me.' Listen to my words." While her words strongly resonated, I hung up the phone thinking, "He knows I know he supports me." In her wisdom, she was trying to prepare me for what she knew would likely happen.

I tried to remember my mentor's framing. In that moment, the Holy Spirit and my counseling skills quickly kicked in as I tried to "step to his side," a strategy attributed to William Ury (1993) as noted by Babcock and Laschever (2003) in *Women Don't Ask*. I acknowledged the feelings that came up for him, but also asked if I could offer a counternarrative. I briefly shared what debasement felt like for me as I described the lengths I had gone to in order to achieve a *successful* search—a search he had previously complimented me on—that had been executed so well. I also communicated the type of mothering arrangements that were being engaged in as I made varied university contributions tied to the amount of responsibilities that were thrust upon my shoulders. I ended my resistance with, "I'm coming to you to ask you to partner with me in figuring out solutions for pay that are more commensurate, given my high level of contributions." I put forth the request for service as an ally and sponsor.

The person's body language and tone shifted. He acknowledged that he had spoken with someone in a position higher in the chain of command, in which he said, "I told them, 'we're killing Jenelle. We gotta get her some help!'" In that room, I gave voice to no longer being willing to simply accept what I was being given (Babcock & Laschever, 2003). Yet, it was also painfully evident to me that the institution knew exactly the type of battle-fatigued position in which I was functioning. They took care of me *just enough* and then put me back to work on the academic corner. Prior to the end of the meeting, the "ally" described above informed me that a joint meeting would be initiated with another person in the chain of command regarding my salary. I was told, "When we get to the meeting, let me do the talking." A month later, when we got to the meeting and after pleasantries were exchanged, the *ally* looked to me to discuss why we were there. Shocked, I stared at him and said, "I'll let you start off." As I turned the floor over to the person who I thought would shift roles and serve as my "sponsor," the reason for meeting was communicated devoid of any passion. The other person in the chain of command informed me of all the reasons why the salary increase, at that time, would not be possible or at least a year off, at best.

Though, I was dissatisfied with the "no" or "not now," I was more disappointed with the actions of my ally/sponsor and how the message was framed from the person higher in the chain of command. "It would be nice to make people happy," in relation to a salary increase. Nice? Being stunned and not quite sure how to find my voice in the moment through the rage and tears that were starting to well up in my eyes, I struggled to find voice which articulated that the conversation was not at all about being "nice," but about being fair and equitable. The moment reminded me of my counselor's recent suggestion: "You look to the institution to take care of you. You must look to you to take care of you." I gave away my control assuming that "this 'someone else' [would] be fair and that … judgments about the value of [my] work [would] be accurate" (Babcock & Laschever, 2008, p. 41). This is a similar mindset that prevented me from negotiating my base salary even before I accepted the position as I naively assumed, "Of course they'll pay me what I'm worth." This perception, when not met with favorable outcomes, can impact self-confidence, self-esteem, subsequent job offers, and quality of life (Babcock & Laschever, 2003, 2008; Thomas, 2001).

Salary differentials among women faculty of color and Black, female faculty, in particular, have been long cited as contributors to job dissatisfaction, decreased retention, and higher rates of battle fatigue and workplace stress (Evans, 2007; Lee, 2011; Reznulli, Grant, & Kathuria, 2006; Wilson, 2012). Though strategies focused on improving my financial situation ensue, I no longer choose to remain silent and continue feeling helpless. As I have been processing the situation with my counselor and outside peer/senior mentors, I contemplate next steps and how I can continue giving voice in academic spaces while I am here. "Any individual Black woman who is forced to remain 'motionless on the outside,' can develop the 'inside' of a changed consciousness as a sphere of freedom" (Hill Collins, 2000, p. 129). Consequently, I have begun to access private and shared safe spaces as ways to increase self-knowledge, empowerment, and self-definition. I vigorously seek out examples of those who give voice as I am unearthing the courage daily to speak up and out.

FINDING VOICE: SEEING, HEARING, READING, AND TRYING ON EXAMPLES

I opened up my e-mail one day to find in my inbox information regarding the Faculty Women of Color in the Academy 2013 National Conference sponsored by the University of Illinois, Urbana Champaign. What I experienced there was life changing. One of the critical incidents I encountered shortly after the poster presentations was a woman whose work had been selected for presentation to the larger group. The woman had recently given birth. When she took the stage, her baby girl was on her hip. And, I'll be damned if she did not move through her research with her child in her arms. It was one of the most powerful things I had ever witnessed, especially when I was at my institution, a few years back, feeling as though I needed to conceal the fact that I had a child—a beautiful, Black, baby boy out of wedlock.

A second critical incident came in the form of storytelling that I encountered during the conference. One panel session focused on moving from associate to full professor and how to position oneself for success. A panelist whose narrative strongly resonated with me was Dr. Elaine Richardson. She told her story of raising her kids, living a life on the streets, getting a doctorate, and transitioning to academia. Her raw honesty and wisdom was unbelievable. I was so taken by everything she was offering to us that I was texting senior and peer mentors to share with them what I was experiencing in the moment, and how empowered I felt.

Throughout the conference, I heard from so many successful women—associate and full professors—as well as women in upper level administration, some who had been single moms at one point or another in their careers, telling their stories and sharing their journey—bumps and triumphs. There they stood, alive with strength and voice, firmly speaking their truth. There I sat, soaking it all in, each and every word. Their stories and that entire space gave me courage later on to open up to my sister scholars at my institution regarding the weariness, the "bling" that I took off exactly 1 year earlier, and my fragmented state as I navigated being a Black, single mom and an academician. As I received support from them, I also listened to their stories and felt connected.

Mentoring happens in different ways and for varying lengths of time. Although I did not previously know any of the senior women at the conference, they provided mentorship. These women served as role models, advisors, consultants, offered psychosocial support, and shared resources. Two such resources that have been added to the list of tools used to empower myself and support other peer protégés of color in the academy include *Presumed Incompetent: The Intersections of Race and Class for Women in Academia* (Gutiérrez y Muhs, Niemann, González, & Harris, 2012) and *Mothers in Academia* (Castañeda & Isgro, 2013). The first text helped reinforce our truth, "we are not crazy," when we encounter aggression from students as we inform them that we are to be addressed by our title of Dr., are mistaken for a student, staff, or secretary—anything other than a contributing faculty member—or simply dismissed. The second text has offered varied perspectives of what it means to be mom and female in the academy. Combining the latter resource with the readings of Audre Lorde, Patricia Hill Collins, and bell hooks is helping me to go inward and discover what it means to be a Black, single mom and a Black female in the academy.

The third critical incident came in the form of song. Surviving in academia is also spiritual. "Tested and tried, I have come through. Shiny and whole, I've been made new. Feel the warmth of my shine were words written by Dr. Ollie Watts Davis and then sang to us at the conference by The University of Illinois Black Chorus. As I sat there weeping, I reflected on my fragmentation and thought, "I am more than who they think I am. I am more than what I've been feeling." Turning to one's religion is not helpful for all Black people, however, for many, the role of faith, religion, and spirituality are ways we buffer the effects of racism, sexism, and microaggressions in the workplace (Holmes, Duncan, Miller, & Holmes, 2011; Smith, 2004). Prayer and meditation are also coping methods and forms of resistance Black women faculty employ (Patitu & Hinton, 2003; Shorter-Gooden, 2004) to minimize the toll that academia takes on one's soul (Rockquemore & Laszloffy, 2008). Needless to say, I was only too happy to receive a song that affirmed my value, offered me strength, and spoke to my spirit in a conference setting, which represented a healing space.

I am still astounded when I encounter individuals in my institutional backyard who try to offer a safe space, while at the same time, engaging in minimization tactics. For instance, while it may be suggested that I speak up about fair and equitable salary given workload intensification, it is often noted that I keep my son out of the conversation manifesting the conflict between *ideal worker* and mother (Williams, 2010). "[Academics] must often suppress their connections to family, community, culture and any other evidence of their corporeal existence in order to be touted as 'ideal workers' within capitalist rational economic models of productivity" (Nzinga-Johnson, 2013b, p. 98). Yet, the ability to provide economically is a historical and cultural component of what constitutes the experience of ideal worker and mother for me as well as for many other Black women (Hill Collins, 1991, 2009).

The space that I inhabit as a Black, female faculty and single mom in academia is a double bind (Jones & Shorter-Gooden, 2003; Stanley, 2006; Thomas & Dey, 1998). Though I am still learning to give voice to my lived experiences verbally and in writing, I am speaking for myself by bringing my son into the conversation and work-related spaces, in large part, because I saw and read examples of other Black women doing so. Sometimes, I come to campus in what Nelly describes, "stomping in my air force ones," particularly when I am in writing mode while sporting my newly garnered kinks and coils since undergoing the big chop. When people comment, I am only too eager to respond, "I'm undergoing a transition." Using my hand to pat my hair, as I tilt my head to one side, I add, "This means change is coming," coupled with a smile. My expression of dress, hair, beauty, speech, writing, and "style [has become] the canvas of [my] cultural yearning" (Hill Collins, 2005, p. 209), in which everything about me craves freedom.

The development of freeing spaces right in one's institutional backyard is critical for supporting Black female faculty (Clark & Davis, 2011). "The right to be Black *and* female *and* respected pervades everyday conversations among African-American women" (Hill Collins, 2009, p. 126). Where do we place that in the walls of the ivory tower when safe spaces are either not prevalent or nonexistent on campus? Supporting attendance at conferences that specifically speak to our embodiment as Black females in academia is vital. However, it is also imperative that home institutions offer support, resources, and the infrastructure needed for the development of nurturing spaces on campus where we work daily.

NAVIGATING SILENCE AND SPEAKING MY TRUTH

I remember sitting in a meeting where one of the agenda items was to discuss how instructors were infusing multicultural content in their courses. As the topic of the hour moved to the top of the agenda and instructors began to share, I was directly asked, "Jenelle, what do you teach in your courses?" Feeling put-off, I stared at the individual who asked the question. This person was not only leading the meeting, but was also an assigned institutional mentor. I immediately felt confused as I was trying to decipher whether a microaggression had occurred. I did not mind talking about what I taught and the pedagogical techniques used, but *something* rose in the pit of my stomach—was I being targeted as I was the only Black (female) faculty in the room? I remained silent. The individual seemed disinterested in what others were saying as a short while later, the question was put forth a second time directly to me. I responded, "I'll weigh in, but I would like to hear how other people are infusing content into their courses." I was upset and felt alone. Where in the hell were my allies and sponsors? Although I said *something* as a way of resisting, it did not represent the breadth and depth of what I wanted and needed to share.

On the way home, I processed the experience with two peer mentors. I wanted to revisit the situation with my assigned mentor, but I did not know how. I eventually decided to write:

> Hi [name omitted] ... I have been processing what occurred ... [and] ... it seemed like questions regarding multiculturalism were directed primarily to me. I have been going back and forth trying to figure out why.... While [instructor name omitted] identified his class as one in which he teaches multicultural content in relation to [topic omitted], I felt like you continued to direct questions toward me. I am wondering if there was an underlying assumption operating in the meeting, and that is, faculty of color either know or ought to know about multicultural content, and they are the ones that are responsible for teaching it. Once ... we were assessing a student, who happens to identify as African American. You turned to me and asked if I thought the student was a good role model. I was baffled, as this question was not posed to anyone else in the room.... As you know, research often suggests that faculty of color undergo unique experiences in academia.... When you continued to direct questions about multicultural content primarily to me yesterday, I felt very alienated as a person of color. Is it not everyone's responsibility to be informed? As my mentor, I am wondering if we can initiate dialogue regarding the above.

While I had other individuals lay eyes on the e-mail prior to sending it out, "I was not expecting a critical avalanche that had the power in its intensity to crush spirit ... [and] push [me] into silence" (hooks, 1990, p. 339). What I received was an e-mailed response that left me feeling more marginalized and isolated. I also became withdrawn as the bullying and toxicity which can be commonplace in academia began (Pitt et al., in press; Wilson, 2012). Exclusion from activities that would support the achievement of goals and objectives related to tenure and promotion initiated. In trying to enlist an "ally," who was someone in the chain of command (i.e., majority female), the person wished not to become involved. Silence hurts. As the mundane extreme environmental stress (Carroll,

1998; Pierce, 1975) worsened, I accessed senior mentors outside the institution, union representative knowledge (to stay informed of my rights), and support from campus diversity champions. I refused to meet with the *aggressor* alone from that point. Efforts to reach out were at best failed attempts (Orelus, 2013).

At the height of the craziness, I remember one day stepping off the elevator to exit toward the rear of the building. I saw the individual, and I stood frozen, as we were the only two there. After a few seconds, I turned around and walked out the front of the building. I realized I was experiencing fear and intimidation. As a way of coping, I initiated therapeutic support and had my family and peer/senior mentors outside the institution keep me uplifted in prayer. I recited scriptures focused on confidence, faith, and forgiveness. I needed to know that my PhD, my worth, and purpose equated to more than what I was experiencing. While, things finally subsided as the assigned mentor became unassigned and eventually left the institution, I think about (missed) opportunities the institution had for individuals to serve in the role of ally and sponsor.

I have been practicing moving my silenced experiences to the center (Patton, 2004) throughout university spaces (e.g., campuswide diversity forums), and thus, also becoming empowered enough to simply "ask the question:"

> I acknowledge the panel is speaking to campus diversity and it's with intention that I ask this question that speaks to a particular segment of our campus. A few years back, I was told that being Black and a single mom in a city like [withheld] ... "[would] not go over well for promotion and tenure." [When] I attended the Faculty Women of Color in the Academy National Conference ... I realized that there [was] another way of existing in this world called academia. I [also] acknowledge that while I'm not a woman administrator of color, but given what [woman administrator of color's name withheld] has undergone recently, I'm wondering if the panel could speak to how [name of university withheld] can more fully support women faculty of color and women administrators of color, so folks are not suffering in silence?

Though time was running short, what I received was a response from one panelist (senior-level university administrator) that indicated a singular entity on campus would look into efforts that would do more to support women administrators of color. It was a response wrapped largely in silence. There I was speaking my flat-footed truth—"a story or statement that is straightforward, unshakable, and unembellished" (Bell-Scott, 1998, p. xix) and encountering minimalism. I was grateful that I turned inward and spoke my truth to power. It was something that needed to be said, given the context of the university conversation that I thought was occurring. In some ways, it was more about putting the focus back on the institution and having them examine, in the moment and over the long haul, prevailing sociopolitical and cultural norms that are not only pervasive in the academy, but also exist as a way of keeping many of us on the margins (Diggs et al., 2009; Orelus, 2013; Patton, 2004).

Interestingly, three specific events occurred thereafter. The next day, I encountered a majority male administrator who seemed to make an intentional effort to speak to me. Though, I saw the person pretty regularly before, on that day, not only were inquiries made relative to how things were going for me, but compliments were also offered regarding service tasks I was engaging in on behalf of the university. The next week, I encountered a majority female administrator who told me privately, "I was going to send you an e-mail … Thank you for standing up for us women in there." The next month, after leaving a university-level service committee meeting, a majority female tenured faculty member and I stood talking in the parking lot. Before we parted ways, she mentioned, "By the way, I wasn't there, but I heard you asked a question at the forum last month and no one really said anything …"

CONCLUSION

Silence can mean many things. While for one person it can signify a struggle to speak truth, for another, it can be perceived as a lack of care or indifference. "When the silence is broken and faculty of color do choose to speak, many … are not yet prepared to listen to the narratives" (Stanley, 2006, p. 702). Finding the courage to speak and being met with silence is a hurtful experience. If institutions of higher education are truly committed to dismantling extant dominant structures and pursuing inclusive spaces with a sense of urgency, then it is critical that our narratives, which are often wrapped in vulnerability, are met with openness and a sense of social responsibility. As mentors move in and out of the roles of advocate, coach, advisor, sponsor, and ally, it is important for universities to not only develop programs that demonstrate an understanding of the lived experiences of their constituents, but to also intentionally seek out opportunities to support those who feel marginalized. I think an important opportunity was missed at the forum. If one institutional member whose traditional embodiment leverages privilege were also standing and speaking alongside this Black, single mom on the tenure track, publicly interrogating pervasive structures that exist in academia, they could serve as a role model for others in power desiring to do the same. In this way, faculty members or administrators of color, in the future, are not standing alone. Individuals who are responsible for developing support programs must be taught what it means to deliver these services and truly function in the various roles in which mentors serve.

As I continue navigating the bumpy terrain of academia, I wonder who speaks for me—out loud, in the open, outside of my group? While I am still holding the institution accountable and *waiting* on a response to the above, I am learning to speak for myself. "The master's tools will never dismantle the master's house. They may allow us temporarily to beat him at this own game, but they will never enable us to bring about genuine change" (Lorde, 1984, p. 112). The transition from flowing in and out of silence to consistently and outwardly speaking truth is coming from the internal fire of rejecting master narratives, discovering who I am, and knowing who I want to be. It is this place of empowerment, self-definition, and self-knowledge that I am stepping into and embracing (Hill Collins, 2009). People have to practice interrupting the status quo. I am talking about people like me who live on the periphery and resist from the margins, but also administrators who expect to retain faculty of color for the long haul. Individuals have to try on the experience of interrupting, stand in that space, and encounter all of what the experience brings. This level of consciousness needs to be everywhere at all times. Effective institutional members who "fight" alongside us as we work to decenter and dismantle sociopolitical dominance that keeps us marginalized are not at all silent. These are the differences between "mentors" and those who radically serve as allies and sponsors.

REFERENCES

Babcock, L., & Laschever, S. (2003). *Women don't ask: Negotiation and the gender divide*. Princeton, NJ: Princeton University Press.

Babcock, L., & Laschever, S. (2008). *Ask for it: How women can use the power of negotiation to get what they really want*. New York, NY: Bantam-Dell.

Bell-Scott, P. (1998). Telling flat-footed truths: An introduction. In P. Bell-Scott & J. Johnson-Bailey (Eds.), *Flat-footed truths: Telling Black women lives* (pp. xvii–xx). New York, NY: Henry Holt and Company.

Benjamin, L. (Ed.). (1997). *Black women in the academy: Promises and Perils*. Gainesville, FL: University Press of Florida.

Berry, T., & Mizelle, N. (Eds.). (2006). *From oppression to grace: Women of color and their dilemmas within the academy*. Sterling, VA: Stylus.

Bierema, L. L., & Merriam, S. B. (2002). E-mentoring: Using computer mediated communication to enhance the mentoring process. *Innovative Higher Education, 26*(3), 211–227.

Bova, B. (2000). Mentoring revisited: The Black woman's experience. *Mentoring & Tutoring: Partnership in Learning, 8*(1), 5–16.

Bryant, R., Coker, A., Durodoye, B., McCollum, V., Pack-Brown, S., Constantine, M., & O'Bryant, B. (2005). Having our say: African American women, diversity, and counseling. *Journal of Counseling and Development, 83*(3), 313–319.

Bushouse, B. (2013). Supporting academic mothers: Creating a work environment with choices. In M. Castañeda & K. Isgro (Eds.), *Mothers in academia* (pp. 213–225). New York, NY: Columbia University Press.

Carroll, G. (1998). *Environmental stress and African Americans: The other side of the moon*. Westport, CT: Praeger.

Castañeda, M., & Isgro, K. (Eds.). (2013). *Mothers in academia*. New York, NY: Columbia University Press.

Chronicle of Higher Education. (2010). *Almanac of higher education 2009–2010*. Retrieved from http://chronicle.com/section/Almanac-of-Higher-Education/141/.

Clardy, P. (2010). "Amazing grace:" Examining one woman's induction into the academy. In C. Robinson & P. Clardy (Eds.), *Tedious journeys: Autoethnography by women of color in academe* (pp. 35–59). New York, NY: Peter Lang.

Clark, S., & Davis, D. (2011). Women of color in the academy. *Equality Diversity and Inclusion: An International Journal, 30*(5), 431–436.

Crenshaw, K. (1989). Demarginalizing the intersection of race and sex: A Black feminist critique of antidiscrimination doctrine, feminist theory and antiracist policies. *University of Chicago Legal Forum*, 139–167.

Crawford, K., & Smith, D. (2005). The we and the us: Mentoring African American women. *Journal of Black Studies, 36*(1), 52–67.

Crosby, F. J. (1999). The developing literature on developmental relationships. In A. J. Murrell, F. J. Crosby, & R. J. Ely (Eds.), *Mentoring dilemmas: Developmental relationships within multicultural organizations* (pp. 3–20). Mawah, NJ: Erlbaum.

Dace, K. (Ed.) (2012). *Unlikely allies in the academy: Women of color and White women in conversation*. New York, NY: Routledge.

Davis, D., Reynolds, R., & Jones, T. (2011). Promoting the inclusion of tenure earning Black women in academe: Lessons for leaders in education. *Florida Journal of Educational Administration & Policy, 5*(1), 28–41.

Delgado, R., & Stefancic, J. (2012). *Critical race theory: An introduction*. New York, NY: New York University Press.

Diggs, G., Garrison-Wade, D., Estrada, D., & Galindo, R. (2009). Smiling faces and colored spaces: The experiences of faculty of color pursing tenure in the academy. *Urban Review, 41*, 312–333.

Edwards, N., Beverly, M., & Alexander-Snow, M. (2011). Troubling success: Interviews with Black female faculty. *Florida Journal of Educational Administration & Policy, 5*(1), 14–27.

Evans, S. (2007). Women of color in American higher education. *Thought & Action, 23*, 131–138.

Gibson, S. (2004). Being mentored: The experience of women faculty. *Journal of Career Development, 30*, 173–187.

Gilkes, C. (1980). Holding back the ocean with a broom: Black women and community work. In L. Rodgers-Rose (Ed.), *The Black woman* (pp. 217–232). London, England: SAGE.

Greene, H., O' Connor, K., Good, A., Ledford, C., Peel, B., & Zhang, G. (2008). Building a support system toward tenure: Challenges and needs of tenure-track faculty in colleges of education. *Mentoring & Tutoring: Partnership in Learning, 16*(4), 429–447.

Gregory, S. T. (2001). Black faculty women in the academy: History, status, and future. *The Journal of Negro Education, 70*(3), 124–138.

Griffin, K. (2013). The calculus of yes and no: How one professor makes decisions about academic service. *Thought & Action, 29*, 35–43.

Griffin, K., & Reddick, R. (2011). Surveillance and sacrifice: Gender differences in the mentoring patterns of Black Professors at predominantly White research universities. *American Educational Research Journal, 48*(5), 1032–1057.

Gutiérrez y Muhs, G., Niemann, Y., González, C., & Harris, A. (Eds.). (2012). *Presumed incompetent: The intersections of race and class for women in academia.* Boulder, CO: University Press of Colorado.

Harley, D. (2008). Maids of Academe: African American women faculty at predominantly White institutions. *Journal of African American Studies, 12*(1), 19–36.

Harris-Perry, M. (2011). *Sister citizen: Shame, stereotypes, and Black women in America.* CT: Yale University Press.

Henderson, T., Hunter, A., & Hildreth, G. (2010). Outsiders within the academy: Strategies for resistance and mentoring African American women. *Michigan Family Review, 14*(1), 28–41.

Hill Collins, P. (1986). Learning from the outsider within: The sociological significance of Black feminist thought. *Social Problems, 33*, 514–532.

Hill Collins, P. (1991). The meaning of motherhood in Black culture and Black mother-daughter relationships. In P. Bell-Scott, B. Guy-Sheftall, J. Royster, J. Sims-Wood, M. DeCosta-Willis, & L. Fultz (Eds.), *Double stitch: Black women write about mothers & daughters* (pp. 42–60). New York, NY: Beacon Press.

Hill Collins, P. (1994). Shifting the center: Race, class, and feminist theorizing about motherhood. In E. Nakano Glenn, G. Chang, & L. Rennie Forcey (Eds.), *Mothering: Ideology, experience, and agency* (pp. 45–65). NY: Routledge.

Hill Collins, P. (2000). It's all in the family: Intersections of gender, race, and nation. In U. Narayan & S. Harding (Eds.), *Decentering the center: Philosophy for a multicultural, postcolonial, and feminist world* (pp. 156–176). Bloomington, IN: Indiana University Press.

Hill Collins, P. (2005). *Black sexual politics: African Americans, gender, and the new racism.* New York, NY: Routledge.

Hill Collins, P. (2009). *Black feminist thought: Knowledge, consciousness, and the politics of empowerment* (3rd ed.). New York, NY: Routledge Classics.

Hinton-Johnson, K. (2006). Choosing my best thing. Black motherhood and academia. In T. Berry & N. Mizelle (Eds.), *From oppression to grace: Women of color and their dilemmas within the academy* (pp. 155–167). Sterling, VA: Stylus.

Holmes, K., Duncan, E., Miller, K., & Holmes, B. (2011). In their own words: Sistah colleague circle embraces womanist collaboration. *Women in Higher Education, 20*(9), 24–26.

Holmes, S., Land, L., & Hinton-Hudson, V. (2007). Race still matters: Considerations for mentoring Black women in academe. *The Negro Educational Review, 58,* 105–129.

hooks, b. (1990). Marginality as site of resistance. In R. Ferguson, M. Gever, T. Minh-ha, & C. West (Eds.), *Out there: Marginalization and contemporary cultures* (pp. 341–343). Cambridge, MA: MIT Press.

hooks, b. (2000). *Feminist theory: From margin to center* (2nd ed.). Boston, MA: South End Press.

Ibarra, H., Carter, N., & Silva, C. (2010). Why men still get more promotions than women. *Harvard Business Review, 88*(9), 80–85.

James, S. (1993). Mothering: A possible Black feminist link to social transformation? In S. James & A. Busia (Eds.), *Theorizing Black feminisms: The visionary pragmatism of Black women* (pp. 44–54). London, England: Routledge.

Jones, C., & Shorter-Gooden, K. (2003). *Shifting: The double lives of Black women in America.* New York, NY: Harper-Collins.

Kendall, F. (2006). *Understanding white privilege: creating pathways to authentic relationships across race.* New York, NY: Routledge.

Kram, K., & Isabella, L. (1985). Mentoring alternatives: The role of peer relationships in career development. *Academy of Management Journal, 28*(1), 110–132.

Lee, J. (2011). Does universalism hold in academia?: Focusing on women and racial minority faculty. *Journal of the Professoriate, 6*(1), 48–66.

Lorde, A. (1984). *Sister outsider: Essays & Speeches by Audre Lorde.* Freedom, CA: Crossing Press.

Lugo-Lugo, C. (2012). A prostitute, a servant, and a customer-service representative: A Latina in academia. In G. Gutiérrez y Muhs, Y. Niemann, C. González, & A. Harris (Eds.), *Presumed incompetent: The intersections of race and class for women in academia* (pp. 40–49). Boulder, CO: University Press of Colorado.

Mannis, V. (1999). Single mothers by choice. *Family Relations, 48*(2), 121–128.

Mullen, C. (2005). *The mentorship primer.* New York, NY: Peter Lang.

Myers, L. (2002). *A broken silence: Voices of African American women in the academy.* Westport, CT: Greenwood.

Nzinga-Johnson, S. (Ed.). (2013a). Introduction: Extending the boundaries. In *Laboring positions: Black women, mothering and the academy* (pp. 1–32). Bradford, Ontario, Canada: Demeter Press.

Nzinga-Johnson, S. (Ed.). (2013b). Resisting with child: Black women's embodied negotiations of motherhood in the academy. In *Laboring positions: Black women, mothering and the academy* (pp. 91–110). Bradford, Ontario, Canada: Demeter Press.

Odhiambo, E., & Charoenpantikul, C. (2011). Marginalization: A continuing problem in higher education. In V. Yenika-Agbaw & A. Hidalgo-de (Ed.), *Jesús* (Eds.), *Race, women of color, and the state university system: Critical reflections* (pp. 62–79). Lanham, MD: University Press of America.

O'Reilly, A. (2004). *Mother outlaws: Theories and practices of empowered mothering.* Toronto, Ontario, Canada: Women's Press.

Orelus, P. W. (2013). The institutional cost of being a professor of color: Unveiling micro-aggression, racial [in]visibility, and racial profiling through the lens of critical race theory. *Current Issues in Education, 16*(2), 1–10.

Ortlieb, E. T., Biddix, J. P., & Doepker, G. M. (2010). A collaborative approach to higher education induction. *Active Learning in Higher Education, 11*(2), 109–118.

Paludi, M., Martin, J., Stern, T., & DeFour, D. (2010). Mentoring women in academia and business. In C. Rayburn, F. Denmark, M. Reuder, & A. Austria (Eds.), *Handbook for women mentors: Transcending barriers of stereotype, race, and ethnicity* (pp. 80–108). Westport, CT: Praeger.

Patitu, C., & Hinton, K. (2003). The experiences of African American women faculty and administrators in higher education: Has anything changed? *New Directions for Student Services, 104,* 79–93.

Patton, T. (2004). Reflections of a Black woman professor: Racism and sexism in academia. *Howard Journal of Communications, 15*(3), 185–200.

Pierce, C. (1975). The mundane extreme environment and its effect on teaming. In S. G. Brainard (Ed.), *Learning disabilities: Issues and recommendations for research* (pp. 111–119). Washington DC: National Institute of Education, Department of Health, Education, and Welfare.

Pitt, J. S., Vaughn, S., Shamburger-Rousseau, A., & Harris, L. (2015). Black women in academia: The invisible life. In J. Martin (Ed.), *Racial battle fatigue: Insights from the front lines of social justice advocacy* (pp. 209–223). Santa Barbara, CA: Praeger.

Pittman, C. (2010). Race and gender oppression in the classroom: The experiences of women faculty of color with White male students. *Teaching Sociology, 38*(3), 183–196.

Reid, P. (2012). Black and female in academia. *The Presidency, 15*(2), 6.

Renzulli, L., Grant, L., & Kathuria, S. (2006). Race, gender, and the wage gap: Comparing faculty salaries in predominately white and historically Black colleges and universities. *Gender and Society, 20*(4), 491–510.

Rockquemore, K., & Laszloffy, T. (2008). *The Black academic's guide to winning tenure without losing your soul.* Boulder, CO: Lynne Rienner.

Rowley, J. (1999). Supporting teacher: The good mentor. *Educational Leadership. 56*(8), 20–22.

Ryu, M. (2010). Minorities in higher education: Twenty-fourth status report. Washington, DC: American Council of Education Publishing.

Shorter-Gooden, K. (2004). Multiple resistance strategies: How African American women cope with racism and sexism. *Journal of Black Psychology, 30*(3), 406–425.

Smith, W. (2004). Black faculty coping with racial battle fatigue: The campus racial climate in a post-civil rights era. In D. Cleveland (Ed.), *A long way to go: Conversations about race by African American faculty and graduate students* (pp. 171–190). New York, NY: Peter Lang.

Stanley, C. (2006). Coloring the academic landscape: Faculty of color breaking the silence in predominantly White colleges and universities. *American Educational Research Journal, 43*(4), 701–736.

Stanley, C. (2007). When counter narratives meet master narratives in the journal editorial-review process. *Educational Researcher, 36*(1), 14–24.

Stanley, C., & Lincoln, Y. (2005). Cross-race faculty mentoring. *Change, 37*(2), 44–50.

Stanley, T. (2005). The one with the baby: Single-mothering in academia. In R. Bassett (Ed.), *Parenting and professing: Balancing family work with an academic career* (pp. 82–88). Nashville, TN: Vanderbilt University Press.

Thomas, D. (1990). The impact of race on managers' experiences of developmental Relationships (mentoring and sponsorship): An intra-organizational study. *Journal of Organizational Behavior, 11*(6), 479–492.

Thomas, D. (2001). The truth about mentoring minorities: Race matters. *Harvard Business Review, 79*(4), 98.

Thomas, G., & Hollenshead, C. (2001). Resisting from the margins: The coping strategies of Black women and other women of color faculty members at a research university. *Journal of Negro Education, 70*(3), 166–175.

Thompson, C., & Dey, E. (1998). Pushed to the margins: Sources of stress for African American college and university faculty. *The Journal of Higher Education, 69*(3), 324–345.

Tillman, L. (2001). Mentoring African American faculty in predominantly White institutions. *Research in Higher Education, 42*(3), 295–325.

Tindall, N., & McWilliams, M. (2011). The myth and mismatch of balance: Black female professors' constructions of balance, integration, and negotiation of work and life. In E. Gilchrist (Ed.), *Experiences of single African-American women professors: With this ph.d., I thee wed* (pp. 59–82). Lanham, MD: Lexington Books.

Turner, C. (2002). Women of color in academe: Living with multiple marginality. *The Journal of Higher Education, 73*(1), 73–93.

Wilder, J., Bertrand Jones, T., & Osborne-Lampkin, L. (2013). A profile of Black women in the 21st century academy: Still learning from the "outsider-within." *Journal of Research Initiatives, 1*(1), 27–38.

Williams, C. (1994). Role models and mentors for Blacks at predominantly White campuses. *Trotter Review, 8*(2), 20–23.

Williams, J. (2010). *Reshaping the work-family debate: Why men and class matter.* Cambridge, MA: Harvard University Press.

Wilson, S. (2012). They forgot mammy had a brain. In G. Gutiérrez y Muhs, Y. Niemann, C. González, & A. Harris (Eds.), *Presumed incompetent: The intersections of race and class for women in academia* (pp. 65–77). Boulder, CO: University Press of Colorado.

RESPONSE

CHANGE AGENTS IN THE ACADEMY

On Safe Spaces, Meaningful Advocacy, and Naming the Leak in the Academic Pipeline

Carol E. Henderson

Jenelle Pitts's narrative is heart wrenching. Not only does it describe the deliberate attempts of colleagues to undermine her personal character, but their calculated and disturbing microaggressive, and I would argue in this case macroaggressive tactics, do exactly what they are intended to do: to inflict undue harm to her personhood; to have her doubt herself and question her intellectual and professional vicissitude; and, had she not utilized her academic street smarts to persevere, Pitts may have even left the profession all together. The ease with which some of these behaviors occur is unsettling and makes very clear that the leak in the academic pipeline comes, not from disciplinary unpreparedness on the part of the scholar (for surely she would not have been hired if she were not qualified), but on the part of gatekeepers, the sentinels who feel they must protect a perverse version of academic reality that is unfounded in reliable data or principled administrative practices. It is this "death by a thousand cuts" that has allowed our academic halls to hemorrhage excellent and

Beyond Retention: Cultivating Spaces of Equity, Justice, and Fairness for Women of Color in U.S. Higher Education, pp. 213–218
Copyright © 2016 by Information Age Publishing

213

talented women of color who refuse to jump over one more arbitrary hurdle, suffer one more humiliating experience, endure one more empty conversation that has no merit. The pain that is expressed here is palpable; the decision to speak, courageous. bell hooks is right when she says that moving from silence into speech is an act of defiance for the oppressed and the exploited, for those in "the struggle" and those in struggle (hooks, 1989, p. 9). Speaking our truths makes the interiority of our being tangibly present in the dialogue of humanity. Dr. Pitts claims her right to be heard here and practices a self-healing ritual that is part of a collective experience grounded in the power of the written and spoken word. In considering the question embedded in her title, "Who Speaks For Me?," it is quite evident that she does a stellar job speaking for herself!

But there is another question that lingers beneath Pitts's rhetorical gesture here. It is a question directed at community, at sisterhood, at common human decency. If we are serious about diversifying the academy both compositionally and intellectually—if we are committed to moving forward into a global era that is more equitable, inclusive, and welcoming—one that represents the reality of the world we now live in—if we hope to model in our faculty ranks what we preach about in our classrooms, to provide for our students the true import of a humane and just world, then we, as a collective, must learn to listen to the counterstories told by fellow sojourners whose unnecessary wounding can become our pearls of wisdom. We must listen in order to acknowledge our institutional vulnerabilities and missteps. We must write down the details of their dreadful experiences in order to develop and reengineer better solutions for progress and mutual respect. We must listen and then be *compelled* to act in order to create safe spaces in the academy that provide avenues for meaningful advocacy and holistic development as scholars, teachers, and as human beings.

I have often said that the way to address the paucity of women of color in the academy is to look at the departments—the chairs and colleagues—who function as the habitus wherein they must thrive. This is the place where her professional development takes place; this is one of the spaces where her scholarly identity will be shaped. Oftentimes, discussion of campus climate is framed as the larger institutional culture, that entity whose organizational demeanor sets the tone for colonized behavior in colleges, departments, campus offices, and classrooms. It is true that what is sanctioned through silence and inaction at the institutional level thrives in multiplicative fashion at intimate points of interaction on the campus. In cases such as Dr. Pitts, the structural collapse of an advocacy network exposes unspoken and spoken customs that function as barriers to one's success and well-being. This relates not only to one's promotion and tenure pursuits, but to one's professional advancement as well. Patching up this infrastructure will not work (i.e., removing a mentor or admonishing an administrator for ineffective leadership and poor decision making); although remedying the issue quickly and decisively is a first and most important step in demonstrating to the injured party that she is valued as a colleague and complete being. Once that remedy has been actioned, however, a more deliberate and calculated reassessment of institutional practices must be undertaken to minimize the occurrence of such inept behaviors in the future. Dr. Pitts does an admirable job laying out the various ways she was wronged and the necessary steps she took to mend herself. She also celebrates the ways the practice of mentoring may be leveraged to counteract departmental and institutional lapses in faculty development processes. Peer mentoring, e-mentoring, and the development of collegial network systems outside of one's inhabitable academic space all serve as viable alternatives of providing sanctuary from one's misuse—a means of cultivating space for one's spiritual renewal and intellectual empowerment.

But what other measures can be put into place—both long and short term—to counteract structural and institutional inequities that form challenges to network building?, to recruiting and retaining a diverse faculty collaborative?, to creating a more equitable and inclusive academic environment? At a more global (administrative) level, a functioning and empowered diversity network provides institutional infrastructure that can be instrumental in establishing sound and sustainable accountability practices by which injured parties can be advocated for and heard (Cantor, 2012, 223; Green Evans & McCloud, 2004; Ackelsberg, Hart, Miller, Queeney, & Van Dyne, 2009). Once these practices are in place, they must be activated. Nothing can be more injurious to an individual than to bare the wounds of one's soul, only to have that hurt ignored in a void of silence (Aptheker, 2012, xiii). At the microlevel, this same infrastructure has the capacity to set institutional climate by undergirding the best mentoring practices, transforming recruitment and hiring processes, redirecting errant colleagues who help to cultivate toxic department environments, and creating formal and informal support systems for faculty of color who struggle with racist and sexist politics in the classroom. Informal collaboratives help stem the feelings of isolation and marginalization that often accompany being the only African American woman in the department or the only Latina on the search committee or the only person of color teaching race and equity (Croom & Patton, 2011).

Administrators need to know when to intervene in extreme cases, as well. In reflecting on my own experiences in the classroom, I am forever indebted to my department chair, who realized my teaching abilities and understood the resistance to change of some unexposed students who felt that an introduction to American literature course meant you studied all dead white male authors. The hostility of those students—attitudes of privilege I will call it—almost had me rethink whether I wanted to teach at that institution. My chair, sensing my frustration, navigated department waters for me so that in going forward, I would not be exposed to that kind of disrespect. When I look back on it, that semester was my rite of passage into the murky waters that would become my "identity performance." Dark chocolate and unapologetically so, I now know I challenged every presumed incompetency they had concerning Black women faculty each time I stood before a classroom. Whether we like it or not, this is the reality of an academy that is still pedagogically rigid, and in some respects, culturally naïve about student demands and expectations. Thus in building allied diversity networks, which can be formed with small gestures such as the one I describe above, we can begin to strengthen alliances across administrative ranks which transform academic communities into learning environments built on academic excellence and inclusivity. This "architecture of inclusion," as Attorney Susan Sturm rightfully calls it, cannot be achieved exclusively through qualitative study and legal protection alone (Strum, 2006, p. 249). These are important, but building a sustainable framework demands that the norms of an institution, a department, and a college change. In changing, the core values and educational mission of an institution make room for a diversity that is intellectually engaging and socially purposeful. As such, these shifts in ways of thinking transform institutional culture incrementally but steadily so that faculty of color do not have to defend the merits of their scholarship, justify what "peer review" means in their specialized journals, or explain why three African American authors are allowed—necessary—in understanding American identity *for real* on a syllabus in an introduction to American literature course.

In closing, I share a kinship with Dr. Pitts. I, too, journeyed through the academy as a single mother of a beautiful son, but I was a single mother on Aid to Families with Dependent Children, just starting graduate school at the master's level. My son was 6 months old. As I reflect on the winding road that would become my academic sojourn through graduate school—a journey that would eventually take me from an assistant professorship to vice provost for diversity—one thing becomes *very clear*: I could not have made the journey without a dedicated and resolute network of change agents who assisted me in my passage through the various challenges and obstacles and joys and accomplishments that is the American higher educational experience. Along the way, I witness and continue to experience the subtle and not so subtle behaviors of an academic world that was not created to accommodate me. This academic world is still primarily white, predominantly male, and markedly classed. Working from the margins has become my saving grace. It is a space that offers a distinct way of seeing reality—a way to envision, as bell hooks (1994) and Patricia Hill Collins (1986) both observe, the outsider-in and the insider-out viewpoints of academic life in order to understand the mutual and contested perspectives of this existence. It is in this moment that one also realizes that depending on the situation, any one of us may be outsiders or insiders regardless of our attempts to circumvent the process. Embracing the tensions of this multidimensional identity is key to maintaining one's sanity and quelling the tide of isolation and resignation. We can change academia as outsiders, argues Nancy Cantor (2012), if we hold on to those values forged in the precipice of struggle. It is these principles that will remind us of who we are, as women of color, despite the assaults on our personhood. We must continue to write, to speak our truths, to act on our own behalf, all in support of our sisters who navigate the treacherous academic terrain daily. Placing their stories next to ours creates a memorable and regenerative energy—a tapestry of living moments—that reminds us that we are not alone in this journey.

REFERENCES

Ackelsberg, M., Hart, J., Miller, N., Queeney, K., & Van Dyne, S. (2009). Faculty microclimate change at Smith College. In W. Brown-Glaude (Ed.), *Doing diversity in higher education: Faculty leaders share challenges and strategies* (pp. 83–102). New Brunswick, NJ: Rutgers.

Aptheker, B. (2012). Foreword. In G. Gutierrez y Muhs, Y. F. Niemann, C. G. Gonzalez, & A. P. Harris (Eds.), *Presumed incompetent: The intersections of race and class for women in academia* (pp. xi–xiv). Boulder, CO: University Press of Colorado.

Cantor, N. (2012). Introduction to section III: Networks of allies. In G. Gutierrez y Muhs, Y. F. Niemann, C. G. Gonzalez, & A. P. Harris (Eds.), *Presumed incompetent: The intersections of race and class for women in academia* (pp. 221–223). Boulder, CO: University Press of Colorado.

Collins, P. H. (1986). Learning from the outsider within: The sociological significance of Black feminist thought. *Social Problems, 33*(6), 514–532.

Croom, N., & Patton, L. (2011–2012). The miner's canary: A critical race perspective on the representation of Black women full professor. *The Negro Educational Review, 62/63*(1-4), 13–39.

Green Evans, C. & McCloud, R. (2004). Finding calm waters during the tenure process: A dozen anchors for success. In C. Y. Battle & C. M. Doswell (Eds.), *Building bridges for women of color in higher education: A practical guide for success* (pp. 157–169). Lanham, MD: University Press of America.

hooks, b. (1989). *Talking back: Thinking feminist, thinking Black*. Boston, MA: South End Press.

hooks, b. (1994). *Teaching to transgress: Education as the practice of freedom*. New York, NY: Routledge.

Sturm, S. (2006). The architecture of inclusion: Advancing workplace equity in higher education. *Harvard Journal of Law and Gender, 29*(2), 248–334.

CHAPTER 8

PUTTING AN END TO OUTSIDE LOOKING IN

It's Time for Women of Color in Higher Education to Create Social Capital

Monica Burke

Background Information

Accessibility to career networks and resources can be essential to the success of women faculty of color and as Combs (2003) suggests, professionals in their quest for more favorable status in terms of position level and earning power require access to career networks. Furthermore, according to Forret and Dougherty (2004), there is a relationship between participation in networking and career outcomes or perceived career success. The duality of race and gender can create a distinctive challenge to gaining access to a career network, which is a crucial component to career advancement. As such, this chapter highlights social capital through the personal narratives of women staff and faculty of color in higher education, describing their mentoring and networking experiences in addition to their access to resources and support. As a framework for this discussion, social capital offers a lens for exploring support and mentoring for women of color in higher education.

Beyond Retention: Cultivating Spaces of Equity, Justice, and Fairness for Women of Color in U.S. Higher Education, pp. 219–241
Copyright © 2016 by Information Age Publishing

To better understand the lived experiences of women of color in higher education, narratives were collected from women staff and faculty of color at institutions of higher education using purposeful homogeneous sampling. Purposeful homogeneous sampling within a particular context is used to gain insight into a specific phenomenon (Smith, Flowers, & Larkin, 2009). Using a homogenous sampling approach, I invited eleven female women of color faculty and staff to participate in this study. Using narrative inquiry, which is a qualitative approach in which the researcher uses stories to study the impact of experiences (Clandinin, 2006), the perspectives and experiences of the participants are explored. Women faculty and staff of color were provided with the opportunity to reflect on their experiences and to tell their stories, including their emotions and feelings. Anonymity was ensured, and therefore, names are not provided in this chapter. To begin, I will share my story.

LIVING MY STORY

Lived experiences, accompanied by a myriad of emotions throughout my career in higher education, sparked my reflection on the role of mentoring and networking in my career as a woman of color in higher education. I came into the field of higher education full of expectations and with a belief that those who looked like me and had successfully ascended to upper ranks would assist me in moving forward in my career, as well as encourage me. This expectation was based on past positive mentoring experiences with people of color. My rose-colored glasses were removed immediately after my supervisor's supervisor, a Black male with over 30 years of experience, informed me that my doctoral degree meant nothing to him during my first week on the job. This was followed by countless demotivating events, including denying my requests for opportunities to gain new experiences that would promote my professional development and career advancement, in addition to overtly giving credit for my work successes to another person he mentored. What was most confounding to me is that these experiences were in stark contrast to his insistence during my interview that he supported all persons of color because he understood what it took to make it as a person of color in the field of higher education.

Subsequently, I felt increasingly drained by all the negativity and obstacles. The excitement that fueled me initially was soon replaced by the perception that my gender and degrees would be consistent barriers to my career advancement and socialization in my current workplace, even by those individuals who were Black or Black females as well. I am far from naïve; I knew that encountering people, even those with the same skin color, who are unwilling to provide support or actively try to create barriers for me was in the realm of possibility. I had encountered these types of experiences in my previous roles. However, I was dealing with a person who openly espoused the value of supporting and promoting upcoming professionals of color in public while only supporting a select few, many of whom produced a modicum of success and several who were not people of color. Additionally, very few people in his career support and mentoring circle were females, and most of these females were in staff support roles without a bachelor's degree.

Consequently, I finally accepted the fact that no matter how hard I worked and in spite of any quality work I produced, my efforts were futile regarding gaining his sponsorship because he did not believe that I was deserving of his support or mentorship. Metaphorically, the final straw came when I was referred to as a "glorified secretary" due to my construction of reports and marketing materials, development of assessment measures and reports, proficiency with publishing software, and continued engagement in scholarly writings. Eventually, I became more intentional in accepting mentorship from individuals in other departments and at other institutions who saw value in my work as well as my potential to develop career-related skills. This decision made a major difference, as I was able to find engaged mentors and have access to support and resources which concurrently elevated my confidence in my professional abilities and provided opportunities for me to learn and grow professionally.

THE RULE, NOT THE EXCEPTION

Through personal conversations and reading scholarly works, I found that the difficulties I experienced as a woman of color in higher education were not atypical. Over the years, as I increasingly listened to troubling stories about the personal experiences of women of color in higher education, I also noticed that few of us were full professors and in key leadership positions. This insight led to speculating if I would ever be in a position to receive effective mentorship and support for my career development and advancement. In addition, a supposition formed that, for women of color, a climate that is rarely conducive to professional support was an often accepted expectation and a common existence which brings forth challenges and prompts the need for a supportive peer culture, mentorship, role models, and access to career networks.

As Patitu and Hinton (2003) have found, many women in higher education report being shut out of groups at work due to their race, gender, or sexual orientation, even at historically Black colleges and universities

(Bonner, 2001). Eventually, the isolation faced by Black women faculty, administrators, and students can lead to stress, feelings of insecurity and invisibility, and the belief that they are voiceless among colleagues (Hughes & Howard-Hamilton, 2003). In essence, the dyadic nature embedded in being a woman and a person of color can directly and indirectly impact a woman of color's sense of belonging and socialization in higher education. Logically, experiencing isolation and indifference in the workplace can make it difficult to gain access to career networks and receive mentoring, sponsorship, or coaching. The duality of race and gender, which are two social constructions rooted in discrimination and accompanied by stereotypes, can create a distinctive challenge to gaining access to a career network (Griffin & Reddick, 2011; Johnson-Bailey & Cervero, 2008; Tillman, 2011), which is a crucial component to promotion and the retention of faculty and staff. Referred to as double jeopardy (Beale, 1979; Fleming, 1996), because women of color fall into two oppressed categories, they also have to contend with stereotypes and possibly being labeled as "sensitive" or "playing the victim" if they voice their concerns about any unequal treatment or isolation. As explained by Bower and Wolverton (2009), "even though the civil rights and women's movements kicked open doors for two previously excluded groups, it didn't mean the welcome mat was out" (p. 3). In addition, Andrews (1993) asserts that "being Black and female, compounded by the attainment of a high level of education, predictably creates problems on both a professional and personal level" (p. 182).

Reflecting on Andrew's assertion, I experienced problems in the workplace while in an administrative role and must add that, interestingly, most of the negative experiences I encountered were at the hands of other Black people. In the initial years of my tenure as an administrator, I was only one of two Black females outside of the faculty ranks with a doctorate. Regrettably, I occasionally heard or heard about snide remarks regarding the superior attitudes of Blacks who had doctorates or dealt with some disparagement about me having a doctorate. Of course, these perceptions and opinions did not help me to receive peer support from some of the other Black females on campus. For example, a colleague informed me that another Black female in her department, with whom I rarely conversed or collaborated, shared with her that she was not fan of mine because it was her opinion that people thought that I was special because I was a young Black woman with a doctorate, and she did not understand why. As someone I worked with routinely, the colleague let me know that she was telling me this to make sure that I watch my back since she had submitted her resignation and was soon leaving the university.

These perceptions and comments, of course, contributed to me being wary of whom I should seek or ask for support and advice and ultimately, my decision to deliberately have a very small peer network during my time as an administrator. This experience also made me uncomfortable about people finding out about my doctorate, and I found myself, for the purposes of equanimity and professional well-being, trying to make sure some of these people who held negative perceptions about individuals with terminal or professional degrees were at ease about my level of educational attainment. A tactic that I would often use was to remain quiet during discussions on certain topics to avoid sounding, as it was once described to me, "too scholarly." At times, this experience also contributed to my feelings of disconnection.

FROM DESPAIR AND DISDAIN TO HOPE AND SUPPORT

Once I segued into a faculty position, I found myself in the company of colleagues with professional experience as well as doctorates and was welcomed into the fold. I received advice and offers of support as well as encouragement from each person in the department and support from the associate vice president of academic affairs/chief diversity officer. In particular, I finally had a Black woman, who is a full professor in the department, provide coaching and counseling to me. Without hesitation, she informed me that she was available to assist me in any way and assured me that I would be successful as a faculty member. She also discussed with me the potential barriers that I could encounter in and out of the classroom while reassuring me that I had the ability to succeed in spite of challenges. Throughout my tenure as an assistant professor, she has been a constant supporter, advisor, and mentor. Due to having my colleagues' encouragement and concern for my well-being, I felt as if I were connecting and part of a supportive career network to assist with my growth and advancement. Concurrently, this connection and helpfulness significantly contributed to my professional growth and as asserted by Van Emmerik (2004), my "mentoring constellations" positively equated with my career and job satisfaction and better career expectations.

Collins (2001) observed that, while Black women in higher education have differing experiences, backgrounds, and beliefs, "they are connected in their struggle to be accepted and respected, and to have a voice in an institution with many views" (p. 20). Often at professional conferences, several of my Black female colleagues from various institutions of higher education and I get together to catch up, seek and provide advice, vent, brainstorm, and lament if needed about our career productivity and trajectories. Common themes are typically derived from these conversations which include the awareness that most of the Black men usually mentor and assist other Black men and not us; the seeming effort in higher education to promote and mentor Black men to higher positions which is not afforded to Black women in the same way; the lack of Black women in the upper leadership pipeline who can bring us on or who are willing to bring us along; the issues with encountering barriers that have nothing to do with our job performance; and the unpredictability of expectations and triviality that will, at times, seep into our interactions with colleagues and students. As an African American woman who is a director of a midsize department at a predominantly White institution shared,

> With over 10 years of experience working in academia/higher education, the last 2 years have been my first true experience with the lack of successful mentoring and social support from both women and men of color in the field of higher education. I have been consistently amazed at the way men of color, specifically Black men, rally around and support one another versus the way Black women show social support for one another. It seems as if there is a constant battle or perception that there can only be one Black woman around the table at a time versus supporting each other and making or helping to prepare a seat for your sister. One of my most recent experiences includes being made aware of a personal relationship that my direct supervisor, a male of color, has with a male staff member that reports directly to me and has submitted a formal complaint to my supervisor about me. It has been a struggle to talk candidly with my supervisor about the professional challenges that I am having with this particular staff member because I am aware of their personal relationship. (Personal communication, June 4, 2014)

As a whole, having access to career network and mentoring is an important component of career advancement, considering these networks offer opportunities, support, and access to information. Unfortunately, for many women of color, access to career networks can be limited, and consistently searching for a support network can be discouraging. Authors suggest that women, in general, in higher education (e.g., both faculty and staff) often experience challenges in the workplace (Blackhurst, 2000; Costello, 2012; Johnsrud & Heck, 1994; Lampman, 2012; Nobbe & Manning, 1997; Timmers, Willemsen & Tijdens, 2010; Ting & Watt, 1999). In an effort to cope with these challenges, it is imperative for women of color in higher education to build their social capital through the development of professional skills and career networks which are necessary to sustain and advance in their careers and establish a lifestyle that creates well-being.

Career networks are central to the success of women faculty of color and as Combs (2003) suggested, professionals in their quest for more favorable status in terms of position level and earning power require access to career networks. An advantage of having a career in higher education is that one is likely to encounter inspiring peers, those who role model, support, and help overcome obstacles, but not every colleague will be affirming and contribute to one's career growth. The fundamental need for a genuine mentoring experience is described by an African American female tenure-track Assistant Professor at a predominantly White institution:

> In the beginning, my experience was not all bad. One White colleague, in particular, made every effort to make me feel welcomed and included. She connected me with Black faculty in the college and across campus. She invited me to basketball games, shared announcements for leadership roles in professional organizations in the discipline with me, and invited me to church. She even attempted to connect me with a successful Black bachelor that was also a professional and a friend of hers. Yet when she and I disagreed on a matter concerning a student in my class and an advisee of hers, around the same time my class schedule was mysteriously changed to accommodate her class; our relationship changed and never recovered. However, her initial efforts made it clear that she knew that I needed mentoring and social support to survive, grow and be successful as an assistant professor at a PWI in a predominately White city. (Personal communication, May 30, 2014)

MENTORING AND SOCIAL CAPITAL

Given the complex intersection of race and gender, Zamani (2003) deduces that membership in both marginalized groups can often make a woman of color invisible in colleges and universities. For example, Catalyst (2006) observed that African American women report higher levels of exclusion from the workplace than their White counterparts. Subsequently, this feeling of invisibility could have a negative influence on a productive and satisfying career and work experience for African American women, in particular.

The conception of social capital is that the people who do better are somehow better connected (Burt, 2001). Accordingly, the role of access to information, resources, and career sponsorship are full mediators of the relations between social capital and career success (Seibert, Kraimer, & Liden, 2001). Gaining access to a support network and being engaged in a mentoring relationship which can aid in the development, promotion, and persistence in the careers of women of color, is a consequence of social capital.

Obtaining a mentor is important to career development as mentoring is a key element to continuing career success. Mentoring serves as an avenue to instrumental or career function (e.g., sponsorship, coaching, organizational culture instruction) in which an individual with more experience and influence, known as the mentor, helps to advance the career of a mentee/protégé (Cunningham, 1999; Kram, 1985). Mentors provide career development, psychosocial support, sponsorship, role modeling, acceptance, counseling, confirmation, exposure and visibility, coaching, protection, collaboration, and tasks to help mentees advance their careers (Kram, 1983). These psychosocial functions of mentoring have an influence on a mentee's self-image and competence (Chao, Walz, & Gardner, 1992). Psychosocial mentoring can also assist a mentee/protégé in developing and refining his or her professional identity (Tonidandel, Avery, & Phillips, 2007). Mentoring also offers social capital, career benefits, and resources entrenched in career networks which impart information, sponsorship, and professional skills afforded through mentoring relationships (Chow & Chan, 2008).

Not having a mentor does not mean that an individual cannot be successful in her or his career, but it does mean that certain resources and opportunities will not be available to that individual (Crawford & Smith, 2005). Accordingly, for women of color, mentoring in higher education is an essential component of recruitment and retention. Consequently, participation in formal and informal networks can be deemed as critical to women of color's persistence in academe (Aleman, 2000). As stated by an African American female tenure-track faculty at a predominantly White institution,

> Unmet mentoring can exist in many different areas. One area in which I struggled to find consistently adequate mentoring support is writing. Frequently, I recall hearing the statement "publish or perish." When I started exploring this phrase further, I discovered that women of color in academia, particularly African American women, often underperform in this domain. For several years, my attempts to identify a writing mentor simply revealed the challenges faced by other academicians. The lack of access to and availability of writing mentors became very frustrating. Therefore, I sought writing support from academics from different backgrounds. Ultimately, I received my best writing support from a select group of mostly male full professors, retired female professors, and female professors connected with other academic organizations. (Personal communication, May 28, 2014)

The challenge for women of color can routinely appear in being offered mentor-initiated mentoring or receiving acceptance in self-initiated mentoring. Searching for or securing a mentor, especially for new faculty, can be a daunting task while simultaneously maneuvering the expectations of teaching, advising, research, publishing, service, and learning the ecology of academia. Obtaining a mentor can also become a challenging task if you add in issues of racism, sexism, identity, and marginalization. Particularly for a woman of color, support from a mentor and a peer support network in the workplace can assist in dealing with the frustration and aggravation that can grow from dealing with challenges. As an African American, female faculty member with 3 years of experience at a predominantly White institution recounts,

> Being a new faculty member at a predominately White institution, I have experienced the full spectrum of human emotion. At times I have been extremely excited about the space and time for all my creative ideas to come into fruition; while at other times I have experienced feelings of loneliness and isolation as I try to incorporate all these things. Obtaining a mentor that supports my ideas and offers genuine feedback while using a culturally relevant approach has been the most valuable component to my success as new faculty. Interestingly enough, this person is an African American colleague that is pursuing tenure and promotion herself. However, I believe that this colleague, like me, understands the challenges of being faculty of color and has taken this place of peer-mentorship to support both of us. I am grateful for this. (Personal communication, June 3, 2014)

LOCATION, LOCATION, LOCATION

Within a network, particular people or groups are connected to and trusting of certain others as well as obligated to support specific others dependent on the exchange with specific others; therefore, holding a certain position in the structure of these exchanges can be an asset which is, in essence, social capital (Burt, 2001). Using a network of peers can be a viable avenue to obtain social and career development and support. Further, if an individual cannot find support in the workplace, it is natural to find mentors outside of the workplace. Clayborne and Hamrick (2007) concluded that Black women are more likely to identify their primary sources of support in religious faith, other Black women, and off-campus resources rather than supervisors or colleagues. An African American female who has worked in higher education for 23 years explains her experience with off-campus support and mentoring as follows:

> Mentoring can come from outside the academy. For example, one of my most important mentors was in the corporate America. She taught me how to navigate political situations with finesse. She modeled effective presentation skills and allowed me to shadow her. Within 6 months, I was codirecting a citywide program with her that was affiliated with a national organization. This experience assisted me with my professional growth as well as provided me with powerful networking opportunities. (Personal communication, June 1, 2014)

McKenzie (2002) claims that if a Black woman is the only Black woman in her department, or one of the few professional Black women on a campus, she is more likely to suffer from physical and/or mental exhaustion than women of other races and/or the other gender. This contention is also reinforced by an African American faculty member who was the only woman of color in her department at a predominantly White institution. She contends,

> Finding social support was crucial for my short- and long-term professional success and personal happiness. The first 2 years of employment at the university, I was the only person of color of 15 faculty members in the department, the only unmarried individual in the entire department, the youngest in my program area, yet the only PhD. The other faculty members in the program area were full-time instructors who had been with the university for years. It was obvious that I was the token minority faculty member that was needed to add "diversity" to the faculty. It was clear that I was different from the others and was in need of a social network of a variety of individuals that could fill the roles of friend, close friend, big sister, mother, constant spiritual voice and guide, good listener, advisor, cheerleader, motivator, accomplice, fun-finder, joke-teller, go-getter, focused intellect, and seasoned academic professional. Interesting, I had several persons in my life that could fill multiple roles; however those people were hundreds of miles away in different states consumed with the challenges of their daily lives. Without regular face-to-face contact with those individuals, I wanted nothing more than to turn in my letter of resignation and leave at the end of each academic year. Had the economy not been so bad, I would have left the end of the second academic year. Luckily, if it had not been for friendship I developed with a seasoned academic professional female of color, I probably would not have made the progress I made nor would I have been able to maintain my sanity. This seasoned professional woman of color understood my situation because she had lived it. Her keen insight, advice and friendship were the support I needed to make it through those 5 years. She connected me with campus and various community leaders and individuals. She was God-sent. Interestingly, I was introduced to this seasoned woman of color during my first week at the university by the welcoming colleague previously discussed. She arranged the meeting. My colleague actually told me that I would benefit greatly from knowing this seasoned professional woman of color. She was right! However, this one person could not completely meet all of my social support and mentoring needs. (Personal communication, May 30, 2014)

CROSSING CULTURAL BOUNDARIES

Although not the only factor to consider, Okawa (2002) alluded that cultural similarity is "a primary though not exclusive consideration" (p. 509) in mentoring. Because women of color are underrepresented in the upper leadership and management ranks on college campuses (Mehra, Kilduff, & Brass, 1998) and because there is often a paucity of faculty of color who can serve as mentors (Thompson, 2008), cross-cultural mentoring is a plausible option for women of color. Considering that the situation is bleak for women of color in faculty and administrative positions (Rai & Critzer 2000) in higher education, it can be difficult for a woman of color to find another woman of color in an upper rank who could possibly serve as a mentor and share similar experiences and worldview. For example, according to Edwards (1998/2001),

> African American women face an interesting challenge in searching for a mentor to monitor their progress and facilitate their professional development. The scarcity of African American women in first line administration on campus makes it difficult to find enough mentors to meet demand. As a result, a functional but ironic professional alliance has often been formed between African American women and White men. (p. 47)

Cross-cultural mentoring relationships in the workplace allow for mutual testing of stereotypes and attributions regarding differences, and also allow for the development of cross-cultural communication skills (Bova, 2000). Furthermore, there is a suggestion that to "seek multiple mentors and role models from a variety of cultural backgrounds, as the diverse perspectives of these individuals can help develop a well-rounded sense of professionalism" (Henry, 2010, p. 10). Johnson-Bailey and Cervero (2004) noted that "Mentoring across cultural boundaries is an especially delicate dance that juxtaposes group norms and societal pressures and expectations with individual characteristics" (p. 7). A Mexican American assistant professor describes one of her professional experiences as follows:

> My first faculty position was in South Dakota—Anglo/White majority with very limited Mexican population. Everyone assumed I was as White as they were. It was awkward for me as students or other faculty would look at me strange when I told them about my heritage. Almost as if it was not a good thing. I was assigned a faculty mentor there, but diversity issues were not really discussed. (Personal communication, June 11, 2014)

Personally, a White male has been one of my most ardent supporters and has worked diligently to ensure that I am prepared for my tenure and promotion review. He has assisted me with publications, served as a cofacilitator on presentations at professional conferences, provided me with opportunities to grow professionally, introduced me to people in his professional network, advised me or consoled me when needed, and encouraged me to step outside of my comfort zone. With his sponsorship, support, and coaching, my job-specific competence and job satisfaction has consistently increased. Similarly, an African American female who is an administrator acknowledges,

> Mentoring is essential in academe for all women. In particular, women of color cannot break the glass ceiling without effective mentoring. Without access to mentors, women of color may languish in junior faculty ranks or as coordinators or directors. With the relative small numbers of presidents, provosts and deans who are women of color, it is not always feasible to have a female mentor of color. Mentoring can come from unlikely sources such as White males. In my experience, a high-ranking African American administrator to whom I reported ended up not being an effective mentor for my professional growth. She did not engage in professional development or networking, thus couldn't expose me to new experiences. A White male administrator and a White female administrator were more integral to my professional growth than my direct supervisor, who was a woman of color. (Personal communication, June 1, 2014)

Further, for a person of color who works at predominantly White institutions in regions with a predominantly White population, finding a culturally similar mentor can be an even more challenging process. A Black female administrator with 10 years of experience in a Rocky
Mountain state with a very low percentage of people of color explains,

> I am engaged in a peer-to-peer mentoring relationship with a Black male because of scarceness of other people of color to potentially serve as mentors and due to the many dimensions they share with being an educated person of color at a predominantly White institution in a small, predominantly White town; despite differences in gender, this mentoring relationship is effective because we are both dealing with many of the same intersectionalities. (personal communication, June 2, 2014)

In spite of cultural dissimilarity, effective mentoring can serve as an avenue to a developmental career network can lead to the fostering of social capital. Ultimately, mentoring relationships have similar elements regardless of the culture or race of the participants in the relationship. This concept is supported by Aleman's research (1986) which found that there were no significant differences reported in the amount of perceived career benefit from a relationship with a Black or White mentor (Brinson & Kottler, 1993). Contrarily, Thomas (1990) noted that same-race relationships were found to provide significantly more psychosocial support than cross-race relationships; however, same-race and cross-race relationships did not differ significantly in the amount of career support they provided.

INTERNALIZING FEELINGS, COPING WITH STRESS

Largely, having a mentor can potentially help to subside the stressors associated with being one of few persons of color at a predominantly White institution. This sentiment is conveyed in a quote from a Black female who has been a faculty member for 6 years and was the only person of color in her department at a predominantly White institution, "I believe my 5 year assistant professor experience would have been more productive and rewarding if I had several regular supportive individuals on the job and in my personal life" (Personal communication, May 30, 2014).

For faculty of color, being left out of the informal networks in their respective departments can lead to feelings of isolation (Stanley, 2006). A research study by Tillman (2001) identified three primary factors that present roadblocks for Black females' successful promotion and tenure— lack of socialization to faculty life, lack of meaningful mentoring, and inability to articulate a viable and sustainable research agenda. As Stanley (2006) advised, "discrimination cuts across many areas of the academy such as teaching, research, service, and overall experiences with the campus community" (p. 705). Therefore, mentoring must become an activist practice (Okawa, 2002), as it is critical to the survival of junior faculty of color in the academic culture, especially at predominantly White institutions, which seem, and in some ways are, uninviting and unfriendly to those who have been historically underrepresented or absent.

IMPROVED PERFORMANCE, ENHANCED RESPECT

In the academic realm, the benefits of mentoring include the lessening of feelings of isolation and alienation, especially for early career faculty (Zellers, Howard, & Barcic, 2008) and can be utilized as a tool to socialize new faculty (Davis, 2008). Further, Boyle and Boice (1998) assert that tenure-track faculty who participate in formal and/or informal mentoring relationships are more likely to persist and succeed in higher education than those who do not. For instance, a study by Patitu and Hinton (2003) found that the African American women faculty in their study who aspired to be tenured believed they are less likely to receive mentoring and direction on their pursuits than White faculty and that they are less likely to be asked to coauthor a publication by a senior White faculty member. Moreover, a study by Thomas and Hollenshead (2001) that focused on the experiences of women of color found that these women are marginalized within the academy and lacked access to mentoring from senior faculty. This extends to social support as well. For example,

Gregory (2001) concluded that an external barrier to academic success for Black women in the academy is the lack of support groups. This finding is supported by the research of Ponjuan, Conley, and Trower (2011) which found that faculty of color receive less social support than White colleagues. A lack of support, feelings of isolation, and the absence of a mentoring relationships can not only lead to feelings of dissatisfaction, but eventually, to faculty women of color leaving the institution. This is exemplified in the following narrative of a Black, female assistant professor. She states,

> I desired official mentoring from tenured faculty. I desperately wanted a mentoring committee to guide me through the tenure process by helping me generate a plan and then providing the support and direction to successfully execute the plan to reach the goal of associate professor in the 5 years allowed. I felt that I needed a committee as a new junior faculty member. I made an appeal to my department chair that was female. She shared with me the names of faculty members across campus she felt would be good "mentors" for me. I contacted them and not one of them responded. I decided to look within the department and was able to receive some unofficial mentoring from faculty members in other program areas. I would go to them if I had questions or concerns. They would listen and provide suggestions and advice but they never really followed up or expressed interest in knowing the outcome. I decided to leave the university while my tenure packet was under review. My decision to leave the PWI was driven by the lack of professional support and mentoring, poor collegiate relationships in my immediate program area, low salary, and the lack of social opportunities in the city. Although the department committee and dean had approved my tenure packet, I did not feel that the work presented in the tenure packet was reflective of my true interest, talent, knowledge and skills. I believed it was time for a fresh new start. In the one and a half year away from the PWI, I have joined faculty at another university and an official mentoring committee was formed during my first semester for my benefit, progress, and professional development. Within 1 year, I have submitted a manuscript and contributed to two grants; one was awarded; the other is under review. I have attended several workshops to enhance teaching, research, and writing. Through the workshops, I have connected with other faculty of various disciplines and ethnicities, and I am enjoying the partnerships and friendships that are developing. The experience at the PWI has made me a better faculty member at the new university where I am employed. (Personal communication, Mary 30, 2014)

In general, there are a number of reasons to anticipate that mentoring enhances a mentee's/protégé's performance as evidenced in the aforementioned narrative. For instance, mentees/protégés often learn new skills from their mentors (Lankau & Scandura, 2002). This relationship also provides a psychosocial function (e.g., serving as a model, a confidant, an ally) in which the mentor provides support and advice, fosters one's professional development, proposes opportunities for career growth, and helps the mentee/protégé develop and refine his or her professional identity. Furthermore, the feedback and reinforcement provided by the mentor could likely boost the protégé's self-efficacy (Day & Allen, 2004), which may correspond in higher performance in his or her career (Stajkovic & Luthans, 1998).

ESTABLISHING A FORMAL MENTORING PROGRAM

A new, Black, entry-level female professional stated that she was promised formal mentoring upon her hiring, but did not receive it once she arrived on campus, which is a "source of frustration" for her (Personal communication, June 3, 2014). Issues such as this could be avoided through the establishment of a formal mentoring system and the support of an informal mentoring system. Formalized university mentorship programs, as suggested by Jackson and Flowers (2003), will enable minority individuals to engage meaningfully with colleagues and administrators who have more experience and can provide advice and feedback to those seeking to advance within the institution. Turner and Myers (2000) affirm the need for mentoring of faculty of color as one of their top three recommendations for faculty retention. Definitely, scheduled "check-ins" with the mentees/protégés and an evaluation to determine the success of its participants, as well as the program, should be embedded into the system. A buddy system, the assignment of an employee as a partner to a new employee during their transition to an institution, can also be initiated to help new faculty and administrators adjust during their first few months on the job.

Participation in professional minority-focused development activities, such as writing circles, symposiums, and professional or research institutes, can provide an avenue for women of color to develop competencies to meet career expectations. For faculty, these activities should be offered as a supplement to typically funded professional development opportunities. An added benefit of professional development is that it presents a possibility for women of color to develop a support network outside of the institution.

Career development can be defined as an ongoing series of stages characterized by unique concerns, themes, and tasks (O'Neil & Bilimoria, 2005, p. 168). Methodical and intensive career planning by women of color in concert with a knowledgeable mentor, which can include a senior academic or administrative leader at the institution, can help build a solid foundation for establishing career needs and the subsequent effect on job satisfaction, turnover intention, and contribution to one's field and the institution.

GETTING CONNECTED, GETTING RESOURCES, GETTING AHEAD

The theory of social capital serves as a framework for understanding the advantage of career network membership. Social capital is described as "the aggregate of the actual or potential resources that are linked to possession of a durable network of more or less institutionalized relationships of mutual acquaintance and recognition" (Bourdieu, 1986, p. 248). This includes the sum of the actual and potential resources embedded within, available through, and derived from a network of social relationships (Nahapiet & Ghoshal, 1998). An individual's ability to access resources depends on the strength of their relationship with another individual (Gaddis, 2012).

Personal and professional sustainability is tandem with developing and leveraging social capital, mastering networking and establishing and maintaining mentoring relationships. A solid foundation built upon interpersonal (e.g., building networking relationships, taking part in informal and formal professional development opportunities, fostering collegiality) and intrapersonal (e.g., establishing parameters for self-care, adaptability, planning, self-motivating) skills and utilizing the benefits of a career network are essential to career success as a professional in higher education.

While in an administrative role in higher education, I observed this trend as a Black male with about the same years of experience as I had was consistently put on key institutional committees, given professional development opportunities, financial increases, and sponsorship for career prospects by his mentor. The sponsorship, support, resources, and access to job opportunities provided to him subsequently propelled him to continual career advancement. In other words, "getting ahead" involves receiving relevant career development advice and support as well as resources from a social network in pursuit of one's career goals. These social ties located in certain strategic locations and/or hierarchical positions can provide an individual with useful information about opportunities and choices otherwise not available (Lin, 1999). The absence of social ties, career development advice, and support can also impact one's motivation in career growth and motivation, as described by an Asian Indian American female faculty member:

> I had obstacles at work where I felt other directors and colleagues did not support me at times and did not take me under wings or help me grow. Even when I worked hard, I did not get recognized, and there were multiple opportunities that I felt I was qualified for; however, it was always somebody else who was recognized or had that opportunity given to them. So, it makes you unmotivated with your career, especially when you have the skills, especially since the department that I teach in is a male dominated field with

very few females, and I am one of the very few minority females. No one ever really sat down and mentored me. I was a young faculty, and I had to figure it out on my own and find people to go to for mentoring and support. I feel that if I had that, I would have maybe grown more in the biology department. (Personal communication, June 12, 2014)

The art of networking is subtle and challenging. Networking includes proactive behavior that aids in developing relationships and enhances career development (Kram, 1985); developing and maintaining relationships leading to career development (Forret & Dougherty, 2001); offering a forum for career information and sharing, as well as serving as a social function (Ibarra, 1993); and affording a cultivation of social resources that positively correlates to salary increases, promotions and career satisfaction (Seibert et al., 2001). As acknowledged by Mehra et al. (1998), the "lack of access to informal networks may be one reason that women and minorities who are entering organizations in unprecedented numbers, are still underrepresented, especially in upper-management ranks" (p. 441). Career advancement involves receiving relevant career development advice and support, as well as resources, from a social network in pursuit of career goals. Network members can possess an advantage personally and professionally by receiving access to information and opportunities, such as promotions, simply based on the privilege of membership.

Taking into account that women of color are often excluded from career networks, how can women of color earn social capital to advance in their careers if they are excluded from the people and networks which provide the capital? The promotion and retention of women of color in higher education requires intentional career planning and the removal of institutional barriers to their advancement. I recall an Asian Indian faculty member who decided to leave a predominantly White institution due to a lack of support and advancement opportunities; she disclosed that the lack of support that she received prompted her to move forward to other opportunities. Sandler (1986) noted that women of color "are simply not retained or tenured at the institutions which hire them as faculty or administrators ... retention opportunities have worsened considerably" (p. 191). As a result, many women of color at times find themselves serving as the only woman of color administrator and faculty.

CONCLUSION

Accessibility to career support networks and allowing women of color a platform to address or release career-related concerns can play a significant role in increasing job satisfaction as suggested in a study by Crawford and Smith (2005) in which all respondents believed that if they had been mentored, they would have had greater job satisfaction. Consequently, support networks and mentorship necessitate the development of social capital. To increase the likelihood for women of color to be retained, institutions of higher education need to be more proactive in supporting and creating higher educational environments that are conducive to bringing about success for women of color and assisting them in building social capital. An intentional focus on the experiences of women of color and the incorporation of strategies, such as creating networking opportunities and mentoring, could have positive impact and inherently, positive returns for institutions of higher education. Of course, this transformation might require a restructuring of the existing institutional design, but if institutional leaders commit to addressing the needs of women of color at their institution, the benefits will be invaluable.

Sustaining a career in higher education entails multiple facets of "career capital." By my definition, career capital is the totality of knowledge, education, prior career-related experiences, interpersonal relationships, innate or developed skills, and personal qualities that one possesses to identify opportunities and use those opportunities for career development and success. Fostering effective mentoring relationships is a complex process demanding flexibility and an understanding of human interrelations (Bova, 2000). In addition, there must be an intentional pursuit of support networks, professional and personal, and the development of a career plan. Having a network to support and promote other women of color, as well as cultivate relationships that would provide connections to influential colleagues and, consequently, more career resources, is detailed in the following narrative of a Black female who reports that she has five women of color in her professional support network.

> When I arrived at this institution some 27 years ago as a first generation college student, my first encounter with a positive university role model was one I shall never forget. She worked for the TRIO Student Support Services Program and shared with me the importance of asking questions when I did not understand, finding individuals who would indeed help me succeed, and believing in myself, regardless of my standardized test scores. Her direction, words, and mentoring helped me to succeed and graduate. I am still guided by her advice in my career aspirations; for asking, finding, and believing are key components/steps, I believe, for a successful career path for women of color. I have encountered many more females such as her, and they, too, have assisted me with my success. They have been there to listen, encourage, correct, love, and believe in me, even when I doubted myself. These women are important to me, personally and professionally. Frankly, I don't know if I would have made it without the many blessings of my social

support system-, mentor-, role-model sisters! (Personal communication, May 27, 2014)

Unfortunately, having a reliable, positive support system is not a certainty for all women of color. Hence, to address the issue of successfully retaining women of color at higher education institutions, intentional approaches for positive support are necessary. Strategies must include or begin with senior leaders addressing the structural issues and cultural milieus that obstruct women of color from professional advancement. They must also implement initiatives to promote networking opportunities and mentoring relationships for women of color. Based on the participants' narratives, some strategies institutions could consider implementing for the retention of women of color include a formal mentoring program, methodical and intensive career development planning, and a professional development enhancement plan. These strategies must, of course, accompany enabling women of color to have a means to convey feelings or concerns about the campus climate. Such strategies will result in genuine opportunities for advancement and professional growth.

REFERENCES

Aleman, A. M. (2000). Race talks: Undergraduate women of color and female friendships. *Review of Higher Education, 23*(2), 133–152.

Andrews, A. R. (1993). Balancing the personal and the professional. In J. James & R. Farmer (Eds.), *Spirit, space, & survival: African American women in (White) academe* (pp. 179–195). New York, NY: Routledge.

Beale, F. (1979). Double jeopardy: To be Black and female. In T. Cade (Ed.), *The Black woman* (pp. 90–100). New York, NY: New American Library.

Blackhurst, A. E. (2000). Career satisfaction and perceptions of sex discrimination among women student affairs professionals. *NASPA Journal, 37*(2), 399–413.

Boyle, P., & Boice, B. (1998). Systematic mentoring from new faculty teaching and graduate teaching assistants. *Innovative Higher Education, 22*(3), 157–159.

Bonner, F. B. (2001). Addressing gender issues in the historically Black college and university community: A challenge and call to action. *Journal of Negro Education, 70*(3), 176–191.

Bourdieu, P. (1986). The forms of capital. In J. G. Richardson (Ed.), *Handbook of theory and research for the sociology of education* (pp. 241–258). New York, NY: Greenwood.

Bova, B. (2000). Mentoring revisited: The African-American woman's experience. *Mentoring & Tutoring: Partnership in Learning, 8*(1), 5–16.

Bower, B. L. & Wolverton, M. (2009). *Answering the call: African American women in higher education leadership*. Sterling, VA: Stylus.

Brinson, J., & Kottler, J. (1993). Cross-cultural mentoring in counselor education: A strategy for retaining minority faculty. *Counselor Education and Supervision, 32*(4), 241–253.

Burt, R. S. (2001). Structural holes versus network closure as social capital. In N. Lin, K. Cook, & R. S. Burt (Eds.), *Social capital: Theory and research* (pp. 31–56). New York, NY: Aldine de Gruyte.

Catalyst. (2006). *Connections that count: The informal networks of women of color in the United States.* New York, NY: Author.

Chao, G. T., Walz, P. M., & Gardner, P. D. (1992). Formal and informal mentorships. *Personnel Psychology, 45*(3), 619–636.

Chow, W. S., & Chan, L. S. (2008). Social network, social trust and shared goals in organizational knowledge sharing. *Information & Management, 45*(7), 458–465.

Clandinin, D. J. (Ed.). (2006). *Handbook of narrative inquiry: Mapping a methodology.* Thousand Oaks, CA: SAGE.

Clayborne, H., & Hamrack, F. (2007). Rearticulating the leadership experiences of African American women in midlevel student affairs administration. *NASPA Journal, 44*(1), 123–146.

Collins, A. C. (2001). Black women in the academy: A historical overview. In R. O. Mabokela & A. L. Green (Eds.), *Sisters of the academy: Emergent Black women scholars in higher education* (pp. 29–42). Sterling, VA: Stylus.

Combs, G. (2003). The duality of race and gender for managerial African American women: Implications of informal social networks on career advancement. *Human Resource Development Review, 2*(4), 385–405.

Costello, C. A. (2012). Women in the academy: The impact of culture, climate, and policies on female classified staff. *NASPA Journal about Women in Higher Education, 5*(2), 99–114.

Crawford, K., & Smith, D. (2005). The we and the us: Mentoring African American women. *Journal of Black Studies, 36*(1), 52–67.

Cunningham, S. (1999). The nature of workplace mentoring relationships among faculty members in Christian higher education. *The Journal of Higher Education, 70*(4), 441–463.

Davis, D. J. (2008). Mentorship and the socialization of underrepresented minorities into the professoriate: Examining varied influences. *Mentoring & Tutoring: Partnership in Learning, 16*(3), 278–293.

Day, R., & Allen, T. (2004). The relationship between career motivation and self-efficacy with protégé career success. *Journal of Vocational Behavior, 64*(1), 72–91.

Edwards, J. (2001). Assorted adaptations by African American administrators. In M. D. Wenniger & M. H. Conroy (Eds.), *Gender equity or bust!: On the road to campus leadership with women in higher education* (pp. 46–50). San Francisco, CA: Jossey Bass. (Original work published 1998)

Fleming, J. (1996). Black women in Black and White college environments: The making of a matriarch. In C. S. V. Turner, M. Garcia, A. Nora, & L. I. Rendon (Eds.), *Racial and ethnic diversity in higher education* (pp. 302–311). Needham Heights, MA: Ginn.

Forret, M. L., & Dougherty, T. W. (2001). Correlates of networking behavior for managerial and professional employees. *Group & Organization Management, 26*(3), 283–311.

Gaddis, S. (2012). What's in a relationship? An examination of social capital, race and class in mentoring relationships. *Social Forces, 90*(4), 1237–1269.

Gregory, S. T. (2001). Black faculty women in the academy: History, status, and future. *Journal of Negro Education, 70*(3), 124–138.

Griffin, K. A., & Reddick, R. J. (2011). Surveillance and sacrifice: Gender differences in the mentoring and advising patterns of Black professors. *American Educational Research Journal, 48*(5), 1032–1057.

Henry, W. J. (2010). African American women in student affairs: Best practices for winning the game. *Advancing Women in Leadership Journal, 30*(24). Retrieved from http://advancing women.com/awl/awl_wordpress/

Hughes, R. L., & Howard-Hamilton, M. F. (2003). Insights: Emphasizing issues that affect African American women. In M. F. Howard-Hamilton (Ed.), *Meeting the needs of African American women* (pp. 95–104). San Francisco, CA: Jossey-Bass.

Ibarra, H. (1993). Personal networks of women and minorities in management: A conceptual framework. *Academy of Management Review, 18*(1), 56–87.

Jackson, J. F. L., & Flowers, L. A. (2003). Retaining African American student affairs administrators: Voices from the field. *College Student Affairs Journal, 22*(2), 125–136

Johnson-Bailey, J., & Cervero, R. M. (2004). Mentoring in black and white: The intricacies of cross-cultural mentoring. *Mentoring and Tutoring: Partnership in Learning, 12*(1), 7–21.

Johnsrud, L. K., & Heck, R. H. (1994). Administrative promotion within a university: The cumulative impact of gender. *Journal of Higher Education, 65*(1), 23–44.

Kram, K. E. (1983). Phases of the mentor relationship. *The Academy of Management Journal, 26*(4), 608–625.

Kram, K. E. (1985). *Mentoring at work: Developmental relationships in organizational life.* Glenview, IL: Scott, Foresman, & Company.

Lampman, C. (2012). Women faculty at risk: U.S. professors report on their experiences with student incivility, bullying, aggression and sexual attention. *NASPA Journal about Women in Higher Education, 5*(2), 184–208.

Lankau, M. J., & Scandura, T. A. (2002). An investigation of personal learning in mentoring relationships: Content, antecedents and consequences. *Academy of Management Journal, 45*(4), 779–790.

Lin, N. (1999). Building a network theory of social capital. *Connections, 22*(1), 28–51.

McKenzie, M. M. (2002). Labor above and beyond the call: A Black woman scholar in the academy. In S. Harley (Ed.), *Sister circle: Black women and work* (pp. 231–253). New Brunswick, NJ: Rutgers University Press.

Mehra, A., Kilduff, M., & Brass, D. J. (1998). At the margins: A distinctiveness approach to social identity and social networks of underrepresented groups. *Academy of Management Journal, 41*(4), 441–452.

Nahapiet, J., & Ghoshal, S. 1998. Social capital, intellectual capital, and the organizational advantage. *Academy of Management Review, 23*(2), 242–266.

Nobbe, J., & Manning, S. (1997). Issues for women in student affairs with children. *NASPA Journal, 34*(2), 101–111.

Okawa, G. Y. (2002). Diving for pearls: Mentoring as cultural and activist practice among academics of color. *College Composition and Communication, 53*(3), 507–532.

O'Neil, D. A., & Bilimoria, D. (2005). Women's career development phases: Idealism, endurance, and reinvention. *Career Development International, 10*(3), 168–189.

Patitu, C. L., & Hinton, K. G. (2003). The experiences of African American women faculty and administrators in higher education: Has anything changed? In M. F. Howard-Hamilton (Ed.), *Meeting the needs of African American women (New Directions for Student Services No. 104*, pp. 79–93). San Francisco, CA: Jossey-Bass.

Ponjuan, L., Conley, V. M., & Trower, C. (2011). Career stage differences in pretenure-track faculty perceptions of professional and personal relationships with colleagues. *The Journal of Higher Education, 82*(3), 319–346.

Rai, K. B., & Critzer. J. W. (2000). *Affirmative action and the university.* Lincoln, NE: University of Nebraska Press.

Sandler, B. (1986). *The campus climate revisited: Chilly for women, faculty, administrators, and graduate students.* Washington, DC: Association of American Colleges.

Seibert, S. E., Kraimer, M. L., & Liden, R. C. (2001). A social capital theory of career success. *The Academy of Management Journal, 44*(2), 219–237.

Smith, J. A., Flowers, P., & Larkin, M. (2009). *Interpretative phenomenological analysis: Theory, method and research.* London, England: SAGE.

Stajkovic, A. D., & Luthans, F. (1988). Self-efficacy and work-related performance: A meta-analysis. *Psychological Bulletin, 124*(2), 240–261.

Stanley, C. A. (2006). Coloring the academic landscape: Faculty of color breaking the silence in predominately White colleges and universities. *American Educational Research Journal, 43*(4), 701–736.

Tonidandel, S., Avery, D. R., & Phillips, M. G. (2007). Maximizing returns on mentoring: Factors affecting subsequent protégé performance. *Journal of Organizational Behavior, 28*(1), 89–110.

Thomas, D. A. (1990). The impact of race on managers' experiences of developmental relationships. *Journal of Organizational Behavior, 11,* 479–492.

Thomas, G., & Hollenshead, C. (2001). Resisting from the margins: The coping strategies of black women and other women of color faculty members at a research university. *The Journal of Negro Education, 70,* 166–175.

Tillman, L. C. (2001). Mentoring African American faculty in predominantly White institutions. *Research in Higher Education, 42*(3), 295–325.

Tillman, L. C. (2011). Sometimes I've felt like a motherless child. In S. Jackson & R. Gregfory Johnson III (Eds.), *The Black professoriate: Negotiating a habitable space in the academy* (pp. 91–107). New York, NY: Peter Lang.

Timmers, T. M., Willemsen, T. M., & Tijdens, K. G. (2010). Gender diversity policies in universities: A multiperspective framework of policy measures. *Higher Education, 59*(6), 719–735.

Ting, S. R., & Watt, S. K. (1999). Career development of women in student affairs. *College Student Affairs Journal, 18*(2), 92–101.

Thompson, C. Q. (2008), Recruitment, retention, and mentoring faculty of color: The chronicle continues. *New Directions for Higher Education, 143,* 47–54.

Turner, C. S. V., & Meyers, S. L. (2000). *Faculty of color in academe: Bittersweet success.* Boston, MA: Allyn & Bacon.

Van Emmerik, I. J. H. (2004). The more you can get the better: Mentoring constellations and intrinsic career outcomes. *Career Development International, 9*(6), 578–594.

Zamani, E. M. (2003). African American women in higher education. *New Directions for Student Services, 104,* 5–18.

Zellers, D. F., Howard, V. M., & Barcic, M. A. (2008). Faculty mentoring programs: Reenvisioning rather than reinventing the wheel. *Review of Educational Research, 78*(3), 552–588.

RESPONSE

WE CANNOT DO IT ALONE

Stacey Pearson-Wharton

I commend Monica for her critical analysis of academia and the relationship between mentoring and social capital for women in higher education. I found her own story familiar, and the other stories she discussed were also reminiscent of my lived experiences. To further elucidate the notion of social capital and the power of mentoring, I will tell my story. I entered the realm of higher education from a nontraditional career and education path. I have my PhD in counseling phycology. My transition into the higher education field was mostly successful, with very minor struggles along the way. Much of my success throughout my career as a young professional was derived from the strong guidance and support of my mentors who were established in the field. Like that of Burke, I firmly believe that throughout your life there will be a package of people who help you move along the way. Those people will vary in appearance based on the location to which you move.

The experience of having my first mentor, Dr. Donnie, at my church greatly influenced how I would develop in my career. My mentor was a psychologist at the University of Pennsylvania. She worked with students who were struggling within the college, and I instantly aspired to do the same. After Dr. Donnie, I had dozens of supervisors to meet with weekly for my clinicals; however, Dr. Donnie and I had a special relationship. I always saw our relationship as more family based. My relationship with Dr. Donnie was very important to my development, because society stereo-

Beyond Retention: Cultivating Spaces of Equity, Justice, and Fairness
for Women of Color in U.S. Higher Education, pp. 243–246

types individuality as strength. Having a mentor can appear as a sign of weakness within the African American culture; yet Dr. Donnie helped me to see past that and to pursue my dreams. She solidified my belief that none of us can do it alone (Kent, Green, & Kochran, 2013).

Upon the commencement of my education, I attended Norfolk University, a historically Black college and university located in Virginia. I continued my education in rural Pennsylvania for my graduate degree. During my graduate experience, I worked as a graduate assistant within the dean of students office. Although I was working within the higher education sector, I was enrolled in courses that pertained to phycology. My supervisor in this role was a Latino male from Cuba. The role of my mentor was more focused on the academic affairs aspect of university life; however, he had previous experience working administratively. My assistantship was the experience which introduced me to higher education. Finally, I moved on to attend Penn State University for my doctorate program.

Mentorship has been so important to me throughout my experience as a professional. Having a supporting mentor is crucial when struggling with issues regarding self-efficacy, like I was during my first job search. When a person struggles with lack of confidence and self-worth, it can lead to depression and anxiety. My mentors taught me that you cannot see racism and sexism as permanent and internal issues. These mentors taught me how to see these issues as external and temporary, and that I could get past it. This life lesson that my mentor taught me is the reason that I was able to transition to a new job in Michigan right after the Ku Klux Klan was causing riots in that same area. Mentors are able to empower us in ways that we cannot always empower ourselves.

After completing my doctorate degree, though I was hesitant, I took a job at the University of Michigan. I took the job at this particular university because I knew that my boss would be a Latina woman. I believed in looking at mentoring as "where, who, and how a mentor mentors mentees" and include the "place (location), space (structure), and face (relationships)" as crucial components to the mentoring relationship (Kochan, 2013). Although I was open to supervisors that came from other backgrounds, I saw having a Latina woman as a supervisor as a great opportunity to connect. Ironically, her boss happened to be an African American woman in the role of the dean of students. These two women, along with another Black Carribean woman, guided and supported me at my first job. These women would listen to me when I was struggling and helped me to see and recognize my own personal strengths and weaknesses. Time was always made for me, and these women's faith in me helped me to have confidence in myself and my ability to be successful. The influence that these three women had on me was significant because they are the reason I decided to consider a career in leadership.

Another lesson that I have learned from my mentors is that if you restrict who you let influence you, you may deprive yourself of wisdom and guidance that could be essential to your development (Marina, 2014). Luckily, I was able to open up to one of the best gifts I was given throughout my career. This particular mentor came in the package of a White male. I truly believe that he was essential to my growth. Coming from a privileged place, my mentor taught me that I could have and want anything within my career. Every week we would have lunch or brunch together, and I was extremely content with being his second in command. Finally, he told me that I needed to leave in order to advance to a director level position.

Although my mentors came in all different packages, I struggled with how I was culturally conditioned to see mentorship based on my background. Culturally, there is an expectation that an African American individual will look out for another African American person and help that individual to grow, solely based on the fact that they share the same skin color. If I solely believed that I could only be helped by an individual that looked like me, my life would be very different. Just like the author of the chapter says, this assumption is not always valid. People are hurt often, just as Burke was hurt by her Black professor. These particular betrayals sometimes make it hard for individuals to trust mentors, leading to what Grier and Cobbs (1968) would call "healthy cultural paranoia." Essentially, healthy cultural paranoia creates a metaphysical barrier for humans to put up in order to prevent being hurt by people who look like you.

Upon reflection, I could not possibly understand why a person who looks like you would not have your best interest at heart. In my role as a mentor, I have always felt compassionate and had a sense of duty to my mentees. However, I am sure there has been a time where I have disappointed one of the individuals that I have mentored. Reflecting on this aspect has challenged me to help others to the best of my ability and not to let them down the way I have been let down in the past by other African American individuals. I also believe that the reason why African American people look out for each other specifically is because they understand the culture of their childhood. Within an African American home, many times, the gender roles do not comply with the status quo. Women are raised to be independent and strong and to avoid being needy, especially around other people of diverse backgrounds. The way these individuals are raised stems from slavery. An African American woman or male is taught not to ask for help and to remain stolid in expression, which at times prevents their needs from being met. On the other hand, if a child of White background cried because her needs were not being met, she may get the help that she needs. Mentors of students and mentees of color need to be cognizant that the needs of their mentees are met.

I truly recognized that my life would have changed drastically if I did not let my mentor into my life because his skin color was White. I would have never advanced to where I am today and gained the social capital I have without his influence. I learned that there is a perfect mentor out there for everyone, but that person may not come in the aesthetic package that you expect. Regardless of apprehensions, people need help to engage in a variety of mentoring relationships, just as I did. We are an "outgrowth of experience with others" (Kochan, 2013, p. 413). The people that mentor us shape us and prepare us for our futures. We cannot do it alone, and luckily mentors are there to give you a little piece of what you need to create the full successful person you intend to be.

REFERENCES

Grier, W. H., & Cobbs, P. M. (1968). *Black rage*. New York, NY: Basic Books.

Kent, A. M., Kochan, F., & Green, A. M. (2013). Influences on mentoring programs and relationships: A critical review of research. *International Journal of Mentoring and Coaching in Education, 2*(3), 204–217.

Kochan, F. (2013). Analyzing the relationships between culture and mentoring. *Mentoring & Tutoring: Partnership in Learning, 21*(4), 412–430.

Marina, B. L. H. (2014). A cultural connection to identity development for graduate female students of color. In F. K. Kochan (Series Ed.) & F. Kochan, A. Kent, & A. Green (Volume Eds.), *Perspectives on mentoring: Vol. 4. Uncovering the hidden cultural dynamics in mentoring programs and relationships: Managing the complexities* (pp. 63–78), Charlotte, NC: Information Age.

SECTION V

CULTIVATING HOMEPLACE

CHAPTER 9

BALANCING
THE CALL TO SERVE

The Costs and Benefits
of Leaving a Legacy in the Academy

**Tamara Bertrand Jones, La'Tara Osborne-Lampkin,
and JeffriAnne Wilder**

Black women doctoral students with faculty career aspirations should be advised of both the benefits and challenges of a future faculty career. For Black women, multiple identities, race and gender in particular, intersect (Crenshaw, 1989; Hill Collins, 2000) in ways that need acknowledgment during the doctoral student socialization process (Bertrand Jones & Osborne-Lampkin, 2013). Often Black women faculty are forced to invalidate stereotypes and legitimize their competence, intelligence, and overall worth (Benjamin, 1997; Hill Collins, 1986; hooks, 1989), especially at predominately White institutions. For these reasons, advising and mentoring relationships can be used to help mitigate the challenges that Black women doctoral students experience and potentially face as new faculty in academe.

Black women have expressed comfort in developing relationships with someone who "looked like" them and someone who understood the

*Beyond Retention: Cultivating Spaces of Equity, Justice, and Fairness
for Women of Color in U.S. Higher Education*, pp. 249–266
Copyright © 2016 by Information Age Publishing
All rights of reproduction in any form reserved.

249

challenges they faced in the academy (Patton, 2009). This notion makes developing professional relationships within the academy more difficult as faculty members are mostly White, middle-aged males (Patton, 2009; Patton & Harper, 2003). And so, while relationships with faculty from any racial/ethnic background, or sex can be effective advisors and mentors to Black female students (Brown, Davis, & McClendon, 1999), Black female faculty are routinely sought out to serve in this capacity. Unfortunately, the lines between mentoring and advising can become blurred for Black female faculty as students seek to find a faculty member with whom they identify. Consequently, Black women faculty members routinely find themselves serving in dual roles for not only their assigned advisees, but for underrepresented students in general.

The literature has documented the unique cultural significance of Black faculty–Black student mentorships. These intraracial relationships are vital to the growth, development, and retention of students *and* faculty of color (Allen, 1992; Kraft, 1991; Sedlacek, 1999). Oftentimes, Black students and other underrepresented students have higher expectations of faculty mentors (Guiffrida, 2005). In fact, research supports the notion that the most successful faculty-student mentoring relationships take place when the student and faculty member share similar characteristics in terms of culture, race, and gender (Davis, Chaney, Edwards, Thompson-Rogers, & Gines, 2004; Guiffrida, 2005; Tuitt, 2012). Yet, at times developing and nurturing these relationships comes at a price for Black female faculty, who already occupy vulnerable positions as underrepresented scholars in the academy.

While we understand that having strong mentoring relationships are invaluable to the success of students of color, the consequences for the faculty who expend their effort and energy in "service" activities can be detrimental to their overall well-being as faculty. To that end, it is imperative to discuss the advantages—and difficulties—associated with Black female faculty who balance the call to "serve" and leave a legacy in the academy. As Moore and Toliver (2010) and Tuitt (2011) point out, these critical conversations are missing from the broader discussion and literature on underrepresentation populations in higher education.

In this chapter, we will discuss two formal mechanisms, institutional and noninstitutional, that can increase mentoring opportunities for students, reducing the load for Black female faculty as they balance research, service, and support to students. Before discussing these mechanisms, we offer personal reflections on how we have navigated our roles as advisors and mentors for underrepresented students. Our narratives focus on the costs and benefits for Black female faculty who serve in these dual roles, both formally and informally. In subsequent sections focused on the intersections and divergences of mentoring and advising and associated faculty responsibilities, respectively—we describe the benefits of these relationships for underrepresented students, and Black female students, specifically.

TO WHOM MUCH IS GIVEN, MUCH IS REQUIRED

Within the academy African American women simultaneously assume the roles of scholars, researchers, educators, mentors, service providers, and social change agents. In addition, as African American women faculty members take the journey in the academy and move toward the tenure and promotion process with aspirations for advancement up the hierarchy of supervisory, management, and administrative goals, they are frequently "tagged as it" or the "go to person" for issues of diversity. (Harley, 2008, p. 24)

As one might imagine, balancing these responsibilities as Harley outlines, requires time and commitment, and is no small feat. In this section, we discuss our individual experiences as faculty members balancing these multiple roles. Moreover, integrated in our discussion is the cultural obligation we feel in carrying out these duties as Black female faculty in academe.

JeffriAnne's Experience as a Faculty Mentor and Advisor

I am a tenured sociologist working at a comprehensive, master's level institution in the Southeast. Black scholars account for only 4% of the total faculty population at my predominately White institution. I am the only African American faculty member in my department of 18 full-time faculty. Thus, I am called on more frequently than my colleagues to serve in a variety of academic service activities, ranging from my current role as the chair of the Commission on Diversity and Inclusion, to the advisor of several cultural student organizations. However, the bulk of my service commitments are dedicated to mentoring and/or advising undergraduate and graduate students. Because of my identity as a Black woman, many female and minority students look to me for guidance, direction, and support outside of the classroom. This domain of my work—oftentimes unrewarded in an evaluative way—requires a great deal of time, effort, and energy that must also be balanced with other duties (teaching and research) that have more tangible professional consequences (i.e., promotion and tenure). Nonetheless, mentoring and advising is undoubtedly one of the most gratifying aspects of my work because I can readily see the fruits of my labor each time a student succeeds.

Although mentoring and advising are conceptualized as two distinctive tasks, in my personal experience, these function as one singular role, encompassing both formal and informal activities. The formal roles include: supervising independent student research; thesis and dissertation committee work; academic advising; graduate school and career counseling; and socializing/inculcating students into the academic system (i.e., sharing the "unwritten rules" of academe). Informally, I have mentored students by writing letters of recommendation for work and graduate school and by serving as a personal "life coach" on a variety of nonacademic issues including, but not limited to, work-life balance, finances, and personal relationships.

In addition to these formal and informal duties of mentoring and advising, there are several culturally significant features of my service built into working with many students of color, particularly Black students. I readily identify with my African American heritage, and like many other faculty of color, my social identity purposefully intersects with my research, teaching, and service endeavors. I feel a cultural obligation and responsibility to ensure the success of students of color at my university. This "oath" of ethics and caring is deeply connected to what Barbara Omolade (1987) refers to as a *Black feminist pedagogy*. For many African American faculty (especially women) the work of teaching and mentoring is done so with a broader concern for African Americans' overall success in higher education. In many instances, students of color expect me to be compassionate and nurturing, consistent with what Guiffrida (2005) and others (see Harley, 2008; Peña & Wilder, 2011) refer to as "other-mothering" in the academy. Finally, because we are both marginalized "others" within a predominately White institution, I serve for many African American students as the "institutional buffer" against racism and other inequities students may face in this environment. It is common for students to share their race-based grievances with me, and my role is to advocate for them in the best way that I can.

Without a doubt, I cannot place a value on the benefits of mentoring students of color who are on the path to attaining undergraduate and graduate degrees. Working with students is the primary reason I stay in the professoriate. I have been fortunate to receive numerous accolades from my institution for excellence in mentoring. Yet, there are significant costs that at times push me to reconsider my career in the academy. In my experience, being good at what you do can be a detriment to your professional livelihood. The better you are as a faculty mentor, the heavier the load can become as more students and colleagues seek you out for service opportunities. This Catch-22 makes it rather challenging to decline these types of requests in favor of focusing on my research agenda. This issue is particularly daunting now as a tenured faculty member because many faculty members at my institution are met with more academic service requests *after* earning tenure: "You've got tenure now, so you can shift your time *away* from research."

I have experienced a tremendous amount of guilt and resentment associated with having to say "no" more often than I would like. In fact, for Black female faculty like myself, there is a considerable amount of mental and emotional discomfort attached to balancing this "call to serve" (see Alexander & Moore, 2008; Griffin, 2013). I have battled "service fatigue" on multiple fronts. The cost of being a role model (I have often heard students say, "*I want to be just like you,*" or "*You are the only reason that I am here and/or made it,*") can place a tremendous burden on faculty to maintain excellence and perfection at all times. Further, it can be isolating for Black female faculty who are not afforded the ability to "turn off" this image of the consummate colleague and professor. Lastly, it is personally defeating to feel that my (in) actions have resulted in the failure of a student of color. I was once scolded by a Black female student's family member for "allowing" this student to fail my class and drop out of school. I was told—in no uncertain terms—that I failed this student because she looked up to me as an African American female professor. It was my personal responsibility to this young woman *and* my race to ensure that she was successful.

In order to combat these kinds of challenges, I have learned to:

- set clear expectations of my mentoring and advising responsibilities,
- respectfully decline service requests that I truly am not able to accommodate,
- develop strong peer relationships with other Black female faculty inside and outside of my institution, and
- find ways to "unplug" from the emotional taxes of mentoring, especially when I am physically away from campus.

Tamara's Experience as a Faculty Mentor and Advisor

One of the aspects of the faculty role I looked forward to most was the interaction with students. I anticipated working with individuals and small groups of students to assist them in their professional development. I understood that I would informally advise many students, with a few formal advisees specifically assigned to me. I recognized that my unofficial roles would include advisor, mentor, and sounding board for the students of color in particular as there were no other women of color in our program when I joined the faculty. I also knew that my previous experience as an administrator would draw full-time professionals and students interested in administrative career options. I thought I was fully prepared to assume these roles; however, the actual load was, and has been, overwhelming at times.

In my first year as an assistant professor, I took on two first-year doctoral students as research assistants, a White female student who had not previously participated in research, and a Taiwanese female student who had engaged in research but for whom English was not her first language. These two women, along with two Black female first-year doctoral students, became my formal advisees. The next spring another Black female advanced doctoral student approached me about becoming her dissertation chair when her chair at the time retired. I said yes and was happy to be the first among the other junior faculty to have a student on track to graduate.

These five advisees did not include the other students, White and students of color, who requested I serve on their dissertation committees or who reached out to me for mentoring. By the end of my first year I had five official advisees and served on five dissertation committees. By the end of my third year, that number grew to nine advisees and 12 dissertation committees. These numbers do not reflect the master's students, or the doctoral students who graduated in these years. Even with accounting for students graduating and my decision to not take on any new advisees, or serve on any new dissertation committees, my chair noted on my progress toward tenure and promotion, "These numbers are higher than we would expect for a junior faculty member in their third year."

My advising load is largely reflective of the "Black tax" (see Cohen, 1998; Griffin & Reddick, 2011). The tax is not only applied for Black students; underrepresented students, women, and other students within my department and outside of my department seek me out. I pay for being Black, female, and what I would describe as "nice" in the academy. I think this is because I am approachable and students can decipher I have their best interests at heart. They sense a familiarity and comfort in my demeanor that encourages them to come to me for advice, or stop by my office to just say hello. While I am humbled and honored, these students exact the tax each time they e-mail, call, or meet with me. At times I marvel at the "back taxes" I've accumulated and owe the Academy Revenue Service because I am tired. The Black tax is real and it is a heavy price to pay for being Black and female in academia.

The cultural significance of my presence, and thus my advising and mentoring, has not escaped me as it ensures that students of color, Black women in particular, have someone who identifies as they do and can support them in their journey. I believe that much is expected from who much is given and as such, I rarely complain, and especially not to students. As a gender-conforming woman, there are certain stereotypes and roles that I unfortunately affirm. I am caring and I am nurturing. The *other-mothering* scholars discuss (see Guiffrida, 2005; Hirt, Amelink, McFeeters, & Strayhorn, 2008) is part of my identity that I do not lament being able to share with students. Unfortunately, the level of care associated with other-mothering is quite taxing, both physically and mentally.

Balancing the multiple roles of advising, teaching, research, and service has been challenging for me. Mainly, because I know that one of the primary purposes I was drawn to academia was my relationship with students. Because I understand the importance of not only having and creating a network of colleagues and mentors (and experienced the benefits firsthand), I rationalized that part of my time would be spent ensuring my students had access to at least my network. However, when I was told to reduce my service (i.e., advising) by my departmental tenure and promotion committee during my third year review, I did. Since I committed to reducing my service load I have received at least five requests to serve on dissertation committees in the last year. Ironically, in the 3 days since I began writing this chapter I have received four requests from students for advising, none of whom are my formal advisees. Navigating these requests and the other responsibilities has left me feeling like academe is an extreme sport indeed (see Davis et al., 2012).

Kimberly Griffin (2013) spoke of the complexity involved in making decisions about service opportunities. I have had to conceptualize my decision making about advising and mentoring in much the same way and develop strategies to support my process. Some of these strategies center on:

- not saying yes immediately;
- pausing and setting aside time to consider the request fully; in saying yes on the spot, I most likely have not yet counted all of the costs associated with this decision;
- consulting my calendar and determining if I truly have the time, expertise, and motivation to be of assistance.

Initially, saying no was difficult for me. Since implementing this strategy, I have said no more times that I have said yes. Students whose work I am interested in, and am able to connect to my own, are ultimately more likely to engage me than others. I felt I was shirking my responsibility as a faculty member by saying no. However, more recently, I have begun to see my "no" responses as freeing up space for me to say yes even more … down the road once I have recovered from all of the previous commitments.

La'Tara's Experience as a Faculty Mentor and Advisor

As a tenure earning faculty member at the same primarily White institution located in the Southeast as my coauthor, I immensely enjoyed teaching and formally advising graduate students. In this capacity, I provided support and developed doctoral students in research by teaching research courses and serving on doctoral dissertation committees. Over the course of my two and a half year tenure at the institution, I cochaired four doctoral dissertations, one which was assigned to me during my first semester when the student's chair "resigned." Under my direction, this student (a Black female) was able to complete the dissertation within a year and half. I also served on 11 dissertation committees, five of which were completed during my tenure at the institution. At first glance, these numbers may not seem overwhelming; however, balancing this commitment along with teaching and research was, indeed, challenging. This challenge was exacerbated by the fact that my research background resulted in both faculty and students actively seeking me out for additional formal and informal advisement. Moreover, the fact that the department was one of two departments that offered one of the two doctoral programs at the institution meant that I was required to support dissertation research, a duty not required of other junior faculty at the institution, including junior colleagues in my department in other programs.

Nevertheless, I embraced this "opportunity," even after being informed by my chair that "dissertation duties were nonevaluative" and "did not count toward teaching, research, or service." Despite this knowledge, as a research scholar, I believed that it was my responsibility to ensure that students were provided opportunities to engage in rigorous, well-designed research. This obligation to students was even more pronounced for minority students who actively sought me out for support, guidance, and validation that they could design and carry out "sound research."

In addition to my advising and teaching responsibilities, I actively pursued my own research agenda and was called upon to serve on various committees at each institutional level. In fact, I actively served on five university committees, five college committees, and four departmental committees, while at the same time serving my profession in various capacities. While my tenure at the institution was, indeed, one of great opportunity and growth, balancing these responsibilities required much effort, stamina, and ingenuity.

I have since transitioned to a research faculty position at another primarily White institution. And, while my formal responsibilities for advising and service have shifted, I have still provided a great deal of informal advising for students through various means. For example, as a research faculty member, I have advised graduate research assistants for the past 3 years. While not their formal advisor, I have served as mentor and advisor for all seven of my research students over the years, in varying capacities. Currently in my role of supervising three graduate research assistants, I have provided mentoring and support that spans from supporting the design of the independent research studies to helping them understand the "unwritten rules" of the academy. One of my most challenging experiences has been informally advising students, both minority and nonminority, who have taken research courses that I taught as an adjunct. I have undertaken this role with mixed emotions, largely due to the fact that assigned faculty should serve in these roles. Yet, these emotions have been countered by an obligation to help students, particularly Black female students, "make it through." The cultural obligation to support students, specifically students of color, has in some instances required me to provide hours and hours of support—time that should be used for my research—given my faculty appointment. So, one might pose the question: Will you continue to engage in this practice? With mixed emotions, I must say, certainly.

making Sacrifices

Despite what is deemed as a "nonevaluative" duty in the academy, I will continue to formally and informally advise students. However, over the years, I have actively engaged in activities to support this work. First, when assigned a graduate student to formally advise my first semester as an assistant professor, I immediately engaged in research to ensure that the advising practices that I employed were actually grounded in the research. As a result of this process, I have implemented the following to manage and support my advising "responsibilities":

- request students send a miniprospectus outlining their research interests and how they envision I might support their work;
- respectfully decline requests that are not clearly aligned with my expertise and, on occasion, my research interests, as well as those I simply cannot accommodate due to other commitments;
- develop informal/formal contracts outlining my responsibilities and the responsibility of the student, including timeframes for deliverables; and
- seek out colleagues to engage in research to identify promising practices for mentoring and advising students to expand my "tool kit" in order to better support students and balance my advising and mentoring responsibilities with other duties.

As illustrated in our narratives, as Black female faculty, we have been committed to the service of advising and mentoring students. And while we have served in these capacities for all students, we have demonstrated an increased commitment to students of color and to Black female students in particular. This commitment has not come without a cost, particularly in terms of time and, in some cases, stress, to balance the duties associated with these roles with our other faculty responsibilities. Yet, we turn now turn to the benefits of our service, specifically to those we have been committed to serving.

BUILDING A LEGACY: THE ROLE OF ADVISING AND MENTORING IN IMPROVING SUCCESS FOR UNDERREPRESENTED STUDENTS

The growth and presence of Black women in the professoriate is inexorably linked to the access, entry, and retention of Black women in doctoral programs (Mabokela, 2001; Moses, 1997). Without strong numbers of Black female students in the doctoral pipeline, the future of Black women scholars—and the diverse voices and perspectives that they bring to the academy—cannot survive and flourish (Evans, 2007). In graduate school, key relationships are developed that aid students in developing social and cultural capital, as well as the personal agency needed for success. The mentoring and advising processes provide vehicles for the exchange of information about graduate school and the academic profession that is critical to student success.

Researchers have long argued that two of the most important relationships doctoral students form in graduate school are with their mentors and advisors (Baird, 1997; de Valero, 2001; Felder, 2010; Gardner, 2009; Golde, 1998; Wao & Onwuegbuzie, 2011). Mentoring and advising relationships influence doctoral student academic and social integration in their disciplines, and also their overall satisfaction (Ellis, 2001; Nerad & Miller, 1996; Nettles, 1990). Faculty advisors play a particularly important role in the persistence of Black graduate students (Milner, 2004). For Black females on the path to the professoriate, doctoral advising is an even more critical determinant of success (Essein, 1997).

For many underrepresented populations in higher education, mentoring and advising have been thought of as effective strategies for increasing retention and graduation rates (Brown et al., 2010; Gregory, 1999; Patton & Harper, 2003; Smith & Davidson, 1992). Students experience many benefits of mentoring and advising when relationships are designed to meet their individual needs. Unfortunately, in research literature and discussions of mentoring and advising, the terms are used interchangeably despite the different functions and characteristics of both processes (Barnes & Austin, 2009; Mertz, 2004; Wao & Onwuegbuzie, 2011). In this section, we discuss the intersections and divergences of mentoring and advising and faculty responsibilities associated with these processes.

Faculty Responsibilities in Advising and Mentoring

In previous work, we detail the distinctions between mentoring and advising (Bertrand Jones, Wilder, & Osborne-Lampkin, 2013) and examine how the terms and functions associated with each process overlap. The roles of the mentor and advisor are different in that the mentoring relationship provides psychosocial and career support and role modeling (Jacobi, 1991; Kram & Isabella, 1985) while the advisor provides programmatic academic support (Bertrand Jones et al., 2013). Much like that argument, our claim here is that careful articulation and observance of the distinctions of the advising and mentoring functions allows for all faculty, regardless of race or gender, to be actively engaged in both relationships with all students.

For example, Mertz's (2004) conceptual model of developmental relationships included both mentoring and advising as separate types of relationships. With support from Mertz's (2004) work, we distinguish advising as a relationship focused on advice about programs of study, academic issues, and working closely with students in planning and conducting dissertation research. These distinguishable roles result in both unique, and overlapping, associated faculty mentor responsibilities. We also highlight the associated faculty responsibilities for mentoring, and propose those specific to advising (see Bertrand Jones et al., 2013).

Mertz's argument that the intent of individuals involved in the relationship, and the level of investment required, distinguishes the type of mentoring or advising relationship. In her pyramid, advising is above and more involved than role modeling, but below and less involved than mentoring. Most times students and faculty are assigned in advising relationships, unfortunately creating mismatched intentions, as compared to advising relationships where both the student and advisor had a say in the match. The advisor may serve as the student's major professor/committee member on the dissertation committee, and may also be a mentor to the student. As such, Knox, Schlosser, Pruitt, and Hill (2006) found that advisors identified their role as mentor, role model, and professional developer. Researchers contend that the differences in intent influence how women and doctoral students (Heinrich, 1995; Ragins & McFarlin, 1990) develop meaningful mentoring and advising relationships.

Given the requirement of faculty time and commitment to the doctoral advising and mentoring, better understanding faculty perceptions of their roles in these relationships can help further extricate the distinctions in mentoring and advising. We suggest using a Black feminist approach to advising not only Black female doctoral students, but for working with all students. The framework we proposed for advising combined many tenets of Black feminist thought with responsibilities, functions, and characteristics of advisors (Bertrand Jones et al., 2013). We expand our argument of a culturally responsive approach to advising to include mentoring. A culturally responsive approach to both mentoring and advising helps to clarify the intent of the relationship and mitigates many of the challenges identified by Black women doctoral students in academe and can positively influence doctoral degree completion and program satisfaction. This approach also extends the responsibility for advising and mentoring underrepresented populations to all faculty, regardless of race, gender, or other identity.

In the final section of this chapter, we go beyond the individual strategies we have employed as Black female faculty balancing the multiple demands of teaching, research, and service with those associated with mentoring and advising. Specifically, we highlight mechanisms and structures that can be used to support faculty and mitigate some of the challenges associated with balancing the demands of the academy, while still ensuring students of color have someone to identify with and the support needed for their academic journey.

Developing Strategies and Creating Networks to Meet and Balance the Call to Serve

The strategies we offer in this chapter would serve all faculty well. However, our identification as Black and female in academia allow for heightened awareness and responsiveness to the quandaries for Black women. We predicate much of our discussion in this section on the mechanisms that may positively influence our own experiences, and those of other Black women in the academy. There are two broader issues that undergird the problem at hand, the success and number of Black women in academia. We offer two main recommendations; one calls for a revisited role of institutional actors in facilitating the success of Black women, and the other involves support from professional organizations in increasing the number of Black women in academia.

Institutional Actors' Role in Facilitating Black Women's Success

The functions that advisors and mentors serve in students' lives, as discussed earlier, can be extended to institutional actors who influence faculty assignments, recognition, and ultimately award of tenure and promotion. Institutional actors, like department chairs, deans, and upper level administrators, should develop awareness of the intersecting oppressions of race and gender for all faculty, but especially for Black women. Black women's status as "outsiders-within" (Hill Collins, 1986) gives us unique perspective of the culture of academia, which in turn allows us to both critique and contribute to knowledge production. Essentially, our presence represents a level of knowledge that not all of our counterparts in academia possess. Awareness of this knowledge enables institutional actors to ensure that our unique position is not exploited, but validated. Validation in this sense ensures that all participants are viewed as equal contributors. Validation builds on the awareness cultivated of Black women's contributions as academicians and cultured beings with the understanding that these "dual-identities" contribute much to departments, colleges, and institutions broadly (Moore & Toliver, 2010).

Awareness

Advocating requires that institutional actors recognize Black women's participation in the advising and mentoring processes by recognizing and rewarding the unofficial and informal mentoring and advising in which Black women engage. In our narratives we discussed the students with whom we were assigned as primary advisor, along with the additional students whose primary advisor we were not. In the current recognition structure in academia, faculty typically get "credit" for those students they are officially assigned to advise. All other advising is "off the record." We argue that institutional actors advocate for the assistance provided to these additional students be considered as part of the official record and devise mechanisms for recording and rewarding this additional load.

Advocating

Institutional actors are primed to educate Black female faculty about the institutional policies and practices that support their advising and mentoring efforts. As evidenced in our narratives and articulated by Kimberly Griffin (2013), Black women use complex decision-making processes to determine what activities in which to engage. Saying no to service obligations, or limiting advising and mentoring relationships is often counter to what many Black women view as one of their purposes for being in academia. As such, seemingly simple advice of "just say no" only serves to privilege one of the complicated dual-identities of academician and cultured being that Black female faculty operate claim in academia. Operating with no or little service mandates forces Black women faculty to choose between a sense of cultural responsibility and professional self-preservation.

Professional Organizations Role in Increasing Numbers of Black Women

This discussion of cultural responsibility and professional self-preservation would be less of an issue if there were more Black women in aca-

Professional organizations

demia. An underutilized mechanism for increasing the numbers of Black women in academia is professional organizations. Professional organizations represent a critical mass of individuals focused on a particular issue, discipline, or cause whose focus can be used to target the underrepresentation of many populations in academia.

Many mainstream professional organizations have subgroups that focus on underrepresented scholars' participation or representation in the organization. For example, the American Educational Research Association, which two of us are members of, has a committee on scholars of color whose role is to provide programming for underrepresented scholars in education. The committee coordinates formal recognition of scholars of color in the larger organization's awards process and provides focused networking and professional development opportunities for scholars of color. This committee, and many like it in other professional organizations of various disciplines, can be used to leverage participation of Black women in academia. Targeted outreach to Black women that provides workshops, trainings, and networking opportunities serve to help Black women develop the skills needed for broader success, as well as create networks the women can draw on thereafter.

Whereas the example above involves a discipline specific professional association, Sisters of the Academy (SOTA) Institute is an example of a multidisciplinary organization that serves to create a network of Black women in particular. Founded in 2001, SOTA's mission is to create a network of Black women to facilitate their success in academia. One of their professional development programs, the Research BootCamp, is designed to assist advanced doctoral students in progress and completion of their dissertation research and junior faculty in the development of manuscripts for publication. SOTA's work, in this capacity, can be leveraged to both increase the number of Black females with doctorate degrees and support the retention of Black female faculty in the academy. An increase in the number of these women broaden the pool from which institutions and students alike can select their advisors and mentors, thus lessening the load for existing Black female faculty.

CONCLUSION

As scholars with similar research interests of mentoring, advising, and faculty development, we have personally benefited from a peer network that has not only strengthen our collective and independent scholarship, but has also enhanced our toolkit with increased strategies for balancing commitments to research, service, and teaching. As three Black women in academia, we have collectively experienced challenges associated with navigating and balancing the demands, therein. Our experiences, both individual and collective, are valid and can be used to facilitate understanding of the ways that Black women survive and thrive in the academy (Hill Collins, 1986).

In this chapter, we discuss our service as advisors and mentors to students, serving in both formal and informal roles. The purpose of our discussion in this chapter was twofold. First, we wanted to illuminate the complexity of weighing our decisions to serve, in some cases, in dual roles as advisors and mentors to underrepresented students, while maintaining other faculty responsibilities. Within this discussion, we highlight the costs associated with these decisions, as well as, the internal and external benefits of serving in these roles. Second, and perhaps foremost, as we recognize that the decision for Black women faculty, in particular, to serve as mentors and advisors is one that is embedded in a sense of cultural responsibility. As such, we provide strategies and propose mechanisms to mitigate the challenges and "tax" on faculty as they seek to serve in these capacities, while ensuring their own preservation and success in the academy.

We acknowledge that mentoring and advising are two distinct roles, yet even we [the authors], struggle with separating them. Understanding the disparate number of underrepresented scholars serving in faculty roles, Black women in particular, we feel a sense of obligation to ensure that students have someone in which they identify with and can provided the support needed for academic success. Implementing strategies that require both us, as faculty members, and students to think through the suitability (i.e., students developing miniprospectus) and feasibility (i.e., faculty reviewing other commitments) of the advising relationships to simply declining requests, can help reduce what can become overwhelming advising responsibilities. Yet, institutional mechanisms that recognize and validate this type of service (i.e., advising and mentoring to students) are also warranted. There is also much promise for targeted supports (e.g., training, workshops) and mechanisms (e.g., SOTA) that can potentially have a broader impact on the retention and influx of Black women in the academy. Employing such strategies can facilitate Black female faculty in leaving a legacy of scholars who "look like us" and who can in turn "pay it forward" without resulting in the detriment of our success as Black women in the academy.

REFERENCES

Alexander, R., & Moore, S. (2008). The benefits, challenges, and strategies of African American faculty teaching at predominately white institutions. *Journal of African American Studies, 12*, 4–18.

Allen, W. R. (1992). The color of success: African American college student outcomes at predominately White and historically Black public colleges and universities. *Harvard Educational Review, 62*(1), 26–44.

Baird, L. L. (1997). Completing the dissertation: Theory, research, and practice. *New Directions for Higher Education, 99*, 99–105. doi:10.1002/he.9909

Barnes, B. J., & Austin, A. E. (2009). The role of doctoral advisors: A look at advising from the advisor's perspective. *Innovative Higher Education 33*, 297–315.

Benjamin, L. (Ed.) (1997). *Black women in the academy: Promises and perils*. Gainesville, FL: University of Florida Press.

Bertrand Jones, T., & Osborne-Lampkin, L. (2013). Early career professional development: Enhancing Black female faculty success. *Negro Educational Review, 64*(1-4), 59–75.

Bertrand-Jones, T., Wilder, J., & Osborne-Lampkin, L. (2013). Employing a Black feminist pedagogical approach to doctoral advising: Preparing Black women for the professoriate. *Journal of Negro Education, 82*(3), 326–338.

Brown, S., Davis, C., & McClendon, S. (1999). Mentoring graduate students of color: Myths, models, and modes. *Peabody Journal of Education, 74*(2), 105–118.

Cohen, J. J. (1998). Time to shatter the glass ceiling for minority faculty. *JAMA, 280*(9), 821–822.

Crenshaw, K. (1989). Demarginalizing the intersection of race and sex: A Black feminist critique of antidiscrimination doctrine, feminist theory and antiracist politics. *The University of Chicago Legal Forum*, 139–167.

Davis, D. J., Chaney, C., Edwards, L., Thompson-Rogers, G. K., & Gines, K. T. (2012). Academe as extreme sport: Black women, faculty development, and networking. *Negro Educational Review, 62/63*(1-4), 167–187.

de Valero, Y. F. (2001). Departmental factors affecting time-to-degree and completion rates of doctoral students at one land-grant research institution. *The Journal of Higher Education, 72*(3), 341–367.

Ellis, E. M. (2001). The impact of race and gender on graduate school socialization, satisfaction with doctoral study, and commitment to degree completion. *Western Journal of Black Studies, 25*(1) 30–46. Retrieved November 11, 2002, from Academic Index database.

Essein, F. (1997). Black women in the sciences: Challenges along the pipeline and in the academy. In L. Benjamin (Ed.), *Black women in the academy: Promises and perils* (pp. 91–102). Gainesville, FL: University of Florida Press.

Evans, S. Y. (2007). *Black women in the ivory tower, 1850–1954*. Gainesville, FL: University Press of Florida.

Felder, P. (2010). On doctoral student development: Exploring faculty mentoring in the shaping of African American doctoral student success. *The Qualitative Report, 15*(2), 455–474.

Gardner, S. K. (2009). Student and faculty attributions of attrition in high and low-completing doctoral programs in the United States. *Higher Education: The International Journal of Higher Education and Educational Planning, 58*(1), 97–112. doi:10.1007/s10734-008-9184-7

Golde, C. M. (1998). Beginning graduate school: Explaining first-year doctoral attrition. *New Directions for Higher Education, 101*, 55–64.

Gregory, S. (1999). *Black women in the academy: The secrets to success and achievement* (Revised ed.). Lanham, MD: University Press of America.

Griffin, K. A. (2013). The calculus of yes and no: How one professor makes decisions about academic service. *Thought and Action*, *29*, 35–44.

Griffin, K. A., & Reddick, R. J. (2011). Surveillance and sacrifice gender differences in the mentoring patterns of Black professors at predominantly White research universities. *American Educational Research Journal*, *48*(5), 1032–1057.

Guiffrida, D. A. (2005). Othermothering as a framework for understanding African American students' definitions of student-centered faculty. *The Journal of Higher Education*, *76*(6), 701–723.

Harley, D. (2008). Maids of academe: African-American women faculty at predominately White institutions. *Journal of African American Studies*, *12*, 19–36.

Heinrich, K. T. (1995). Doctoral advisement relationships between women. *Journal of Higher Education*, *66*(4), 447–469.

Hill Collins, P. (1986). Learning from the outsider within: The sociological significance of Black feminist thought. *Social Problems*, *33*, 514–532.

Hill Collins, P. (2000). *Black feminist thought: Knowledge, consciousness, and the politics of empowerment*. New York, NY: Routledge.

Hirt, J. B., Amelink, C. T., McFeeters, B. B., & Strayhorn, T. L. (2008). A system of othermothering: Student affairs administrators' perceptions of relationships with students at historically Black colleges. *NASPA Journal*, *45*(2), 210–236.

hooks, b. (1989). *Talking back: Thinking feminist, thinking Black*. Boston, MA: South End Press.

Jacobi, M. (1991). Mentoring and undergraduate academic success: A literature review. *Review of Educational Research*, *61*(4), 505–532.

Knox, S., Schlosser, L. Z., Pruitt, N., & Hill, C. E. (2006). A qualitative examination of graduate advising relationships: The advisor perspective. *Counseling Psychologist*, *34*(4), 489–518.

Kraft, C. L. (1991). What makes a successful Black student on a predominately white campus? *American Educational Research Journal*, *28*(2), 423–443.

Kram, K. E., & Isabella, L. A. (1985). Mentoring alternatives: The role of peer relationships in career development. *Academy of Management Journal*, *28*(1), 110–132.

Mertz, N. T. (2004). What's a mentor, anyway? *Educational Administration Quarterly*, *40*(4), 541–560. doi:10.1177/0013161X04267110

Mabokela, R. O. (2001). Introduction: Soaring beyond boundaries. In R.O. Mabokela & A. L. Green (Eds.), *Sisters of the academy: Emergent Black women scholars in higher education* (pp. xiii–xx). Sterling, VA: Stylus.

Milner, H. R. (2004). African American graduate students' experiences: A critical analysis of recent research. In D. Cleveland (Ed.), *A long way to go: Conversations about race by African American faculty and graduate students* (pp. 19–31). New York, NY: Peter Lang.

Moore, P., & Toliver, S. (2010). Intraracial dynamics of Black professors' and Black students' communication in traditionally White colleges and universities. *Journal of Black Studies*, *40*(5), 932–945.

Moses, Y. (1997). Black women in academe: Issues and strategies. In L. Benjamin (Ed.), *Black women in the academy: Promises and perils* (pp. 23–38). Gainesville, FL: University of Florida Press.

Nerad, M., & Miller, D. S. (1996). Increasing student retention in graduate and professional programs. *New Directions in Institutional Research, 92*, 61–76.

Nettles, M. T. (1990). Success in doctoral programs: Experiences of minority and White students. *American Journal of Education, 98*, 494–522.

Omolade, B. (1987). A black feminist pedagogy. *Women's Studies Quarterly, 15*(3/4), 32–39.

Patton, L. D. (2009). My sister's keeper: A qualitative examination of mentoring experiences among African American women in graduate and professional schools. *The Journal of Higher Education, 80*(5), 510–537.

Patton, L. D., & Harper, S. R. (2003). Mentoring relationships among African American women in graduate and professional schools. *New Directions for Student Services, 104*, 67–78.

Peña, M., & Wilder, J. (2011). Mentoring transformed: When students of color see diversity in leadership. *Diversity in Higher Education, 10*, 345–363.

Ragins, B. R., & McFarlin, D. B. (1990). Perceptions of mentor roles in cross-gender mentoring relationships. *Journal of Vocational Behavior, 37*, 321–339.

Sedlacek, W. E. (1999). Black students on white campuses: 20 years of research. *Journal of College Student Development, 40*(5), 538–550.

Smith, E. P., & Davidson, W. M. (1992). Mentoring and the development of African-America graduate students. *Journal of College Student Development, 33*(6), 531–539.

Tuitt, F. (2012). Black like me: Graduate students' perceptions of their pedagogical experiences in classes taught by Black faculty in a predominately White institution. *Journal of Black Studies, 43*(2), 186–206.

Wao, H. O., & Onwuegbuzie, A. J. (2011). A mixed research investigation of factors related to time to the doctorate in education. *International Journal of Doctoral Studies, 6*, 115–134.

CHAPTER 10

EXPRESSING CIVIC VIRTUE INSIDE A CROOKED ROOM

A Call to Awareness for Women of Color at Predominantly White Institutions

Mahauganee Dawn Shaw

One morning, as a first-year doctoral student, I found myself essentially chasing a young assistant professor across the parking lot. I was attempting to engage her in conversation and make a connection to a potential mentor. She perceivably was attempting to avoid getting engaged in a conversation that would interrupt her morning routine. I only got a few words from her and one glance as she hurried away from me. As I watched her enter the building that we both called our academic home, I thought "She's going to be my friend, and doesn't know it yet. I'll follow up with an e-mail." In the pages that follow, I explore this experience and others through a discussion of organizational citizenship and how Black women approach the task of claiming citizenship within predominantly White institutions (PWIs) of higher education. So, this chapter begins at the end of this story with two questions: How do we get to the point where (a) a Black female doctoral student is so desperate for connection that she is chasing potential mentors across campus, and (b) a Black female faculty

Beyond Retention: Cultivating Spaces of Equity, Justice, and Fairness
for Women of Color in U.S. Higher Education, pp. 267–286

member is so protective of her time that she is avoiding all possible distractions? This chapter offers perspectives that will help dissect the above scenario—in which one person takes on the role of chasing or seeking potential mentors and resources while another becomes chased, making their time a sought after commodity—and others like it.

As the mere existence of this book proclaims, women of color (Asian, Black, Latina, etc.) are known to have marginalizing experiences within predominantly White environments at institutions that have yet to identify and implement effective methods of fully integrating women of color into campus operations. Building on these foundational ideas and claims, this chapter is not written as a call to action for PWIs to shift policies and practices in a manner that will acknowledge the needs of all members of the campus community. While there is no doubt that policies and practices need to shift, the focus of this chapter is the empowerment of women of color as members of predominantly White campus communities. Throughout the pages that follow, I offer a call to both awareness and action for women of color that belong to PWI communities to develop and maintain methods of asserting our presence on campus, inserting our voices into campus conversations, and reflecting on how our experiences and actions communicate our rights as institutional citizens.

Before offering the call, I will introduce the concept of organizational citizenship and the metaphor of the crooked room. Together, these two ideas will help provide a framework for making sense of the experiences of women of color in predominantly White spaces. More specifically, these concepts will be used as a foundation for examining the experiences of women of color working, teaching, and learning on PWI campuses. Personal narratives will be used to provide examples of how women of color embody their roles as citizens of predominantly White organizations and operate within crooked environments.

Introduction to Relevant Concepts

Central to this call to awareness and action is the concept of organizational citizenship, and the behaviors which suggest that someone maintains citizenship status within an organization. However, to fully understand the difficulty that women of color may experience when attempting to display organizational citizenship at PWIs, it is also important to understand how PWIs resemble a crooked room. The sections that follow provide an introduction to each of these concepts and set the stage for the narratives that follow.

Organizational Citizenship Behavior

Many researchers have studied organizational citizenship over the years; the result of this body of research is a defined set of citizenship behaviors displayed within the workplace. In his seminal work on organizational citizenship behavior (OCB), Organ (1988) defined and explained OCB as follows:

> Individual behavior that is discretionary, not directly or explicitly recognized by the formal reward system, and that in the aggregate promotes the effective functioning of the organization. By *discretionary*, we mean that the behavior is not an enforceable requirement of the role or the job description.... Thus, college professors who prep for their courses, teach, do research, and write are not, by our construction, exhibiting OCB, no matter how good their teaching and research is judged by others. (p. 4)

Thus, organizational citizenship is defined through the expression of behaviors that lie outside of one's expected job functions. OCB consists of the informal actions performed in addition to one's work responsibilities. It is posited that these actions truly communicate one's investment in the success of the organization. Recent research has begun to question individual motives behind engaging in OCBs and how time spent engaging in OCBs influences the completion of work assignments and the achievement of organizational goals (e.g., Bergeron, Shipp, Rosen, & Furst, 2012; Bolino, Klotz, Turnley, & Harvey, 2013).

Organ's (1988) *Organizational Citizenship Behavior: The Good Solider Syndrome* looked across various areas of scholarship to compile previous work that helped to provide a foundation for the developing area of study focused on OCBs. In so doing, Organ identified four categories of OCBs that were emerging from the literature at that time: altruism, conscientiousness, courtesy, and civic virtue. In a more recent analysis of the extant literature on OCBs, Podsakoff, MacKenzie, Paine, and Bachrach (2000) again reviewed previous research that identified various forms of citizenship behavior. Their result was the compilation and definition of the following "seven common themes or dimensions: helping behavior, sportsmanship, organizational loyalty, organizational compliance, individual initiative, civic virtue, and self-development" (p. 516). The growth in number from four OCBs to seven is a testament to the amount of attention OCBs received from organization researchers over the years since Organ's (1988) book. Each of the four OCBs originally identified by Organ has been mapped into one of the seven previously listed categories. Of the seven, this chapter will specifically focus on one of the original four OCBs, civic virtue. Civic virtue will provide the framework for how women of color can boldly assert their citizenship status within their PWI homes.

In Podsakoff et al.'s (2000) analysis, the following citizenship behaviors are combined into the theme of civic virtue: organizational participation, making constructive suggestions, protecting the organization, persisting with enthusiasm and extra effort, volunteering to carry out task activities, and job dedication. Those who exhibit civic virtue are thus believed to express:

> a macrolevel interest in, or commitment to, the organization as a whole … shown by a willingness to participate actively in its governance (i.e., attend meetings, engage in policy debates, express one's opinion about the strategy the organization ought to follow, etc.); to monitor its environment for threats and opportunities (e.g., keep up with changes in the industry that might affect the organization); and to look out for its best interests (e.g., reporting fire hazards or suspicious activities, locking doors, etc.), *even at great personal cost* [emphasis added]. These behaviors reflect a person's recognition of being part of a larger whole in the same way that citizens are members of a country and accept the responsibilities entailed. (Podsakoff et al., 2000, p. 525)

Citizenship, by definition, implies that one has inherent rights and privileges. Throughout this chapter, I will explore the rights and privileges that citizens of PWIs are entitled to, and how women of color can take ownership of these rights and privileges by expressing civic virtue within their work lives. The expression of civic virtue is not the safest form of citizenship expression. Organ (1988) notes that civic virtue potentially "carries the risk of disapproval, [and] hence some personal cost" (p. 13). While the expression of civic virtue may be inherently risky, it also carries with it the potential for great reward—both the accomplishment of influencing change in the organization and the intrinsic pride associated with doing one's part to encourage organizational advancement.

The Metaphor of the Crooked Room

In discussing Melissa Harris-Perry's (2011) *Sister Citizen: Shame, Stereotypes, and Black Women in America*, Tejada (2013) discusses the significance of Harris-Perry's metaphor of the crooked room. She states:

> the metaphor of the crooked room, a place of misrecognition that is filled with stereotypical myths of Black women … [is used by Harris-Perry to help] readers [understand] the structural constraints that mainstream White society imposes on Black women and [to analyze] Black women's fight to be authentically recognized. (Tejada, 2013, p. 269)

This metaphor, born from research on field dependence attempting to investigate how individuals find an upright position within a space that has been tilted, provides a foundation for the issues addressed in this chapter. Reporting on the findings of a field dependency study where participants were positioned in a crooked chair inside of a crooked room, Harris-Perry (2011) notes:

> To the researchers' surprise, some people could be tilted by as much as 35 degrees and report that they were perfectly straight, simply because they were aligned with images that were equally tilted. But not everyone did this: Some managed to get themselves more or less upright regardless of how crooked the surrounding images were. (p. 29)

In many ways, PWIs—institutions that were not established with the intention to serve women or people of color and ascribe to missions that were often penned prior to the admission of the first female or person of color to the student or faculty ranks—are representative of crooked rooms. People of color who belong to a PWI community must attempt to, figuratively, stand up straight inside of the crooked room they call their academic home.

One's awareness that the room (campus environment) is crooked (structured in a way that is marginalizing or alienating) affects how one interacts with others and embodies citizenship behavior. Therefore, in order for us to truly understand the experiences of women of color on predominantly White campuses, we must understand how these campuses are askew and how that angle influences the experiences of citizens who do not belong to the dominant culture. As noted by Harris-Perry (2011), "We can better understand sisters [in this case, all women of color] as citizens when we appreciate the crooked room in which they struggle to stand upright" (p. 32). To assist in this understanding, I turn now to a brief description of the higher education landscape and the presence of people of color within the faculty ranks.

Higher Education as a Crooked Space

In 2011, the most recent year for which data are available from the National Center for Education Statistics, there were 761,619 full-time instructional faculty in degree-granting institutions (Snyder & Dillow, 2013, p. 419). Women comprise 44% of this number, and are more highly represented in lecturer and instructor positions than in tenure track positions. Women of color only represent a small percentage of the female faculty: Black (4.5%), Hispanic (7.7%), Asian (7.5%), Pacific Islander (0.22%), and American Indian/Alaska Native (0.53%). Women belonging to two or more racial or ethnic categories were too small of a group to calculate an accurate percentage.

Education, my field of study, is one of the fields in which female faculty outnumber male faculty. However, the racial/ethnic distribution of Education faculty is similar to those reported for the entire teaching population. Education faculty members are mostly White (85.1%), with 6.6% Black, 5.1% Hispanic, 1.6% Asian/Pacific Islander, and 1.5% American Indian or Alaska Native (Snyder & Dillow, 2013, p. 429). While these statistics are able to paint a general picture of faculty life within U.S. institutions, they do not define campus environments and what is possible within those environments. Now that we have a brief overview of the higher education landscape, the rest of this chapter will focus on how citizens can take ownership of their organizational homes and make an impact that defies the statistics.

When presented with a crooked space, each person will individually adjust themselves as needed to fit into and navigate through the space. So, how does one operate within a crooked environment while neither being blind to the crookedness nor blinded by the adjustments that have been made, either by oneself or others? This is the overarching question with which I approached the writing of this chapter and which I attempt to answer through sharing my own personal experiences of attempting to "stand up straight in a crooked room" (Harris-Perry, 2000, p. 29).

ENCOUNTERS WITH CROOKED SPACES AND ACTS OF CIVIC VIRTUE

Personal narratives are used below to illuminate the topic of organizational citizenship and examples of women of color carving out and claiming space within PWI settings. While many of my meaningful experiences in academe have involved men and women of varying racial and ethnic backgrounds, I only share relationships involving other Black women in this section. Focusing specifically on these relationships provides a platform to discuss encounters with crooked rooms and acts of civic virtue from the multiple positions that Black women occupy within the academy. The narratives that follow highlight some of my experiences of attempting to assert my citizenship within PWI environments and learning how to locate the upright position as a Black female citizen of a predominantly White campus. These experiences range from my orientation to PWI citizenship as an undergraduate student to my current experiences as a PWI faculty citizen. In this discussion of citizenship, marginalization, and civic virtue, there are traces of the other six OCBs; however, these will not be directly explored. Brief definitions of each of the six remaining behaviors from Podsakoff et al. (2000) are included in Appendix A.

The foundation for my perception of what it means to be a Black female operating within a predominantly White academic space was formed throughout my high school and undergraduate experiences. Leaving high school, I had certain perceptions of what it meant to be educated in a predominantly White environment; despite the fact that many of these perceptions made me uncomfortable, I opted to attend a predominantly White university. Based on my previous educational experiences, I entered college believing that I would only have rare occasions to see aspects of my culture reflected inside the curriculum and environment and that I would likely encounter people who would impose preconceived beliefs of me based only on my outward appearance. On the other hand, I knew that I could use elective experiences to supplement my prescribed curriculum in ways that I would find "culturally nourishing" (González, 2000), and I understood that there were support services and people in place to help me navigate difficult situations as they arose.

I began my undergraduate experience enrolled in an intensive academic program, the kind where they sat us down at orientation and told us that there had been seven applicants for each of the seats we were filling in the room. Those of us entering that program totaled approximately 120 students. Our program required that we took most of our classes together as a cohort and shared an academic advisor. Of that cohort, eight of us had Black heritage—five females and three males. My father would jokingly refer to the eight of us as the "minority participation." Those of us within the minority participation cohort who needed each other to feel supported and comforted banded together as a fairly tight-knit group and helped each other the best we knew how. Although there were other people in our individual social networks, we would study together, attend class together, spend a nice chunk of our free time hanging out with each other, and occasionally plan our own "prayer breakfasts" in the cafeteria on the mornings when we had major exams. When we struggled through a particularly difficult course one semester, four of us even hired a tutor together and would do joint tutoring sessions. With this group, I was able to blend academic spaces with social spaces. Rather than seeking out the cultural spaces on campus (e.g., the Black culture center or the minority student affairs office) as places where we could feel at home and at ease, having the minority participation cohort together helped us to make otherwise alienating campus spaces much more welcoming and comfortable. To sit in a large lecture hall alone with 119 other students would have been a challenging experience for me. However, to sit in that same lecture hall flanked by three to six other people who shared common perspectives and my cultural background was a nourish-

importance of finding community

ing experience for me. Those experiences helped me to lay the keystones to my understanding of my placement and positioning within my PWI campus.

Supplementing my education through cocurricular involvement and predominantly Black social spaces helped me to navigate the collegiate environment. In my secondary and undergraduate educational experiences, each time that I chose an African/Black-centered elective or social experience, it was an attempt to locate the spaces on campus that felt a little less crooked. Every time, during my collegiate career, that I became the sole Black member of a student organization or was elected or hired into a student leadership position on campus, I saw that as an opportunity to help make the campus a little less crooked for other Black students. It was the way that I expressed my civic virtue. By being present in spaces where people of color were not well-represented and inserting my perspectives and opinions, I was able to influence campus programs and policies.

People of color in the United States often learn from an early age to bend themselves to fit into the dominant culture. We learn this from watching our parents, guardians, and community members change their word choice or vocal inflections or accents or language from one space to another. The power of observation allows us to notice the differences in our parents' body language and communication tactics from one situation to another—when they are on the phone with their siblings versus a telemarketer versus the church pastor, or in the safety of the car with the immediate family versus inside of a parent-teacher conference. Observing the people around us provides some of our first lessons on how to change ourselves to assimilate as seamlessly as possible into the expectations and norms of the dominant culture. The fact that we learn to go back and forth between our own culture and the dominant culture, moving between environments where our behavior oscillates between higher and lower levels of comfort and informality, is an indicator that we both believe there to be benefits to the ability to assimilate into White culture and see fault with the perceived need to assimilate. The ability to assimilate by softening accents, altering body language, and changing word choice, allows people of color to engage in the dominant culture, offer critiques and ideas, in a manner that is more readily received. Even as we bend to fit into the crooked room presented to us by predominantly White environments, we do not forget that there is an environment that feels more upright and inviting, more nourishing.

It was not until my graduate school experience that I had a Black female take an uninvited interest in me and my future path. There had been several Black female mentors in my life prior to that point, but this time was different. My previous mentors were people who were often assigned to me through some community program or group in which I was participating. This time, however, there was a Black female faculty member who taught in my program of study and wanted to see me succeed. Her interest in me and my success felt genuine, and although I had always engaged with and appreciated my previous mentors, I welcomed her mentorship even more because she identified me on her own. No one assigned her to me or me to her; our relationship was organic, and that was a new experience for me. I was drawn to her. She was poised and graceful in a way that I did not often see modeled, and that I had come to think of as rarely expected of Black women within predominantly White spaces. Her presence commanded attention, and yet she was soft spoken. My introduction to this mentor ignited my quest to observe Black women who were navigating the PWI environment in professional roles. This particular mentor remained in contact with me when I went off to work full-time after my master's program and was helpful in my process of applying to doctoral programs once I decided it was time to return to academia. Now that I have joined the faculty ranks, she is a senior colleague who I see at conferences where she introduces me to other senior scholars in our field of study and continues to uplift and encourage me.

I share this particular relationship because it highlights one way that faculty members exert their civic virtue and locate the upright in their work spaces. As a tenured faculty member, this mentor identified me as a promising student and took a vested interest in my future. In studying the experiences of Black faculty at PWIs, Stanley, Porter, Simpson, and Ouellett (2003) found that "the opportunity to be a role model to students of color is a mixed blessing to faculty of color in predominantly White institutions" (p. 166). Their participants "indicated a desire to give back to the African American community" (p. 166), but found that the low enrollments of students of color hindered the ability to do so. Although there were other students of color and other Black females enrolled in my program of study, this reasoning may have also held true for my mentor. I interpret her readiness to adopt me as a mentee as an expression of her "desire to give back." By investing time, energy, and resources into me, she certainly made my perception of the campus less crooked.

In addition to her influence on my experience, I believe that her interest in and adoption of me as a mentee influenced her own work life as well. In order to fully explain the influence of our relationship on my mentor, it is important to distinguish between the individual and collective impacts that an expression of civic virtue can have. When one completes an act of civic virtue with the goal of impacting a crooked room, there is both an individual and a collective effect. In the case of my mentor described above, the individual effect of our interactions was that I was able to stand more upright within the crookedness of our campus. Her

experiences within different crooked spaces likely led her to better understand what my future experiences in the academy might be and to offer
me advice that would help me best navigate those experiences. As someone who had already maintained citizenship in various crooked spaces,
however, I believe she received a personal individual effect. Having
already learned to stand herself upright within the crooked spaces of
PWIs, our relationship allowed her to maintain her upright position. It is
possible that learning to steady oneself in an upright position in a
crooked room is a temporary accomplishment. In order to maintain the
upright position, one must continue to engage in the types of actions that
originally led to the ability to stand straight in spite of the crooked images
that fill one's daily spaces. Therefore, I believe that my mentor's decision
to adopt me as a mentee was both of personal benefit to herself, helping
her to maintain the upright position she had previously achieved and a
show of a helping behavior (see Appendix A) with me as the beneficiary.
The collective benefit of her actions throughout our relationship was that
they also served to make the campus a more inclusive place, thus helping
to straighten the crooked room around us. By helping me to become
more upright, working toward the maintenance of her own upright positioning, and helping to tilt the campus environment toward the upright
position, her adoption of me and her continual involvement in my life has
been an act of civic virtue.

I decided to pursue my doctorate at a large research institution. It
remains the most expansive campus I ever called my academic home.
Understanding that I could easily get lost on this campus, I immediately
set out to meet administrators and faculty of color. One evening, my first
semester there, the school of education brought Dr. Gloria Ladson-Billings to campus as a featured speaker. I eagerly attended the lecture and
felt at home in an audience that was more racially diverse than most campus spaces. I had the good fortune that evening to be introduced in passing to a young Black assistant professor who taught in the school of
education, and in the same department where I was enrolled (you may
remember her from the opening paragraph). When she learned that we
were in the same department, she mentioned that I should enroll in a
seminar course she was slated to teach. I thought that a rather straightforward request, and confused about how her course would fit into the program of study that I did not fully understand at the time, responded that
I would look into her course. That was the extent of our first meeting, and
yet I decided at that moment that I should probably target her as a potential mentor. A major benefit of having mentors is that they become part of
your personal network, help to expand your network, and help to connect
you to important (and often hidden) resources (Baker & Griffin, 2010;
Reddick & Young, 2012). As a young Black female professor in my gen-

eral area of study, I assumed that she could add to my life in these basic ways and potentially in others.

The next time I saw this professor was in the school's parking lot one morning several weeks after our first meeting. I figured that I needed to seize the opportunity to remind her of who I was and to begin laying the groundwork for her to adopt me as a mentee. I ran across the parking lot attempting to flag her down and engage her in conversation about anything that would help her notice me. When she seemed to take little interest in me, I tried to pull her in by expressing interest in the course she mentioned at our first meeting. She quickly noted that the syllabus had yet to be finalized and continued to speed walk toward the building. In my memory of that day, which I now find quite comical upon recall, I was begging for her attention and chasing her across the parking lot. At the time, I figured that she may have been overrun with students of color wanting her time and attention and that she was not interested in adding me to that roster. In her memory of that day, she was probably running late for a meeting or class and was attempting to not get caught up in a lengthy conversation. Either way, I ended up enrolling in her course that spring semester and eventually being the largest recruiter of other doctoral students of color into her courses.

My experience in her course taught me that it was possible to have a classroom experience that was both educational and culturally nourishing; this is exactly what I would tell other students of color in my attempts to get them to enroll in her courses. I saw it as my civic duty to inform other students of color that they should take her courses, as I believed that being a student in her classroom would (a) empower them to pursue research topics that blended personal and academic interests, and (b) help spark their civic virtue fuse. Her classes provided students of color the encouragement needed to hone and use their voice to influence both their own academic experience at our institution and the experiences of the students of color who would come behind them. While I was learning valuable information in my other courses, I was not receiving this type of cultural nourishment and empowerment from them.

My relationship with this professor helped to lay the groundwork for my eventual professional leap into academe. The summer after I completed my first course with her, she hired me as a research associate to help collect data for her new book project. It was in those research team meetings that I was introduced to many aspects of qualitative research and the process of working within a small team of researchers to help develop and advance a project. The following year, I assumed the presidency of our campus's Black Graduate Student Association, and recruited her as our advisor. She became a wonderful support to the executive board and I was able to nominate her for a faculty mentoring award that she won later that year. She and I later became conference roommates for a few years at the major research conference in our field. When I tagged along with her between conference sessions and to evening socials, she introduced me to scholars within her network. Watching her interact with other conference attendees and eventually presenting a session alongside her were valuable educational experiences. I did not realize at the time that, through all of these experiences, she was helping to prepare me for academic life by providing me a front row seat to how she organized, worked, and networked as an academic. Now that I have transitioned into a faculty position, I often rely on my memories of how she navigated certain situations to help guide me through my own daily minutiae. Over the years, this professor has become one of my closest and most treasured mentors and friends.

Before moving on, I want to return briefly to the questions posed in the opening paragraph of this chapter. How does one become the chaser or the chased, the seeker or the sought after, in that scenario? Those of us who are traversing life in a crooked room—otherwise stated, academics of color positioned within PWIs—learn to employ certain survival tactics. Within the scenario offered, both people are drawing upon a survival tactic. For the chaser or seeker, the survival tactic being used was seeking and identifying sources of support (people, services, resources) and reaching out to connect to them. For the chased or the sought after, the survival tactic in play was remaining focused on the task at hand and protecting one's schedule from people and tasks that may defer the end goal. Both are valid tactics and methods that academics are taught to use in order to be successful. Having encountered the same crooked room, my mentor and I were both using our survival tactics to approach the day's work. In the moment, those survival tactics clashed, keeping us from making a sustained connection in our initial meetings. However, given both of our desires to connect to sources of support, we eventually developed a symbiotic relationship and were able to aid, rather than hinder, each other's success.

This professor was only one of the many sources of support throughout my doctoral studies. Another valuable source of support came when two Black females in my program decided to develop and coordinate the "Sister Scholar Circle." The Sister Scholar Circle was a group designed to help support the experiences of Black women matriculating through our doctoral program. Based on their own experiences in the program, these two women conceived a support space for themselves and other Black women, both students and faculty, to connect on a regular basis, share their accomplishments, debrief their experiences, and offer each other academic and social support. In the email announcing this idea to the other Black women in the program, they wrote: "[We] discussed how much the sisters need a support system to help us through the humbling experience of becoming a scholar. It is our hope, that by creating the Sister Circle, we will build a space for encouragement and scholastic inspiration" (N. Njoku & J. Rogers, personal communication, September 1, 2011). Although they did not use this terminology, the sister circle was a method of strengthening the bond between women of color who inhabited the same crooked room and laying the groundwork for us to support one another.

Sister circles have been noted to be useful resources that offer Black women an outlet for fellowship and support (Patton & Harper, 2003). While the Sister Scholar Circle is not the only sister circle to which I have belonged over the years, it stands out because it included both faculty members and graduate students. It offered a unique opportunity for faculty and students to provide support for one another without the power differential that usually exists within those relationships. The result of the combined membership was a space that provided participants with the support, encouragement, and inspiration that the group's coordinators envisioned. Even though the women in the circle already had one-on-one relationships with one another, meetings of the circle were a time to engage in collective support and celebration. In recent conversations with those currently matriculating through that program, I have learned that the Sister Scholar Circle continues to offer these same benefits and has been expanded to include other women of color. Additionally, one of the original two coordinators has stepped back from organizing and has shifted that responsibility to newer doctoral students. While developing and coordinating the circle was itself an act of civic virtue, passing the torch epitomizes the type of sustained impact that can be initiated by an act of civic virtue. The Sister Scholar Circle is an initiative that produces tangible benefits for participants and will be sustained over the years through the act of passing on the coordination task to other women of color who share citizenship in a crooked space.

After completing my doctorate, I moved to Ohio to begin my teaching career. Of the many people I met upon moving to Ohio, a few stand out when I think about help in making the transition. I want to continue my focus, however, on the Black females encountered along the way, sisters who reached out to encourage and support me as I navigated both the path as a new faculty member and as a new addition to our institution. The first was an assistant professor in my department. Her first message to me was that we should schedule regular times to commune over dinner, as it would be a helpful experience for the both of us. In the two years that we shared at the institution together before she moved on, we had many meals together. Although we participated in some of the same weekly events, such as faculty meetings and writing groups where we could share

Shared meals—
safe space

Critical
friend

knowing glances, our shared meals allowed us to offer each other a time and space where it was safe to give voice to unspoken thoughts and to debrief difficult interactions without judgment. Given her experience and wisdom, I used her as a sounding board for my thoughts. I shared tales of encounters that I found odd or troubling and sought her opinions. She cautioned me of certain pitfalls of faculty life and gave me advice on how to sustain a research agenda while also fulfilling my teaching and service expectations. I came to think of her as my big sister in the department, looking out for me and helping to direct me, while also knowing that she could rely on me when support was needed. Through my conversations with and observations of my big sister, I have learned how advocating for oneself and others can move one closer to an upright position in a crooked room.

The second Black woman who quickly befriended me was a campus administrator who was also enrolled as a doctoral student in my department. When I arrived at the university, she was collecting her dissertation data and considering different qualitative software programs to assist in the analysis. After she decided to use a program that I had suggested to her, she and I met to help her get oriented to the program and its various features. At the time, I considered myself to be paying forward the time and effort that others had poured into me as a doctoral student without realizing that I was also endearing myself to her as a frientor—someone who is both a friend and a mentor.[1] I believe that frientorships are important to the success of people of color in the academy. It is helpful to have people who you trust enough to call a friend and respect enough to either receive their critiques of your actions and work or to offer your critiques of theirs. While I have listened and offered advice as this particular frientor has navigated her doctoral journey, she has done the same for me as I have navigated my entry to the professoriate and institution. Our debriefing conversations are opportunities to share stories of recognizing crooked elements within the campus environment. As frientors we are able to either provide an alternate perspective on the story shared or validate each other's identification of crookedness. Having company in the crooked room has proven to be an invaluable resource as we both attempt to find the upright and help each other to maintain less crooked positions.

The combined effect of my relationships with these two women on my transition to a new institution has been an effective orientation to my role and the institutional culture. One participant in Stanley et al.'s (2003) study of Black faculty experience noted: "Because there are so few African Americans here, you don't get a chance to talk to anybody else to see if they feel what I feel" (p. 165). Thanks to these two women, this is not an experience that I can echo. The unsolicited nature of their support is reminiscent of the mentor from my first graduate program, adopting me as an act of civic virtue. As defined earlier, the basis of civic virtue is a commitment to taking an active role in an organization's development and advancement. The example behaviors included in the definition of civic virtue from Podsakoff et al. (2000) do not include the behaviors that these two women exhibited; yet, their actions are born of their commitment to organizational development and advancement. Their intentionality in seeking me out, offering advice and providing me with safe spaces to debrief my encounters with tilted images on our campus is an example of how Black women express civic virtue. By voluntarily reaching out to assist another Black woman in the transition to an institution and through the process of navigating institutional policies and personalities, these women represent a commitment to institutional progress. Their civic virtue and the sense of responsibility they feel as institutional citizens are evident in their actions to help another woman of color acclimate to the campus environment, thus helping that individual succeed and helping the institution to sustain an increase in the number of employees from underrepresented racial and ethnic groups.

My stories have heavily highlighted my role as the recipient of mentoring relationships. As a new faculty member, however, I have begun to take on the role of the chased/sought after from the opening scenario. There are students who want and need my support as an advisor and instructor, and sometimes, simply as a cheerleader. Given my experience as the chaser/seeker in the faculty-student relationship, I attempt to make myself available to students who seek me out as a resource. While I have connected with students of various racial and ethnic backgrounds, I have noticed that students of color who seek me out for advice and counsel—regardless of whether I am their assigned academic advisor or whether or not they are enrolled in my courses—can become a large draw on my time. I am not outside of the norm as a Black faculty member who feels a responsibility and desire to act as a source of support for these students (Stanley et al., 2003); neither am I outside of the norm as a faculty member who, in efforts to avoid distractions, sometimes attempts to avoid engagement with students who chase after me. My goal is to balance between these extremes in order to both support students of color and remain cognizant of my responsibilities as a faculty member with schedule constraints. Luckily, I have the examples of mentors like the women I have described in the pages above to rely on when I am uncertain of how to properly strike that balance. Having those examples at my disposal and those women within my network allows me to stand a little bit straighter inside a crooked room and encourages me to have the civic virtue required to reach back when students of color reach out.

ISSUING THE CALL

Writing about the experiences of Black women in America (a crooked room), Harris-Perry (2011) posits that awareness may influence how Black women "understand themselves as citizens, what they believe is possible in their relationship with the state, and what they expect from their political organizing" (p. 35). This statement translates seamlessly to the PWI environment: Awareness of the structural deficiencies within a campus culture and environment can influence how Black women in that situation view their citizenship within the institution, the institution itself, and their assumptions about their own political influence within the institution. Stated otherwise, when people are aware of how their environment does not support them, they gain a deeper understanding of their own positioning and can move forward with tempered beliefs about how they can impact that positioning.

My goal in this call to awareness and action is to assure readers that women of color hold citizenship power within their PWI environments. Regardless of one's role or function at an institution—whether student or employee—there is a certain amount of power that is held as a campus citizen. People of color can and should exercise their citizenship in ways that will help make the crooked room straighter. In so doing, it is important to acknowledge the slow pace of organizational change. Scholars of organizational development have written about the challenges of implementing and sustaining change within institutions of higher education (e.g., Boyce, 2003; Kezar, 2001). To be clear, this call is not to suggest that women of color should seek to cause anarchy within their institutions and issue demands to be seen, heard, and understood. Instead, it is a two-pronged call to both awareness and action. First, moving forward with an awareness that recognizes crookedness, it is a call to ascribe to a mission of helping to straighten out crooked spaces a little bit at a time. Second, it is a call to commit to the personal development that will happen during that process. The results of accepting and acting on this call will be varied and have both personal and organizational effects. In the process of helping our institutions become better places to live and work, we also take bold steps toward becoming who we are and embodying that image publicly.

How we each go about acting on this call may be different from person to person. Each person reading this chapter and accepting this call will likely have different motivations for expressing civic virtue. For some it may be one of the statistics offered at the front of the chapter regarding the presence of women of color on predominantly White campuses. For others it may be an experience as a student, staff, or faculty citizen of a PWI that has left a vivid memory of just how crooked the campus environment can be. For many, it will be one or more other impactful experiences. In explaining the metaphor of the crooked room, Harris-Perry (2011) also cautions readers to not assume that the crookedness is experienced similarly by different people. She writes:

> Sisters are more than the sum of their relative disadvantages: They are active agents who craft meaning out of their circumstances and do so in complicated and diverse ways. Despite important commonalities, all African American women do not share the same ideas, beliefs, and feelings. (p. 46)

This statement is true of all women of color occupying PWI campuses. Although there are common disadvantages and common experiences, each unique person will experience the environment in a unique way. How one decides to display civic virtue or enact citizenship within that space will be unique to that person's "ideas, beliefs, and feelings." *values*

The acceptance of this call will appear differently for each person. Referring back to and considering the personal examples shared earlier in the chapter, it may appear in the coordination of a sister circle or in the development of a one-on-one frientorship with another sister on campus. However the call is enacted, it should be in a format that makes sense within the institutional environment and for the position that one occupies (i.e., level of study and employment) on the campus. As someone who has held membership (ranging from temporary to permanent positions) within five PWIs, I believe this is a key distinction—the institutional context matters and one's positioning matters in the determination of how to make a sustainable influence. For example, while a sister circle could be helpful in many situations, the Sister Scholar Circle is especially impactful because (a) it was created in a space where there is a critical mass of women of color concentrated in one area of study, and (b) it is student-driven despite the presence of faculty members. Identifying one's sphere of influence and a compelling need within the campus context can help to clarify ways to act on the call presented in this chapter.

CLOSING THOUGHTS

This chapter ponders and sparks several questions: What does it mean to be a Black female citizen of a predominantly White institution? How does one become a willing citizen of an environment that (you are aware) lacks the "cultural nourishment" (González, 2000) you require to truly flourish? Does maintaining organizational citizenship in ways that differ from the norm change what it means to be a member of the campus community? In exploring the questions posed above, the crookedness (i.e., marginalizing aspects) that often exists within the PWI environment has to be acknowledged and considered.

By calling for women of color to stand upright within the crooked spaces of PWIs, I am suggesting that women of color should act as change agents within their campus environments. Through acts of civic virtue, women of color can spark discussions and initiatives that serve to straighten crooked spaces. The easiest way to operate inside of a crooked room is to adjust oneself to tilt to the same degree of the room. Adapting to the room allows one to achieve alignment quickly, as it is easier to tilt oneself than to shift an entire room to the upright position. Rather than tilting oneself to align with the campus environment, we should all attempt to locate and maintain the upright position. Once one has managed to stand up straight in a crooked environment, it will likely take continued individual and group efforts to maintain the upright position. It is my hope that you will answer this call by joining myself and other women of color at PWIs in asserting our institutional citizenship and attempting to maintain an upright position.

APPENDIX A: DEFINITIONS OF THE SIX REMAINING OCBS

This list includes definitions of the six organizational citizenship behaviors not explicitly addressed in this chapter. These definitions come from Podsakoff, MacKenzie, Paine, and Bachrach (2000).

1. Helping behavior—"involves voluntarily helping others with, or preventing the occurrence of, work-related problems" (p. 516).

2. Sportsmanship—"a willingness to tolerate the inevitable inconveniences and impositions of work without complaining" (p. 517).

3. Organizational loyalty—"promoting the organization to outsiders, protecting and defending it against external threats, and remaining committed to it even under adverse conditions" (p. 517).

4. Organizational compliance—"a person's internalization and acceptance of the organization's rules, regulations, and procedures, which results in a scrupulous adherence to them, even when no one observes or monitors compliance" (p. 517).

5. Individual initiative—"involves engaging in task-related behaviors at a level that is so far beyond minimally required or generally expected levels that it takes on a voluntary flavor" (p. 518).

6. Self-development—"includes voluntary behaviors employees engage in to improve their knowledge, skills, and abilities" (p. 525).

NOTE

1. I was introduced to the concept of frientor
   created by the University of Southern Calif...
   lence in Teaching (2003):

   > Frientoring addresses the asymmetrical nature of mentor-protégé
   > relationships by establishing a collegial tier in which each party can
   > contribute as equals.... Frientoring allows both participants to feel as
   > though they are giving of themselves and simultaneously receiving
   > intellectual and emotional reinforcement" (p. 5).

REFERENCES

Baker, V. L., & Griffin, K. A. (2010). Beyond mentoring and advising: Understanding the role of faculty "developers" in student success. *About Campus, 14*(6), 2–8.

Bergeron, D. M., Shipp, A. J., Rosen, B., & Furst, S. A. (2012). Organizational citizenship behavior and career outcomes: The cost of being a good citizen. *Journal of Management, 39*(4), 958–984.

Bolino, M. C., Klotz, A. C., Turnley, W. H., & Harvey, J. (2013). Exploring the dark side of organizational citizenship behavior. *Journal of Organizational Behavior, 34*, 542–559.

Boyce, M. E. (2003). Organizational learning is essential to achieving and sustaining change in higher education. *Innovative Higher Education, 28*(2), 119–136.

González, K. P. (2000). Toward a theory of minority student participation in predominantly White colleges and universities. *Journal of College Student Retention: Research, Theory, and Practice, 2*(1), 69–91.

Harris-Perry, M. V. (2011). *Sister citizen: Shame, stereotypes, and Black women in America.* New Haven, CT: Yale University Press.

Kezar, A. J. (2001). Understanding and facilitating organizational change in the 21st century: Recent research and conceptualizations. *ASHE-ERIC Higher Education Report, 28*(4).

Organ, D. W. (1988). *Organizational citizenship behavior: The good soldier syndrome.* Lexington, MA: Lexington Books.

Patton, L. D., & Harper, S. R. (2003). Mentoring relationships among African American women in graduate and professional schools. *New Directions for Student Services, 104*, 67–78.

Podsakoff, P. M., MacKenzie, S. B., Paine, J. B., & Bachrach, D. G. (2000). Organizational citizenship behaviors: A critical review of the theoretical and empirical literature and suggestions for future research. *Journal of Management, 26*(3), 513–563.

Reddick, R. J., & Young, M. D. (2012). Mentoring graduate students of color. In S. J. Fletcher & C. A. Mullen (Eds.), *The SAGE handbook of mentoring and coaching in education* (pp. 412–429), Thousand Oaks, CA: SAGE.

Snyder, T. D., & Dillow, S. A. (2013). *Digest of education statistics 2012* (NCES 2014-015). Retrieved from: http://nces.ed.gov/pubs2014/2014015.pdf

Stanley, C. A., Porter, M. E., Simpson, N. J., & Oulett, M. L. (2003). A case study of the teaching experiences of African American faculty at two predominantly White research universities. *Journal on Excellence in College Teaching, 14*(1), 151–178.

Tejada, K. (2013). Book review: Sister citizen: Shame, stereotypes, and Black women in America; For colored girls who've considered politics when being strong isn't enough. *Humanity and Society, 37,* 269–271.

University of Southern California Center for Excellence in Teaching. (2003). *Mentoring university students.* Los Angeles, CA: Author.

CHAPTER 11

ANSWER THE CALL

Brenda L. H. Marina

Similar to the researcher/scholars of these chapters, many of us have experienced the challenge of balancing the demands of our teaching, research, and service. Women educators of color must be prepared to deal with the expectations of serving as role models and leadership roles while balancing career and personal ambitions. Up to this point, one might consider that these woman are "persisting in the journey toward self-definition" (Collins, 2000, p. 121). Brock (2010) captured the essence of this journey as each searches for a personal place, a personal identity when she stated:

> Throughout my teaching career I have agonized over how to better understand myself and use this to more effectively teach my students. And as I work for this understanding, I question, *Where do I begin my journey?* I have been searching for the connection between the personal me as a Black woman and the pedagogical me as a Black woman teacher. (p. xv)

We have explored concrete experiences and acts of women of color, while at the same time striving to understand and extrapolate wisdom and meaning. As educators, writers, researchers, and mentors, our concrete experiences, uniquely individual, are at the same time intersecting and are collectively connected. Rogers (2002) adds to our assertion by saying:

> Perhaps the most compelling stories that have emerged from generations of political leaders are those that involve personal transformations in which

Beyond Retention: Cultivating Spaces of Equity, Justice, and Fairness for Women of Color in U.S. Higher Education, pp. 287–290
Copyright © 2016 by Information Age Publishing

individuals move from fear to fearlessness, and from individual discontent to a sense of collective unity and strength. Such changes often involve individual development and transformation in an interactive and collective context. (p. 365)

To further contextualize the intersections and critical geography of the call to serve and a call for awareness, we can consider three levels of awareness: an awareness of self, interpersonal awareness, and systemic awareness. At level one, an awareness of self, women of color must understand the dynamics of their personality and how they contribute to the systems of knowing (Marina & Edwards-Joseph, 2014); at level two, interpersonal awareness, we must have an appreciation of other women's reality without being judgmental; and at level three, systematic awareness, women of color must be able to accurately understand how other women's development is impacted by their environment. Women of color need to have knowledge of how to advocate at the systemic level in an effort to alleviate barriers that may impede the psychosocial development of the women following similar crooked paths (Dinsmore, Chapman, & McCollum, 2000; Lee, Armstrong, & Brydges, 1996).

I ask you the reader to explore the intersections of these levels of awareness as you consider the following questions posed by authors Jones, Osborne-Lampkin, and Wilder:

1. How many informal mentoring relationships are you currently directing?
2. How many formal mentoring relationships are you currently directing?
3. Are there institutional mechanisms at your institution that support programs such as Sisters of the Academy?
4. What strategies might you employ to facilitate Black female faculty in leaving a legacy of scholars who "look like us" and who can in turn "pay it forward?

Furthermore, Shaw challenges us with a call to awareness and action. She asks some very poignant questions at the beginning of her story, and these questions remain to be answered:

• How do we get to the point where a Black female doctoral student is so desperate for connection that she is chasing potential mentors across campus?

• How do we get to the point where a Black female faculty member is so protective of her time that she is avoiding all possible distractions?

At the end of her chapter, the questions are even more provocative:

- What does it mean to be a Black female citizen of a predominantly White institution?
- How does one become a willing citizen of an environment that (you are aware) lacks the "cultural nourishment" you require to truly flourish?
- Does maintaining organizational citizenship in ways that differ from the norm change what it means to be a member of the campus community?

By celebrating the multiple voices and perspectives, we will better serve our field as we undo the idea of archetypes and find clarity in our own career and scholarship trajectories in the academy (Marina & Edwards-Joseph, 2014). Chapter authors Jones et al. noted that Black women faculty are forced to invalidate stereotypes and legitimize their competence, intelligence, and overall worth (Benjamin, 1997; Hill Collins, 1986; hooks, 1989), especially at predominately White institutions. As we continue to examine our own identity location and construct more informed and authentic paradigms for ourselves, we also will deconstruct the boundaries and norms of conventional social science (Marina & Edwards-Joseph, 2014). To deconstruct such boundaries, Shaw asks for women of color to stand upright within the crooked spaces of predominantly White institutions and act as change agents within their campus environments. However, Jones et al., lament over the complexity of weighing decisions to serve, highlighting the costs associated with these decisions. They recognize that the decision for Black women faculty, in particular, to serve as mentors and advisors is in essence, a cultural responsibility. It appears that women who make it to the top are not reaching out to mentor others coming up the ranks behind them (Goodson, 2000). As such, the *tradition* of the "glass ceiling" is still an invisible and intangible phenomenon that is pervasive throughout the United States in the academy (Marina, 2012). If we consider the intersecting levels of our awareness and our journey up the ladder as we tap on the glass ceiling of success, my coeditor Sabrina Ross and I add the following questions for your contemplation:

- Are we as women responsible for the glass ceiling in higher education (and at primarily White institutions)?
- Are we pulling up the ladder behind us once we make it to the upper echelons of the academy?

It has been well documented through many voices in the field that there is a disparate number of underrepresented scholars, women of color

and Black women in particular, to serve as advisors and mentors while fulfilling our other duties. It also has been documented that many
researcher/scholars "often categorize Black women as 'noise' if they are
few in number, and eliminate Black women from their analyses" (Chin,
2007, p. 292). I ask you the reader, to hear the noise, visualize the invisible, and critically examine the intersections of your space and place. This
discourse, these counterstories, this "noise," should not be relegated to
the margins.

handwritten note in left margin: "noise"

REFERENCES

Benjamin, L. (Ed.) (1997). *Black women in the academy: Promises and perils.* Gainesville, FL: University of Florida Press.

Brock, R. (2010). *Sista talk: The personal and the pedagogical.* New York, NY: Peter
Lang.

Chin, J. L. (2007). *Women and leadership: Transforming visions and diverse voices.* Mal-
den, MA: Blackwell.

Collins, P. H. (2000). *Black feminist thought: Knowledge, consciousness, and the politics
of empowerment.* New York, NY: Routledge.

Dinsmore, J. A., Chapman, A., & McCollum, V. J. C. (2000, March). *Client advocacy
and social justice: Strategies for developing trainee competence.* Paper presented at
the annual conference of American Counseling Association, Washington DC.

Goodson, S. (2000). Are women responsible for the glass ceiling? *USA Today.*
Retrieved November 5, 2010, from http://findarticles.com/p/articles/mi_
m1272/is_2659_128/ai_61586738/

Hill Collins, P. (1986). Learning from the outsider within: The sociological significance of Black feminist thought. *Social Problems, 33,* 514–532.

hooks, b. (1989). *Talking back: Thinking feminist, thinking Black.* Boston, MA: South
End Press.

Lee, C. C., Armstrong, K. L., & Brydges, J. L. (1996). The challenges of a diverse
society: Counseling for mutual respect and understanding. *Counseling and
Human Development, 28,* 1–8

Marina, B. L. H. (2012). Academe's glass ceiling, trend or tradition? A cross-
cultural briefing. In S. Fullerton & D. L. Moore (Ed.), *Global business trends
contemporary readings* (pp. 10–13). Ypsilanti, MI: Academy Business Administration.

Marina, B. L. H., & Edwards-Joseph, A. (2014). Religiosity and spirituality in educational leadership programs: perspectives and reflections from black educators. In N. Witherspoon Arnold, M. Brooks, & B. M. Arnold (Eds.), *New
Directions in Educational Leadership: Innovations in Research, Teaching, and Learning Series, Vol. 2: Critical perspectives on Black education: Spirituality, religion, and
social justice* (pp. 231–250). Charlotte, NC: Information Age.

Rogers, K. L. (2002). Life questions: Memories of civil rights leaders. *The Journal
of African American History, 87,* 355–368.

CHAPTER 12

WHERE DO WE GO FROM HERE

~~Concluding~~ Emerging Thoughts

Sabrina L. H. Ross and Brenda N. Marina

In this final section of *Beyond Retention*, we resist the traditional idea of offering concluding thoughts and instead discuss emergent themes from the text as well as a tentative framework for moving forward. As in our introduction, we situate our discussion of emergent themes related to women faculty of color and academic space within the framework of critical geography. As a critical geographic project, the calls of various women of color working within higher education institutions poignantly identify structures of oppression that act as barriers to the full incorporation of women of color in predominantly White academic contexts. Similarly, the responses of senior women faculty of color and women of color administrators working within predominantly White institutions (PWIs) also serve emancipatory goals. The theoretical contributions, personal advice, and insights from these women provide practical strategies for improving the current context of higher education for women of color in academia and also function as markers for moving forward toward higher education spaces that genuinely reflect equity and social justice for all.

What follows are salient themes that emerged from the calls and responses of the women featured in this text. Consistent with the precepts

Beyond Retention: Cultivating Spaces of Equity, Justice, and Fairness for Women of Color in U.S. Higher Education, pp. 291–299

of critical geography, these themes reference the geographic and symbolic space of predominantly White, U.S. higher education contexts. The first three themes (geographic metaphors of PWIs, social justice sites, and safe spaces) present emergent themes from the chapter writers of this text. The fourth theme (toward higher education spaces of equity), summarizes insights and recommendations from the writers of chapter responses.

1st 3 themes *4th Theme*

Geographic Metaphors of PWIs

Our decision to use critical geography as a framework for this text was based on the subject matter of this book, the emancipatory goals of critical geography, and the geographic metaphors many of the chapter authors enlisted when describing their experiences. This reliance on geographic and place-specific metaphors is common in the narratives of women of color seeking to illuminate their racialized and gendered experiences in academia. For example, Robinson and Clardy (2010) titled their edited collection of autoethnographic accounts of women of color working in higher education *Tedious Journeys*, to emphasize the perilous routes through tenure, promotion, and administration that women of color must navigate within predominantly White higher education institutions. Similarly, Annette Henry's (1993) notion of dangerous terrain in her article "There Are No Safe Places: Pedagogy as Powerful and Dangerous Terrain" captures the hazardous nature of the work that women of color engage as they teach in ways that challenge oppression in predominantly White higher education classrooms. Still other geographic metaphors used by women of color comparing predominantly White institutions of higher education to slave plantations (e.g., Ladson-Billings, 2005; Paul, 2001; Williams & Evans-Winters, 2005) underscore the vulnerable positions and exploited labor of women of color working in academia.

Like the scholarship cited above, four of the authors of this text also invoked powerful geographic and spatial metaphors in their chapters. Wilder's "Ripple Effects and Shockwaves: The Impact of a Black Faculty Member's Open Letter to her Institution" invokes geographic metaphors of water and air to convey the psychological impact of her open letter that chronicled her experiences within a predominantly White Southern university. Like the ripple effects of a pebble skipped across water, the positive effects of Wilder's speaking truth to power emanated out in ever widening circles of her university; however, like the sharp change in air pressure occurring after an explosion, shockwaves from Wilder's letter challenged the rhetoric of diversity espoused by the university and, in doing so, created a palpable change in her academic environment.

Smith's "Walking the Tightrope of Academe With No Net" applies the spatial metaphors of a playing field that is not level and of tightrope walking without the protection of a safety net to convey the treacherous ground that women of color are forced to traverse in higher education. Furthermore, Burke's "Putting an End to Outside Looking In: It's Time for Women of Color in Higher Education to Create Social Capital" utilizes a barrier metaphor to underscore the structural and psychological obstacles that women of color have difficulty breaking through within predominantly White institutions.

Finally, Shaw's "Expressing Civic Virtue Inside a Crooked Room: A Call to Awareness for Women of Color at Predominantly White Institutions" utilizes the metaphor of the crooked room to describe the inequitable conditions under which women of color are required to work. She chronicles the actions that she and other Black women faculty working in PWIs took to survive within the "crooked rooms" of academia and the actions they took to assert their citizenship and create more upright working environments for themselves. When taken together, these geographic and spatial metaphors communicate the continued persistence of marked difficulty for women of color in their journeys through predominantly White higher education contexts.

Social Justice Sites

While each of the chapters in this text written by women faculty of color represent calls for equity and justice, three of these chapters also reflected the desires of the authors to cultivate their own social justice sites within the academy. For example, Jones, Osborne-Lampkin, and Wilder's chapter "Balancing the Call to Serve: The Costs and Benefits of Leaving a Legacy in the Academy" discusses the importance the authors hold for mentoring students of color. Significantly, they present their efforts to mentor and advise college students of color as a cultural obligation that helps to ensure that students of color attempting to withstand the stormy environment of higher education will have support and protection.

Garcia-Pusateri's "*Soy Latina, Donde Estás mi Gente?*" articulates the multiple spaces of difference that she occupies as a Latina woman and an "only" (i.e., administrator and student, Latina who does not speak Spanish fluently, etc.) within her predominantly White institution. Rather than a liability, she uses her intimate knowledge of White culture and White space as resources when she raises difficult questions about power and privilege and advocates for diversity and inclusion. The multiple spaces of difference that she occupies allow her to skillfully navigate the White space of her institution to cultivate academic spaces that are more just. Similarly, Meyer's chapter "Triple Threat: Multiple Identities in the Academy" details her multiple markers of identity as a Black woman and member of the LGBTQ community with a focus on the ways that the intersectionality of her identities sensitizes her to mutually influencing sources of oppression and encourages her to use knowledge gained from attention to her multiple identities to foster change and cultivate social justice within her academic institution.

Safe Spaces

For many women of color in academia, ways of understanding their lived experiences in U.S. higher education are intimately connected to their knowledge of other historical and contemporary women's experiences of racial, gender, and class discrimination, their strategies of survival, and their wisdom cultivated to resist and transcend these intersecting forms of oppression (Collins, 2000; Marina & Fonteneau, 2012). Knowledge of and support from these women constitute safe spaces where women of color can construct and maintain empowering definitions of self. A common theme in research on women faculty of color is a reliance on self and others for support and guidance. Such actions are often responses to missing or inadequate formal mentoring (Fries-Britt & Turner, 2005; Myers, 2002). In three of the chapter responses for *Beyond Retention*, the safe spaces developed through women of color's mentoring relationships with each other served as a predominant theme.

In their chapter titled "I'd Rather Be Harriet: A Counterstory of Two Sister Scholars," Njoku and Rogers discuss ways in which they are sustained by both a historical memory of the activism of Harriet Tubman and their support for and mentoring of one another. This inherited tradition of activism and their unwavering support for each other operate as emotional safe spaces that enable them to withstand the discrimination and discouragement that they experience as doctoral students in a predominantly White Southern university. A similar theme of mentoring safe spaces is found in Johnson, Robinson, Staples, and Daoud's chapter titled "Preparing to Lead: The Socialization of Black Women for Faculty and Administrative Careers Through Graduate School." In their autoethnographic accounts, the authors describe the importance of both faculty mentoring and peer mentoring in the cultivation of an academic space that allowed them to thrive. The theme of peer mentorship is revisited again in Pitt's chapter "Who Speaks for Me?: Learning to Resist With Marginalized Statuses in the Academy." Pitt describes the power of peer mentorship outside of her university to combat the racist and gendered discrimination and attempted shaming she experiences as a Black unmarried mother. Pitt also describes the power of other mothering by women in her community who help her navigate academia and motherhood. Thus, in Pitt's chapter, both the peer mentoring network and the group of community mothers served as safe spaces that allowed her to cultivate self-definition and resist the oppressiveness of her university environment.

Toward Higher Education Spaces of Equity

In this final section of emergent themes, we present common topics offered in the insights of senior women faculty of color and women administrators of color who responded to chapters in *Beyond Retention*. Fittingly, these responses were as diverse as the women who wrote them, employing a wide range of strategies to respond to the calls made by chapter authors. Many respondents recognized similar themes in the chapter authors' narratives and their own journeys through academia. Many used stories of their own personal experiences to contextualize the advice they offered. Some respondents specifically chose to broaden the scope of their responses to address not only the specific chapter to which they responded, but also to women faculty of color in general who are currently traversing the rocky terrain of PWIs. Some of the responses are highly theorized and others are more informal, but all provide valuable insights and wisdom gleaned from the lived experiences of the respondents.

Despite the diversity of approaches taken to the responses, a number of common and sometimes overlapping themes became evident. These themes include: (a) learning from the experiences of women faculty of color, (b) the significance of mentoring, (c) addressing feelings of isolation and alienation, (d) the role of administrators, and (e) what women of color can do for themselves. These themes are discussed below. The section concludes with a recap of the advice offered by the respondents.

Learning From the Experiences of Women Faculty of Color

The experiences of women faculty of color can be used to educate the campus community about issues of diversity and to highlight needed areas of change. Many respondents praised the chapter authors for sharing their personal stories as a way to enact change in higher education. Significantly, respondents pointed to the transformational power of these stories. They noted the ways in which stories by chapter authors initiated complicated conversations (Pinar, 2004) about race, gender, class, sexuality, ability, and diversity that are necessary to shift the current academic culture. One respondent hoped that the counter stories written by chapter authors could serve as "pearls of wisdom" that alert us to institutional vulnerabilities regarding women faculty of color and which also serve as springboards upon which solutions to their negative experiences can be grounded.

Addressing Feelings of Isolation and Alienation

Feelings of isolation and alienation are commonly expressed by faculty of color working within PWIs (Stanely, 2006a). Many respondents shared their own feelings of isolation and alienation at being "an only" within their department, college, or administrative ranks. Respondents also replied to chapter authors' discussions of experiencing isolation and alienation in creative ways. Several respondents emphasized the general development of community and of sisterhood to stave off feelings of isolation and alienation. A number of respondents recognized the lack of a critical mass (Collins, 2000) of women faculty of color at PWIs and discussed alternative forms of community to prevent women faculty of color from feeling alone. One respondent argued that the stories of women faculty of color shared in this text informally create a positive space of healing, renewal, and solidarity for women of color in higher education. Two respondents noted the importance of cultivating peer groups for support, encouragement, and informal education. What these responses have in common is recognition of the lack of community that is often available for women of color in higher education and the provision of creative solutions for addressing the feelings of isolation and alienation.

Significance of Mentoring

The importance of mentoring for faculty of color success is a prominent general theme in literature about women of color in higher education (e.g., Niemann, 2012; Stanley, 2006a) and in the chapters written by authors of this text. The theme of mentoring was also prominent in the responses of women of color administrators and senior faculty members. All but one of the respondents discussed the importance of mentoring for the success of women faculty of color. Many of the respondents attributed successful mentoring to their own achievement and work in their current roles to informally and formally mentor women faculty of color across their respective universities. Some respondents cited a preference for mentors who "looked like them" but advised faculty of color to be open to mentorship from other individuals (e.g., mentors from other ethnic groups and/or genders) if such individuals were well intentioned and qualified. A few respondents noted a lack of available female mentors of color and suggested that peer mentoring, e-mentoring, and the development of collegial network systems outside of one's academic space could serve as suitable alternatives when formal female mentors of color were not available.

The Role of Administrators

It is perhaps not surprising that many of the administrators who provided responses echoed existing literature on the retention of faculty of color by focusing on the need for members of university leadership to take decisive and proactive steps to support and retain faculty of color at PWIs (e.g., Stanley, 2006b; Turner & Myers, 2000; Williams & Evans-Winters, 2005). Several respondents to chapters in this text emphasized the importance of having an Office of Diversity, a university diversity officer, and/or a university diversity council with the power and influence needed to address challenges experienced by faculty of color. Respondents viewed these institutionalized diversity networks led by a chief administrator of diversity as vital to defining and ensuring that strategic goals for diversity, inclusion, and equity are implemented. Respondents placed priority on the role of administrators in establishing accountability practices for aggrieved faculty of color, changing recruitment and hiring processes, managing learning opportunities related to faculty of color and White privilege, and spearheading initiatives to improve the overall campus climate for faculty of color. Respondents also noted that administrators genuinely interested in improving the campus climate for faculty of color must ensure that they have aligned themselves with the core values of diversity espoused by their universities and have educated themselves on issues of power and privilege. One respondent noted that such education involves knowing when to intervene in cases of faculty of color mistreatment. Another respondent offered that it is the role of university leadership to create spaces of dialogue that help faculty from majority groups to better understand and support faculty of color.

What Women of Color Can Do for Themselves

While respondents recognized the limitations that racism, gender discrimination, and other intersecting oppressions placed on the career advancement of women faculty of color, they also emphasized the necessity of personal accountability for women of color and discussed the things that women of color can do to protect themselves, develop professionally, and sustain their spirits. A common response was that women faculty of color need to know themselves in order to recognize when they are being compromised or taken advantage of, to know when an academic space is no longer healthy or viable, and to be able to better connect with and teach their students. Relatedly, one respondent urged women faculty of color to deepen their understandings of the ways in which they are, at different times, marginalized and privileged by their identifications and group membership. Knowing oneself in this way can help to ensure that women of color can use aspects of privilege that they possess to fight for social justice. Respondents also noted that women of color working in higher education should be open to change and able to take risks in order to capitalize on unexpected or previously unconsidered opportunities for career advancement and happiness. Another respondent suggested that women faculty of color must hone skills in time management in order to balance competing demands on their time; just as importantly, the same respondent noted that personal time must be guarded for women faculty of color who often put the needs of others before themselves. In addition to this general advice on what women faculty of color can do for themselves, respondents provided specific practical advice for women faculty of color that is listed below.

Practical Advice From Respondents

- learn negotiation skills for an equitable workload and salary;
- learn leadership skills for career advancement;
- actively seek out mentors, role models, or "dedicated change agents" and nurture those relationships for long-term sustainability and benefit;
- use professional conferences as opportunities to network, build relationships, and publish;
- participate in ethnic minority writing retreats to break isolation, discuss work, and network;
- coauthor with others with similar research interests to expand your publications;
- if given the option, teach courses that can be used to support your research agenda; and
- enhance your vita by actively seeking out work assignments that increase your marketability.

REFERENCES

Collins, P. H. (2000). *Black Feminist thought: Knowledge, consciousness, and the politics of empowerment.* New York, NY: Routledge Classics.

Fries-Britt, S., & Kelly, B. T. (2005). Retaining each other: Narratives of two African American women in the academy. *Urban Review, 37*(3), 221–242. doi:10.1007/s11256-005-0006-2

Henry, A. (1993). There are no safe places: Pedagogy as powerful and dangerous terrain. *Action in Teacher Research, 15*(4), 1–4.

Ladson-Billings, G. (2005). *Beyond the big house: African American educators on teacher education.* New York, NY: Teachers College Press.

Marina, B. L. H., & Fonteneau, D. Y. (2012) Servant leaders who picked up the broken glass. *Journal of Pan African Studies, 5*(2), 67–83.

Myers, L. (2002). *A broken silence: Voices of African American women in the academy.* Westport, CT: Greenwood.

Niemann, Y. F. (2012). Lessons from the experiences of women of color in academia. In G. Gutierrez y Muhs, Y. F. Niemann, C. G. Gonzalez, & A. P. Harris (Eds.), *Presumed incompetent: The intersections of race and class for women in academia* (pp. 446–500). Boulder, CO: The University Press of Colorado.

Paul, D. G. (2001). *Life, culture, and education on the academic plantation: Womanist thought and perspective.* New York, NY: Peter Lang.

Pinar, W. (2004). *What is curriculum theory?* (2nd ed.). New York, NY: Routledge.

Pinar, W., Reynolds, W., Slattery, P., & Taubman, P. (1995). *Understanding curriculum: An introduction to the study of historical and contemporary curriculum discourses.* New York, NY: Peter Lang.

Robinson, C. C., & Clardy, P. (2010). *Tedious journeys: Autoethnography by women of color in academe.* New York, NY: Peter Lang.

Stanley, C. A. (Ed.). (2006a). An overview of the literature. In *Faculty of color: Teaching in predominantly White colleges and universities* (pp. 1–29). Bolton, MA: Anker.

Stanley, C. A. (Ed.). (2006b). Summary and key recommendations for the recruitment and retention of faculty of color. In *Faculty of color: Teaching in predominantly White colleges and universities* (pp. 361–373). Bolton, MA: Anker.

Turner, C. S. V., & Myers, S. L. Jr. (2000). *Faculty of color in academe: Bittersweet success.* Boston, MA: Allyn & Bacon.

Williams, D. G., & Evans-Winters, V. (2005). The burden of teaching teachers: Memoirs of race discourse in teacher education. *The Urban Review, 37*(3), 18.

ABOUT THE CONTRIBUTORS

ABOUT THE EDITORS

Brenda L. H. Marina, an associate dean for the division of academic affairs at Baltimore City Community College. She has served as an associate professor, teaching graduate courses in educational leadership and higher education administration at Georgia Southern University. Her scholarship explores women in leadership, mentoring for leadership, multicultural competence in higher education, and global education issues from a womanist perspective. Dr. Marina is a board member for the International Mentoring Association and a peer reviewer for the *International Journal of Mentoring and Coaching in Education*. Dr. Marina has published book chapters related to identity development for female students of color, religiosity and spirituality in leadership programs, managing diversity in workplaces and society, as well as journal articles on cultural competence and the glass ceiling. She recently published a book entitled *Mentoring Away the Glass Ceiling in Academe: A Cultured Critique*.

Sabrina N. Ross, PhD, is an associate professor of curriculum studies at Georgia Southern University. Her scholarship explores intersections of race, gender, and power within educational contexts. Dr. Ross has published articles in journals such as *Educational Foundations, The Journal of African American Males in Education, The International Journal for the Scholarship of Teaching and Learning*, and *Teaching in Higher Education*. She has served as a guest editor for special issues of *The Journal of Curriculum Theorizing* (with Ming Fang He, 2012) and *Vitae Scholasticae* (with Donyell Roseboro, 2011) and is coeditor (with Svi Shapiro and Kathe Latham) of *The Institution of Education* (2006). She is currently working on a book detailing Black feminist and womanist orientations to curriculum.

ABOUT THE AUTHORS

Nina Asher, EdD, is a professor in the Department of Curriculum and Instruction at the University of Minnesota-Twin Cities. She was department chair from July 2011–June 2014. Dr. Asher is also an affiliate faculty member in the Department of Gender, Women and Sexuality Studies. She writes in the areas of postcolonialism and feminism, globalization, critical perspectives on multiculturalism, and Asian American studies in education. She has published over 30 articles and book chapters, and her work has appeared in such leading national and international journals as the *Educational Researcher, Teachers College Record, Postcolonial Directions in Education, International Journal of Qualitative Studies in Education,* and *Discourse: Studies in the Cultural Politics of Education,* among others. Dr. Asher was the recipient of a 2014–15 Fulbright-Nehru Academic and Professional Excellence Award (Research) for her project, "Examining the Intersections of Globalization, Privatization, and Education After Two Decades of Economic Liberalization in India," and conducted this research in India during her sabbatical in the 2014–15 academic year.

Monica Galloway Burke, PhD, is an associate professor in the Department of Counseling and Student Affairs and the assistant to the chief diversity officer at Western Kentucky University. In addition to teaching, she actively plans and conducts various seminars, presentations, and workshops, primarily related to diversity and social justice. Dr. Burke has also presented, researched, and published scholarly works locally, regionally, nationally, and internationally on the issues of cultural competence, diversity in higher education and the workplace, group dynamics, gender dynamics, and student success.

Nina Daoud, MSEd, is a doctoral candidate in the Department of Counseling, Higher Education, and Special Education at the University of Maryland, College Park. Her research examines issues of diversity and equity within higher education with two main foci: (1) diversity within Black collegians; and (2) college access and choice among underrepresented students. For her work on Black collegians, Ms. Daoud has been the recipient of numerous awards, including the 2015 Caribbean and African Studies in Education Outstanding Graduate Student Research Award at the American Educational Research Association. Additionally, she has received both national and institutional-level funding to pursue scholarship on diversity within Black collegians, and has spearheaded several manuscripts and conference presentations on the experiences of underrepresented students in higher education.

Elena Flores, PhD, is an associate dean of academic affairs and faculty development and professor in the Counseling Psychology Department, School of Education, at the University of San Francisco. She is a Spanish-speaking, Latina clinical psychologist with several years of experience providing mental health and human services to adolescents and families from diverse cultural backgrounds. Her research and publications focus on Mexican American and European American family functioning and adolescent health risk behaviors, Latino adolescent sexual behavior, ethnic/racial discrimination stress, and obesity prevention and intervention among Latinos. She has received National Institutes of Health funding as a coinvestigator to study Latino adolescent relationships and condom use, and to examine parental influences on obesity among Mexican American children. Her publications have appeared in such journals as *Journal of Counseling Psychology, Cultural Diversity and Ethnic Minority Psychology, Journal of Adolescent Health, Hispanic Journal of Behavioral Sciences*, and *Journal of Marriage and the Family*.

Yvania Garcia-Pusateri, MS, is an assistant director and coordinator of diverse student development in the Office of Diversity Affairs at Miami University of Ohio. She is also a doctoral candidate in the educational leadership program at Miami University of Ohio. Yvania provides a critical lens to her experience as a Latina in higher education. She speaks about her intersecting identities which have impacted her place within the Latino community as well as within White culture. While her experiences have been challenging, her passion for students and her work in equity and inclusion remain unscathed.

Tara T. Green, PhD, is professor and director of African American and African Diaspora Studies at the University North Carolina at Greensboro where she teaches literature and gender studies courses. She is the author of *A Fatherless Child: Autobiographical Perspectives of African American Men*, which won the 2011 National Council for Black Studies Outstanding Publication Award, and the editor of two books, including *Presenting Oprah Winfrey, Her Films, and African American Literature* (2013). Her full-length study on the life of activist, journalist, and creative writer, Alice Dunbar-Nelson, is under review.

Carol E. Henderson, PhD, is a professor and serves as vice provost for diversity at The University of Delaware. She is the author of many publications, such as *Scarring the Black Body: Race and Representation in African American Literature* (U of Missouri Press, 2002); *Imagining the Black Female Body: Reconciling Image in Print and Visual Culture* (Palgrave MacMillan 2010); *America and the Black Body: Identity Politics in Print and Visual Culture*

(Fairleigh Dickinson University Press, 2009); and James Baldwin's *Go Tell It on the Mountain: Historical and Critical Essays* (Peter Lang, 2006). She teaches courses in African American literature and culture that focus on representations of the Black body in print, film, and art. She is the recipient of several community, professional, and research awards, such as the University of Delaware's Excellence in Teaching Award (2006, 1996) and the Richard "Dick" Wilson Mentoring Award (2002).

Jennifer M. Johnson, PhD, is an assistant professor in the Department of Teaching, Learning, and Professional Development at Bowie State University. She is an experienced teacher and academic counselor specializing in enhancing the academic and social experiences of persons traditionally underrepresented in higher education. Her research interests include precollege access programs, historically Black colleges and universities, students in science, technology, engineering and math programs, and high-achieving students of color. This scholarship explores the ways race, gender, and class intersects to shape the educational experiences of students across diverse institutional contexts.

Tamara Bertrand Jones, PhD, is an assistant professor of higher education in the Department of Educational Leadership and Policy Studies at Florida State University. Dr. Jones' research builds on interests developed while conducting dissertation research, her own academic and social experiences during graduate school, and her previous professional roles as an evaluator and college administrator. Her current work explores the socialization experiences of Black female early career scholars—doctoral students and pretenure faculty. Dr. Jones is a cofounder of Sisters of the Academy Institute, a national organization created to facilitate the success of Black women in the academy.

La'Tara Osborne-Lampkin, PhD, is an associate in research at Florida State University, and former assistant professor of educational policy and leadership at the University of North Florida. She has an array of professional experiences in the university, private and public sectors, and extensive experience in building collaborative partnerships with an array of stakeholders to conduct and use research evidence. As a policy and research scholar, over the past 5 years, she has also led multiple, large-scale federally funded projects examining federal and state policies and reform efforts designed to increase educational outcomes for diverse student populations in K–12 settings, with a recent focus on principal-related reform efforts. Dr. Osborne-Lampkin also explores formal and informal policies and structures that impede and/or enhance the persistence and success of faculty and graduate students in higher education institutions. Dr. Osborne-Lampkin has published work in the *Journal of Research Initiatives, Educational Evaluation and Policy Analysis, Educational Administration Quarterly,* and *Journal of Leadership and Policy in Schools, Journal of Negro Education, The Negro Educational Review,* among other peer-reviewed journals.

Lakeisha Meyer, PhD, is an assistant professor of education serving in her sixth year at Bucknell University, a predominantly White liberal arts institution in central Pennsylvania that serves approximately 3,500 students. Dr. Meyer is the only Black tenure-track faculty in the department of education where she works. She is also the only faculty member in her department identifying as a member of the LGBTQ community. She is a first-generation college student from rural Kentucky; her research pertains to issues of identity and education.

Patricia Turner Mitchell, PhD, is the present chair of the Department of Leadership Studies, a past chair of the School of Education Faculty Association, and a member of the University of San Francisco Faculty Association Policy Board. Dr. Mitchell is also an accomplished writer and has published in the areas of organizational management and leadership, women's issues, curriculum development, reading and language arts. Her book, *Ten Stupid Things Women Do to Mess up Their Careers*, has become a best seller for the publisher. Her others books, *Cracking the Wall Twenty Years Later: Women in Higher Education Leadership* and *Collaboration and Peak Performance: A Multidisciplinary Perspective for Emerging Leaders* were published in August of 2013.

Nadrea R. Njoku, MSEd, is a doctoral candidate in the higher education and student affairs program at Indiana University. She is a native of New Orleans, LA, and a proud graduate of Xavier University of Louisiana. Her research interests focus on the intersections of race and gender issues in higher education, with a specific concentration on the student experiences at historically Black colleges and universities. As an artist, her visual work explores historical and contemporary narratives of African American women. She has exhibited her work around the United States.

Ramona Ortega-Liston, PhD, is an associate professor at the University of Akron, Department of Public Administration and Urban Studies. The foci of her research agenda are the career variables influencing the employment and promotion of Latinos in public service and women in higher education. She teaches leadership and decision making, ethics in public service, the MPA Capstone course, and she created the Washington

D.C. Summer Seminar for graduate students. She has been appointed to three presidential commissions: the Army Command and General Staff Board, the Air Force Board of Visitors, and the Student Financial Assistance Advisory Board. She currently is a board member for the Akron Community Knight Foundation, and is active with the Summit County Salvation Army and the Harvard Club of Northeast Ohio.

Stacey Pearson-Wharton, PhD, serves as assistant dean for student life and director of the Counseling Center at Susquehanna University. Dr. Pearson-Wharton has also worked in private practice providing individual psychotherapy. She has sought to advance issues of equity and inclusion on college campuses and the field of higher education. Very active in the American College Personnel Association, Dr. Pearson-Wharton was a member of the governing board as the association's director of equity and inclusion. Now, as a professional speaker, she works with campuses across the country to inspire and educate students on taking steps for positive change in their lives and for their communities. She has been a role model for women with experience teaching, publishing, and presenting on issues related to college student development along with diversity and exclusivity.

Jenelle S. Pitt, PhD, is an associate professor in the Department of Counselor Education and Rehabilitation at California State University, Fresno. Dr. Pitt has 16 years of experience in working with persons with disabilities from marginalized backgrounds. Her research interests include cultural diversity and multiculturalism, counselor training and preparation, and organizational behavior practices in state vocational rehabilitation programs. Dr. Pitt has seven peer-reviewed publications, two book chapters, and one published work focusing on building multicultural competence through the use of service learning. The National Council on Rehabilitation Education named her Rehabilitation Educator of the Year in 2014. In 2015, she received recognition from both the National Rehabilitation Association and National Association of Multicultural Rehabilitation Concerns for her work on multicultural and disability advocacy in education.

Tykeia N. Robinson is a doctoral student studying higher education at the University of Maryland, College Park. She also serves as the academic counselor for the Ronald E. McNair Post-Baccalaureate Achievement Program. She has worked for several years as an administrator of programs designed to support underrepresented students at various points of the academic pipeline. Her research focuses on how underrepresented students experience their graduate programs and the various sites/contexts where graduate socialization and training exist. She is also interested in exploring the graduate student experience as it relates to the paucity of persons of color in the professoriate.

Juhanna Rogers, MA EdM, is a doctoral candidate in the higher education concentration at the University of Maryland, College Park. She also serves as the academic counselor for the Ronald E. McNair Post-Baccalaureate Achievement Program. She has worked as an administrator of programs designed to support underrepresented students at various points of the academic pipeline for close to 10 years. Her research explores the processes of existing research traineeships and other developmental programs in STEM graduate education in order to better understand the varied and nuanced ways that students are socialized and trained in graduate school. Her work specifically focuses on illuminating the experiences of underrepresented minority students both within and beyond these programs and identifying strategies employed by university faculty and administration to support and retain underrepresented minority students to and through graduate programs in STEM fields.

Donyell L. Roseboro, PhD, is the department chair and associate professor in the Department of Instructional Technology, Foundations, and Secondary Education at the University of North Carolina Wilmington. Her scholarship engages critical race, feminist, and identity theories to explore the ways in which democratic education might create more equitable learning opportunities for students and more heterarchic governance processes for teachers. She has 22 publications including a 2014 journal article (with Candace Thompson) entitled "'To Virgo or Not To Virgo': Examining the Closure and Reopening of a Neighborhood School in a Predominantly African American Community," a book chapter published in 2013 entitled "Rethinking School Reform and Neighborhood Schools," an edited book (with Dennis Carlson, 2010) entitled *The Sexuality Curriculum: Youth Culture, Popular Culture, and Democratic Sexuality Education* and a book published in 2008 entitled *Jacques Lacan and Education: A Critical Introduction*.

Mahauganee Shaw, PhD, is an assistant professor in the Department of Educational Leadership at Miami University, where she teaches in the student affairs and higher education program. Her research focuses on improving organizational effectiveness within higher education, with emphasis on implementing and sustaining organizational changes. This agenda is aimed at producing findings and tools that can be incorporated into practice and used to enhance both institutional operations and the collegiate experience.

Michele D. Smith, PhD, is an assistant professor in the Department of Counseling, Leadership, and Special Education where she teaches and serves as the program director for the Student Affairs in Higher Education Program at Missouri State University. Her scholarship explores mentoring African American women doctoral candidates, women in leadership, and the intersection of race and gender in athletics focusing on African American men in football and basketball. As a faculty member, she brings to this book the unique perspective of intersecting the worlds of higher education and athletics as one who has coached and continues to officiate at the high school and collegiate levels.

Candice L. Staples, MSEd, is a doctoral candidate at the University of Maryland, College Park. She has over 10 years of experience in working with students of color and programs advocating on behalf of public historically Black colleges and universities in the nonprofit arena. She enjoys participating and assisting in the process of students achieving their dreams and seeing their "aha" moment. Ms. Staples' research interests include faculty development, diversity and equity, organizational culture, and the presidential pipeline.

JeffriAnne Wilder, PhD, is an associate professor of sociology and the founding director of the Institute for the Study of Race and Ethnic Relations at the University of North Florida. In addition to her studies in sociology, Dr. Wilder also completed a PhD concentration in women's studies and gender research. As a race scholar specializing in issues of cultural diversity, her primary areas of research include race and ethnic relations—specifically the contemporary experience of Black Americans, the intersections of race, class, and gender, and the experiences of Black women in higher education.